the truth about rape

RapeRecovery.com
Gold River, California

Published by: RapeRecovery.com
2377 Gold Meadow Way, Suite 100
Gold River, CA 95670
email: Teresa@RapeRecovery.com

Lauer, Teresa.
    the truth about rape: emotional, spiritual, physical, and sexual recovery from rape / Teresa Lauer. —Gold River, CA: RapeRecovery.com, 2002.

        p.   ;   cm
    ISBN 0-9662078-1-5

    1. Rape—Psychological aspects. 2. Rape—Physiological aspects.
    3. Rape victims—Counseling. 4. Rape victims—Services for.
    5. Rape victims—Mental health. I. Title. II. Emotional, spiritual, physical and sexual recovery from rape.

RC560.R36 L38   2002   2002-100500
362.883   —dc21   CIP

06 05 04 03 02 ■ 5 4 3 2 1

Project Coordination by Jenkins Group, Inc. • www.bookpublishing.com
Cover Design by: Dunn+Associates
Cover Photography by: Eyewire.com

Printed in the United States of America

This book is dedicated to my husband, Phil.
You are my angel, my savior,
my best friend, my lover.
You are my air, my water.
Without you, there is no me.

Contents

Section III: Resources

Acknowledgments

A book exists due to effort from a number of people. For this reason, I give sincere and humble thanks to those who have contributed so much:

Thank you to my husband, Phil. He has saved my life, and while he doesn't fully recognize or appreciate it, he will in his own time. Until then, I say to him thank you again from the bottom of my heart.

Thank you to my mother, Lillian with whom I have a relationship that has gone from mother and guide to treasured friend.

Thank you to Dr. Gary Bushweiler, a wonderful friend, who I thank for living through this with me. Though difficult, he never wavered or deserted me, for which I'm eternally grateful.

Thank you to Dr. Dennis Hinkle for his unwavering support and belief in me.

Thank you to Sheila Kriefels for her direction and empathy.

And last, but certainly not least, thank you to those who helped me produce a book of words and images of which I can be proud:

I'm grateful to Kathi Dunn and Susan Kendrick for their artistic visions; Kathi for her assistance in producing a cover with intensity and drama and Susan for writing cover text that captures the very essence of my story.

I'm also grateful to Rebecca Chown for her superior critique and editing skills and for helping me convey words and thoughts that matter, and to Nikki Stahl and Mareesa Orth for helping make this project come to life.

Thank you again.

Teresa

A Letter to Rape Victims

There's no doubt in my mind your rape was one of the most traumatic experiences of your life. It's likely that you have experienced, or are continuing to experience, a myriad of emotions that have you confused and frightened. There are words that I can say to you to make you feel better—momentarily. But for your own recovery, you must become knowledgeable about what your rape has meant to you personally and learn the effects that it has had on your own life.

I want to save you time—precious time. Time to spend, comfortable in your own skin, secure in your emotional health. Time to explore your spiritual recovery and to reach the heights of your potential. Time to spend physically healthy so that you may live life to the fullest. And time to savor your sexuality as a woman; free to receive loving touches without the pain of past memories.

I wrote this book to fill a pressing need. As you are all too well aware, you may have experienced overwhelming confusion after having been raped. If you're like me, and many of the women I've counseled and spoken with, you have a million questions following your rape. From basic survival techniques, such as how to get out of bed in the face of overwhelming sadness, to long-term concerns, such as reclaiming your sexuality.

Words are my salvation—words that others have penned so carefully, words that others have whispered softly in my ears, words that have eased my suffering, words that helped me know I cannot only survive, but thrive—and this is what I give to you: My own experience as well as others who have experienced rape. Soak them in, massage them to make them yours, learn and grow. Whether an hour ago, or twenty years ago, it is never too early—or too late—to begin taking care of yourself.

I've lived through and understand your pain, however I can't pretend to know the effect the rape has had on your life. Do you still trust men? Are you in a happy and secure relationship? Do you function well in your daily life but feel a lingering sadness?

While reading this book, please keep in mind that at no time do I intend to imply that healing from rape is easy, quick, or effortless. There are steps you must go through as a victim of rape. No one is better suited than you to determine the speed with which you move through these steps.

I also want you to keep in mind that you are not alone. There are a great many people who care about you, who care if you heal from this rape, who love you and want nothing else but for your suffering to end, from your family and friends to professionals who have devoted their careers to alleviating suffering from rape, to other rape victims who are available for support and a shoulder to lean on. Open your mind, your body, and your heart to healing.

I must be truthful and say that my rape has never fully left me. There are too many emotions in everyday life—there are too many things that remind me, for me to ever forget that it happened. However, I've come to realize that this is a good thing. While the rape was physically and psychologically painful, it's as vital a part of who I am today as any of my other experiences.

I have one further caveat as you read through the following questions: I am unable to do justice to the plethora of information available on recovery from rape. I humbly admit that I've tried my best to include questions that will serve as a good cross section for the concerns of rape victims, however, the information is presented as a stepping stone for you to seek more advanced help.

And, if at any time you feel overwhelmed, stop reading. Take care of yourself and work at your own pace.

Please feel free to email me at any time at Teresa@RapeRecovery.com; I answer each email personally. I'm with you in spirit as you begin your recovery.

Best Regards,
Teresa

How to Use
The Truth About Rape

Section I

Section 1 contains over 50 actual sessions with my therapist for rape therapy. I have included these sessions to serve as a model for how therapy progresses, for there are very predictable stages of therapy: A distinct beginning, middle, and end. These stages of recovery are more easily recognized through a topographical view, such as the journal I've presented. For this reason, I suggest that you keep a journal, if at all possible, to record your own thoughts and feelings, and also progression, through therapy; the emotional value of looking back at one's progress is enormous.

Section II

The five chapters located in this section of *The Truth About Rape* have been designed to provide you with focused information to help you identify areas in your life you need to address. Your time is valuable. You have a life, family, friends, hobbies and interests, desires, and goals. Your rape has probably taken valuable time away from these things that you enjoy; and my goal is to focus your energies on your recovery.

During my work in rape recovery, I've been asked numerous questions on how others have recovered. The short answer is: Hard work, perseverance, blood, sweat, and tears. The good news is there are people in the world who care about you, who have empathy and compassion for what you're going through, and who want to help you. The chapters in this section include questions that others have asked and that you may be wondering about, too.

This is a very hands-on book; it addresses four important cornerstones of psychological health: Emotional, spiritual, physical, and sexual. It's designed to provide you with vital information, whether your rape occurred twenty days ago or twenty years ago.

At the same time, the book is interactive in that if there are questions or concerns that are not being addressed here, I encourage you to email me at Teresa@RapeRecovery.com and discuss your concerns. I will personally answer each email.

The following chapters are highlighted in this section:

Emotional Healing

Is there a void somewhere deep inside you that you've been unable to fill? Do you feel that many of your current behaviors are due to the fact that you were raped and never fully addressed your feelings? Do you suffer from relentless nightmares and flashbacks? Do you feel "stuck" in the rape? What do you need to do to become all that you can be? Are you in a happy, committed relationship? Have you told your story to those you feel should know? Are you suffering from guilt, shame, or anxiety? Feelings are never wrong—nor right. They just are. We examine these questions and more in "Emotional Healing." An overview of this chapter includes:

- Your Rape: A Traumatic Event
- Re-Experiencing Your Rape
- Avoidance Symptoms
- Arousal Symptoms

Spiritual Healing

For the purposes of this book, I refer to "spiritual" as the recovery process from rape. I believe there's a very strong spiritual component to rape; yet how does one integrate such a significant event into an otherwise normal existence? How do we wake one morning with our trust and self-image intact and then experience rape and not have it affect us? We read about rape all the time in the newspaper but the stories don't do justice to the importance of the crime to the victim. It's an intrusive experience on our minds and bodies and recovery must begin as soon as possible.

Do you wonder what kind of man could have done this? Do you find yourself not wanting to talk about it, just hoping these feelings go away? Are you concerned about your own rage and anger? Are you confused about therapy and wonder if it's worth the time and money? Do you want professional help but don't know where to start? Do you wonder if group therapy or support therapy might be for you? We look at these questions and more in "Spiritual Healing." An overview of this chapter includes:

- Becoming Educated
- The Stages of Rape Recovery
- The Recovery Process

Physical Healing

Your physical healing is paramount. You must educate yourself on the medical and physiological effects of the rape in order to properly locate professionals who will help you as an informed consumer. Are you anxious about seeing your gynecologist for the first time since your rape? Do you wonder exactly what takes place during the exam? Are you wondering if you have an eating disorder and if it's related to the rape? Do you injure yourself and need to know how to stop? Are you apprehensive about your safety? We consider these questions and more in "Physical Healing." An overview of this chapter includes:

- Medical Concerns
- Physiological Concerns
- Safety Concerns

Sexual Healing

Your sexual health is vital to your well-being. One's emotional, spiritual, and physical needs are often addressed, however our sexual needs often go unmet. You've experienced a decidedly intrusive event where a penis was used as the weapon. While we understand that rape is a power-motivated crime, still the tool used to commit the crime is sexual in nature.

Confusion over your sexuality is to be expected. Do you feel as if you were "too sexual" (as many women do) and that's what caused the rapist to act? Have you changed your appearance to appear less attractive? Do you wonder how you're ever going to be able to have intercourse without thinking about the rape? Do you have little interest in sex? Are there some positions that are just too difficult for you because they remind you of the rape? Are you wondering how you're going to be able to communicate your needs to your partner? Are you wondering if sex therapy might be beneficial but don't know how to go about it? Did you respond sexually during the rape and are suffering from guilt and shame? Do you want to see a massage therapist to re-orient yourself to touch? Do you have scars from the rape that have resulted in embarrassment? Do you suffer from vaginismus? Do you suffer from chronic pain or disabilities from the rape and need a way to help yourself? We consider these questions and more in "Sexual Healing." An overview of this chapter includes:

- Intimacy Concerns
- Body Image and Sensuality
- Your Sexual Healing

Family and Friends

Family and friends can accelerate your healing and can be your biggest allies in your recovery. This section is designed to help them help you with your emotional, spiritual, physical, and sexual concerns. In addition, they can find information on providing support to you following your rape with resources designed to address their concerns.

The Format of Section II

In addition to answering a number of questions on Emotional, Spiritual, Physical, and Sexual Healing, each chapter follows a format for providing the information you need in a clear, concise manner.

Question & Answer

The following is an overview of the contents of each question:

A Personal View

This section is perhaps my favorite. In the work I've done in rape and recovery, I've met a number of extremely courageous women. Prior clients, friends, strangers who have become friends—all have been giving of themselves, their hopes, their dreams, their struggles.

I feel very privileged that they've shared their lives with me, and now, with you. Their motives are completely unselfish as they share firsthand what has worked for them—and in some cases—not worked, in order to save others time and pain. I thank them all from the bottom of my heart.

A Clinical View
This section provides clinical information regarding each question. Admittedly, due to the astounding amount of information available on each of these subjects, the information is intended to provide an overview only.

The very real limitation of space forces me to cleanly edit the information so as to provide succinct, valuable information that you can build on through your own self-directed study or with your therapist.

Resources

General Resources
These resources are made up of governmental and non-profit agencies, when possible, and provide superior information.

Even though they may be out of your geographical area, contact them or visit their web sites to further research your current issues.

Web Resources
In the comfort of your own home you can take the time you'd like to peruse our web resources. A great deal of care has gone into the selection of these sites; however, as fluid as the Internet is, there is a possibility that site addresses have changed or become obsolete. I will be providing updates to this information on my Web site at RapeRecovery.com; please visit often to obtain new resources.

Book Resources
The written word means a great deal to me. It has allowed me to cry, to laugh, to share, to learn. I'm grateful to rape victims who have written their memoirs as I've learned much about myself from them.

Also, I'm grateful to the many professionals who have obtained further education in trauma in order to provide comfort and care to those affected; my library of their work is extensive and the books well-worn. My colleagues have invested years of their professional lives to alleviate the pain of rape victims and for that I'm indebted. Their compassion and empathy has motivated them to make symptoms more tolerable, relationships more rewarding, lives more fulfilling.

Video and Audio Resources

Video and audio resources are becoming more plentiful and for that I'm appreciative. Again, please visit my Web site, www.RapeRecovery.com for updates to the existing resources.

Section III

General Resources, Book, Video and Audio Resources

This chapter is a complete resource and referral list of resources in all previous chapters.

State Sexual Assault Coalitions

This section lists each state's sexual assault coalition. Please utilize this section to obtain information on crisis counseling in your area, victim compensation, and legal remedies.

Section I

Therapy Sessions

Introduction to Therapy Sessions

I have an excellent memory. This ability to remember people, places, and events throughout my life has proved to be beneficial as well as detrimental. I envy those who cannot remember, though I'm certain they envy my ability to remember. However, the burning in of memories and, even more frightening, the actual emotions I've experienced, led me to therapy in an effort to move beyond these intense feelings and to become "unstuck" in that particular place and time.

In addition to an excellent memory, I've had the sometimes maddening habit of writing down everything that occurs in my life on a nearly daily basis. I feel compelled to chronicle events so that they retain their effect and so that I may later judge how they shaped my eventual behavior.

So it is that during my three years of therapy, I chronicled my relationship with my therapist, my emotions, and my progress. Heightening the intensity of therapy was my propensity to relate events in my journal in present tense. This is how I remember, in present tense with raw emotion. My breathing becomes shallow, my eyes dilate, and my skin feels as if it's on fire. This is how I remember, so this is how I've written my journal. I'm physically, emotionally, and psychologically present in that particular place in time.

What follows are excerpts from the journals I kept at the time of the rape and afterward. To have included all 652 pages would have proved cumbersome and perhaps tedious to you, my reader, so I made the decision to include selected entries that chronicled important events or in which I made significant progress and gained insight, sometimes significant, and to omit other, less meaningful, entries.

My most profound insight, and one that I hope everyone reading this book takes to heart, is that help is as near as your spouse, your family, your friends, and a community of therapeutic professionals. There's no reason to suffer through the aftermath of a rape alone, or in silence. There are people who can provide empathy or who have experienced the same trauma or who are trained to provide support and care at this difficult time. You are worth the compassion and understanding that others have to give.

Please feel free to visit my Web site at www.RapeRecovery.com or email me with your questions regarding information and referrals. Or simply reach out; I'm sincerely interested in your recovery and will answer each email personally.

Thank you,

Teresa

Session #1

I leave home at 7:30 a.m. for my 9:00 a.m. session to go ten miles. I don't want to be late, but I needn't worry. I arrive in a half-hour and drive around the neighborhood and then around again until the building opens.

All the time I've spent calmly recalling facts, rehearsing my story over and over in my own mind during the past five weeks, has been a waste of time. All I can think as I wait for the office to open is that being here is a big mistake. My mind is a blank.

The waiting room is painted soothing colors and contains a plethora of green plants, but is still too bright; I catch myself thinking that perhaps table lamps would be more comforting. I feel as if I'm on display to anyone who happens past.

I pick up a magazine but can't concentrate well enough to read an article, so I sit flipping through the pages. I glance around the room, wondering what has brought the other patients in. A couple in the corner is turned toward each other and the woman is hanging her head. The man is holding her hands in her lap and is speaking gently in her ear. He's comforting her as if she's just suffered a loss of some kind. Perhaps it's a mistake for me not to have asked Phil to come to this session. As always, I have to prove that I can do it alone, but now seeing this couple and the comfort that the man is providing makes me want Phil by my side.

Another man sits in the corner, wringing his hands. He looks terribly lonely and disheveled, rumpled almost, like he hasn't been to sleep or changed his clothes in several days. Something about him makes me feel tender towards him, almost motherly.

One by one the other patients are called for their sessions until I'm alone. It isn't long before a tall attractive man appears in the doorway and calls my name. He introduces himself as a psychologist but asks me to call him by his first name, Gary.

He motions the way down the hall to his office and invites me to walk ahead of him. His office is spacious and comforting and has a beautiful view of the mountains beyond. And a benefit of living in California with its mild Mediterranean climate, even in January: Bundles of brilliant flowers snuggle against the building outside his window.

I like Gary immediately. He has a confident, self-assured manner, his eyes meet mine, and his smile is shy and engaging. I know him to be the head of the department but I'm surprised to see that he's only about ten years older than I, if that. A part of me hoped that he'd be older and unattractive, but he's quite the opposite.

He offers me a seat and a glass of water and, while he's gone, I take a moment to look around his office. An overflowing bookshelf gives me the sense that he's built a robust library of differing schools of therapeutic theory.

He returns with my glass of water and sits in front of me, leans back in his chair, and casually crosses his legs.

I can't force my eyes to meet his when he returns—uncharacteristic for me. I feel so anxious that I worry my words will tumble from my mouth and I won't be able to stop talking once I start. Or won't be able to stop crying once I start that.

His records state the reason for my session, but he asks me to elaborate.

A sexual assault a number of years ago, yet of course this doesn't tell the full story. In answer to his questions regarding my present symptoms, I tick off the list: flashbacks, anxiety, sleeplessness, but I feel my voice becoming flat as if I'm trying to lessen their impact on me over the past five weeks.

I carefully respond to his questions, providing him with basic descriptors: *Yes—I'm married to a wonderful man for eleven years—together for eighteen. His name is Phil. Software designer. We own our own computer software company. No—no children.*

I hear myself talk as if I'm a different person. Looking into his eyes and revealing myself is uncomfortable, and although he's friendly and keeps the conversation moving forward through my too-sparse account of my history, I nonetheless feel intimidated by him. I'm self-conscious of my nervous laughter and feel out of place, and I worry that he'll find me weak or stupid or, worse, crazy.

I hear the words I've carefully rehearsed, yet they're disconnected and strangely lack emotion. I feel nauseous and want to tell him that I've made a mistake in coming to see him and that I'm sorry for taking his time, but I don't say it. In truth, I'm desperate for his help.

Gary asks how it is that I'm seeking help after this length of time and I tell him about the day I called his office for today's session.

⌐⌐

It's about a week before Thanksgiving and I'm becoming overextended and tired between work and preparations, for we're having company for Thanksgiving. I lie awake at night, my mind turning over with rambling thoughts.

5

One evening, I'm exhausted and am able to fall asleep relatively early. In the early morning hours, I wake in a cold sweat, paralyzed with fear. I lie motionless, unable to open my mouth and scream for help, or to reach out for my husband asleep beside me. I can hear the soft rhythm of his breathing and feel his breath against my cheek, but I can't open my mouth or lift my arms. It takes perhaps a half-hour or maybe a bit longer before I can move again and while it's still dark, I wander through the house, unable to lie down again for fear that I won't wake up. I feel as if I'm dying.

The smothering sadness that encompasses me when daylight comes makes it all the more apparent that I must speak with someone—soon.

I call as soon as Phil leaves for a client. I'm strangely disconnected to the act of my fingers dialing the phone, as if the decision has been taken out of my hands. I speak with a woman named Anne. Her voice is a welcome relief; she's kind and compassionate and I'm glad that I've called. The cool wood of the cabinet feels good against my back as I slide to the kitchen floor.

I feel my heart pounding in my ears as I speak to her. Calming and gentle, she asks how she can help.

Words tumble from my mouth, hesitantly at first, then in a torrent.

Assault—recent—but that isn't the problem; really it isn't. My problem is a rape that occurred a number of years ago.

I ask to see a man, although I've no idea why I've said this. She doesn't question my request but insists that I wait for Gary. She instills trust in him and I tell her that will be fine. She talks to me for about ten more minutes, calming me and making sure that I'm all right. She assures me that she's there—if there's anything I need, just call. I'm grateful for the time she has taken to put me at ease and hesitate to hang up and let my connection with her go, but of course I do.

I feel apprehension almost immediately. I've made a decision but am disappointed in myself that I need help. I'm terrified at sharing my feelings with a stranger, but more terrified at not doing so.

I surrender.

To my surprise, having given myself over to someone else, I feel an odd sense of non-responsibility, an unexpected benefit, surely. I can allow myself to think and to feel anything now. I can slide over the edge because now there is someone to break my fall.

Gary's name and phone number land on the calendar and are circled in red ink with a count of the number of days until we meet.

⌒

Our first session is over; my initiation to the 50-minute "hour" and I'm disappointed that the session has ended so quickly. I wanted to share more of myself with Gary today—I've kept everything inside for so long. I so anticipated this session, and now it's over nearly before it began. I waited hundreds of hours for this one small one, and I'm exhausted. I'm also disappointed that I won't be seeing Gary for several weeks.

I have the sense that we are evaluating each other and our ability to work together. He's determining, I suppose, how he can best help me and I'm deciding whether he's the best person on whom to build a foundation of trust so that I can tell him that which I've kept silent for so long.

Session #3

I'm here, I tell Gary in answer to his question, to talk about a rape that occurred a number of years ago. I'm unable to cope with the emotions I'm feeling now. To my relief, for this session, he steers me toward my present life—my work, Phil, who I am at this point.

⌒

Phil and I sit at the dining room table. It's Sunday—a favorite day of the week. We share the paper and eat orange rolls hot from the oven while we drink coffee. There are days when we don't get up from the table until two or three in the afternoon.

The sun warms the room through the lace curtains. There's no need for the fireplace but we light it anyway. We sit in our bathrobes around the huge oak table as the world goes by outside. We listen to soft jazz and the crackle of the fireplace while we read, but I'm preoccupied, thinking about my next meeting with Gary.

I'm concerned that I'm unprepared for therapy. This isn't typical of me, so I set about forming goals to be accomplished during therapy, both inside and outside of the therapy hour.

First, I decide that I have to know more about the process of therapy. There are so many questions for which I need answers: What may I expect from Gary? What does he expect from me? While my three most pressing goals are to tell Phil about the assault that took place here in our garage, to alleviate my fears, and to better handle my flashbacks, I know that there is deeper, more important, work to be done.

I need to use this opportunity to uncover other issues that have bothered me but I feel selfish concentrating on my wants and needs. In the back of my mind, I wonder how therapy will affect my marriage. Phil is my entire life, but there's a great deal he doesn't know about me. While I know he loves me completely, I'm fearful of what his reaction will be when he knows the truth. At the same time, I'm realizing that I can't keep all this inside any longer—my sadness—and fear—overwhelm me. I need to be free, and I need Phil to know who I am.

I wonder sometimes how I've managed to keep all this from him. Doing so is so ingrained that I don't know how to begin telling him the truth. But, as much as I love him, I feel a distance between us because he doesn't know. I used to feel relief at this, but my relief has turned into a sadness so acute I am afraid I will die of it. Phil senses that I'm distracted and asks if I want to sit in the living room. I do— Christmas and New Year's have passed and I've taken a big step in starting therapy. I feel I've got a lot of work to do, but today I just want to sit and be held.

I love our home, but feel safe only when Phil's with me. This lovely Victorian, painted a soft pastel pink with slightly darker trim and with pretty roses nestled against the old-fashioned wrap-around porch, is very much the dream house and very much worth the time and effort necessary to make the dream ours. One of four painted in colors of candy—soft pink, green, yellow, and orange—our tiny development looks like a child's play set of Victorian dollhouses.

A huge, two-story foyer with warm, taffy-colored hardwood floors is framed on one side by the kitchen and then, two steps down, is a cozy family room. On the other side is the dining room and then, two steps down again, the living room. On all the paned windows and on the beveled stained-glass front door hang delicate lace curtains, allowing the softest glow of fading sunsets to rest on the inside of the house.

I'm privileged to have Phil in my life. He's tall and handsome and sure of himself and his abilities. His strengths are the things that first attracted me to him.

His brown eyes convey his feelings completely, and the way he holds me encourages me to let him take the lead, for I'm safe with him. A furtive smile defines his lips, like he has a secret only the two of us know.

Logic mixed with tenderness, practicality with a large dose of compassion; that describes my husband.

My life in a chaotic house as a child is little more than a memory now and I'm constantly surprised by Phil's solid, calm nature. He has a rare union of left-brain, right-brain abilities; the right traits surface at just the right moment along with an engaging sense of humor.

I've admired his personality, always. His strengths are my weaknesses. I know guilt and shame intimately while he doesn't subscribe to those concepts at all. I'm hypercritical of myself in terms of my body and my accomplishments whereas he presents the polar opposite. On the occasion when he is at fault, he accepts responsibility, rectifies the situation quickly, and moves on with no loss of self-esteem. Whereas he's extremely extroverted and outgoing and rarely edits his past, I'm more introverted and moody, desperately trying to re-write mine.

When I tell Phil that it's time for me to learn a different, more effective, way to deal with my feelings, he's supportive, as I knew he would be, and I'm grateful. I'm relieved when he tells me that he's noticed my sadness in the last couple of weeks and to take the time I need. The package into which I've neatly tucked my rage and shame and covered with beautiful fabric is slowly beginning to unravel.

Though I hesitate beginning the work of therapy without Phil's approval, I've placed him in a somewhat uncomfortable position. There's a part of me that hopes he'll protest so that I may hide from my feelings a while longer, but the rational part of me knows that Phil will support whatever I feel is best for me. He knows me and is confident that I don't rush into situations without thinking first. He respects my ability to think through a problem.

⌒

Gary stops me, telling me our time is up. As I get ready to leave he asks about our company—a software design firm, I tell him. I love my job but feel, along with being a good partner from a business sense, that my greatest responsibility is towards my husband in regards to our marriage. I am, I tell Gary as I leave, moving backward rather than forward. I suppose these are the things that all people discuss in therapy—the mundane, small things that happen in everyone's lives, the relationships with people they love and who have influence over them, but I'm frustrated at talking about surface things instead of getting to the point of why I'm here. I'm realizing how vital it is to come prepared and keep myself focused.

Session #4

Gary asks if I've given therapy any further thought since our last meeting. I have, I tell him. Specifically, I've thought about the year I lost so much and how it affects me still. And I tell him about how even the smallest task becomes clouded under the recollection of emotions. These are the moments I'm here to resolve—those moments that oppress me and leave me feeling inferior to others because of the rape and I decide to tell him about last week.

After meeting Phil for lunch I stop at Barnes and Noble for the books that Gary suggested. I don't leave for several hours. A trip to this cavernous bookstore dictates that I have a cup of coffee and watch people as they walk by me on their way to who knows where. The dark mahogany beams rise high above my head and the deep green sofas with leather already worn beckon—this is the place to be on this moody, rainy Thursday.

I walk past the huge computer book section, my second home, and instead work my way back to the psychology section. I take the tattered paper on which Gary's written several titles but am unable to find even one. After checking the women's and then the recovery sections, I'm left with having to ask a clerk.

I hand the paper to the only person at the counter—a man. The first title is suggestive of the subject matter and I'm aware of that fact as he looks down at the title, then at me, then down at the title again. My discomfort is evident as he hands the paper back to me, telling me that he has no copies in stock, but would I like to have him order one and call me when it comes in?

I return to the recovery section after placing my order and find several books that look interesting. It occurs to me that I've never read anything on rape or sexual assault before, recovery from or prevention of. I'm a voracious reader in every other subject and have an almost perversely curious mind about things I don't understand—why not this?

I sit along the edge of the interior café in the center of the reading area and begin reading the table of contents of one of the books. I turn it over to look at the author's photograph on the back. Has she been raped, I wonder. One never knows. A person can present one face to the world and hide a world of pain.

Gary turns to face me as we walk to the door. Is it important, Gary asks me, if the author has been raped? Is it important to me that she's experienced the same event? Does that give what she has to say more weight?

I think about his questions for a moment and reply that yes, I suppose it does.

But then, why come to me? He returns the volley.

Why have I chosen a man who clearly has no experience in how it feels to be a woman who has been raped?

I choose not to tell him of a devastating visit to a female psychologist a number of years ago, shortly after the rape, and instead pull a tattered sheet of paper from my pocket that he gave me at our first session.

He's surprised that I carry it with me and smiles as I hand it to him: *"I did the best I could." "I had no choice." "I'm not a bad person because things happen to me." "Things may feel worse for a while as we take the 'lids' off of what you have repressed or denied." "Panic comes from the sense or feeling of loss of control." "All these feelings are me."*

I recall, I continue, the one caveat he made when we first met: That relating my history is vital in order to facilitate healing. While it sent a shiver up me then, I feel a sense of urgency now. I've been complacent in my role here in his office.

Session #7

Gary notices immediately that I'm distressed and, though I suspect he has some other subject in mind for today, asks if I need to talk about something in particular. I do, I tell him. One of the most terrifying symptoms that I'm experiencing—flashbacks—is becoming more frequent; in fact, I had one last night.

He asks that I tell him about the first flashback I experienced.

It's late November of last year, and is the reason I'm here.

My past—suddenly and irrevocably—collides with my present and with great force I'm slammed between the two.

It happens while I'm shopping. That's the last thing I remember, in any case. It's a little more than a week before Thanksgiving and the mall is humming with excitement. Being Tuesday, most of the other shoppers are young moms with kids. Red and green glimmering tinsel winds its way around the upper level rails and flows over, raining on the Santa and elves and playing children below. Along with holiday music, this is the most wonderful sound this time of year—children playing. The sounds today, though, make me sad.

I'm running late but decide to make one more stop at a large department store. The display in the window of the gourmet candy store next door is enchanting. Gold foil packages of luscious chocolate candies woven between red and green silk strands invite me in, but my eyes move past the window to a rack of silk blouses inside the department store. They're exquisite: Golds and reds and greens, like the colors in the candy store. I look to my right, suddenly bombarded with too many images, too much movement in front of me. The colors from the candy display streak in front of my eyes and move as I turn my head.

I move toward the rack of blouses. My hand reaches out to touch one of them and keeps going. Farther and farther, it stretches toward the silk fabric until my hand is no longer a part of me. It moves away from me as if disconnected from my arm. The colors of the blouses melt together, forming a horrid, ugly concoction. The patterns, beautifully flowing a moment before, now push and claw against each other, forming grotesque shapes I can no longer make out.

My breath catches suddenly, as if I've been pushed hard against my back, but I'm still standing. I look behind me, expecting to see someone, but instead experience a cacophony of sights and smells and sounds—particularly sounds. I feel as if I'm laboring hard to comprehend something vague and disturbing. I sense myself being

13

half in, half out. Half "here" and half not. The sensations frighten me. An impression of myself, young and naïve and blissfully ignorant, surrounds me. I don't want to disturb that image and so remain perfectly still.

Two older ladies shake my shoulders and tell me that I've been staring into space for twenty minutes. I feel as if I've awakened from a nightmare. I fumble for words in answer to their puzzled looks, but give up and run out of the store into the mall. I'm trembling and drop the packages I clutch in my hands. I turn to pick them up. My heart beats wildly in my ears. I glance around, sure that someone is near me, but see no one.

Reaching my car takes forever. I'm in a familiar nightmare where, with great effort, I place one foot in front of me, then the other, then the other, but with each step, the aisle stretches farther from me. I'm loaded with packages and my feet feel as if they're blocks of concrete.

I reach my car at last. Inside I'm safe so I stay, motionless, with the doors locked, trying to figure out what's happening to me. My heart is racing still and I can feel the blood pounding in my ears. I try to calm myself by taking deep breaths, but my efforts are futile. I look in the rearview mirror. I'm sweating and my eyes are dilated. I panic—I need to go home. I need to see Phil.

⌒

This is, Gary confirms, a classic flashback.

It has a name. For this I'm grateful and know that if it has a name, others have experienced it, and if others have experienced it, I'm not crazy. If I'm not crazy, I can recover.

I continue with my story. I've lost interest in everything but Phil, I tell him, and am content sitting in an empty, dark theatre with him and a huge tub of popcorn watching movies all day. I feel ashamed of my lack of motivation and scared when I can't modify my behavior with willpower. I've endured ugly times before, as everyone has, but this is different. When anxious I long for numbness, and vice versa. My feelings swing wildly from polar opposites.

His diagnosis, Gary tells me, is severe Post Traumatic Stress Disorder, PTSD. He's given my symptoms and current state a great deal of thought. Due to the duration and severity of my symptoms he's confident with this diagnosis and is just as confident that he can help me. He gently delivers this information as a doctor would when informing his patient that he has a serious illness, but moves quickly from the emotional to the educational aspects of the diagnosis.

He pulls a book from the shelf and moves his chair close to mine, turning to the section on PTSD. He gently moves me from the emotions of having received this diagnosis to going through the symptoms with me.

The first set of symptoms in meeting the diagnosis of PTSD addresses exposure to a traumatic event. Exposure in this case relates to having witnessed or been confronted with an event, either natural (such as a flood or hurricane) or man-made (such as rape, war, physical, or sexual assault), in which one is actually injured or threatened with injury or death. These traumatic events cause the victim to experience an intense response, such as paralyzing fear, terror, or helplessness. Yes, we both agree, I meet these criteria.

The next set of symptoms addresses the persistent re-experiencing of the trauma in the form of nightmares, flashbacks, insomnia, intrusive thoughts, becoming panicky and shaky when thinking of the trauma, and becoming upset around the anniversary of the event. Understandably, re-experiencing is often terribly confusing and distressing.

Flashbacks, Gary tells me, are particularly terrifying to a trauma victim. They strike suddenly and are extremely emotional events in themselves. One doesn't black out but there is a feeling of having left oneself temporarily, causing a sort of numbing effect. Flashbacks can be so vivid that one can smell or see or feel the event happening to them again. Individuals experience different triggers for these flashbacks and other forms of re-experiencing, but these symptoms are often what convince them of the need to seek help.

Gary continues. The re-experiencing of feelings, such as fear, shame, and guilt, among others, leads to avoidance of the pain of re-experiencing the trauma and, as a result, leads to a greater need for help. Avoidance can take many forms, such as not wanting to talk or think about the trauma and avoiding certain places or activities in order not to be reminded of the trauma.

In my case, duration and disturbance to overall functioning are what have led Gary to diagnose severe PTSD.

Each day, I tell Gary as I leave his office, I pick up the phone to cancel our next session, and each day I put it back down. I'm frantic and incapable of making decisions, even tiny ones. I vacillate between being relieved that I'm seeing him and terrified at uncovering feelings that might be better left alone. I feel the need to hold onto what I know, as negating and oppressive as it is, because it's known.

Session #9

I've learned quickly that time is of the utmost importance in the therapy hour—what can be resolved elsewhere should be. I've decided it's not yet time to tell Gary of the recent assault. I'm not ready, even though it's clear that it's opened up a very old wound.

In truth, I probably don't trust him yet. Gary's allowed a brief period of becoming acquainted, but I can sense he's making attempts to get down to business. In an effort to prove to him that I'm trying, I tell him today of my efforts to reacquaint myself with my "memory boxes."

I make another cup of coffee, grab my cordless phone, and make my way upstairs to the guest bedroom. This small bedroom in the front of the house is a womb-like refuge. While a winter cold snakes through the first floor, this guest bedroom remains toasty warm. Golden sunlight streams through the window, nourishing the deep green ivy, grown huge with tender loving care.

The colors are in sharp contrast to the rest of the house. Deep hunter green and vivid burgundy meld together to invite our guests to relax and enjoy their stay. Phil and I joke that we must have been hungry when decorating, buying curtains and furniture with colors like French Vanilla and Sweet White Chocolate. An elaborate patchwork of designs echoes off the thick, goose down comforter and again off the curtains.

Sitting cross-legged on the bed, I stare at a group of boxes in front of me. The rain taps ever so softly against the windowpanes and the room grows darker still to match my mood. The sun moves deeper behind the clouds.

Anniversaries come and go—they are important as a means of measurement. Mentally, I tick away weeks since—then months—then years. I glance at my past, not to savor, but to judge.

My means to that end, to stealing a glance into my past, is a secret journey I take every now and then through boxes that have moved with us to each new house, like prized possessions. They sit innocently, covered in pretty, flowered fabric. I've stacked them in a pyramid and topped them with a menagerie of stuffed animals.

My stuffed animals sit in front of me now, guarding the boxes. A furry family brought together mostly by difficult times in my life, they fulfill a promise from the gift giver: Warmth, comfort, love, and nurturing to soothe a tender heart. A fuzzy, sweet bunny with a pink bow and collar—my first from Phil. The smallest: a cream-colored teddy bear with soft brown eyes. A playful panda that Phil brought me perched atop his shoulders to cheer me after surgery.

⌒

Gary listens politely but cocks his head slightly, as if to say: *Interesting—but what does this have to do with the rape?* I feel silly having spoken to him of these childish things that still provide some sort of comfort to me, but tell him that these are boxes full of tangible links to my past and if examining the past is important, then this is where my past lies. This is how I must accomplish the task he asks of me. He assures me that indeed the past is important and I resolve to finish my work in opening the boxes when I return home.

Session #10

I feel cautious today, talking to Gary. The stuffed animals guard my memories for me, memories contained in boxes that have become a metaphor for how I've dealt with pain in my life. Wrap it in pretty fabric, let it stack up, put it away where I'm sure not to see it.

Examining my past is important, Gary assures me again. We'll identify thoughts and feelings that I've experienced both during and after the rape. Doing that allows us to separate *thoughts* from *feelings*. A reconstruction of the rape in some form, written or oral, is necessary. It's important that I identify the "triggers" for the nightmares and flashbacks.

I see our goal much more clearly now. He encourages me to use my analytical skills and intelligence on this highly emotional issue, and I'm flattered. I'll approach this in a much more organized fashion.

I tell him of my work since our last session.

~

I wander through the house, trying to figure out why I'm restless and irritated, until I realize that it's because I've been putting off the task of looking in the boxes. My resolve following our last session has dissipated.

I grab a soda and go upstairs to the guest room. It's unseasonably warm and I open a window to let a soft breeze blow in through the lace curtains. I watch the sun dance off the comforter and become aware of a pressing need to look through the boxes. I have to in order to move to the next step with Gary. I don't have a choice.

I lay back on the bed, taking a moment to assess the job ahead of me. At times I feel an almost overwhelming lack of emotion and at other times my sensitivity is razor sharp. I'm uncertain which is worse, but am terrified that once I allow myself to experience the feelings, I won't be able to stop. The cards, letters, photographs, legal papers, and journals in the boxes are all my secrets. They define the person I've become.

I turn to my task of opening the first box. I approach my job as impartially as possible as I plan my strategy: Take off the cover. Look inside. Address the contents. Deal with the feelings. Simple. Clean. Over. The boxes are meticulously wrapped. I've taken care to cover every inch in a glorious union of deep hunter green and vibrant burgundy to match the rest of the room. And I've titled them in secret as well: Crime. Death. Birth.

~

Gary looks at me as I finish. Perhaps, he says, it's best to go slowly. And he gives me an assignment: Reconstruct the events of the rape and attempt to identify the feelings I experienced. This frightens me, but I say nothing. It's clear to me that I'm taking baby steps.

I wait for him to ask the magic question that will draw my truths out of me, yet he can't know what that question is. Even I don't know. I'm in a loop and becoming discouraged at my lack of progress after three months. Perhaps looking at the rape head-on as he has suggested will help.

When I tell Phil that I'm thinking of cutting back on therapy or perhaps stop going altogether, he wraps his arms around me, encouraging me to stick with it a bit longer.

Session #11

Gary continues to try to put me at ease and I want to say what's on my mind, but find that I become pithy and insightful when by myself and quiet when with him. *This is backwards*, I think to myself.

The thought that he's judging me is with me always, serving to reinforce my resistance. I cannot articulate what I need from him. I've no practice in asking, so my needs go unmet. It isn't his fault but mine, yet the result is the same. I like him though, and am curious what he thinks of me.

How will I know when I'm done? I ask. *How am I to measure our success?*

He gives me a quizzical smile, as if I'm a dinner guest getting up to leave after having been served the soup. I understand the look. We haven't even finished our appetizers and I'm ready for my coat.

He questions why this is important to me and my only response is a curiosity in knowing how one *does* know. I live in a world of facts, figures, measurables, and quotas, of criteria and proof. Of standards and tests. This is all very gray to me. To the extent that I can understand the process we're undertaking, I need an explanation.

Just as important to me in this process is the desire to bridge his world to mine and so I rely on the solidity of familiarity. To step outside myself and hear my words, I'm certain it seems as if my head is on straight, yet this isn't the truth. I'm deceiving myself, or trying to, and he'll have none of it.

What of reverse engineering? I ask. It's a process I partake in on a daily basis in my work: Look at the desired end result and work backward. Develop a flowchart and determine the steps necessary to reach that result. This, Gary tells me, isn't possible in therapy. He encourages me to move away from that which is familiar and to accept the process that we're undertaking.

Conflict is evident in my every action. I feel like screaming, yet smile politely and nod. I feel like reaching out to him, yet keep my distance. I feel like getting serious, yet make nervous jokes, hiding (in *my* mind, anyway) my discomfort. I'm conscious of a particular feeling of being trapped and needing to escape. When my freedom is in danger of compromise, I choose retreat.

I dance around during the session, goof off basically, in order not to be asked about the assignment he gave me. During the week I tried a hundred times to do as he asked but couldn't face looking at the details of the rape in black and white, either mentally or on paper.

Now, I chide myself for having thrown us off track and wasted valuable time.

Session #12

I want to talk to you, I tell Gary this morning, about something that's happened to me. This declaration, out of the blue, arouses his curiosity. His legs are crossed and he lifts himself up to sit higher, bringing one arm over and crossing his hands.

I go on to explain that I must tell Phil something but need to talk to him, Gary, first in order to feel my way through this. The news will be devastating to Phil, and I need to protect his feelings. And, I say, lowering my eyes, I must tell him in a way that doesn't make him feel betrayed. I never meant to do that—my silence was necessary to protect, not designed to betray. And, I admit, I wanted to keep Phil from feeling as if he wanted to leave me.

I have every intent of telling Gary what happened, but am surprised to find myself instead telling him of the day last week that I finally worked on the assignment he gave me.

It's completely still in the house. It's early and overcast and I turn on the lights in the den. I'm alone and have promised myself that I'll take the entire day, if necessary, to complete the assignment. I prepare: The temperature is just right, I've made coffee, and I have Phil's fisherman's sweater on—I can smell him and feel protected and safe.

I sit looking at the computer screen before me. My memories are compartmentalized. They're arranged in a certain sequence of events so that I may protect myself. I envy, in a sense, those who can block out memories, for I've never been able to. I liken my memories to the stinging jellyfish on the bottom of the ocean floor. They're lying in wait, and while I'm unsure of when I'm going to be stung, I know it's going to be painful.

The past is etched into my mind, but I question how I might take Gary into a journey inside myself. How am I to provide him with the colors, the sounds, the smells? How am I to relate the feelings that tear at me? I'm anxious for the sake of my marriage—and my sanity—to do whatever is necessary, but I haven't a clue as to how to go about it.

I title three columns on the page: What Happened, Feelings, and Emotions. I busy myself setting up rows, shading, bordering. Then I get down to work and compartmentalize the fourteen hours. Every excruciating detail lands in the What Happened column. I don't attempt to assign a feeling or emotion at this time.

This takes me several hours to complete. I disconnect completely and simply type the words onto the paper, dealing only with the facts. It's just before noon when I finish. After eating lunch, I return to my task. I try to stay disconnected as it seems to be the only way to get through this, but when I return to the paper and see the words I've written in the first column, I start to shake. Eating lunch may have been a mistake; I'm nauseous and light-headed. I take a minute and walk around, trying to calm my stomach and return to my work.

My next column, attaching feelings to what I experienced, is a challenge. I try words like "scared" and "frightened" but they lack depth. I finally pull out my the-saurus and tackle one of the entries, find an appropriate word, then tackle another. I'm shaking as I read my words and relive the rape, but finally am able to assign the feelings: Frantic, panicked, ashamed, tortured, violated.

I can't stop. Though I don't want to endure this any longer than is necessary, I must continue. I complete the column and move on to describing the emotions. As I finish, I find myself crying softly and finally my tears turn into wracking sobs. Fear and anger—these are the emotions I've assigned to the feelings. That man took a great deal from me, is still taking a great deal from me, but I feel the string that's tied my heart up so tightly for so long release ever so slightly.

Gary notices that I digress from my original intent and tells me that though our time is up for this session, we'll be talking about what I alluded to earlier at our next session. He believes it's important and doesn't want to let it go. I remind him that I'll only be seeing him for one session next month, but now as I sit writing this, I realize this was an attempt to secure another session with him. I'm scared.

Session #13

Gary is late for our session this morning. He mentions that a client needed him and I feel small and insignificant, as if I don't matter at all. Familiar feelings.

I feel disjointed. Memories of particularly ugly times in my life are with me, but in a vague and chaotic way. I feel restless and trapped and upset, and then more upset because I suspect I'm taking this out on Phil.

I'd planned on talking to Gary about the rape but decide that I don't have sufficient time to get into it. My doubts overwhelm me. Am I worth this trouble? Are my problems any more intense, any more difficult to endure, than others'? And what of this person who needed him? I consider giving up my therapy hour for her, thinking perhaps she could benefit more from his being with her.

This is a familiar pattern, looking out for others, putting myself second. But what am I hoping to gain from my actions? Finding that I question the motives behind my actions allows me to realize just how beneficial therapy has become.

I decide not to give the other client my therapy hour but compromise slightly by asking if she is all right. Yes, he tells me, and gives me an out—this time—by saying that my time is important and that it's only he and I at this moment. He reminds me that we've agreed to talk about what I've been avoiding.

I begin to shake as I relate what happened.

⌇

It's about two o'clock in the afternoon, November 11 of last year, when I return home from lunch with a friend. I turn into the driveway, a shared courtyard with three other homes, open the garage door, and pull in. I get out of the car and turn to pick up several packages from the backseat when I hear someone addressing me, asking if I have the time.

I'm startled but not particularly afraid. Our house is on a busy street and seeing people is not uncommon. I put the packages back into the car and turn toward the man, at the same time bringing my arm up to look at my watch. In a split second, he grabs my wrists and holds them together, pulling me away from the car and pushing me back on the ground. He lets go of my wrists as I fall to the concrete.

He's on me in a moment. He unbuckles my belt and unsnaps and unzips my jeans, holding me down with the other hand. I look to my left and realize that although my keys have fallen to the ground, they're close—if I stretch I'll be able to grab them and activate the car alarm. I'm focused and know exactly what I must do.

He's brought my jeans down lower and is trying to push his way inside me as I struggle for the keys. I'm undaunted by how far he's getting—I'm concerned only with the keys. I reach them finally and feel one thrust, then another.

In an effort to make me comply, his fist lands first against my jaw and then he rears back and punches me in my eye. I don't feel pain, just a jarring inside my head. I see the roof of the garage and the garage door opener and feel dizzy, as if I'll pass out, but fight to remain awake and focused.

Frantically I start pushing buttons on the key fob. I hear the doors make a locking sound, then push what I believe to be another button—this time the doors unlock. Another button—the trunk pops open. Another frantic push against the fob and, finally, the alarm sounds. He's startled and pulls out of me, ejaculating on my abdomen and jeans.

With a frantic twist he's off me, standing, pulling up his pants, running from the garage, and it's over.

I try to get up and walk but make it only to my knees. I reach my hands up the garage wall to the door opener and slam the palm of my hand against the wall to close the garage door, and then fall back onto my butt and sit. I bring my knees up and hug them, afraid that he's still outside the house. I back myself into the corner so that he can't see me through the garage window and stay plastered into the corner of the garage.

It's much later that I find myself standing in the shower with blistering hot water running over me. I bring my hand to my jaw—it's not too tender at the moment and doesn't feel swollen. And, it doesn't feel broken.

But my eye is injured—badly. Scared, I get out of the shower and look in the mirror. From the outside there is barely anything visible, just slight bruising. It's from the inside that I sense the damage—liquid pools have filled my eye. It's like looking through opaque stockings, but with big globs of black.

I pick up the phone to call Phil—my doctor—the police. Then put the phone down. His words over his shoulder as he ran from the garage explode inside my head: "Tell anyone and I'll come back and kill you and your husband." My hands are shaking so badly the receiver falls to the floor.

I fold myself into a fetal position on the large overstuffed chair near the patio window, drawing my knees up and covering them with the fisherman's sweater that carries Phil's smell. I try, unsuccessfully, to stem my shaking.

I keep the lights off, even though the clouds are quickly moving in front of the sun again, making the sky darker. The family room is my refuge. I've descended into a nurturing safe place and don't want to leave. I look out at the lovely garden where we've planted rosebushes between Victorian-style benches. I remember when we planted them last summer—the rosebuds reminded me of tiny red kisses with plump, red lips, all strung in a row along the branches.

I watch as the sun moves behind the clouds. The leaves on the patio swirl and dance and lift themselves toward the treetops as a soft, misty rain stains the patio.

I feel almost euphoric that I've cheated death—again.

⌒

I stop talking and look up. Gary is incredulous. Suddenly my symptoms—quite intense when we began therapy, although becoming less so—make a great deal of sense. This most recent assault has acted as a trigger for the rape so long ago. Issues that lay dormant for so many years have surfaced, making it even more vital that they be discussed and resolved.

I begin to speak but Gary stops me, saying that we are out of time. The symptoms that initially brought me to therapy are secondary now to the necessity of telling Phil about the assault. This is too significant, too important to our relationship, to keep from him.

I'm pleased that I've told Gary about the assault and that I've put aside my feelings of worthlessness in order to take care of my own needs.

My irrational fear that Gary will feel I'm unable to grasp what's happening in therapy is with me still, but I'm here for me, not him.

Session #15

Gary asks if I've ever discussed with Phil the rape that occurred many years ago.

No, I tell him. It happened a year before we met and I felt that if he knew the extent that I was injured, physically and emotionally, he would be scared away. This isn't an excuse, I tell him, but rather a reason for my silence. I was so overwhelmed with what had happened during the year that all I wanted was to forget. Phil knew nothing of it and I wanted to keep it that way. Besides, it was in the past. Prior to the first time we were intimate, I told him only that I was raped. No explanation was offered on my part and no explanation was requested on his. He respected my privacy.

But I've been unable, I confess, to keep the rape in perspective. My image of my body and of the person I know myself to be has changed. I find myself relating to Gary some of the ways the rape has affected me in my everyday life.

The first change is apparent when I'm faced with any type of confinement. After the rape, anxiety attacks became more and more frequent, first when traveling. Confined spaces, such as an airplane, made me feel imprisoned. It wasn't the fear of a crash but rather the finality of the door shutting and trapping me inside that was the source of my anxiety. Other types of spaces that others might not even have noticed as restricting during travel terrified me, such as tunnels, bridges, or anything else I couldn't get out of or off of easily.

Another type of confinement that raised anxiety were enclosed areas, such as stores and theatres. Several years after the rape, I walked into my bank while an armed robbery was in progress. The bank robbers corralled the customers behind the manager's desk and one held a gun on them as the other two collected the money from the tellers. As I entered one of them turned toward me, pointing the gun at me while shouting instructions. As a consequence, banks became confining to me and then restaurants as well. Any area where I could be imprisoned and not allowed to leave caused me severe discomfort.

Today, confronted with something as innocuous as a simple argument, I feel an overwhelming anxiety and retreat into, I'm ashamed to say, my closet. I have to get as far away from conflict as possible.

To say that this is perplexing to Phil is an understatement. And the fact that my behavior is so illogical only serves to make me feel more isolated from him. I've internalized the rapist's anger so completely that a raised voice can bring me, figuratively, to my knees. I consider this behavior so far outside the norm that I fear I will be labeled crazy. I have to keep my silence, I rationalize, so that no one will find me out.

This has become a serious detriment, I admit, because one of the rewards of an intimate relationship is the trust that develops through sharing yourself with another person. I've seriously compromised that with Phil and missed the fact that when something good—or bad—happens, I can't share it with my best friend.

Also, I tell Gary, my body has changed dramatically. I gained weight in an effort to keep myself safe. The assault in November proved that thinking to be a gross misjudgment on my part. I'd already gained weight before meeting Phil, but he never commented negatively about it.

Life continued and I did the best I could to manage my anxieties. Phil and I became inseparable. We worked at having an intimate relationship and the kind of marriage that had eluded our parents.

Still, there is confusion on his part when I retreat. He never fully understands and I don't go out of my way to explain, fearing that if he knew the truth, he'd leave. It's not that I don't want to tell him; in my mind I simply can't and continue to have my marriage.

My motives are innocent, I tell Gary, and I wish to hurt no one, but this silence about the assault and subsequent turmoil over my past may be destructive to my relationship. I know there should be no silence about something of this magnitude.

I do feel guilty, I tell Gary, that in preparing to disclose my history to Phil, that he and I have reached a certain level of intimacy. How am I able to discuss this with another man and not my best friend?

Gary's response is accurate, of course: I've nothing to lose in telling him about the rape and everything to lose should Phil decide to leave me. But, he asks me, how realistic is my thinking? Is Phil really the kind of man to leave me, giving up a nineteen-year relationship?

I'm forced to look at our relationship closer. Gary softly suggests that perhaps I've repressed my feelings about the validity of our relationship. Or perhaps, he states tentatively, Phil's love for me.

His words ring true, but not in the way he's suggested. I'm in a struggle with both Phil and Gary to make them believe I'm as unworthy as I feel I am, but neither will. They provide me with compassion, but it's a drug. While I feel heady and wonderful when I receive it, I'm more discontented when it fades.

Gary brings up another valid reason to tell Phil. The sudden, overwhelming nature of rape leaves a victim incapacitated, as if they just can't think straight. Could this perhaps be the reason, he postulates, for my not seeking help for the injury to my eye?

I sit looking at him through the veil of film that has covered my eye since the rape. A plethora of shapes, sizes, and intensities, from opaque gray to deep, deep black, flood my eye as they have every day since. At first the lack of noticeable bruising on the outside of my eye seemed a blessing; I could keep what happened in the garage to myself.

But there have been times since when I've wished there had been more outside evidence of the assault so that I'd be forced to tell Phil and to seek help. Now, with nearly daily migraines, I recognize the need to see a retinal specialist to determine if serious damage may have been done. I know in my heart that it's time to tell Phil what happened but I ache inside just thinking about how to form the words. He will be devastated.

Session #16

All I want to do at our session today is talk about the books I've been reading on rape. I realize this is an effort on my part to avoid talking about the details of my rape, but I ask that Gary bear with me. I want answers, answers that I'm unsure he, or anyone, can provide.

Reading about rape is how I'm able to function at this time and place, by utilizing my logical mind and educating myself on the subject. I read all that I can find on the subject and still find no answers to why men rape. Or, rather, why some men rape.

And what of the source of shame that a woman feels following rape? Why does this occur? Why does a woman feel shame for something that clearly isn't her fault?

That some women feel shame is a fact. That rape is a power issue and not a sexual one is regarded as fact, but is one I can't seem to accept. And besides, facts mean nothing to me without being able to apply them to myself personally. I read even more books. Perhaps they will contain a clue as to what kind of person the rapist was and how the intersecting of our lives affects me.

There are, I learn, four different categories of rapists. I recognize mine (mine?) from the description as having been sadistic. Aren't they all, I think to myself, but continue to read. Sadistic rapists use implements like cigarettes, sticks, bottles, whips, and electrical shock devices and aren't satisfied with just inflicting pain. Sadistic rapists commit strangulation and mutilation more readily than other categories of rapists. They direct their violence at body parts with sexual significance: breasts, buttocks, mouth, anus, and genitalia.

With only fifteen minutes left of our session, I inform Gary that I told Phil about the assault in our garage. I told him at a restaurant, coward that I am, and he was stunned. Tears welled up in his eyes and he was grieved beyond anything I've experienced with him before. He found it hard to fathom that I kept silent about something so profoundly intrusive to our relationship and, while he didn't express it in words, his eyes expressed a feeling of having been betrayed, something I'd hoped would not occur.

But since telling him, we're taking steps to recover from this together. Phil took charge, as I'd anticipated. He helped me obtain the name of a retinal specialist. But there's a difference in him. He's more protective, more conscience of where I am at any given moment. One evening when we were unable to sleep, his hand reached for mine in the dark. This rape, he whispered to me, was on his "watch." He'll make sure, he told me, that nothing bad will ever happen to me again.

Also, we're making plans. Staying in our home is impossible, so we'll begin looking for another. I'm frightened to be alone, terrified that the man will return, a situation made worse by the fact that I work from home. In fact, we'll most likely move out of our community altogether.

I can tell by Gary's expression that he is confused as to why I started out chit-chatting about the books I'm reading and suddenly began talking when we had so little time left about something so significant.

I'm sorry that I confused him, but my dependence on him is unsettling and his approval too significant. This is my way of remaining in control. With that realization comes another: A pattern is emerging in that I hold back with Gary as I've done with Phil. Once I realize this, I'm faced with the fact that it's my behavior that must be amended.

I continue to remind myself that Gary isn't my father or a personal friend, but a professional whom I've sought to help me help myself. The line that distinguishes me from others is sometimes blurred. I don't seem to recognize where I end and they begin and feel chaotic. I dread being left, but I've exposed myself quite completely to him at this point. And isn't that the goal of our relationship? For him to leave me? Won't that be the consequence of our success?

The need for Gary's approval runs deep. I take a breath and tell him something that I wasn't able to until this moment. I tell him I'm in graduate school, working towards my graduate degree in counseling psychology.

I brace myself for his disapproval, but there is none. In fact, he reacts quite the opposite, asking how long I've been studying, where I'm going to school, and with whom I'm training. I breathe a barely audible sigh of relief that my ego is still intact. Gary says he wants to discuss this further, but he's encouraging and supportive. I'm elated that he feels I'll be of help to those with similar issues to mine, following my own therapy and training.

But having begun therapy, I feel damaged somehow, I tell him. I fear that I won't be able to contribute to my clients' mental health if I'm going through difficulties myself, but he's assured me that therapists who have experienced issues in their own lives are often particularly valuable to their clients.

Session #17

A suffocating need engulfs me to rid myself of the memory of the rape that occurred so many years before. Gary assures me that relating it to him with as much detail as I can manage is the first step to healing from it. And so with this session I begin to tell him of the day I was raped.

⌒

It's Thursday, June 17, 1976, at 4:30 in the afternoon. I'm nineteen years old. The air is sweet and clear and San Francisco is at its most beautiful. A soft fog has returned to blanket the city in a delicate shroud.

A sudden violent push against my back forces me into the bushes on my hands and knees, tearing my tights and making my hands bleed. My face falls forward toward the ground and I scrape my cheek. Angry, I twist my head around, glimpsing the face of a man I don't recognize. He grabs my long hair around his hand and pulls me toward him. He stands upright, pulling me to my feet, twisting my arm around my back. My other hand grasps the air in front of me for my purse and the book I've been carrying.

We rush across the street as he scolds me, my feet reaching for the ground. He's screaming obscenities and speaking to me as if we know each other. I think for a moment that he has me confused with someone else until I notice a man on the street turn away upon seeing us. I panic when I realize that he's intending to give the impression that we know each other—that I'm his girlfriend or wife so that no one will become involved. His words become noise, static in my brain. My head is pounding so loudly that I can't make out individual words.

He motions to a house we're walking towards and says something. I try to nod, but he has such a tight grip on my hair that my head won't move. I try to cry out but produce nothing. We're moving quickly toward the house and are almost at the steps. Terror keeps my voice locked inside me. He's moving me—controlling me. My feet barely touch the pavement. He hurries me up the stairs, kicking the front door open and dragging me inside.

With my hair still wrapped around his hand, he turns me around to face him. My eyes, perhaps my brain, make a quick assessment. He's tall, perhaps 6'2" or 6'3", and has curly blond hair that falls to his shoulders. His green eyes are bizarre and lock onto mine with an angry, stabbing hate. I feel a chill run the length of my body. I know he's going to hurt me. He's wearing a cream-colored fisherman's sweater. The sleeves hang too long, even though he's tall. Blue shows from underneath the round collar of his sweater, like a jean shirt.

31

His hands are on my shoulders as he looks down at my face. I expect him to say something but instead find myself flying backward, experiencing a weird sensation as he moves further from me, his eyes still locked onto mine. My arms reach behind me, searching for the floor, but my butt hits first, then my elbows, then my head hits the hardwood floor.

I wake lying on a thin mattress on the floor. I'm overwhelmed but orient myself quickly and am able to remember what took place. He's tied my hands in front of me and taken off my underpants and tights. My jean skirt, with snaps down the front, is still fastened but just barely. Only the top snap is fastened. He's unbuttoned my blouse and opened it to my sides, exposing my breasts. My raincoat hangs off my shoulder on one side and is completely off on the other side.

It's quiet and I feel acutely aware. I try to focus on the room. Renovation is taking place in the house. A noxious mixture of fresh paint and stain used to refinish hardwood floors fills my head, making it ache. I don't hear him around me, which only serves to make me more anxious.

⌒

I sense Gary moving in his chair and lift my head to face him. He focuses his attention squarely on me, gently telling me we are out of time.

32

Session #18

I'm tentative as I walk into Gary's office for today's session, wondering if he'll remember where we left off. I've been stuck in that place and time since I saw him last and am anxious to move on. He motions for me to take a seat and asks if I'd like to continue to talk about the rape. I take a deep breath and take him back in the house with me that Thursday afternoon.

⌣

There is no furniture in the room except the mattress on which I'm lying. An unlighted lamp without a shade is shoved against the corner. The mattress is old, with blue and white stripes, and is thin, scrawny enough to feel the floor underneath. A rancid smell from beneath my face—stains, sweat, and dirt mixed together—overtakes the other odors in the house, making me nauseous.

Heavy tasseled shades cover the bay windows and it's darker now than before. Sounds are different. There's a kitchen to my right and a pass-through above me. The barrel of a small handgun is visible over the edge of the counter. Another wave of panic washes over me and I tremble uncontrollably, although it isn't cold in the house. My fear is palpable and I'm certain he can smell it. I try to calm myself as one would if a dangerous animal were near.

Except for a light shining through the frosted windows in the rear of the kitchen, there's no other light. I see him out of the corner of my eye at the same time he notices me move. I try to be still, but it's too late. In a moment he's on top of me, struggling to push my legs apart and get inside me. I'm paralyzed and my heart is racing. I'm so petrified that drawing a breath is nearly impossible.

His body is hot, almost burning, but his hands are like ice, rough, violent, and tearing into my flesh. My hands are bleeding from cuts made while tying me up and the blood drips onto my stomach. The skin on my arm against my stomach feels familiar and warm, a sharp contrast to his cold hands. His skin feels repulsive. He lies on top of me with nothing on, his penis against my leg, trying to push himself inside me. He isn't hard enough so tries to push his fingers in instead.

The muscles in my thighs ache. Instead of yielding to his demand to spread my legs, I squeeze them tighter together. He continues to struggle with me. I feel as if I'm an animal with a primal need to survive. I'm just a receptacle—no longer human. I strain to get out from underneath his body but can't get leverage. Pushing my head against his shoulder, I try to get up. Words escape from my mouth with no connection to my brain. I hear pleading, begging. It sounds like my voice yet I'm horrified to realize that it's only in my brain. Only a whisper escapes. I can't com-

33

prehend the words he's saying. They run together and fall on my ears like gibberish. Am I going crazy? Why can't I understand and follow his directions? Doing so may save my life. I don't have any other option, yet my thoughts just bounce off the insides of my brain. A massive scream starting way down deep has stopped short. He struggles to pry my legs apart as I struggle just as hard to keep them together. The effort is so intense that my thigh muscles feel as if they're on fire.

His face is close to mine; he's pushing his tongue into my mouth, his hands pulling at me. My breath quickens and turns to panting. One of his hands is between my legs; the other is holding my jaw, forcing me to face him and stop twisting.

He's furious with me. He backs up and sits on his calves. He's found his leverage and, with one final pull, has pried my legs apart. He sits straighter up on his knees and brings his left hand back. I know I'm going to be hit but when his fist finally slams straight into my chin, I feel shock just the same. I'm overwhelmed at the force with which he hits me, dazed by my own lack of power over his strength.

I take a deep breath, sucking in some of the blood that's already begun to pool in my mouth. My tongue instinctively takes inventory. My bottom teeth are holding on by thin threads so I work them around and stand them up, pushing against them with my tongue on the inside and keeping my lip stiff. Cut and bleeding, my lip swells right away. I turn my face to the left and spit blood onto the mattress, choking on some that has run down my throat. I bring my head back around and his fist slams again into my face, this time into the right side of my jaw. The sound of my bone breaking sickens me.

My eyes stop focusing as the pain of his punches reach me. He keeps pounding my body, legs, chest, stomach, face. Breathing is difficult and becoming impossible. Anticipation of where his fist will land next is impossible, and agonizing when it finally makes contact with my body.

His words bring me around. He's imploring me, then threatening me to give him what he wants. I'm confused and angry. It's not I who am hurting him—he's in control. He spits vial words toward me to degrade me and questions why he can't get inside me. I whisper that I've never been with a man. This proves to be a mistake and he grows even more excited.

His physical assault is constant and his verbal description of what he's going to do to me is malicious and grotesque. I hear only words, disconnected from any meaning. Exhaustion overwhelms me. I'm consumed with the simple act of anticipation. No resistance meets him when he spreads my legs this time; my muscles give way under his force.

Surprise registers on his face when he hears the muted, animal sounds that escape me. Anticipating that he will penetrate me with his penis, I surrender, but *instead he pushes something sharp inside me until it stops. Pulling it out, he repeats the motion again and again.*

Instinctively I try to grasp the object but can't with my hands tied. My fingers claw at hands that are unaffected by my scratches.

Gary stops me. Shock doesn't register on his face, for which I'm grateful, but he looks away as he tells me we are out of time, but gently touches my elbow on the way out of his office. I'm numb as I sit writing this, careful not to allow the tiniest tear to be shed, lest I'm unable to stop.

Session #19

Today is gray and rainy. I wear Phil's fisherman's sweater to my session with Gary so that I will feel warm and comforted. I have a hard time meeting his eyes, and without the normal pleasantries that usually take place, I fall onto his couch and continue where I left off last session.

My face is horribly swollen and my breathing raspy and labored. Blood trickles down the back of my throat. Lying on my back is extremely difficult. Raising my hands to him, I plead with him to untie me. To my surprise, he does. I raise my hands toward him again but can't reach his body. He sees my hands reaching up and backs away, his arms being long enough to hold me at bay. I sink back into the mattress.

The cramps in my back grow more intense. He continues pushing the object into me and gives me little room to move. He grows tired and starts to pull it out; I can sense what he's doing and grow restless. Squirming, I want it out of me now.

I bring my legs up and roll onto my right side, holding my stomach. I feel the blood rush out of me. The pain in my face is excruciating—tears well up in my eyes and roll down my cheeks, falling onto the mattress. I feel desperately, horribly alone.

Exhausted, he leaves me alone and falls against the wall at my feet. I'm not his priority for the time being. The respite is welcome but leaves me terrified as I antic- ipate his next actions. I try to think about how to get out of the house but can't form thoughts. I want this to be over. I try to move but can't so I lie on my side as he left me. Looking at him is nauseating but I can't move any of my muscles. I'm frozen in this time, in this place.

Paralysis works its way from my feet up my legs, my thighs, my stomach, and squeezes my chest tight. I'm alarmed and panic—what if this feeling strikes my throat, my breathing? Could my breathing simply stop? Is this where I'm going to die? I can't move, not even to save my life.

He picks himself up and moves around the kitchen, standing behind the counter. He brings back some items and tells me what he's doing as he begins freebasing cocaine. I fight to remain coherent as smoke fills the room, but the sweet aroma of the cocaine makes me dizzy and light-headed. Desperate to surrender to the sleep it might bring, I'm frightened nonetheless to lose control. My eyes feel heavy, opening and closing ever so slowly. I'm unsure whether it's the effect of the cocaine or what he's put me through, but each time they close I fight the urge to sleep. I'm afraid he'll kill me.

Letters appear in front of my eyes, at first just floating in space. I try to make words of them, to concentrate on the words the letters are forming. Vibrating, spinning letters, huge in size. While I focus on them, I'm unable to focus on him and what he's done to me.

Finally the letters slow and stop spinning. I'm able to right them in my mind, to strip away the garish colors and the wild patterns that fill and surround them. I go over them and make them the same size. I go over them again to line them up. I go over them once again to put them in proper order. My mind is consumed with my work. Words of a book I started reading last week come to me now. Their beauty so impressed me at the time. My heart aches to be reading it now, to be outside this house.

I struggle hard to remember the words. The author spoke of houses like this one where people live and experience life. One word comes—then another. The effort is intense and exhausting but I have to make the words come. I deplete my resources, but can't stop.

The words that I grasp turn brilliant in color and wave and pulsate. They run together and back away from each other as if they have a life of their own. Patterns fill my mind with colors and shapes and feelings and sizes and fonts and—another word. Then another and another. Like a gift, I have an entire sentence. The tiny trickle of tears down my face turns into wracking sobs that burn my cheeks.

A noise surprises me. I look toward him and see him rise to his knees. The blackness of the room makes him appear ghostly. I can see his face more clearly now but don't feel anything at all. The absence of emotions for just a moment is strangely calming and I suppose this is how a person feels just before they die—as if they have nothing to lose in sweet surrender. That whatever comes next will be a relief compared to this particular moment in time.

The absence of emotion passes quickly. I draw a breath, smelling the blood on my lips, and realize that I've forgotten to breathe. The terror returns and I try to remember my parents, my dog. I fear that I'll never see them again.

Hands—silken—more words float into and out of my grasp. Pulsating and spinning in my head, they grow large and blood-red, then creamy and soft, almost translucent. I can see the paper that the words are on, too: The soft, sweet color of vanilla ice cream and the fragrant smell of the trees from which the paper was made. I've lost my dignity at the hands of this man. I need words in front of me to survive— comforting words to assure me that I will get out of this house.

These words take an eternity to form. One lies upon the other. I'm in a dream, walking farther and farther out of my body. I stare at him now as if it will erase all that has happened. Being outside of myself brings liberation. He can't hurt me now. I'm calm—untouchable. The feeling doesn't come from within, but rather sur-

rounds me. I try to comprehend something incomprehensible; I can't ask why at this moment.

⟂

Gary stops me, noticing that my breathing has changed. My chest feels as if it's on fire and I can't quite get enough air in. He asks that I place my feet on the floor and takes me through relaxation exercises, trying to return my breathing to normal. Remembering is physically painful. There's sadness in Gary's eyes as he walks me to the door. I'm sad as well when I leave, a feeling that has not lifted even now as I write this.

Session #20

I decide not to tell Gary of the intensity of my nightmares since I began talking about the rape. He may slow me down or stop me altogether in an effort to alleviate them, but there is a freedom as well in being able to talk about what happened. I'm sorry for the burden I'm placing on him—I know this can't be easy to hear, but I'm desperate for his help.

I continue where I left off at our last session and take him back into the house with me.

⌒

I notice parts of his body for the first time. He doesn't look like a rapist. He doesn't look like the monster he is. He's supposed to look different. He's supposed to look like someone whom the rest of us know to stay away from. Otherwise, we're not safe. Slumped against the wall, he looks like any other man on the street.

The streets are quieter now. Sounds are muffled, like they are when the fog lowers into the crevices of the buildings and descends like cat's paws onto their roofs. This time of night usually brings comfort and solace, but I'm filled with sorrow when I realize I'll never experience this time of night with the same innocence again.

Worse, sounds that comforted before, that I hadn't even fully heard, are now alarmingly absent. Only after they're missing do I realize I hadn't noticed them fully—sounds of people, of traffic, of televisions and radios in houses nearby. Now there is only silence except for a foghorn moaning long and low in the distance.

Because it's quieter outside, I feel even more alone. Normal life continues around me but I'm not a part of it. The person I was this morning no longer exists. Overwhelming loss devours me. No one will hear me, even if I gather the courage to cry out.

I'm so lost in myself that I barely recognize he's speaking to me. His tone has changed and he starts an apologetic diatribe that enrages me. He asks for understanding, declares concern for me, as if he has no complicity in what he's done. His green eyes, dilated nearly full, eclipsed by large, black pupils, stare at me. This is a cruel joke.

Questions he's asking go unanswered. Statements he makes pass over me without reaction. He meets my quiet rebellion with hostility, telling me that I'm even more beautiful when in pain. I lay staring at him. We're at a stalemate. We both understand it's he who has the power in this room. We both know that he can force me to do what he pleases.

His sudden silence frightens me and I know he's going to hurt me more tonight.

He reties my hands. A candle he'd placed on the pass-through while in the kitchen earlier flickers each time he slumps against the wall. I'm terrified that it will fall onto the mattress and burn me alive, but I try not to become mesmerized by staring at it. He notices me looking up and realizes he's found a tool to use against me.

He berates me for looking where I shouldn't, for being bad, and pushes me onto my back. He reaches up for the candle and pours the melted wax pooled in the hollow of the candle over my chest. Burning, intense pain radiates through me. The wax falls onto my breast and rolls down into the center of my chest, blistering my skin as it flows down. Pulling my hair back and baring my throat to his mouth, he bites into my neck and whispers that I'm going to wish I were dead.

He encounters no resistance as he pushes my legs apart to penetrate me. I want him to get this over with so I can go home and take care of myself. He slams into me, again and again, but can't ejaculate. My hands are still tied in front of me and the movement pushing against my arms and breast is sheer agony. I feel my skin pull on my bones, he's so rough. He grunts like an animal and we fall into a sick, disgusting conspiracy in which we both have the same goal: For him to come.

He's frustrated by not being able to and pushes me onto my left side. He stands up and kicks me in the back, then moves in front of me and kneels down. Reaching around my head, he pulls me to him, trying to push his penis into my mouth. I'm swollen and my jaw is broken but that is of no matter to him. I can't help choking and pull back. Fresh blood flows from my teeth and jaw; he's upset the delicate bracing of my teeth. It's physically impossible for me to open my mouth wide enough and I push my hands against his thighs and abdomen. The thought of him in my mouth is repulsive.

I make resolutions with myself minute by minute. If I make it through the next ten minutes . . . the next fifteen . . . He tests my limits for enduring pain. He doesn't want sex from me but defilement. He's enraged that I can't take him in my mouth and falls away from me. I roll onto my back. I press my pelvis into the mattress and bring my legs closer together to try and stop shaking but the need to go to the bathroom is urgent. I push against my lower abdomen. I can't afford further humiliation. It becomes a stubborn show of preventing him from seeing what he's doing to me.

I whisper that I have to go to the bathroom but try to sound calm as I say it, as though it's not as pressing as it really is. He motions down a hall but tells me he won't untie my hands. I've won a small victory. I struggle to stand, but it's impossible. Even if my hands were untied I wouldn't have the strength, so I crawl the twenty or so feet to the bathroom on my knees and the outsides of my hands, dragging my clothes behind me.

Gary stops me. I sit shaking uncontrollably as Gary whispers that our time is up. I'm devastated at having to relive all of this, to reveal these things to another person and then to have to go out into the world as if everything is all right when it's anything but.

Session #21

It's been nearly a month since our last session and I find myself anxious to see Gary. Everything seems to be unraveling lately: I have nightmares when I *can* fall asleep, insomnia on too many other nights. I tell Gary none of this but, at his urging, continue to tell him about the rape.

~~

I'm shivering, afraid that I won't make it to the bathroom. I wait for him to grab me at any moment from behind and take me back to the mattress. I don't feel his hands on my body so I keep moving slowly along the floor, afraid to look back. I feel each wood grain on the hardwood floor as I methodically place the outsides of my hands down onto the cold floor, then one knee, then the other, then start all over again.

When I awake, I'm on the mattress again, having no recollection of returning to the front room or even of reaching the bathroom. The top snap of my jean skirt is still fastened, keeping my skirt around me. My eyes burn and my face is flushed. I'm lost and no one knows that I'm here or what's happening to me. No one is going to rescue me.

He claws at me, trying to open my legs. I hear yelling that must be from him, but I have a hard time focusing on his face. I can't open my mouth enough to say that I'm trying to do what he says. He kneels between my legs and grabs me by my ankles. He draws me toward him, pulling me up by my hips. He's going to sodomize me.

He turns me over, crushing the right side of my face into the mattress, laying me against my jaw. I twist my head down and to the right and bring it back around to lie on the left side of my face. My hands are still tied in front of me so my head is at an angle again. I can't catch my breath and whisper, pleading with him not to do this and to please untie my hands. I stretch my mouth as much as I can to make him hear me. My jawbones grind together. I become disoriented again and feel as if I'll pass out.

He reaches underneath me and unties my hands, stuffing the blood-soaked cloth into my mouth. Shaking, I keep swallowing to keep from becoming sick. He has both my hands in his, still behind my back, making it impossible for me to get leverage. It seems like forever that I'm sucking in air and, along with it, dirt and blood on the cloth. No air escapes. I stop resisting. My whole body engages in trying to get air out of my lungs. I have an eerie sensation of my muscles going limp and soft. Again, I feel this is what it must be like to die, to grow soft and feel your mus-

cles relax their grip on life. Suddenly he grows tired and lets my hands go. The desire to take another breath is stronger than the enticing blackness and, as soon as he releases my hands, I'm able to reach up and yank the cloth from my mouth.

He pulls my skirt up around my waist and sodomizes me. No preliminaries. The pain is sudden, vicious, and raw. He keeps pushing, chastising me for the blood that's running down the inside of my thighs. I fear that he'll break me in two and force myself to hold on, to take deep breaths. Animal grunts now escape from deep inside me.

Suddenly, I'm astounded to feel myself flow out of my body. In sharp contrast to his hard, vicious movements, mine, in moving outside of myself, are softened and gradual. I move to a corner in the room and watch what's happening to me. The disorientation is excruciating; the confusion at what's happening too much to bear. Disconnection from the girl lying on the mattress leaves me with the feeling of having abandoned her, as if she's truly all alone.

My body moves to accommodate the pain but instinctively, not with any consciousness, because I'm no longer in it. I have to leave my body in order to remain sane. I see myself push against him and rise up on my hands and knees. I'm relieved to be able to breathe again. He taunts me, threatening to go deeper inside. My insides are burning and my muscles close around him as much in rage as in pain. I reach out in front of the mattress to the hardwood floor. Hard and real, it's something that I can touch. My fingers dig into the wood.

Panic-stricken, I realize I'm inside my body again. A disconcerting feeling of being able to simultaneously experience this and look at myself overwhelms me. Frightened of him, I'm even more terrified of what's happening to me. I'm sure he's driven me insane.

He pulls me toward him with a ferocious jerk that lifts my hands off the floor and then back down with a thud. A bolt of pain shoots up my back. I claw at the floor, stretching my fingers in front of me, frantically trying to get away. My hands are surreal. Disembodied and disconnected from my arms, I see them in front of me as if they're not mine. I don't recognize them. They appear opaque and I can see the blood flowing through them and the bones and nerves. Shards of the hardwood floor mix with blood underneath my fingernails.

He comes inside me with furious energy, convulsing again and again. He pushes against me, holding onto my hips, bringing them towards him. Pulling out of me doesn't bring the measure of relief I long for. The torment is beyond words. He falls against the wall and passes out almost immediately.

Without his hands supporting my hips, I drop to my stomach, then onto my right side on the mattress, unable to move. I'm exhausted. All I can do is lie motionless, staring into space. I notice the wall before me, the small brush strokes on the newly painted surface and the way it intersects with the ornate baseboard. How very intricate and pretty. A deep black sleep overtakes me.

I awaken to the sound of my heart beating loudly in my ears and pounding in my throat. I don't move a muscle. I'm afraid that he will hear and I draw a breath in order to calm myself. As happens when one is going underwater, not knowing when air will be available again, my breathing becomes short and barely audible.

It's difficult, but I keep my eyes closed when I hear him stir. I don't want to see him again. Don't want to look into his eyes. I open my eyes when I hear him move toward the kitchen. He stays there for some time; he's saying something to me that I can't understand. I don't respond and in a moment he's back in the room with me. He makes demands I can't accommodate and I whisper that I'm going to be sick.

Becoming angrier, he grabs the gun from the pass-through and puts it under my chin, threatening to blow my face off if I don't do what he says.

His hand slams down hard onto my neck, his fingers squeezing into my throat. Vile admonitions pour from him, but the pressure against my neck and chest make him seem far away and hard to understand. I move in slow motion. Bringing my hands up to his, I dig hard into his flesh and feel his blood seep onto mine, moistening my flesh.

His sudden, spastic movement frightens me. He brings the gun to my cheek and, without hesitation, pulls the trigger. My breath—my heart—stops.

⌒

Gary stops me. Our time is up. I've come to resent those words, to resent the fact that he's asking me to relive this pain. I crawl off his couch, spent. I want to tell him of the nightmares I've been having but there's no time. There's never enough time.

Session #22

Gary calls me into his office. I'm sure he can see that I don't want to continue and I'm certain he doesn't want to hear any more, but we're in too far to stop now. I tell him I feel as if I have to get poison out of my system. And so, I continue where I left off at our last session.

⌁

Our eyes lock as we wait for the bullet to rip into my face and blow my head apart. The next second feels like a lifetime of agony; my entire life in this action, in this house, this man, this rape, this moment.

There is no sound.

I expect to hear a thunderous blast rip through my head but there is no sound. He pulls back from me and stands upright, emptying the bullets into his hand. He counts them—one, two, three, four, five—a cruel laugh erupts from him as he flings the gun and bullets onto the counter in the kitchen.

My eyes lock onto his again as he comes toward me. I've no energy left. No fantasies of escape, no hope, no resistance—just numbing nothingness. He falls down on me and pushes himself inside. I'm a piece of flesh. He knows it, as do I. His penis reaches up high into me. He ejaculates, arching his back and holding tightly onto me. A moment later he starts again and then again, ejaculating each time.

My eyes stare straight into his. He turns his face away from me and continues. His face, I fear, is the last I'll ever see. I see distorted, chaotic images and strive to see more clearly but am grateful that I can't. I feel numb and my skin moves over my bones again like before with each thrust inside me. My skin is a dress a couple of sizes too big. I lose my focus on him and slip into the blackness.

I awake. I'm cold. He's off me now and a light is shining ever so softly along the edges of the shade, not as if the sun is shining, but as though it's just becoming light. Muted passages from songs come from nearby homes; people are getting ready for school and work. Am I really hearing these sounds or have I gone crazy?

My eyes move around the room. He's slumped against a different wall farther from me, his head in an agonizing, unreal position. I stare for what seems like forever, picking a spot on his chest and then another on the wall to see if he's breathing.

I lift my head. Move ever so slightly. Stop. Move ever so slightly. Stop. This goes on for what seems like forever until I'm on my knees. I'm dizzy and feel nauseous. Still, I keep moving, slowly but methodically. I keep moving my eyes between his body and the door. My knees are underneath me and I'm able to sit on them. I bend forward, pull myself along on the outside of my arms, much like before, but I use my arms now instead of my hands. The goal of getting toward the door makes it easier to endure the physical pain.

On and on I move—methodically, excruciatingly, slowly. I wait for him to grab me from behind, then move again, the slightest amount, then am very still, waiting for him to grab me from behind. My coat and skirt drag behind me.

Finally, I reach the door and stop. I haven't looked behind me for some time. I reach for the doorknob and turn it ever so slowly. I'm close now and fearful of what he'll do to me if he sees me trying to leave.

Just as quickly as I was in the house, I'm out. Out of the coffin and standing on my own. Blood is caked onto my body, everywhere. I realize that my clothes are hanging from me and pull them around me. I want to go home. It's so near, only a couple of blocks, and I stumble at first, trying to orient myself to the outside.

It's early—barely anyone is on the street. A man stops me only steps from my apartment, grabbing me by the shoulders, asking if I'm okay. I nod frantically. I have to go home—I'm terrified to look behind me. Please don't hurt me—don't hold me back—don't touch me. I just want to go home. Probably just as frightened, looking at this mess of a young woman in front of him, bloody and bruised, clothes half off, he lets me go.

〜

I stop and look up at Gary, who looks away. I feel as if my heart is lying bare on the floor. I want to scream to him to help me, to save me, but we say nothing as he leads me to the door.

Session #23

I feel awkward prior to our session today. Over the past sessions while relating the story of the rape, I'd been successful at containing my thoughts and feelings to our time together. Now, a full week of emotions pours forth from me as soon as I see him.

I interrogate Gary as if he has the answers I've been looking for all these years, either as a psychologist or as a man, and become agitated when he remains silent. How could the man on the street just let me go? How could he look in my eyes and see how badly I was hurt and let me go? I suppose I'm asking Gary if he could do that to me— could he let me go? Am I not worth saving?

Respectful silence. It's not that Gary doesn't want to provide me with answers; it's simply that there are none. There is no answer for why the man on the street didn't help me, or for why I was raped in the first place. I've driven myself nearly mad looking for answers only to be left with a nagging, restless feeling that I was somehow deserving of this.

Gary asks me to talk more about the man I saw on the street.

I'm steps from my apartment. It's cold still—what little sun there is hasn't reached the sidewalk yet because of the old, Victorian apartment buildings lining the street. I must traverse the hill, go past the small grocery store, then the steps. I plan a strategy on how to get home.

I have to get there before the rapist realizes I've escaped. I fight feeling nauseous and the feeling that I'll pass out any moment. I wrap what I'm wearing around me to keep my clothes from falling to the ground.

My breathing is labored and my chest feels as if it will explode when I see the man coming toward me from my left. He seems to have come from nowhere and I turn to face him straight on. I can see my shattered body reflected in his expression.

He grabs me by the shoulders, looks into my eyes, and asks if I'm all right. His swift action in pulling me towards him frightens me. I feel my head snap back and my eyes roll back into my head. When I open them again I see only sky.

I panic. Somehow I'm able to form words and plead with him to let me go, as much from a feeling of dread that he will hurt me as from the need to get off the street so the rapist won't find me. The physical act of his putting his hands on me seems to make me more aware of my surroundings, and when he lets go of my shoulders, I stumble slightly and reach out to grab his arm to keep from falling.

He backs away.

I look down. I have my coat over me, but just barely, and a shirt underneath that's unbuttoned. My skirt, with snaps down the front, is scarcely on and the ones I've somehow fastened are mismatched.

All down the front of me, where my shirt and coat don't cover, my chest is covered in blood. Most is old and dried but some, along the right side of my chest and shoulder, is new, red blood. I touch it with my finger. It's still warm and wet.

⌒

I'm shaking and nauseous as Gary gently tells me that our time is up. I feel relieved that I don't have to go on. My words seem to come in slow motion today. Disconnected and halting; the session seemed as if it was four hours long.

The look on the man's face torments me even now, so many years later.

Session #24

Gary's empathy for the brutality that I endured in the man's house leaves me feeling disconcerted. Not wanting to be labeled a victim and hating the reality of what that implies—lack of control—I'm strangely uncomfortable now in having told him the details of the rape. Still, there's more to say and since I began the journey, I must finish it. I take a breath and continue where we left off during our last session.

I finally make it home, bleeding and raw.

I find myself standing in my bathtub. I've turned on the shower but don't recall the steps exactly or even how long I've been standing there. It has to be nine in the morning, perhaps ten. I hear no sounds of people leaving for work—no sounds at all, in fact, save for the pounding in my ears. I try to make sense of what has happened but it's too soon. Something is terribly wrong—instead of hearing my own voice inside my head, I hear that of the rapist, his words scorching my ears.

Words run through my head that I don't recognize, louder and louder still, until I fear I'll go mad. Terror grips me around the neck like a noose. The water is scalding, but still not hot enough. It will, I hope, burn the memory of this man off me and peel the skin from where he has touched me.

Leaning my hands against the tile, I shift my weight from one foot to the other and back. I feel no emotions, just numbness that seeps from my flesh into my bones.

I stare straight ahead at the wall of the shower until a droplet of water demands my attention. Focusing intently, I watch as it maps a path along a band of grout and on along each tile until it plunges ever so softly from the faucet to join the blood and water pooling in the tub around my feet.

I watch hundreds and hundreds of these tiny droplets fall to their demise though I'm unsure of how long, in fact, that I stand there watching. Well into my study, it occurs to me that it's my blood that I'm watching pool around my feet and swirl into the drain. How much can I lose, I wonder, until I pass out or die? My hair, matted and wet, comes out in clumps as I push it back from my face.

Each small drop of water blisters my skin as it lands, but I barely feel it. Looking down, I bend my elbows and bring my palms up, turning them over and back again. They're foreign to me and are the only area on my body, save for my feet, that don't have a bruise, a cut, or a burn.

I feel along my sides, taking an inventory of my injuries. My hands become my eyes. I can't bring myself to look at what he's done.

My breasts are tender—my right excruciating. I feel the pain of the candle wax he poured over me more intensely in the shower than I had in his house.

My hands move down my stomach, then further down. I bring my hand along my hips, then inside me. I'm caked in blood.

Simple movements are piercingly painful. My thigh muscles burn and grow heavy—I'm tired and start shivering. My knees buckle, but I don't make an effort to catch myself and float slowly to the floor of the bathtub.

Sitting is impossible so I kneel on the floor as if in prayer. The irony isn't lost on me. I bring myself onto my hands and knees and stay that way, with my head down, the water beating against my back, for hours. Vulnerable—open—violated.

As comforting as the shower had been at first, it becomes unbearably irritating. Dizzy and suddenly nauseous, I must get out. My muscles are stiff and no longer cooperate with me so I crawl up and over the side of the tub and lie on my side on the bath mat, holding my stomach.

Terror grips me once again as a host of memories floods me. The thought that perhaps the rapist followed me and knows where I live seizes me. Perhaps he's in my apartment at this moment—perhaps outside my bathroom door, waiting for me. Wait—how had I gotten in the door? Where are my keys? Still in the door?

Afraid to move, I lie there forever. Motionless. Breathless. Terrified to make a sound. I'm afraid even to towel myself off for fear of him hearing me should he be outside. Surely he hears the pounding of my heart. Nausea grips my stomach when, without warning, I become violently ill. Fluids pour from me as my body tries to purge the brutality the rapist inflicted.

I can't stay on the bathroom floor any longer. Slowly, painstakingly, I begin my work. My movements are minute, I so fear throwing up again. Each time I open my mouth, my bones grind together, doing further damage. Because I've been sodomized, sitting up is impossible. A large wound on my right hip makes leaning on that side unbearable. Each movement becomes a new way in which to relate to my body, each movement the discovery of a new injury.

Five minutes stretch into ten, then fifteen without another movement. Then, when my stomach feels more calm, another movement. Twenty minutes this time— another movement—and then another. I roll up the bath mat and clean up the blood and vomit and urine on the floor as best I can.

I gather my courage and painfully make my way into the hallway. The man isn't in my apartment but on the floor in front of my bedroom door are my clothes in a pile—the clothes I'd put on yesterday morning—the clothes I was raped in. They're bloody and torn and I don't want them in my home.

I look up, finally, from a spot on the floor. I know that our time is up but say to Gary that I've become successful at one thing, at least: Restricting my feelings to this one small hour of the week. I can't feel any more than I'm feeling or I will go mad.

Session #26

I struggle to keep the purpose of relating my history to Gary in the front of my mind. There are feelings surrounding the year that we're discussing that I have to accept and I find myself at today's session anxious to tell him about Saturday, June 19, the day following the rape.

⌒

I pass out on my bed after the shower but awaken later in the afternoon. When I do, I'm shivering and cold with my face puffed up into a grotesque balloon. The pain in my mouth makes me nauseous and the fear of what might happen should I leave it another moment makes me take action. Though it's late I call my dentist and, through clenched teeth, get a session for late in the evening. I avoid the looks I get on the bus but am more focused in any case on not becoming sick. My mouth is clenched tightly to steady my lower teeth.

Sitting is impossible so I stand, holding onto a pole. I concentrate on making sure I get off when necessary, but am suddenly aware that I'm on the outside, looking in. Fragmented and chaotic feelings floor me and suddenly I'm in fear that I'll see the man who raped me, though I'm headed in a different direction from his house.

My dentist, whom I've been seeing for two years since arriving in San Francisco, is suspicious that my injuries aren't a result of a car accident as I had mentioned on the phone. Such injuries, he tells me, aren't consistent with a car accident. He starts to push me for answers until he notices tears welling up in my eyes. I suppose he feels sympathy for me because he gives up his questioning and readies me for surgery to stabilize my lower teeth. After that, he sets and wires my jaw.

The anesthesia and medication for pain bring a hazy feeling, then suddenly a feeling of exhaustion. My dentist and his nurse ask if there's someone they can call to help me get home, but I write on a pad they supply that I have no one. They take the elevator down with me, the nurse giving me instructions all the while. As I watch them walk into the parking garage, I feel a sense of betrayal towards myself. I've not told them the truth about the rape, the beginning of many years of shame and silence.

Arriving home, I lie on my bed, too tired even to take my clothes off except for unzipping my jeans, and fall into a deep, deep sleep.

Suddenly, the phone jolts me awake. I'm in the netherworld between sleep and awareness, and yesterday and the day before do not exist.

The words come through the phone in bits and pieces, like in a dream: Dad—air show—plane accident—killed—huge crowd—no one else hurt.

My face is cracked and bloody from sleeping and wires hold my jaw tight so that speaking is difficult. The nurse on the phone interprets my whispers as shock and hands the phone to one of my dad's friends who reiterates what the nurse has told me with no further details for me to digest. Her next words come in garbled spurts: Will take care of arrangements—come right away—I saw him crash—come right away. She, and I, are crying as the phone goes dead.

I'm crying softly now as Gary tells me our time is up.

Session #28

The grief I'm trying to work through in my therapy with Gary is inexplicably tied to a number of events during the year I was raped. Far-reaching implications are only now becoming clear.

Gary urges me to talk further about my dad, although at first I fail to see how this will help in alleviating the pain of the rape, but I place my trust in him and tell him about my dad's funeral.

⌇

It's June 25, only several days following the rape, and I've finally arrived in Michigan after traveling several days. Due to a constant state of lack of funds, I'm forced to take the train—a long trip, considering what I've just been through.

The funeral home is crowded, but the faces of the people who've come to pay their respects, faces I've grown up with, are a blur. Friends and relatives have come whom I've not seen since moving to California.

The casket is closed when I arrive. I whisper through the wires to the funeral director to let me see him, but he insists he will not because of the extent of his injuries. Although a number of people witness the crash, I need to know that he's dead. I'm far too fragile, the funeral director tells me, and refuses to do so.

My aunts pull me aside, asking how I've come to look "like this." They, too, hear it was a car accident, a mistruth designed to allow me privacy and to make my own decisions concerning my future. This is a decision I come to regret.

As I sit looking at my dad's coffin, I'm struck by the bundle of desires and cravings and needs and longings that is the relationship I remember with my father. I can't separate my dad's death from the rape; they're stitched together as surely as thread through cloth.

⌇

Gary stops me. It's only now that I realize I've been sobbing. I look down toward the floor; I can't let him inside me any further than I've already let him— I don't want to need him. He's respectful of the distance I place between us but still there's a huge canyon that needs to be filled. I stare at the blinds covering the window and press my body deeper into the couch.

My feelings, so artfully repressed, are those of shame and guilt and disgust and they're unrelenting. I'm numb and unable to work although I don't mention this to Gary, as I feel his respect for me is somehow related to my accomplishments and not to the person I am.

Though I've worked hard and kept my goal at the fore, to develop compassion for the girl on the mattress, it eludes me.

Session #30

Gary remembers my reaction when talking about my dad and begins our session this morning with, "You seem to feel a great deal of compassion for your dad, but not much for yourself."

His statement irritates me and I'm in no mood to discuss what he clearly has on his mind. In truth, I've come to the session angry. In fact, I'm enraged. I'm practiced at hiding my feelings usually, the power of which fill me with fear, but a huge red "R" is burned into my skin and I'm reminded of it daily, hourly even, because of therapy. I'm tired, and want to either get better or stop doing what I'm doing.

I hear the rapist's voice in my head when it's quiet. I feel his face close to mine and his mouth against my ear. He's so close to me that I can smell him. He talks to me in a low, guttural voice, telling me the things he's going to do to me.

I look into Gary's eyes. They're soft and kind and understanding of pain I can't even fully express. Tears roll down my cheeks as I try to find words that will make sense, words that will make a difference if I say them, but I say nothing. My eyes burn from my tears.

I wonder for a moment if I should tell Gary about the voice I'm hearing, but decide against it and start talking about the issue he's raised: the time I spent in Michigan following my dad's funeral.

~

It's several days before the Fourth of July and my attorney tells me I must stay for at least several more weeks.

I'm staying with a close friend and, though she's offered her home for as long as I'm in town, I'm uncomfortable with the thought of not contributing and so have arranged for a stipend from my dad's estate. She works late into the evenings and isn't home when a deliveryman brings my dad's wallet from the funeral home.

I'm on the second floor looking out of the front windows along the tree-lined street when I glimpse the man as he walks to his truck. I fight the urge to open the window and call out to him to come back—take this and go—but of course, I don't.

Instead, I sit on a soft, buttery leather chair and place his wallet on my lap. Inside is a credit card, membership cards to various pilot associations, his driver's license, and his pilot's license. And tucked behind it all, a picture of me at twelve. I turn it over. On the back I'd written, "To Daddy. A loving, wonderful, and nice man. Love, Teresa."

I stop, unable to talk through my tears. A girl's relationship with her father colors each of her subsequent relationships with men, I tell Gary. And before I realize what I've said, I tell him I've come to see him as a father. I leave the session embarrassed and consider changing my next appointment.

Session #31

Gary agrees to see me today on very short notice. I'd been certain that I'd be different from his other patients, that I wouldn't need his help between sessions, but I was wrong.

He sees immediately how upset I am and helps me take several long breaths before I speak.

One of the most disturbing symptoms has returned with alarming intensity. I don't want to talk about the past. I want to talk about what's happening now; I need relief from symptoms that only seem to be getting worse the deeper I go. I tell him about something that happened today, something that's starting to happen *every* day.

I'm on my way to the store when I jump out of the car. Suddenly an alarming thought has come. Did I turn off my curling iron? I yank my eyes from the ignition and run to the bathroom. Yes, it's turned off. I turn and walk to the garage door. I sit in the car and put the key in the ignition. Is it really turned off? I get out of the car again, unlock the door to the house, and run to the bathroom. Yes—it's turned off. I turn again to go to the door. This time I don't make it to the car before turning around. Is it unplugged? What if it's not? A fire could start. Back I turn toward the bathroom where I wrap up the cord and place it on the counter. I touch the end of the cord. I touch the curling iron itself. I turn to leave but back I turn toward the bathroom before I realize where I'm going. Yes—it's turned off!

I go through the whole ritual again and again and again.

I'm exhausted. I feel as if I can't believe what I see any longer, as if I can't believe what I know to be true. I place my hand over the outlet in order to make my body believe what my mind can't or, rather, won't.

I hang my head in the bathroom sink off the family room. I'm nauseous and clammy. My elbows press against the sink and grow tender after a few moments, but I can't move. I stay this way for what seems like hours, staring into the sink, down the drain, out of our home, into the river, out to sea. I'm lost.

Lately I've started to involve Phil in my sickening ritual. Before leaving the house, I check to make sure all the appliances are unplugged. Not certain that I've turned them off, I go downstairs, then return upstairs, then down, then up, then down, then up. Ten times—fifteen—twenty. No matter how many times I return to check out the appliances, I don't believe what I see.

So I work around the problem by leaving the house with Phil. Then, further into the behavior, I tell him, then show him physically, that I've unplugged all the appliances. My behavior disintegrates into me asking him to check the appliances for me. He can't comprehend why I've become so irrational. I panic at the thought of leaving the house because something might happen, and then panic at having to stay home alone.

I look at Gary like I've seen him for the first time today. Obsessive-compulsive disorder. His diagnosis of my present state is rapid and he assures me that this behavior, though particularly uncomfortable, is natural while I'm trying to gain control of emotions previously buried. Further, this effort is manifested in a desire to control my environment. This is a complex symptom that has caught me by surprise but is one, Gary tells me, that requires patience in order to work through. Patience. This is a virtue of which I'm in increasingly short supply, I'm afraid.

The road I'm taking in therapy isn't linear but circuitous, and I feel that taking a pause to catch my breath is best. I tell Gary as much, but he seems to recognize this as an attempt to go underground once again and respectfully tells me that he won't allow lingering sightseeing on these side trips. I must go forward in order to make progress. I know this, but I wonder sometimes if he realizes how difficult this is for me.

Session #33

Early in my therapy, I tell Gary today, I anticipated moments of awareness, but it's clear to me now that it isn't one moment but rather a collection of moments that lead to insight. Periods of clarity and truth, of lightness and confidence in myself and the actions I've taken, were fleeting and few in the beginning, but are slowly becoming more frequent and lasting.

Even so, I've reached a level of desperation heretofore unknown to me and I find myself pleading for Gary's help in getting out of the house that keeps me prisoner still.

Phil's sweater hangs to my knees. I feel small and childlike and crawl up on Gary's couch and begin crying. The weather, stormy, mirrors my mood. I tell Gary that I'm sure I'm going to die a violent death at the hands of someone. All or nothing. On or off. Black or white.

He tells me that the rape I endured was brutal, which takes me aback. A feeling of shame washes over me. No, I say, other people have been through worse. I don't want to talk about the rape today, tomorrow, or ever again. Or what it did to me. Or about my dad's death. I just don't want to talk about anything any more.

The momentary feeling of lightness I felt after telling Gary the details of the rape is fading and old feelings of restlessness have returned. I feel resistance of where I am in this process and disappointment that I'm not yet "better." There's a moment during the rape that I obsess over and I can't relate it to Gary, so I run from it.

My guilt, Gary tells me, is irrational. The mood swings, the feeling of terror, the inability to relate to others, the flashbacks, won't go away right away, he reminds me. In fact, my symptoms may not be alleviated for some time since we're taking the lids off feelings that have been repressed.

I can't go on, I tell him as I sit and cry for the remainder of the hour, saying nothing more.

Session #34

It's been quite some time since our last session due to a very ill-timed (in my mind) vacation for Gary. During the time he is away, I dip into self-pity with regularity. Does he really not know how his being away—unavailable—affects me?

Of course, this is my irrational self, that self which, if given the option, would have him all to myself.

He looks rested and content upon his return and I'm envious of his peace of mind, for I have none. He's able to leave me with my demons almost too effortlessly. I launch into a monologue about a puppy I had as a teenager. At first the subject seems disconnected to anything we've been working on.

⌐

It's 1974. I'm seventeen and living in the town in which I was born along Lake Michigan.

And finally, after much acrimony and endless arguments, my parents separate.

My isolation following my parent's divorce is self-imposed. I need to be alone— nearly alone anyway. Each week after picking up my paycheck, I visit the animal shelter, pick out the most pitiful, malnourished package of fur I can find, and take it home. I'm determined to nourish it back to health, to love it like no one else has, and to add the little one to my menagerie, or in some cases to find it another loving home.

I bathe them first, softly lathering their fur, then rinsing them, massaging small circles of love into them. As they wildly shake the water from their fur—even the smallest of puppies—the others in the menagerie and I watch as the new kid runs playfully through the house. I want them, need *them, to be loved and taken care of and to feel safe.*

I take them into the backyard to play until they're tired and then we all troop back into the house for dinner. As we get ready for bed all the puppies join me on the bed. Very Dr. Doolittle. And it works well, until Dana.

She's the tiniest puppy I've ever seen. Abandoned by the side of the road at six weeks, she's barely alive. She's sweet, the color of taffy, with huge, dark brown pools of chocolate for eyes that beg me to take her home. She still has puppy breath.

The staff at the shelter anticipates these Friday afternoon visits and has come to know whom I'll gravitate towards. They aren't surprised to see me staring at Dana through the chain fence and one warns me against adopting her, but his counsel comes too late. She's mine. I've already decided I'm the one to give her what she needs. I take her immediately to the veterinarian, who confirms what the staff related—that she's really quite ill and may not make it. But you don't understand, I say to him; this is what I do. I rescue.

I listen intently to his instructions and ask if I may give her a bath when I get home. No problem, he says, and with the other puppies and Snowball (the queen) watching, she runs through the house as the others had, delighting in the water flying off her back.

She grows tired easily. While the others play on the lawn, she crawls up on my lap and craves my caressing. When I stop she gently nudges my hand with her nose and I begin again. Unwilling to disturb her rest, I allow her to enjoy the loving attention she's getting for the first time in her short life.

We stay nestled in the cool grass long into the evening until it grows cold. One by one, the puppies grow tired as well and join Snowball, Dana, and me until we're surrounded.

⌒

Gary brings me back to the present with his ill-timed, "We're out of time." If only I had him for a moment more. And then another and another. Then everything would be okay. Do I realize yet the significance of telling him about Dana, he asks? No, I tell him, but I experience the pain of losing her as freshly as if it had taken place a moment ago.

Session #36

The connection between talking about Dana and the losses I've experienced in my life yet never fully grieved is vague and, for the moment, unrelated to the rape. For this reason, I question the necessity of talking about it at today's session until Gary guides me back to the subject but I relent when he asks me to talk about Dana.

⌒

The struggle for Dana to regain her health—she has a devastating condition known as heartworms—is arduous and difficult for me to watch. There are times when I see that her illness is getting the best of her. In the five weeks since she's been with me I've grown to love her more each day, perhaps all the more because of her courageous fight.

The session with the veterinarian is difficult to get to. A snowstorm, unexpected so early in the season, has roads blocked but it only serves to strengthen my resolve. She's taken a turn for the worse and I'm frightened that she won't make it. I need to hear the vet's reassuring words but instead hear that I've done all I can and that she's no longer able to fight. Perhaps it's time to put her out of her misery . . .

I see his kind eyes through my tears and nearly give in, but no—if she dies, when she dies, it will be in my home with Snowball and the other puppies she's played with. It'll be with my loving arms around her, not a stranger's. I pay for the visit and another week of medication and wrap her in the baby blanket I keep around her constantly now.

The weather is even colder when we get to the car. She's shivering so I put yet another blanket over her and place her on my seat close to my leg. I aim the heater vents down to warm her and we start home. The streets are icy and the car slips every which way. I'm used to driving in sleet, snow, and ice, but this is so treacherous even I'm frightened.

I'm still three miles away from home when I feel the car slide to the right. I have no steering and reach down to hold tightly to Dana, frantically trying to keep the car on the road. I feel the tire dip ever so slowly down and know that it's a long drop into a ravine. It seems like slow motion as I straighten out the car and bring it to a stop along the side of the road. I drop my head onto the steering wheel, still holding tight to Dana.

I look down at her—her beautifully expressive brown eyes are looking up at me as she gives her tail a wag visible under her little baby blanket. She's getting tired and I must get her home.

Repeated attempts at starting the car bring no results. The road we're on isn't traveled often, particularly in winter. Unable to start the car, I have no other choice but to walk and hope that someone will pick me up. I can't leave Dana by herself, even though it will be warm in the car. I gather her up, talking the entire time, and place her against my chest, then wrap her in my shirt, my sweater, and finally my thick winter parka. I hold her bottom and zip my parka as high as I can, leaving a tiny space for her head, which I place next to my face.

I take a breath and look at the clock, relieved to see that our time is up. I can't go on any longer, feeling this overwhelming grief. I long for, indeed would welcome, the numbness that I've felt all these years, and fear that now I've ventured too far inside myself.

The numbness is gone and all I feel is pain.

Session #37

I'm only interested in small talk today and Gary allows about ten minutes for general chitchat before asking what finally happened to Dana. I begin, somewhat reluctantly, to speak about that day.

⌒

We start out for the walk home. I gently whisper to Dana that we'll be home soon. The wind feels like shards of glass landing against my face and a soft flurry has progressed to full-fledged snow. We've been walking only a half-hour yet it seems like two.

The side of the road drops off sharply on both sides so I walk in the middle of the road most of the time. The heavy treads on my boots make no difference in the ice and we slip and slide. I jab my thumb out when the only two cars to go by pass me. No one stops.

I look down at Dana but she isn't looking back at me as she had been. Placing my hand on the top of her head, I caress her fur. More briskly now. Nothing. Please don't do this to me.

I bring her chin up and look into her eyes—they're drooping and look exhausted.

I stop walking and hold her to my chest. Tears well up in my eyes, making it difficult to focus. I bite hard into my lip to keep from crying. A sigh emits from her tiny body—an immense sigh for how tiny she is—and a shudder shakes her body. I take her outside my parka and hold her toward me. Her eyes are closed and her head flops ever so softly to the left. Sobbing, I cry toward heaven for her to come back, but hear only my lonely wails mixed with the wind. She has left me.

⌒

I'm sobbing as I finish the story and reach for a tissue. Gary's eyes—affectionate and comforting—convey empathy.

He asks the questions that I ask over and over in so many of the instances in my life: Did my actions affect the outcome of what happened? He's referring not only to Dana, of course, but also to the rape. Buried in the issue of self-blame is that of my actions. Had I made my situation worse by my actions or, rather, my inaction? Could I have alleviated, can I now alleviate, my own pain and suffering?

The realization that I alone am responsible, not for what happens *to* me, but for my actions and behavior following an event, comes to me. Of course, I know this on an intellectual level, but I'm upset with myself as my actions have proven to be in direct opposition to the intelligence I consider myself to possess. It's disturbing to realize that although I'm aware of the proper actions I should have taken—report the rape, have Dana put to sleep—I allowed my feelings to overwhelm my ability to do so and thus caused myself further distress.

Session #38

I'm anxious to see Gary this session. I realize, I tell him, that I never learned how to grieve over anything. I just bury feelings deeper and deeper. Your grief seems to overwhelm you, he replies, but what of the anger? Where is the anger for all that has happened?

His question is valid. Of course I feel anger—anger due to the rape, anger due to my dad's death, anger for things we haven't even discussed—but it's deep inside. I've experienced true anger firsthand, directed *at* me. The several times I've expressed my anger, I've felt a sense of disconnection from my actions, a loss of self-control that was disconcerting. I continue to tell him about that year.

It's mid-August, nearly two months after the rape.

Most of the tasks connected with settling my dad's estate are complete. I sit at the dining room table in his house looking at the planks of hardwood floor that he recently refinished. The evening sun shines so beautifully on them. Where before there was a heavy woolen carpet, pools of butterscotch swirls invite me to walk upon them, to stay and enjoy. I recall ripping up the carpet after my parents' divorce, the huge, stifling mass simply a metaphor for all that was wrong at the time. I recall tugging at the baseboards, snapping tacks along the edges, watching as they twirled toward the ceiling, somersaulted, and caught the light like diamonds and fell back to earth like little stars.

While most of my dad's affairs are in order, there are several that are pressing. My attorney calls to tell me that because there is no will, I'll have to stay and testify that I'm his only child in order to inherit his estate, which may take months. It may be tomorrow. In any case, I have to stay.

I'm in a netherworld. I can't stay. I can't go.

My relationship with my friend is becoming strained. I continue to pay her monthly for allowing me to stay, but this can't go on forever. Just knowing I can't go home makes me tense and cranky. I apologize to her but she can see that I've changed.

I can't—won't—tell her about the rape.

I tell Gary that prior to seeing him for our very first session, I considered two possible scenarios.

One possibility: That he would recognize my muted cry for help, sit back in his mahogany leather chair, and declare me pitifully weak and self-centered. He would proceed to inform me that I was taking valuable time from others who truly needed his services.

The other possibility: Alarm would register on his face and he would declare me over the edge, a danger to myself. Before I knew what was happening, I'd be confined to a padded room.

Then, as now, my logical mind brews beneath the surface, but I'll have none of it.

Session #40

I didn't want to come to today's session. I feel completely incompetent in relating my feelings and overwhelmingly sad that I can't ask him for the help I need. I don't want to talk anymore. I don't want to feel. I'm fidgety and cranky and my arms are crossed, a signal that Gary picks up on. Instead of being sidetracked by my small talk, he asks what happened during the rest of my stay in Michigan.

It's early September.

The call is from my attorney's secretary: A full inventory of everything in the basement is needed immediately.

I drive to my dad's house. Sitting in the driveway, I'm transported in time to when I was a little girl, running around the huge oak tree in the front yard, ankle-deep in the cool, misty grass. The beach is but steps away and the humid air hangs heavy.

The house is small—two bedrooms—and old. The front windows look out on a grove of pine trees that line the lake. Cobblestones run up the length of the small road leading past the house. I don't realize how long I've been sitting in the driveway until an old-fashioned lamp guarding the front yard turns on.

I walk with resolve to the basement door and open it. I never liked this basement and don't like being here now, but the inventory needs to be done. Down several steps, then a turn to the right to the basement, but first I must check that the door on the landing leading outside is locked. A skeleton key hangs lopsided out of the keyhole, just as it has for years.

Rows and rows of manuals line the shelves on the left-hand side of the basement, photographic darkroom equipment on the right. An old Royal typewriter and a record player my dad bought years ago are on the table at the back wall.

I sit on the steps and recall all the memories of being in the basement helping him build experimental airplanes. I'd do anything to be near him.

I discover a forgotten photo in the pages of a book of monographs. I run my fingers across the black and white photograph of my dad. He stands beneath a palm tree dressed in a light-colored uniform that fits smoothly over his chest and stomach. His arms, visible from under the short sleeves, don't appear as muscular as they were in real life. The memory of how they felt when wrapped around me is all but faded, but the feverish energy I felt at such times remains.

The photograph doesn't capture the bronze hue of his skin, almost light ebony, against his soft, azure eyes. It does show his eyelashes, long and black and curling toward the sky. His eyes danced and drew one in when he laughed, and his smile was infectious. I drank it in when it was directed at me.

⌁

I stop, remembering that the photo is still in my purse and show it to Gary. It alleviates, somewhat, my embarrassment at having told him he's become something of a father figure to me. After all, as he reminded me, he's far too young.

And what of my relationship with my father? Gary's question catches me off guard. We moved close, became too close, then backed away, I answer. Elusive.

Gary smiles softly. Much the same, he says, as our relationship. He gently tells me that our time is up.

Session #41

There's more, I tell Gary at our session today, that happened while I was in Michigan following my dad's death, making the pain of the rape so much more difficult. I look at Gary and begin to cry, then to sob. He seems surprised to see that we're moving into a subject that's difficult for me and allows me to cry for a time, then gently urges me to continue.

It's mid-September and the rape continues to dull ever so slightly. There are no physical reminders of the rape here in Michigan.

I'm unsure whether I've had my period. I haven't stopped bleeding since the rape and while I know I should see a doctor, I'm scared. I call a clinic and am told that they won't see me without my consenting to a pregnancy test. I don't tell them about the rape and protest the pregnancy test but to no avail.

The woman at the clinic isn't much younger than me. She's speaking to me, saying my name over and over, but her words seem far away. She starts shaking my shoulders.

You're pregnant, she states. And, she adds, the test was performed twice. Her statement leaves no room for questions. Her eyes search mine for reaction. Is this pregnancy expected? Or not? She wants me to provide the right follow-up proclamation but I can't. I'm stunned and remain silent.

My mouth aches and the blood drains from my face. The urge to put my fist through the wall is nearly impossible to ignore, but instead I turn away from the pamphlets I've been staring at and run to my car. I sit crying with my head on the steering wheel.

Her words bring the rape back into sharp focus. I'm still being raped in the house. All I sense is blinding fury, then an astonishing elixir of confusion and chaos.

After leaving the clinic, I drive and drive, finally finding myself at the sand dunes near my house, always a place of comfort for me. I'm almost invisible here between two towering mountains of sand.

The water is beautifully blue as far as I can see. What would happen, I think to myself, if I just started walking—down the dunes—across the road—down the beach—into the water—and in and in and further in until I no longer existed?

I can't breathe and instead pant.

I've been bleeding since the rape. Perhaps the test gave a false reading. I look down at my stomach. There has to be a mistake. God can't be this angry with me.

Four hours go by and still I can't move. I'm losing time again, just like after the rape. I'm numb. Overwhelmed. Alone. And so very sad.

My days after getting news of the pregnancy are filled with calls to clinics but the answer is always the same: I'm too far along; nothing can be done. A condescending "dear" always follows their statements, intending, I'm certain, to be an admonition. I hear myself pleading. I'll take my chances, I tell them. I want to do what's right, but I become terrified thinking that I'll have to deliver this child. I'm certain, but am unaware of how I know, that it's a girl. I can't imagine looking into her face and seeing the man who raped me. I'm Catholic with all that implies, but I don't know if I can do this. I'm trapped.

The answer to this dilemma, should a friend have asked, would have tripped lightly off my tongue. I find, as is so often the case, that the answer isn't as black and white when I'm faced with the situation of having to decide.

The pain of becoming pregnant is overwhelming, yet the sanctity of life, however conceived—I find myself going in circles.

The baby is the only person more innocent than I in this nightmare.

⌇

I stop relating my past and tell Gary that I went back into the memory boxes again. I'm apprehensive, and clearly more comfortable with the complacency of not facing what they have to teach me than with the pain they awaken.

The box marked *Birth* contains a rattle and several small bibs. Also a book on birth that I bought in my fifth month of pregnancy, with photographs of women giving birth. The look of deep concentration and supreme effort on their faces is no less than beautiful to me. And along with all of that is a stack of pamphlets that I'd paper-banded together. I can't begin to speculate why I brought them back from Michigan, or what purpose they serve.

My head begins to ache.

Therapy must be working, I tell Gary with a wry smile. Now I know when I'm in denial.

Session #44

A sight I've not seen in Gary's waiting room before—a baby. The new mother wants only to share every small detail of her pregnancy and birth with me, a total stranger. I politely excuse myself, go to the ladies' room, and cry.

Gary is concerned by the time I return, late for our session, because he'd glimpsed me coming in. The emotional costs of the rape, I tell him, are beyond what I could have imagined.

Sensitive to the fact that his partner's client has her baby with her, he urges me to continue where I left off last week.

       ⌒

It's October and I remain in Michigan.

The pregnancy, I whisper to my friend in answer to her question, feels mysterious and strange. I've decided to have the baby and put her up for adoption. My feelings? They're a patchwork of regret and wonder.

Emotionally I'm in chaos. I'm fascinated at how my body is changing yet I'm in tremendous pain over how she was conceived. I'm incredulous that I'm pregnant due to the rape.

My friend raises my nightgown and lays her hand on my bare stomach. Her hand is warm and soft and her fingers move ever so lightly across me. The baby has grown so large that my skin is pulled taut. I cry softly as my friend traces small circles onto my stomach. Her tenderness is welcome and I don't want her to stop touching me.

She buries her face deep inside my hair, next to my ear. Her breathing is steady but raspy and matches the pressure she exerts against my stomach. The sensation of having the child inside me, closer than any other human being, is one that I ache for. It's what's missing from my life—the closeness of another human being. The softness of the baby's movements is in contrast to the violence of her conception. Contrast and conflict—this has been my life since the rape.

My friend brings my hand up and places it ever so gently on my stomach, then moves my hand in circular motions against my skin as she has been doing. I feel parts of the baby inside my body—astounding! I've avoided touching myself but now that I have, I'm grateful for the sensation.

I move my hands to my breasts. They've grown large. My nipples are tender and hard. I touch the baby inside me and let my hands come down around my stomach. She and I are one and the same.

My friend continues massaging my thighs ever so softly until I fall asleep.

I stop. I sense that our time is up, but don't feel like talking anymore. I want to remember that moment in time. Physically I'm in Gary's office, but the warmth of my friend's hands, the tenderness we shared that evening, are as real to me now as they were so many years ago. My sexuality heightened, I tell him, as the pregnancy wore on, something that I didn't understand and about which I still experience great conflict. The horrendous nature of the rape is with me always, yet the pregnancy—I simply don't understand my feelings.

Session #46

I've avoided this issue, but I want to release myself from its grip.

Suicide. Yes, I tell Gary today—I thought about it. And yes, I attempted it. I feel great shame and humiliation saying it out loud, yet once said, I feel as if a thousand-pound weight has been lifted from me.

In speaking the words, Gary and I have reached a level of intimacy that leaves me entirely vulnerable. I'm at risk, just as surely as when I was in the rapist's house, but I take a deep breath and continue.

It's early November.

I'll remain in Michigan, it appears, through the winter.

I stand at the top of the stairs this late afternoon. I'm silent and unmoving. One small step, one small gesture, and this baby and I will no longer exist. I stand without sound or movement, gathering my courage. I'm the only one home. If I'm to do this, it has to be now. The only sound is a slight rustling of leaves from a soft November wind. The image of leaves—soft muted tones of burnt ginger and gold and brown, feather light, catching the wind and falling to the deep green earth— brings tears to my eyes.

The staircase is long, thirty-five steps in all. Leading from a once-used funeral parlor to the living quarters above, it's in keeping with the rest of the home now used exclusively as a residence. Its huge mahogany railings, stained deep through decades of use, frame blood-red wallpaper and reach high up into the living quarters. An off-hand remark from my friend one day as water from the snow on our boots pooled on the landing just five steps from the top fuels my actions: Be careful—a fall down these steps could kill you.

The warm tears cloud the fist approaching my face. It slams first against my front teeth, then against my jaw. Disconnected from a body, it's gone as fast as it appeared, but leaves me reeling.

My hand gropes in front of me, finding only air. My heart beats wildly. The wallpaper on the opposing side framing the staircase blurs, then spins wildly out of control. My hand clamps down hard, finding the huge wooden ball at the top of the banister. Still holding on, I drop to the top step and fall onto my back.

I tell Gary I must use the restroom and stand in the stall, motionless, crying for the remainder of my session, and then some.

75

Session #47

I'm anxious to see Gary today after his having cancelled our most recent session due to illness. I'm concerned about him and while I want to speak with him about my feelings last week I feel almost guilty talking about myself. He looks well, assures me that he's okay and takes the attention off him placing it back on me. He gently re-directs our discussion to the thoughts of suicide that we spoke about last week.

It's several weeks later and I'm still in Michigan, waiting for a trial day for my dad's estate hearing. Days turn into weeks, which turn into months. Daily I think about returning to San Francisco and am told it may be any day now.

The feeling of being unable to leave is much like being in the house with the rapist. I'm trapped—there's no way out of this house and out of the predicament in which I've found myself.

I walk to the kitchen sink and look out at the yard below. It's late afternoon; the skies are dark and rainy. Children splash in the puddles beneath the window. I'm running out of time. I look to my left at the knives on the counter. One swift slice— one straight, strong slice across my stomach—and it would be over. I pick up the largest knife and feel the blade with my thumb. I can't hear the children outside playing anymore, just my breathing.

I'm wearing a shirt I bought yesterday. It's soft and pink and baggy with plenty of room still to grow and it has a little kitten playing with a mama cat. The word MOM is written across the chest.

I pull the shirt up over my stomach and press my hand over it, feeling her body inside me. She's quiet—sleeping. I press the knife into my skin, making an impression. Suddenly I pull my hand back—quickly. I stand, my heart pounding, my skin on fire, as I feel her move inside me. She has saved my life.

I sink to the floor and become sick. I try to stand to go to the bathroom but can't. I lay on my side, crying.

Gary's gaze is sweet and tender and kind, but he and I both know there's nothing he can do to heal this hurt inside me.

Session #48

Gary asks that I continue to direct our efforts at the consequence of the rape and I decide, after some hesitation, to go into more detail about the pregnancy.

⌐

It's mid-January, 1977.

I'm home in San Francisco from Michigan at last. My duties as my father's heir to his estate are complete, taking a total of five minutes on the witness stand. An insurance settlement allows me to take time off work until after the baby is born.

It's cold, colder than I remember it being in San Francisco, and being home brings a mixture of sweet and sour memories. Before the rape I'd walked endlessly through the city, from the waterfront to Chinatown and out to Golden Gate Park. Now, fear has taken away my sense of adventure. Mere days seem to have gone by, in my mind, since the rape, although in reality it's been almost seven months to the day. Most of my physical injuries have healed and only scars remain, but the pregnancy reminds me of the rape every moment of every day.

I avoid the area around the house in which I was raped, although it's only blocks from my apartment. Upon returning home, two blocks become four into which I won't travel, four become six, and six become eight. My apartment is my prison and I worry about the rapist constantly. Where is he now? Is he watching me? Has he raped again? And I die a little bit each time. "I should have" runs constantly through my mind, and I fear I'll go mad from my "should haves."

I make a session with a hospital in my community, telling the nurse that I'm unmarried, seven months and a few days pregnant, and that I'd like to place the baby for adoption. Her voice rises in pitch. She's clearly excited and I mentally picture her telling the lucky couple about the newborn baby they'll receive shortly.

I'm brought back to the conversation by her question. Will getting the father's relinquishment of his rights be a problem? Unprepared, still, to tell of or say the word "rape," I stall and ask for a session.

The smell of age and illness in the building overwhelms me. This is a religion-based university teaching hospital and the nurse-nun meets me at the top of the stairs. I'm surprised to see that she's wearing a habit, looking more severe than she sounded over the phone. I can't imagine her giving me an exam and wonder if this is the right place for me, as well as the baby.

She has me wait in the lobby until my admission card is prepared and tells me that she'll return and give me a tour of the delivery room and explain how labor and delivery will proceed. I find myself shaking when she returns as she tells me how we (we?) will turn it (it?) over to the adopting couple.

My visit is endless. Tears well up in my eyes as I recount the circumstances that have brought me to this place. I'm giving away a child that's coming out of my body. The facts, laid so bare, make me wonder if I'll ever recover emotionally.

As I stand at the receptionist's desk, the nurse stands next to me with her hand outstretched, asking for the five hundred dollars. Hadn't I been told, she asks me, that there is a five-hundred-dollar fee for the labor, delivery, and adoption process? No, I assure her. I hadn't been told. I would have remembered. I hurry from the room, promising to return with the money, but suspect that we both know the truth—she'll never see me again.

On a logical level, I suppose, I recognize that talking about, feeling, living through, and grieving over the baby is necessary, but the pain is intense. I don't hesitate to tell Gary this at the end of our session as if he has some complicity in it being so.

Session #50

I sit in Gary's office this afternoon, not wanting to talk, not wanting to reveal myself any further than I have. I'm tired. There is psychological pain from the rape that can't be undone no matter how many times I talk about it and no matter how much I think about it.

Gary sits patiently, but ten minutes pass, then twenty, and I'm still staring at the same spot on the floor. I fear that once my emotions are released, I'll be unable to contain them. This lack of control, especially for one who aspires to total control over her life, suffocates me.

Glancing at the clock, and I suppose being the kind of person who's only comfortable taking money for services rendered and not simply for being in the room with me, Gary urges me to tell him more about the baby.

⌐

Following the visit to the hospital, I make a decision: If I place the baby for adoption, I won't tell the agency or the adoptive couple how she was conceived. My logic is that I know nothing of the rapist. Medically, psychologically, and emotionally he is a blank. I know nothing about him other than what he was capable of on the day he raped me. These blanks leave me with horrible thoughts, particularly at night: Will the baby suffer from mental problems? Physical? Emotional? And then when I'm unable to sleep, more chaotic thoughts come to mind. After the delivery will I want to touch her? I'm more tired when I wake than when I go to bed.

Still, the adoptive parents have a right to know and this unwillingness to provide disclosure to them twists my stomach into knots. But I'm more concerned about the baby's future and feel if they knew how she was conceived, they might reject her. And if she finds out she was conceived during a rape, the consequences might prove disastrous for her. It's better that no one know.

I have other concerns regarding my health, too. From the age of sixteen, I've been aware that I was exposed while in utero to diethylstilbestrol (DES), a synthetic hormone prescribed to pregnant women between 1940 and 1971 in an effort to reduce the risk of miscarriage. For years I suffered no ill effects.

It was during an exam that I was told I had the early stages of clear cell cervical cancer. Perhaps because of my age, I was alarmingly naïve and failed to grasp the severity of my condition, but because of my doctor's swift action, I underwent a surgical procedure immediately, a cone biopsy, the preferred procedure at the time for this type of cancer. Fertility, pregnancy, and future health problems were discussed, but frankly not digested. It's not this doctor, the one who most probably saved my life that I go to first but rather to the hospital that I mentioned earlier, my shame is so deep.

～

I'm vaguely discontented now, having revealed all this. Feelings that I could have reached higher potential, greater spirituality, if this "thing" hadn't happened are not and never were sufficient to bring me to therapy. I even felt a certain pride at having dealt with my feelings following the initial rape, but truth be told, the feelings were suppressed, never grieved over and conquered.

My level of discomfort peaks and wanes, but I've always been able to look and function quite normally. No one suspects.

Session #53

Gary faces me squarely this morning and crosses his legs; I shake as I continue to tell him about the pregnancy. I don't want to do this but I want to get it over with; there's no easy way but to walk through it.

⌒

Monday morning I awaken in pain and my bed is stained in blood. I'm frightened and call my friend whose mother is a nurse. Because the pain is becoming more intense, I'm unable to sit and so return to my bed.

As soon as my friend's mother arrives, she gives me an exam and takes my vital signs, but I'm unable to focus on what she's saying to me. She asks for my gynecologist's name and number and I point to a phone book on my desk. After a brief consultation, I'm told it's best for me to get to his office right away.

I'm shown to his office immediately. Confusion is evident on his face as he walks in and sits before me. The last time I'd seen him was for treatment of the cervical cancer several months before the rape, almost ten months ago. At the time he'd been specific in his instructions regarding follow up and he's anxious now for explanations, not only on why he hasn't seen me, but more importantly because I'm pregnant and having problems.

I begin to shake and bite my lip, drawing blood. The rape, my symptoms, all of it comes tumbling out in an almost apologetic manner in an effort for him to understand why I couldn't come to him.

While he's interested in speaking with me, it's more vital that he examine me immediately so he helps me lie back on the table. This position is uncomfortable for me and my chest feels very heavy. He inserts his fingers and presses against my abdomen, causing me to catch my breath.

His manner becomes crisp and measured. He calls to his nurse to get the hospital on the phone and then shouts requests for several others tests as she walks out of the door. He turns back to me, his face as gentle as I remember months ago, and says that he's sorry.

He's holding my hands in his as he explains the procedure he's about to do but his words barely register. I'm in shock at what he's saying and hear only bits and pieces. Because of my physical problems, the baby and I are in trouble. My uterus has expanded as much as it's able and the placenta is separating from the wall of the uterus, which is the source of the bleeding. While the bleeding has abated and I'm currently stable, my situation is tenuous and I'll be expected at the hospital shortly.

He tells me that during his exam he found that my cervix, already compromised from the cone biopsy, had sustained injuries from the rape and is now beginning to dilate. A third-trimester loss is not uncommon for someone with these anatomical problems, he explains softly. I hear the words but they make no sense to me. I stammer, telling him that the baby isn't due yet, not fully comprehending the meaning behind the words a "third-trimester loss."

People move around me with lightning speed, but the room is surprisingly quiet. I again bite my lip hard enough to draw blood when someone lowers me onto my back again. My doctor moves his chair in close between my legs. In one swift motion his hand is inside me, inserting something. I later learn that it is a lapidary and is intended to help my cervix dilate. The baby is dying, and I'm going to have to deliver her.

He helps me up once again and looks into my eyes. The pounding in my ears barely allows me to hear his words but I respond to his questions: Yes, I'll be at the hospital tomorrow morning early. Yes, I have your pager number. Yes, I'll have someone come with me.

A counselor leads me to a small room and hands me a pile of papers. She asks if I have any questions, barely taking her eyes from my stomach. I reply that I don't, which is the truth. I'm overwhelmed by what my doctor has told me and scared of what's going to happen next.

⌐⌐

I become quiet. I don't want to talk about this. I fold into myself. Gary is aware of my non-verbal cues as I cross my arms and bend over, laying my head on the arm of his couch. We are quiet as I cry softly for the rest of my session.

Session #55

I'm aware that the establishment of a safe haven in Gary's office during our sessions is foremost in his mind always. Also on his mind, I know, is the need to move forward, to examine fears as a compassionate being here only for me.

The impact of what he says to me today—*I'm sorry I hurt you*—registers on my face, I'm sure, but makes his previous question no less invasive. Yes, I answer him, she was a child to me, and yes, I named her.

I feel like a pathetic mother animal searching for her baby. I fear that it will be so for the rest of my life. My anger forces me into an impossible position that is intense and never-ending. My agony lingers on and on.

Gary doesn't allow me to back away from this powerful emotion today as he can see so clearly its significance. There are times, such as today, that I don't fully appreciate his tenacity.

I tell him her name, Sarah, and of her birth.

At last it's 6:30 and I'm at the hospital.

The sheets are clean and pressed and feel cold against my skin. I have a slight fever, the admitting nurse tells me, which makes the sheets feel all the more cold. I'm shaking as the orderly lays me back on the bed. A flurry of activity goes on around me in the room, with one nurse taking my blood pressure while another tells me that the doctor will be right in.

My doctor's somber mood is contagious. The room grows quiet when he enters. He's businesslike as he takes a solution from a nurse and shouts several orders. The orderlies leave the room and the doctor, the nurses, and I remain.

He holds onto my hand and looks into my eyes for a moment as he helps me to the edge of the bed. Spreading my legs, he examines me while the nurses take my hands. My heart beats loudly in my ears. No one speaks. The nurses hold onto my arms as I clutch the bed rail. Moments seem like hours. I look to the nurse to my right but she avoids my eyes.

The doctor feels along my pubic bone, coming up slightly into my abdomen, and begins inserting the needle. Painstakingly, he starts emptying the solution into me. The steel beneath my hands is cold. I hold on tightly and ache for it to be a warm hand that I'm holding.

The pain is slow, agonizing torture. My fingernails dig into the palms of my hands; the skin pulls taut over my knuckles. I close my eyes and try to manage the pain but see lights throbbing behind them. The doctor pushes against my abdomen, keeping me still. The stab is more intense as he pushes the needle against me, emptying the contents. He carefully pulls the needle back and rubs a burning solution into my skin as the nurses release my hands. I feel open and raw.

I roll onto my left side, bring my legs up, and hold my stomach as the nurses speak to me. Their words are vague and fade into the air, but I hear ever so softly that the heartbeat is faint—barely perceptible. I'm exhausted and want someone to take care of me.

One of the nurses covers me with a warm blanket and turns off the lights as she leaves the room. I'm alone. A soft, misty sleepiness comes over me. The contractions that started shortly after leaving my doctor's office yesterday haven't subsided but are manageable. I feel flushed, feverish, and start having fragmented, disconcerting dreams. Words gel in my head and then become porous and dissipate before I can make them out.

Thrashing inside me tears me from my sleep. The contractions are still not terribly strong, making these new sensations even more distressing. I hug my stomach and start crying. It's still dark and I want to turn on the lights but can't move.

I wonder what time it is and reach over to my left, feeling along the cold wall, but can't find a buzzer for the nurse, so I lie back feeling the baby tear away from me. The thrashing is unbelievably uncomfortable. Trying to breathe through the contractions and control my breathing becomes difficult. I sense the baby is dying inside me and begin to panic, unsure of whether something has gone wrong. I force air into my lungs but can't release any.

⌒

I glance at the clock on Gary's end table and see that it's five minutes to three. Gary tells me to take my time as I grab my purse and keys, but I don't want to linger any longer than necessary. I remember hearing another client come into the outer office. My time is up. I don't meet his eyes as I hurry to leave his office.

Session #56

I'm terribly embarrassed seeing Gary for our session today. How does a woman explain the experience of birth to a man? He is respectful and quiet while I relate my story, but I have to wonder if, as a man, he's uncomfortable with the level of detail I'm relating in these sessions. I've no other way to express myself but with the facts as they come. He's always shown a willingness to understand my experiences, so I continue where I left off, in spite of my discomfort.

I stretch my legs out and lean back on my hands, trying to ease the furor inside me. I don't understand what's happening. The light snaps on, yanking me from my state. It's a nurse who's asking me to lie back—she and several other doctors are going to examine me.

Tears stain my cheeks as she inserts her fingers inside me. Images of the rape flood me. I'm on my back again with strangers violating me. The doctors speak to each other as if I'm not in the room. They discuss my progress and press against my stomach. They feel the storm inside me, turn off the lights, and leave me alone once more.

Hours pass in the dark. I lie on one side, then the other, trying to get comfortable. There is no rhythm to the contractions. I can't regulate my breathing enough to get on top of them, to work with them instead of against them.

My doctor returns and is concerned. It's difficult for me to focus on what he's saying. The pain is relentless and I struggle to understand as he holds my head and looks into my eyes. He tells me that I've been here for thirty hours and that the pain I've described to the nurse signals that something might be wrong; they're bringing in an x-ray machine. I'm stunned at how long I've been going through this but even more bewildered by the fact that I spoke to the nurse and remember nothing of the conversation. Anything, I tell him. Do anything to end this.

A machine appears, taking up nearly all the space in the small room. The technician is trying to take an image but every movement is agony. He makes demands to move this way, then that way. I try to comply, but become irritated that he doesn't care about the pain I'm in and recognize my efforts. Finally he's satisfied with the images and leaves.

There is evidence, my doctor tells me when he returns, of a break in my tailbone and asks how it happened. I tell him that during the rape the man sodomized me and I felt a snap and bolt of pain that reached into my back. Sitting, standing, walking have all been painful since. Tears pool around my eyes. Please don't leave me alone, I want to say to him, but instead say nothing.

He moves around to the foot of the bed, talking to the nurse, too low for me to hear. I want to yell for them to tell me what to do to get this baby out of me. My doctor returns to the head of my bed, telling me he's sorry as he pushes my hair from my eyes.

I can see the power of my words reflected in Gary's face. He is always a compassionate keeper of my emotions for the hour we're together, but what of when I leave? We're locked in an intimate embrace for one hour but then I return to my normal life as if nothing is amiss. I want to tell him how abandoned I feel when I leave his office.

I'm resentful today that our time is up. I'm not finished and am anxious to release my toxic memories.

Session #57

Gary sits before me today in his relaxed, casual manner and is completely, wholly there for me, as I know he will be for his next client, and the next, and the next. I'm perplexed, still, as to how I can be expected to experience the overwhelming sensations that I do in his office, then go out and live in the real world.

I can choose, I decide, to utilize his expertise at this moment in time or I can pout over not having enough time with him. It occurs to me that I'm relying on a defense mechanism (one I've particularly mastered) in an effort to avoid discussing a subject packed full of emotions over which I'm powerless.

I choose to get down to work.

⌒

I'm still in labor. Minutes turn into hours. The physical pain I'm feeling is justification to cry out, but I do not. My anger turns inside me as the reticence to express my pain becomes more and more a part of me.

My doctor returns, estimating another ten hours or so if we (we?) proceed as we have been. I feel like giving up. He may as well have said another hundred hours. I can't do this any longer. I want to go home. My body isn't cooperating. I fight losing the baby forever but need to have it outside my body.

A nurse joins us. "Let it out, honey," she prompts. "Cry, scream. This is the one time you're allowed." I can't tell her the source of my not crying out: During the rape it meant I might have been killed. I couldn't then, and I can't now.

I grab her arm as she turns to leave. I plead with her to give me something for the pain. She says she's sorry, but she can't. The medications I was given earlier have already prolonged my progress.

A wall of white with blue lights slams into my face. A huge contraction shakes me, though the baby is now still. My left hand clutches the steel bed rail and the other grips the sheets. My knuckles turn white and my fingernails dig into the palms of my hands. I begin shaking uncontrollably. My head throbs so badly that I feel as if I'm having a stroke. Everything goes black.

⌒

I'm exhausted as I sit looking into Gary's eyes. As always, they are comforting and warm and empathetic to the pain of my past. I need him at this moment. There is nothing more to say; my soul is open to him. He looks so sad, and it occurs to me that his face probably reflects how very sad I must look to him.

The memory of my body during the birth, of it imploring me to work with it, is intrusive and not something I'm comfortable feeling. I let it come, though the pain has been buried for too long. Relating the baby's birth to Gary allows me to feel my body again—a feeling unfamiliar at any time other than when Phil and I make love.

I'm sorry for the time I've wasted in not relating these feelings to Phil, but now I understand it just wasn't time.

Session #60

It's the resistance to incredibly intense feelings, I tell Gary today, that is so exhausting. I continue talking to him about the birth of the baby.

⌒

When I awaken I'm shivering. Everything is spinning around me. I lie still, on my side, and try to straighten my elbow when I feel the baby's head push against my cervix. I yell for a nurse, the only time I remember raising my voice.

Incredible. I feel shaky and weak but knowing it will be over soon renews my strength. The nurse comes in, telling me that the doctor is out of the building. I don't care where he is; the baby is coming out.

The contractions are intensely uncomfortable and the pressure nearly overwhelming. My breath catches without exhaling. I don't want anyone with me now; I just want to be left alone to do this. I have an urge to kneel on my hands and knees to relieve the pressure but there's no room on the bed. I feel the baby's body making its way through me.

The feeling of her half in and half out is too much. Tears well up in my eyes. Each contraction brings an urge to push yet I feel her recede a little into me each time. My doctor is suddenly in the room and those around me make room for him between my legs. He spreads them further apart and moves in close to me, putting his hand against my abdomen.

Orders to bear down and to push—my doctor brings my knees up closer to my chest and tells me to pull them toward me. I grab his arm. My muscles tighten around her as she moves through me. I hold tight the only way I know how. I reach down and feel her flesh between my legs but can see nothing. I'm not letting her go.

Shaking, I push her body out of mine. A tremendous force, the entire world, is moving through me. A nurse reaches down to take her from the doctor, ignoring my outstretched hands. I beg for her to let me see the baby but she says nothing. The silence is deafening.

I realize for the first time, or perhaps it's the first time I've accepted it, that the baby is dead.

⌒

I turn to Gary, my eyes full of tears. I suffered for her. I suffered for nothing, I announce to him. Finally, in an office with a man who started as a stranger but has become so much more, the impact of Sarah's death is finally realized.

I'm honest with him: If I put all the experiences of the rape together, they do not equal the excruciating moment when I heard only silence, instead of the cry of life. I've never recovered from that experience, I say, and probably never will.

Session #61

I know that my intimacy with Gary is necessary for movement, but I feel uncomfortable nonetheless. I'm fragile having discussed the baby, but no longer embarrassed. We've also talked about the physical injuries from the rape: a broken jaw, broken tailbone, cuts and burns that left scars, the pregnancy. I relax my body into his couch, ready to talk now about the consequences of the rape and the source of my sadness.

⌒

It's June of 1979, two years after the rape.

Phil and I sit in my doctor's office. It's another time and another town, but I've learned from past mistakes: I've located a doctor who specializes in treating women who've been exposed to DES and have become more responsible in terms of my health.

I nervously wait for my doctor and the results from the colposcopy, for I'm pregnant again. Phil holds my hands in my lap and leans into me, gently brushing my hair from my shoulder.

My doctor taps softly on the door as he walks in, tossing my file onto his desk. His red, tousled hair and ever-present green bow tie are the first things I notice as he takes a seat across from us.

I'm sorry, but—

Time stops. Again.

His voice trails off and he looks out the window. I know this is difficult for him, and for a moment I feel like rescuing him from having to say the words but I don't. He and I know what's coming.

The pain that's progressed over the past several days from a dull ache to a stabbing pain, he tells us, is because the pregnancy is ectopic; the fetus is implanted in the fallopian tube, not the uterus. I continue looking at him, not taking my eyes from his as he quotes statistics:

DES-exposed daughters are nine to twelve percent more likely to—

These types of physical abnormalities are more than thirteen percent more likely to—

Because of the injuries caused during the rape, the situation is more complicated—

Miscarriage is more likely in this situation by over twenty-eight percent—

Pre-term birth in—

I want to tell him to shut up, that I don't care about statistics, but I don't. I

91

lower my head and let the words hang in the air. He's finished and the three of us become painfully aware of the silence.

Another pregnancy, but surgery is necessary immediately to remove the fetus from the fallopian tube. I will remain a childless mother. Phil tells me that it's me he loves, not my ability to have children. He's content having our family limited to just the two of us or, if I'd like, to adopt, but I desperately want to give birth to a live child and so am left grief-stricken.

⌐

I look at Gary with tears in my eyes as if to say, "Do you see? Do you understand what I'm going through?" I'm faced with the question of whether Gary can understand the sexuality of being pregnant and giving birth but decide it's a subject I'm unwilling to discuss with him. I try to remain open and honest for that's the way in which I move ahead, but I meet with significant resistance on my own part. I want to tell him what women know to be the secret of birth: That it's the most astounding feeling—that as the baby comes out of your body you feel a connection to something that's more significant than yourself, that because of you another person exists.

But I don't tell him any of this. Instead I tell him I'll never recover from the loss of two babies and that I'll never recover from not being able to have children with the man I love. Never. This is the source of my suffering.

Session #62

Our last session made me feel as if I've reached bottom. There's no more to say. Now the only thing left is to grieve, but I question the wisdom of doing this in front of someone, even as intimate as Gary and I have become.

There seems no more to say, so I tell Gary the dream I had last night.

It's an incredibly detailed, loving image, I tell Gary. When I close my eyes, I see no grotesque figures, no nightmares, just my dream.

~

My husband and I are living along the ocean. The scene is always the same in my mind. The room, a library next to a kitchen in which my husband and I sit, is bathed in a soft glow from the fireplace. The walls are covered from floor to ceiling with books, making the room seem dark and warm. There are shutters on the windows. They're opened slightly, but it's gotten dark early because it's wintertime.

I'm lying stretched out on a huge, hunter green leather chair with my feet up on an ottoman. Both have the look and smell and feel of soothing comfort, the look and smell and feel of one of my dad's old bomber jackets. A couch is at a right angle to the chair and a soft, ecru fleece blanket is tossed over it. In front of me is a large, square coffee table made of mahogany that holds books of our favorite artists and some candles that I've lit. My face is flushed as the flames from the candle and fireplace dance toward me.

Phil is sitting behind me in a leather chair that matches the other furniture, behind a huge mahogany desk. I hear his fingers methodically clicking the keyboard and I hear him humming softly to some music in the background. He's trust and security and warmth and love. He's my soul and I know that, should we live that long, we'll be friends and lovers into our eighties, nineties, and beyond. I look forward to knowing him, to learning even more about him than I know now.

Beside me is a beautiful Irish setter, so close to me that I can feel her breath on my leg. I run my hands along her fur. It's silken and warm. She's loyalty and absolute friendship, judging me not by how I look or what I accomplish. She loves my touch and stays near me.

The smell of something good fills the air, and we're waiting for friends who are visiting for the weekend. And as always in this dream, my hand falls to my stomach, full and large. I'm pregnant.

~

Gary asks if I understand the significance of the dream. No, I reply. I'm tired—I don't really care. I'm just thankful when I don't wake up shaking and screaming. I'm appreciative of any night when I actually sleep instead of my usual nightmare where I stand, in the rapist's house, looking at myself on the mattress.

So no, I don't understand the significance, nor do I want to. I just want to sleep.

Session #64

My relationship with Gary is intense and intimate. I know our time together is his job, but it's my life. He's right when he says there's unfinished business yet. I tell him of another dream I had last night.

⌒

It begins as a dream, but quickly turns into a nightmare.

It begins as a heavenly dream of dazzling, erotic, ethereal images. I'm naked, sitting with my legs under me and my arms in the air. I'm in ecstasy. Spinning about my head are tiny lights, like fireflies. They're swirling about me, drawing me into a concentric circle. They're gentle with me at first but become more and more frantic, more and more painful. My hair, falling below my waist, is lifted up—up—up. The swirling motion lifts me higher, straightening my back and then, when it will stretch no further, it arches under the pressure.

I feel tremendous pain in my tailbone. A chilling, stark pain travels up my spine inch by inch. I arch more to relieve what's beyond pain. Each fraction of my spine is more intolerably painful than the last. Cramping spasms move up to my neck and head. My arms, still raised, grasp the air in front of me for relief from the agony, for deliverance.

Please, I scream, make it stop. My head and arms are forced down by heavy air. The intensity is painful yet orgasmic. The air pushes my head down toward my chest and presses my arms tight against my sides. It swirls about my body, engulfing me like a cocoon. Pushing my pelvis deep into the floor, I feel a sensation like giving birth. A movement through me descends along my spine. A strand of DNA, golden, now silver, now golden again, dazzling and brilliant, engulfs me until a powerful orgasm brings it twisting around my neck, strangling me.

⌒

My eyes open. I look into Gary's eyes, then down at my hands in my lap. Suddenly it's clear that the rape is about my sexuality.

I'm sweating and feel like I'm going to choke. I bring my hand to my throat and rub it, trying to calm my breathing. I sit exhausted and cry softly as Gary tells me our time is up.

Session #65

There's unfinished work for you to do, Gary tells me when I sit down. I know he's right and tell him that I must go into the house again. I close my eyes. I'm still uncomfortable asking for help. I bite my lip and taste my blood, salty and warm.

Relax, he tells me, as he instructs me to put my feet flat on the floor and close my eyes. His voice grows warm and soft and comforting and I know that I'm safe with him.

He leads me into a soft, almost hypnotic state in which I experience the sensation of being in the house. Although I'm able to hear him through the exercise, I feel as if I'm a spectator watching what is happening. Familiar with the details of my surroundings in the house, he encourages me instead to describe what I'm experiencing while watching for signs that I'm becoming overwhelmed.

I return to the exercise we have tried on numerous occasions, although I'm becoming discouraged at my lack of success. A wretched wreck of a girl is lying on the mattress, bleeding. I'm unable to move, unwilling to help, but am confused as to why. If this were a friend or a relative I wouldn't hesitate, but I'm unable to help this girl and stand staring at her.

Gary's soft voice interrupts the noises in my head. Can I bring Phil in to help me? It's the same question he has asked before. No, I'm unwilling to let Phil see me like this. He presses further this time: There is something you must do, he insists, and tells me that he will not leave me in the house alone.

His words are suddenly clear to me. Their meaning is concise and true and I comprehend in an instant what he has been trying to accomplish: At last I realize that I'm not alone in the house, that he's with me and won't allow me to suffer any longer. His compassion is overwhelming and I feel tears on my cheeks but make no effort to wipe them away. For the first time, thanks to his help, I feel compassion for the girl on the mattress. For the first time, I allow myself to stay with her, knowing she will be okay. For the first time, I truly feel that she will be okay.

I feel as if Gary has allowed me to use him as my therapist, my friend, my mentor, for my own healing. He has allowed me to bring him into my own experience and to use our relationship to find the strength to be there for myself. What he has really provided for me is the insight that all we have, truly, is our own selves, but that there are resources all around us—people who care about us or who move through our lives only for a short period of time who can provide us with what we need.

Gary begins to pull me from the relaxed state, but I feel resistant. I'm exhausted but don't want the euphoria of the moment, one of true insight, to dissipate. Since the beginning of therapy, Gary has encouraged me to face my own resistance of which I've become master. We've formed a powerful alliance against the very defenses that previously protected me, defenses that have since outlived their usefulness.

I've brought a clumsy, halting nature to our endeavor, but Gary's tenacity and perseverance to accomplish our shared goal has rewarded us with this one moment in time.

Session #67

I still feel euphoric about our session several weeks ago and imagine that today we will perhaps begin talking about the end of therapy. I've accomplished all that I hoped—to leave the house—so Gary's question catches me off guard: How do I feel about my weight?

I reply that most times I'm frightened by what I feel is an uncontrollable urge to eat. The impulse to force something down my throat with food is intense. I can't regulate myself and don't know whether I'm hungry or satiated. I don't know whether I can stop or not—and if I can stop, whether I will exist. It's a painful feeling that consumes many of my days.

I feel, I tell him, as though he's just thrown me to the ground. In all the time we've been together we haven't discussed my weight. Why now? Instead of answering my question, he asks instead if the rape affected my weight.

As always, Gary asks intuitive questions. I answer, unsure of whether I really want to talk about this admittedly tender subject.

It's the Monday before the rape. I look in the mirror at myself. I've reached an astounding goal—I've lost one hundred pounds. Amazing. An entire person. This is my first significant accomplishment as a woman. I'm wearing a dress I bought ten months before during the previous winter when I was still heavy. It has an empire waist and is yellow and white with white piping at the edge of a soft, round neckline. My hair, long and dark, frames a smaller face than I've ever seen looking back at me. I feel pretty and something I've never heard describe me before—petite.

I can't help crying as I stand looking at the girl in the mirror.

Gary has an incredulous look on his face. It's difficult to imagine me petite, I guess. I'm irritated that we've taken this detour and leave our session disappointed that the progress I've made isn't signaling the end of therapy.

Session #68

It's been nearly a month since Gary and I have seen each other, enough time for me to appreciate his recent line of questioning and know he was right in pursuing it. Yes, I've had a serious weight problem for most of my life. Yes, I abuse myself with food. Yes, with every bite of food I'm able to push feelings further and further down. Yes, I've practiced this behavior before. Yes, I'll tell him about it.

⌒

I'm five, perhaps six years old. My parents have left me with a babysitter for the umpteenth time.

I want only to be at home with them, but instead am here in this house, which I despise. It's small and stiflingly hot. It has vinyl flooring throughout with sparse furniture and no reading material. There are no lamps, just a ceiling light that remains off most of the time.

The light from the television bathes the living room in blue-tinted light. Movies play throughout the night. My babysitter sits at the edge of the couch. Her favorite endeavor while watching stories of lives she'll never know? Digging the pulp out of lemons and eating it—disgusting.

There's a small, closed-in porch in the front, which I frequent. In fact, I spend hours in there, waiting for my parents to return. There's a huge digital clock across the street at a car parts factory with large bulbs that light up the sky and scream the time: 11:57—11:58—11:59.

I want time to stand still. The rule: If my parents aren't home by midnight, I'll stay the night.

My babysitter starts her verbal assault at midnight exactly. She knows I won't be going home. Do I hear the siren waiting in the distance? That's my parents. They've been in a car crash and won't be coming home.

Finally she yells to me to come back into the living room. She's angry that I'm crying and wants me to stop. It's only 12:30 or so by this time and her mother won't be home until around 2:30. There's still plenty of time.

I'm kicking and screaming as she grabs my upper arm and walks me through the dining room, doubling as a nursery for another of her siblings. We go through the kitchen and to the basement door. She flings it open, slamming it against the wall, and plops me down on the top step.

Although I fight her all the way, she's stronger than I am and I'm deposited exactly where she wants. In a moment, she has the door closed behind me and I'm in complete darkness. All is silent—I can't even hear the sounds from the television. But I do hear the click of the lock behind me.

⌒

Gary looks at me quizzically, cocking his head. He doesn't see yet how this relates to my lifelong habit of abusing food, but I don't care. I'm irritated that we've gone down this road.

Session #69

The weather is balmy today and I'm tired at our session this afternoon, not really interested in talking, and certainly not in talking about my weight, but by this time I know the drill. I take a breath anyway and start where I left off at our last session.

⌒

This activity goes on for a number of weeks: I sit on my babysitter's porch waiting for my parents to return home. They don't come, the clock reads midnight, I begin to cry, and I'm put in the basement.

I'm scared to death. It's dark and dank and I stay on the top step with my back pressed tightly against the door. I push against it so hard that I fear my bones will break. I don't know what might be in the bowels of the basement, what creatures may be hiding.

I know the basement well during the daylight. It's half-finished with concrete floors and a wall on one side and dirt leading up the hill on the other. On the side that's finished are rows and rows of canned vegetables and fruits, stored for the winter. My babysitter's mother arranges them by color—deep reds, oranges, then sunshine yellows. As the shelves round the corner, deep greens.

I hear tiny squeaks and noises from below me, but it's too dark to see. I wait for tiny feet to run across mine, up my legs and arms, onto my face. I stop crying and become still. Having survived several weeks, I bring ammunition—inside my pocket is a soft chewy chocolate chip cookie.

The squeaks sound closer now so I break off a tiny bit of cookie and throw it toward the noises as hard as I can. That will keep them occupied so they don't come after me. Silence—then more squeaking—silence—and on and on.

⌒

I stop and look at Gary with tears in my eyes. As time goes on, I tell him, I bring more and more cookies and while throwing one bite into the void, I eat one myself—and then another. They comfort me somehow, or anesthetize me; I'm not sure which. In any case, I find they lessen my fright in being in the basement.

My babysitter's abuse becomes much worse and much more physically and sexually invasive over the years; but this is not something, I tell Gary, that I want to discuss.

Eating is, as it has been since the beginning, an anesthetic. I eat in order not to feel.

I keep my body hidden under a suit of armor, I tell Gary, but the assault inside my garage showed me what a gross error that was in my thinking. I need to feel safe and be assured that no one will hurt me again, but even being over-weight failed to protect me.

Session #71

The research, I tell Gary at our session this morning, is there: manners of rape, methods, some information, but not enough of motivation—true motivation—on why men rape. There's also precious little about why women—why I—responded as I did after experiencing rape.

Little about why I cling to the need to change my body in order to feel safe.

Little about how I integrate such a painfully intrusive experience into my everyday life, even my sexual life.

Little about when I can expect to feel good again.

Though my journals are difficult to read, all of my memory boxes have been opened, examined, and explored. Still, there are things I don't understand.

The consequences of the rape, the pregnancy, my weight gain, my infertility—I can find nothing that provides the key to understanding. The consequences of what happened still need to be addressed or at least the results must be addressed.

My life is divided into "before" and "after" that year.

My lack of confidence and self-worth is evident in my journals, and I regret that what talents I do have lie in writing and not painting or photography. I recognize that being able to express oneself is key to healing, but words are so inadequate.

I've bought into the view that my body size is tied, inexorably, to my worth as a human being, but perhaps it's as a colleague has said: It's my choice to take the road to hell; it's my choice to hurt myself; it's my choice to allow others to hurt me. Or not.

Is it that I'm on autopilot, as my colleague says? Do I not realize yet that I have a choice? For if I do realize that I have a choice, why do I continue to cause harm by thinking less of myself? What is the payoff? What are the rewards?

Gary agrees, nodding his head slightly, but says nothing. He allows my words to hang in the air and waits for me to process them. I'm experiencing something vague and nearly indescribable. Suddenly a word comes to me: boredom. I'm simply bored by my unwillingness to move past what is. Bored by asking "What if?" Bored talking about it. Bored not talking about it. While at first I'm almost alarmed by being bored, I start to realize this is a good thing. This, finally, is acceptance.

When finally I name this feeling out loud, I see a look in Gary's eyes that conveys to me that we will be terminating therapy soon. I'm uncertain how I've come to realize it, but feel a lightening of my mood I hadn't felt at the beginning of our session.

Session #72

Many are the sessions in which I've felt like crawling up on Gary's couch and being a little girl, but he has always forced me to be the woman I am—to take responsibility for my feelings and to understand and gain insight. In return for the work I've done, he's provided me with an intimacy that has, at times, made me uncomfortable, for how can it last? Won't this be just another loss when therapy ends?

This thinking places me in a box and I'm faced with a dilemma: How am I able to present my real self to someone, stripped bare of the mask that we all wear in front of one another, without having first achieved intimacy? How can it be done? And so, I've come to the conclusion that it couldn't have been done without the fits and starts, without the embarrassment and the humiliation—it just simply couldn't have been.

Intimacy with others—or perhaps lack of it—keeps me silent. For when one is intimate, one is vulnerable. This, then, is what I have to face, even in my marriage. I have to face the possibility that Phil will find the truth about my history and who I am completely overwhelming and unacceptable and that he will leave me. I face it, though, with the knowledge of the man I know him to be, confident in the love he has for me and I for him.

I decide to talk about my sexuality and a recent trip I took with Phil.

⌒

We settle into our room at the lodge and are fortunate to get one in which we see the beach stretching to the ocean. It's warm and inviting, with cathedral ceilings stretching skyward and a crackling fireplace.

Phil and I stand on the deck looking at the view. The sun has set but we recognize the stately figures of reed grass blowing ever so softly by the light of the moon. Their gentle sway and the soft licking of the water on the beach further down are soothing. Phil turns toward me and takes my face in his hands to give me a kiss.

We enjoy a long, relaxing supper at a restaurant just down a gentle slope from our room, and when we return Phil suggests I take a hot bath.

As I run the water, the steam forms a soft mist in the room. I look at myself in the mirror. A woman's body but a child's emotions, at times. I'm silhouetted against the sea green shower curtain and run my hand over my breasts, over the scars, and am surprised at how much I long for a baby to hold to my breast, to nurture and feed and love.

I draw the bath much hotter than necessary. I still cross the line between a pleas-

antly warm bath and an excruciatingly hot one as if to burn the memory of the rape off my skin. I dip my toe in first, then my leg, and watch as they grow rosy pink, then angry red. I force myself into the water. Soon, I've fallen into a soft, hazy sleep.

Phil wakes me with a sharp rap on the door and comes into the bathroom, helping me from the tub. He grabs a thick terry cloth robe from behind the door and wraps it around me, pulling my hair out from the back. He wraps his arms around me and I'm safe again. Without a word, he walks me into the bedroom and lays me on the bed. When we make love I participate with the passion of someone who's been imprisoned for a very long time. With my orgasm comes release from everything.

Later, I can't sleep and listen to the waves break on the rocks outside our room.

Phil sleeps beside me, his soft breath blowing against my skin and his chest rising and falling ever so slightly. The indentation he makes in the bed is almost imperceptible for such a tall, large man. I feel sorry for all I've put him through, for the years that I've spent in isolation. He deserves better. He never understood my need to retreat, my feeling of being trapped in the corner. He does know the lengths I've gone to avoid these feelings, and he's been there for me always—my savior in the most true sense.

⌐

Gary lets my words land in the air and allows me a moment to remember that day.

You're standing on a high diving board, he tells me. You're alone. Phil and I watch you from the sides; we cheer you on, but you're up there alone. Don't be afraid. You can take care of yourself.

Words such as these are my comfort. Written, spoken, they're opportunities for intimacy, if only for a moment. Even my own words are slowly beginning to comfort me—ever so slowly.

Each of us is alone in our experiences, I say to Gary as I raise my eyes to his. We can empathize, we can develop compassion for each other, but we can't live each others' lives. We can't know how another person truly feels without sharing our feelings. I need that intimacy.

And he, knowing just the right thing to say, assures me that I do have it— with him.

Session #74

I've worked hard, really hard, for the progress I've made, I tell Gary today at our session.

I look around his office. I feel comfortable and safe here and I like the smell; it's familiar and I've come to associate it with Gary. I'll miss coming here and feel a sadness creeping in. I push that feeling aside and instead slide effortlessly into talking about Phil.

When his hands, lips, and body are on top of me, I need to feel *him*—experience *him*.

I've found my way during our relationship, albeit clumsily, and have made so many mistakes along the way. Little by little, I'm gaining awareness of how the rape, the pregnancies, the infertility, and finally my weight affect our relationship and my sexuality.

My identity, though negative, is at least familiar. It dictates my behavior because it's my view of how I believe others see me and judge me—how they identify me—or so I've come to believe.

Phil isn't cognizant of the part he plays in my sexuality, but it remains steadfast and true. He can't know what it means to me that my fantasies returned to a semblance of normalcy after we met; those that had grown so violent and gruesome. Phil taught me the meaning of sexuality, of intimacy, and of love.

He's the least intrusive person I've met. He respects my privacy completely and while he assures me he's there for me no matter what, he never pushes me. I can look into his beautiful brown eyes and see my world. He holds my heart.

Looking at Gary, so attentive and caring, the feeling of sadness returns. It occurs to me that I won't have him to guide me much longer and that I'll have to learn to find my own way.

Termination. I know it's coming. Still, I feel lost when I think of not having him to help me interpret these feelings. I will, he told me, have to chart my own course.

Session #78

I'm anxious to see Gary this morning and tell him about something disturbing that happened since our last session.

⌒

I'm treated to a day at a spa. It's beautiful, decorated in a Roman motif with muted apricot and soft gray colors, and is extremely inviting.

My masseuse leads me upstairs to a private area in the building. She's young and has beautiful skin and long, straight black hair. She opens the door to the room we'll be using; it's even more beautiful, decorated in the same muted apricots and grays and has two huge columns not far inside the door, between which is a soft sheer drapery.

Lovely dark green ivy coils its way up one column, across the drapery, and halfway down the other. Between the two columns hangs a painting of a woman, Rubinesque, languishing in a Roman spa.

In front of the columns are two overstuffed oyster-colored chairs. She invites me to take off my clothes and put on a fluffy terry cloth robe and slippers. She offers coffee before disappearing around the drapery. I hear her turning on machines and then the stereo. Soft sweet music fills the room. When she returns, I notice that she's removed her street clothes and has on a smock. She isn't wearing shoes.

She leads me to one of the massage tables. First, she explains, she'll be doing a hot wrap. In getting ready, she'll give me a rubdown, then spread hot oil over me, then wrap me in a warm foil. While she's doing that, she'll give me a facial. Then, following that, a massage. It sounds wonderful.

She asks that I lie on my stomach. Her hands are soft and sensuous as they traverse my legs, up my thighs, my hips, my back, shoulders, arms, and hands. When she's finished she asks that I turn over and starts the same motion. Up my legs, my thighs, my abdomen. I mention that I'm going to start my period and wonder if the massage will help release tension. She tells me that she has many women who ask that she concentrate on their legs, thighs, and abdomen when having their periods or right before.

Her hands move to my hip bones. Her fingers, on both hands at the same time, make small circular motions over the bones and down into my abdomen. I seem tense in my abdominal muscles, she says, and presses hard. She moves over to my left hipbone and works again, rubbing, soothing, massaging up higher, then over. One hand over the other, she works her way to the other side and then deep into the abdominal muscles once again. I feel the cramps subside ever so softly, like tiny rip-

107

ples on water. Tears well up in my eyes. I'm as surprised as she is and she asks what's wrong. I tell her that I'm emotional because of other things going on, but am thinking about the baby. About having something with me at the time of her birth and about how I longed for someone to touch me like she's touching me now.

⌒

I'm sobbing when I finish.

"You have to let your baby die; *you're* keeping her alive." Gary's words bring me back into his office, into the present.

Tears stream down my face. I think about her, in some form or fashion, nearly every day. I allow myself to continue to be raped, to continue to be pregnant, to continue to miss her.

I've held her inside me for years and he's right. It's time to let her go, but my body yearns to finish the job it started. I felt her come out of me but couldn't hold her or put her lips to my breast. Surely I've held her inside me for a reason.

Session #82

The most profound learning and insight occurs when I least expect it, when I'm most afraid, when I'm most discouraged. And so it is with this most recent real-ization. Simple, yet profound: My guilt served a purpose. I needed it, because if I felt guilt, then it meant I had control over everything that happened to me. If I had no control, then my life itself didn't make sense.

I'm agitated and confused when I see Gary at our session today because even though I want to explain this to him I can't seem to properly explain it to myself. I start by telling him what happened.

I'm lying on my bed, incredibly tired after a stressful day and not feeling very well at all. I figure if I can just relax for a couple of hours, I'll be okay to get up, make dinner, and do some more work. I pull back the covers and lie down with my clothes on.

Suddenly, something happens.

It isn't a flashback or a nightmare. It's a recollection, an intense memory. I'm back in the house. It's a moment, just a moment buried in the fourteen hours.

I'm inside myself. For so much of the time in the house I feel as if I'm on the outside looking in, but I'm inside my skin now. I'm on my back, lying on the mat-tress. I can smell it—musty, horribly dirty. My knees are bent. My underwear and tights are off, and my jean skirt is held on by the first snap only. It's after he broke my jaw because when I try to talk, I can't move it. I can feel my lip has swelled and tastes of blood. My blouse and skirt are open and my hands are tied.

The man is on his knees and to my right. He has one hand inside me and a tool in the other. We struggle. I try to get up on my left elbow and grab his sweater. I can feel the material between my fingers.

I whisper that he's hurting me. He looks at me, directly into my eyes. I remember them now, so clearly. The coldness and lack of emotion terrify me. He brings his left hand back and brings it down hard against my left hip, puncturing my skin through my skirt.

I recall realizing, knowing, that at that moment I didn't matter.

This became my philosophy, I tell Gary. It became my attitude, my claim, my belief, my position, and my opinion. It became my doctrine, my sentiment. It became my conviction about myself. It became me.

109

Session #83

I'm euphoric about the events that took place following our last session and begin spilling words before even settling into Gary's couch.

～

The experience of reliving that moment in time, such a small moment during the fourteen hours I was in the house, allows me to experience amazing insight. I was privy to it prior to that moment, but it's the naming of my suffering that makes a difference: That I didn't matter.

The realization is intense and painful but it's also a turning point. I've seen the monster in the closet and am astonished to see that it's me. The way I've treated myself has been the cause of my own suffering.

The evening of our last session I stood looking at myself in the mirror. I have disfiguring scars on my hands, breast, and hip. My jaw is permanently damaged, and even though I found a retinal specialist and can see again nearly perfectly thanks to my surgery two spots remain in my eye due to the blood that leaks through a small hole in the retina and continues to fill the eye. I've had physical and emotional experiences I wouldn't want anyone to experience.

Instead of seeing a survivor when I looked in the mirror through the years, I saw a damaged, young woman.

Instead of seeing the courage and tenacity that I'd pulled from deep inside myself, I saw failure.

This, I realized at that moment several weeks ago, was my choice, and it must end.

As I stood looking in the mirror, I felt blessed to be married to my husband. He accepted me with my scars, inside and out. He loved me and cared for me and never told me, not even once, that I didn't matter.

It was time, I decided that evening, to put our relationship to the test.

I prepared him at dinner several evenings later, taking him to our favorite restaurant along Monterey Bay. I updated him on the last several sessions and, while he was interested, he was also careful not to ask intrusive questions.

I slid my journals toward him across the table. I told him I was aware they'd be difficult to read but that I was ready to share them with him.

The wait was long. He took an entire Saturday to read them. Though I was anxious to learn his reaction, I couldn't be in the same room with him while he was reading.

It was eight o'clock by the time he came into the bedroom for me. Tears stained his face, a sight so totally foreign to me that it momentarily scared me and I began to cry. He stood holding me tightly for the longest time, saying only that he'd had no idea what I'd gone through.

We talked late into the evening and Phil went through a range of emotions: Rage at the people who hurt me; empathy, sympathy, and admiration for how far I'd progressed. I was elated that I'd taken the chance to confide in him, my best friend, after so long, and so thankful that our relationship was strong enough to survive the truth. He shared with me the overwhelming grief I feel at not being able to bear his child, and while that grief will be with me always, I now know that it will not rule—or ruin—my life.

⌐

The intense work of therapy necessary to reach this point was vital, I tell Gary. Every moment of it. Every tear shed, every fear brought to light, every thought shared. Every moment of it has been crucial to reach where I am today.

I reach for a tissue. Gary uncrosses his legs, signaling that it's time for me to leave, but doesn't stand to show me to the door. Instead, we share a moment of intimacy that I've come to recognize: He's honored that I've placed my trust in him and shared myself. And I'm honored to have him in my life.

Session #89

Much of the past several months have been busy with fulfilling the last require-ments necessary for my graduate degree and so my sessions with Gary have been few and far between, with most of our discussions focused on how I can best integrate my experience into my practice. While he's clearly still my therapist, his role is becoming more of a mentor.

We discuss termination of therapy once again. It's time. I've learned what Gary had to teach me, a fact of which we're both aware.

Gary seamlessly handles the termination tasks. I'm almost unaware of them, he's so skillful.

We begin with a review of the progress we've made, in particular the periods of silence (I refuse to call them "secrets" as that conveys negativity) I needed to discuss with both Phil and him. There are four: The assault in our garage, the rape, the pregnancy, and my resulting infertility. I'm extremely proud of the fact that I've told Phil all I need to. An added bonus is the issue of my weight and how it relates to the rape and my sexuality. While this issue has been raised, it's outside of therapy that I want to address it, but I feel able to now with the skills Gary has taught me.

And what of my problem-solving abilities? These, we both agree, have always been strong. One of my initial goals was to transfer the problem-solving skills that I use each day in my work to my personal life. I'm confident that I've met this goal and will be able to continue to solve my own future problems.

And I anticipate them, of course. But I'm secure in my relationship with Phil and can speak with him about any subject. Second, I'm able to analyze the defense mechanisms I employ when I do encounter problems and can determine how best to solve them. My alternatives are varied and extensive.

Session #94

We've prepared for the end of therapy for some time. As Gary ushers me into his office today for this, our next to last session, I expect a range of emotions. Sorrow perhaps, even grief that our relationship is coming to a close, but I don't. Looking into his eyes, I feel only contentment. The strong sense of longing I'd anticipated isn't present.

I feel gratitude for the time he's been in my life and for the energy he's invested in helping me reach my potential emotionally and psychologically.

Today is the anniversary of my dad's death some twenty-two years ago. I can think of that day so long ago and cry, not tears of sorrow and loss, but tears of gratefulness that he was in my life. Gratefulness for his idiosyncrasies, most of which I've inherited, and for his habits, for his love, for his laughter. So it's my father whom I'm thinking about as I sit in Gary's office.

When I began therapy, I tell Gary, I knew that all wouldn't be revealed in the first session, or the fifth, or even the twentieth. There were weeks when I had nothing new to contribute or was simply tired and felt as if I were wasting both our time and my money. Yet these periods, too, served as teachers. Was I denying pertinent feelings? Repressing emotions too close to the surface? Yes, in most cases. It was with his attentive, empathic nature that I was able to finally recognize and attach meaning to these periods as well.

Prior to meeting him, I continue, I ached to be out of that house. I wanted nothing more than to forget the image of seeing myself on a mattress being raped.

But, I came to realize, that wasn't my reality. Even if I could have moved myself out of the house, it wouldn't have freed me. I had to help myself through the fourteen hours I spent on the mattress in order to gain acceptance of my feelings, my thoughts, and particularly my actions on that day and others that followed. Only then could I comprehend the evil that I went through and provide myself with compassion.

Gary tells me that I'm welcome to return to him. This is a safety net for which I'm particularly thankful. Just knowing he's available gives me strength.

I know that I'm leaving a treasured friend, and while I'm filled with pride at the work I've accomplished, I miss him already.

Session #95

My independence day has come with this, our last visit.

While we chitchat a bit and say our good-byes, I relate to Gary an encapsulated version of what I learned during our time together. This is what I'd say to the nineteen-year-old girl I was if she were to see me for therapy:

I'd tell her that it wasn't her fault. Not then. Not now. Not ever.

I'd tell her that there's a spectrum of emotions that occur during her hour with me, but that their meaning is often assigned elsewhere.

I'd tell her that no matter what she wore, no matter what she said, no matter how she acted, she didn't deserve to be raped.

I'd tell her that the nightmares, when she can sleep, *do* go away . . . eventually. But that they may come back when she least expects it.

I'd resist the urge to present my own three years of therapy as if they made any sense to me at the time, because they didn't. There were ragged edges, muted lines, and confusion.

I'd tell her that the raw, vulnerable emotions that feel so overwhelming when alone and contemplative will feel less so when she's able to share them with someone.

I'd tell her that it's extremely difficult to accept the unacceptable and that resistance is exhausting.

The work of therapy for post-traumatic stress disorder, I'd tell her, is intense but crucial. And, I would tell her, it may get worse before it gets better.

I'd tell her that she will experience intimacy and love in her life again, perhaps where she least expects it.

I'd tell her that guilt and shame may be emotions she'll experience as most rape victims do, but not to invest in them. They won't serve any purpose whatsoever.

I'd tell her that she will begin to let people into her heart again in her own time. Acceptance, I'd tell her, will come; again in her own time. And taking the time she needs is vital.

But most importantly—I'd tell her she's not alone.

Epilogue

I sit looking out over Monterey Bay as I write this. The clouds are a soft, dreamy gray and hug the bay, ripe at this time of day with otters and seals and pelicans. Next to my window, climbing up the hill toward a bed and breakfast next door, is an English garden with hummingbirds wildly moving from plant to plant. I'm four hours away from where the rape occurred, yet a lifetime away. It no longer has power over me. It's now only a memory, nothing more.

My husband sits across from me working, his fingers tapping the keyboard as in my dream, and I have one thought: I'm safe and no longer feel alone. I've shared myself completely with Phil and we're more intimate, our relationship more cherished, than I ever could have imagined.

Since finishing my therapy three years ago, my work in helping others recover from rape has extended far beyond counseling. However, the information I've learned from clients has been vital in helping me direct my efforts.

Therapy is complex to be sure and while I experienced a very positive outcome to my therapy, I realize this isn't always the case. Putting aside the emotional element of asking for and receiving help, the thought of therapy can be overwhelming in terms of the time, energy, and money that must be invested.

I found when providing counseling to rape victims that there are universal concerns and questions that accompany this particular type of therapy. Nearly all of my clients asked if I were a victim of rape—a question that reminded me of the discussion I had with Gary at the beginning of my own therapy. While speaking of one's own experience and self in general isn't done, I always answered honestly that I am. In each client who asked, I sensed an inaudible sigh of relief. They'd found someone who understood, who had experienced similar physical events, and as a result, someone with whom they could speak a sort of shorthand.

When my clients learned that I was a victim of rape, they invariably had a number of questions for me: How did I approach therapy? Was it difficult? What helped the most? How long did it last? I was impressed by their courage to ask difficult questions. I kept my answers to a bare minimum as we were there for them, not me. However, these exchanges served to make me aware of the need for more information concerning rape recovery.

I developed goals designed to reduce many of the obstacles that face my clients and other victims of rape, whether that rape was perpetrated by a stranger or an acquaintance and whether it occurred twenty minutes or twenty years ago.

Writing afforded me the unique opportunity to reach more women than I could ever hope to see personally. *The Truth about Rape* is the second book I've written. The first, *Hours of Torture, Years of Silence*, told about the rape itself and its subsequent effects on me; it was specific to the rape itself and did not chronicle my journey through therapy and the healing I ultimately found.

In addition, RapeRecovery.com is a Web site-based source of information specializing in recovery from rape, allowing access to information in the privacy and comfort of their own homes.

Please visit our site at www.RapeRecovery.com to search for a therapist in your area, learn more about rape recovery resources, or to share your own story, and please feel free to email me at Teresa@RapeRecovery.com if I may help you in any way with your own recovery. I wish you the best.

Teresa

Section II

Your Emotional, Spiritual, Physical, and Sexual Healing

1

Emotional Healing

Many women experience various degrees of Post-Traumatic Stress Disorder (PTSD); it's important to realize that PTSD is a medical diagnosis and shouldn't be perceived as being a weakness on your part but an expected response to a very unexpected event that has occurred in your life—your rape.

The following is a summary of the symptoms necessary for a diagnosis of PTSD. Along with a length of time for symptoms of at least one month and that they are significantly affecting your life:

1. Exposure to a trauma

2. Re-experiencing of the trauma in the form of nightmares, flashbacks, dreams, and intrusive memories

3. A numbing of your emotions; reduced interest in your family, friends, social and work activities

4. Hyperarousal symptoms, such as irritability, sleep disorders (insomnia or sleeping too much), rage, exaggerated startle responses

Not everyone who has been raped suffers from Post-Traumatic Stress Disorder (PTSD). We're all individuals with different responses to extreme stressors, such as rape, and are influenced by a number of factors, such as our age and maturity level at the time of the rape, the length and severity of the rape, the extent of our injuries. In addition, factors such as the response from family and friends and our contact (or lack of contact) with those in the criminal justice and mental health system can have a tremendous effect on the severity of symptoms that we experience. That being said, studies have shown that nearly a third of all victims develop some degree of rape-related PTSD.

*Reprinted with permission from the Diagnostic and Statistical Manual of Mental Disorders, Fourth Edition, Text Revision. Copyright 2000 American Psychiatric Association.

"Have I been raped?"

✍ A Personal View

It seems ludicrous now that I didn't realize I'd been raped, but I was so confused. I'd known my best friend's brother for years and I had been attracted to him, in fact, we'd even flirted, yet I felt violated when his advances, which had previously been innocent, turned forceful.

Perhaps the most liberating moment since the rape occurred when my psychologist diagnosed me with PTSD, Post-Traumatic Stress Disorder. I felt if someone had a name for what I had been through then perhaps I could recover. It's like when you're waiting for medical test results, the last thing you want to hear is that they couldn't find anything. A diagnosis feels like a cure is possible.—Zoe, 25

✚ A Clinical View
The Definition of Rape

We often think of a rapist as a faceless monster who grabs his victim off the street, however more women are raped by an acquaintance than a stranger. The definition of rape is very clear: You have been raped if someone performs a sexual act against you without your consent. Period. Make no mistake that your body is your own. No one has permission to do anything you don't want them to do and they should be made to experience the consequences if they do.

Though society's boundaries are becoming more blurred, we have the option and obligation of defining our own boundaries.

You may not have been able to provide consent if you were:

- Forced to engage in the activity
- Threatened
- Drugged or drunk
- Unconscious
- A minor
- Developmentally disabled
- Undergoing a medical procedure

In addition to intercourse, the following may be considered sexual assault:

- Penis, mouth, tongue, fingers or objects inserted into your anus or vagina if you are unwilling
- Kissing, fondling, touching, unwanted bodily contact
- Oral sex (either forcing you to perform or receive)
- Masturbation (either forcing you to masturbate or perform masturbation on them)
- Unnecessary internal examinations by a medical professional

"Is date rape really rape?"

✍ A Personal View

Yes. I slowly began to realize that I'd been raped when I went on a date with what I'd hoped would be a new relationship. Dinner was wonderful, the movie was really nice, but he started groping me toward the end and I grew uncomfortable. When I asked that he take me home, he said that he was sorry he'd been so forward and that we should drive around for a bit down by a lake in our town. He seemed so sincere about being sorry but as soon as we got to the lake, he seemed to change—he grew cold and, well, mean almost. I kept telling him not to do what he was doing but he kept up until he ejaculated inside me. I was devastated and started crying, which made him more angry.

For the longest time, I blamed myself but my therapist made me see that I had in reality been raped. Rape is when someone does something to you against your will.

The difficult part for me to accept was that I had so misjudged him. I have a lot to learn. —Jolene, 19

✚ A Clinical View

The Definition of Rape

Absolutely. Rape, which is any sexual act performed against you without your consent is rape whether you know the person (acquaintance rape), are dating the person (date rape), or are married to the person (marital rape).

Date rape has numerous issues that stranger rape does not and is by far the most underreported method of rape. Victims may be concerned about retribution from friends and family of the rapist if charges are filed. In addition, victims may fear further traumatization by secondary victimization by the criminal justice system and feel a sense of blame and humiliation.

Lack of trust and questioning of one's own judgment is often seen in victims of date rape and acquaintance rape.

It's important to note that alcohol and drug use is often a factor in date rape and that it occurs on campuses nationwide. This issue is of great concern as the vast majority of date rapes committed are not reported because of the guilt and shame experienced by the victim.

In addition the miscommunication that occurs between genders, that is, the "she wanted it" (her mouth said "no" but her eyes said "yes") attitude is prevalent and a factor in many date rapes and in fact some men experience heightened sexual response when the woman struggles.

Do what you can to avoid situations that can lead to date rape:

- Set your own limits and time period for your sexual encounters
- Be firm and direct in regard to communicating this to your date and alert to how you're being perceived
- Remain independent during your date; don't go places where you're uncomfortable and always carry enough money to get home on your own
- Remain sober and in control of your actions
- Trust your instincts; remove yourself from any situation in which you're uncomfortable
- Get help immediately if you feel in danger

"What are date rape drugs?"

✍ A Personal View

I learned that I was raped one evening when my friend and I went to a bar, not because I remember what happened but because the guys who took us home took photographs of us. These photos actually made the rounds in several of my classes. I was humiliated and couldn't believe that they'd actually done this to us and that we were too drunk to realize.

I can't remember a thing; I feel like I lost a lot more than those hours that evening. I'm too embarrassed to even go to the police. What could I say? That I was raped while I was drunk? We suspect that they may have slipped something into our drinks, but we can't prove it. Who would believe me in any case?

What they did was deplorable but it taught me never to drink to excess or to leave my drink unattended. My friend and I learned a valuable lesson.—LeAnne, 21

✚ A Clinical View

Date Rape Drugs

Rohypnol (flunitrazepam) and Gamma Hydroxy Butyrate (GHB) are colorless, odorless sedatives that dissolve when placed in liquid. Possession of Rohypnol is illegal in many states and the U.S. Customs Service has banned its importation into the United States.

When used in the capacity of a "date rape drug" they leave the victim extremely vulnerable and sleepy. Rohypnol has additional side effects, such as difficulty with motor skills and speaking, blackouts, and amnesia. These latter side effects make criminal prosecution especially difficult.

It's important to seek help immediately if you feel you've been a victim of a sexual assault. Urine tests can determine the presence of the drug in your system and medical exams can collect evidence of a sexual assault if too much time hasn't elapsed.

"I was raped on my campus; who can help me?"

✍ A Personal View

I'm completely devastated by my rape and the effect that it's had on my life. Anger—picking fights indiscriminately—I need to be rescued from this pain. And so, I'm seeing someone from the counseling center at my university.

I considered changing schools but came to see that as a victory for the rapist so I'm not going to do that. I'm a shy person by nature and making the friends that I have on this campus after three years is not something I'm willing to walk away from. My counselor at the rape center told me about the Campus Sexual Assault Bill of Rights which was invaluable to learning about services available to me.
—Andrea, 22

✛ A Clinical View

Campus Sexual Assault Victims' Bill of Rights

As a victim of rape on a campus, you are entitled to a number of rights due to the Campus Sexual Assault Victims' Bill of Rights. Signed into law by President Bush in July of 1992, this law requires that all colleges and universities (public and private) receiving federal student aid afford sexual assault victims basic rights as follows:

1. Accuser and accused must have the same opportunity to have others present.

2. Both parties shall be informed of the outcome of any disciplinary proceeding.

3. Survivors shall be informed of their options to notify law enforcement.

4. Survivors shall be notified of counseling services.

5. Survivors shall be notified of options for changing academic and living situations.

Colleges and universities found to be in violation of this law may be fined up to $25,000 and lose their eligibility for participation in federal student aid programs.

"I think about the rape all the time. Why aren't I over this yet?"

✍ A Personal View

This is a question I asked myself over and over again.

Why was it taking me so long to put this behind me? Why did it have such a lasting effect on me? Both the best and the worst part of the rape was that nobody could see what had happened to me. The best because I didn't want anyone to know; the worst because I wasn't able to get the empathy and compassion that I needed.

My leg was pretty severely broken in a car accident several years before my rape. It was traumatic at first to talk about it, but the more concern that others showed me—genuine concern for my welfare—the better I felt; almost as if the good out-weighed the bad. And the more I talked about it, the less "large" it was in my mind.

The opposite occurred with the rape. I'm still not 'over it' and it's been three years.—Pam, 33

✚ A Clinical View

Over what—one of the most devastatingly intrusive crimes that a man can commit against a woman—a crime of such lasting influence that it affects women ten, even twenty, years later?

This is not a cakewalk that you have gone through; it's a serious, violent crime during which you may not have known whether you would survive. This is an issue that I think is often overlooked when considering the lasting effects of rape: In many rapes, the victim doesn't know if she will survive or if the last face she will see is that of her rapist.

No matter how long it's been since your rape, you needn't feel unworthy of your feelings or of the lingering pain you may be experiencing and it's never too late to seek help. The next time you ask yourself this question, stop and ask yourself this: *"If my best friend had been raped, when would I expect her to 'get over it'?"*

We all process information and experiences quite differently and there is a reason that we remember what we do. Our neurobiology is extremely complex and the following is, admittedly, a simplistic explanation, however it serves to remind us that we are who we are and none of our responses are wrong.

Left-Brain/Right-Brain Response to a Traumatic Experience

Victims who engage the left side of their brain are sequential, logical thinkers and, even though they may be terrified, are able to avoid being paralyzed by fear. They are likely to remember details and plan how to contact authorities, etc.

Victims who engage the right side of their brain are more sensory and emotional. The entire rape may be experienced at once with all sensations greatly intensified. They are likely to be frozen with fear; you'll often hear of women being unable to scream during the rape and unable to realize their next move. Victims who engage in the right-brain response have been more likely to develop Post-Traumatic Stress Disorder (PTSD).

"What does a flashback 'feel' like?"

✍ A Personal View

A flashback feels like you're stuck in hell. Everyone is living life around you but you're not there. My first flashback was so terrifying to me—I thought I'd lost my mind. I saw, experienced, lived through a portion of the rape all over again; as if it was happening at that very moment. I learned that my rapist had been watching me for some time from his apartment. One evening when my husband was out of town, I woke and found this man sitting at the foot of my bed. I've never experienced a moment like that—except in these flashbacks. Everything becomes all black like it was in my room and then my eyes seem to adjust and I'm able to make out his form on the bed. I can even smell him. My fear is palpable, just like that night.
—Shauna, 30

✛ A Clinical View

The Definition of a Flashback

A flashback is exactly that: A sudden recollection of the event, accompanied by strong emotions as so aptly described above; it's just like seeing a movie in your head playing over and over and over.

Taking Control of Your Flashbacks

1. Acknowledge that what you are experiencing is a flashback (a normal reaction to your rape) and that you are not crazy or weak. It's simply what you are going through at this point in your recovery.

2. Remind yourself that you're watching a movie of what happened; it's not happening to you right now, so you're safe. You have survived the rape and you will get through this as well.

3. Ground yourself by making contact with your body: stomp your feet, feel your clothing, touch an object next to you, such as a desk or sink to bring yourself into the present.

4. Try to return your breathing to normal by counting to five as you breathe in and out. Remember that if you breathe too deeply you may become disoriented and dizzy, so take care with this step.

5. If you're with someone who understands or if you can call someone, talk about what you've just experienced so that they may help you realize that you are in the present and are safe.

6. After you've experienced your flashback, congratulate yourself on surviving an extremely stressful situation. Take a hot bath or listen to some music to further relax. Write in a journal if you'd like to compare this to a previous flashback. Was it shorter in duration? Easier to bring yourself into the present? Perhaps you feel strong enough to jot down a few words about the actual scene that you experienced; it's valuable to discuss this in therapy.

"When am I going to stop having nightmares?"

✍ A Personal View

My nightmares are astoundingly real—astoundingly intense beings. They have a life of their own. I'm restless before I fall asleep, not wanting to be bombarded by the deeper experience that I know is coming in the form of a nightmare. I have no inkling that it's coming—some nights are tranquil and I'm able to descend into sweet, lovely, sleep and other nights are horrendous.

I don't always relive the rape but rather the aftereffects of the rape in some form or other. Fear in the form of black shadows, large hands, pinpoint eyes. Just glimpses rather than whole images. Other nights it's a feeling of powerlessness—perhaps in the form of looking up as one would from the bottom of the pool. I can see the sun shining on the surface and reach my hands out to pull myself up but can't reach the surface—I just can't reach the surface. I wake gasping for breath from these nightmares.

I've stopped questioning when the nightmares are going to end and instead accept them for what they are: My mind trying to accept an unacceptable act. The only thing I've been able to accept is the fact that I have no control. Then there are the nights that I experience the rape all over again—in great detail. It's quite like a flashback, only I'm asleep. Those are the most frightening because for those few moments that I try to wake up, I'm being raped all over again. —Anonymous, 44

✚ A Clinical View

The Definition of Nightmares

The first nightmare described above could be termed an "ordinary" nightmare in that it doesn't replay the actual rape that was experienced. In fact, people who haven't experienced trauma at all in their history may be familiar with the fear and powerlessness as described.

Nightmares in which the rape are experienced again are termed "traumatic" nightmares and are distinguished by their repetitiveness and content.

Taking Control of Your Nightmares

There are a number of ways in which you can help alleviate the devastating effects of nightmares:

1. Make an effort to speak with your therapist, husband or boyfriend and certainly friends if you're comfortable, about your nightmares and the effect they're having on your sleep patterns. Enlist their support in helping you through this.

2. Make your sleeping environment as soothing and pleasant as possible; if you have a favorite stuffed animal or pillow, don't feel shy about having it at hand.

3. Record your nightmares in your journal with as much factual information as is comfortable.

4. After recording the facts, try to describe the thoughts that you had during your nightmare.

5. Try to describe what was happening in your body; both during the nightmare and after.

6. Re-write your nightmare so that you are in control. What do *you* need to feel powerful?

"Why does a smell remind me of the rapist?"

✍ A Personal View

A smell, a sound, even a color—I've learned that these are all considered "triggers" of the rape. A trigger is anything that reminds you of the rape and brings up feelings and emotions. It was a smell for me as well that "triggered" the incredibly angry, hostile mood.

The man who raped me had the smell of paint and sweat on him and for months I reacted when I smelled it without even realizing its origin.

When I became more aware through therapy of when I was experiencing these feelings I was able to trace it back to the rape; I was surprised that my subconscious was so attuned and that I experienced this behavior even before I consciously become aware of it. There are ways to cope with triggers, both before they occur and during but they are terrifying. Just giving a word to it made me feel better though and feel as if I wasn't crazy.—Maggie, 28

✚ A Clinical View

The Definition of Triggers

You're re-experiencing the rape—and all that's associated with it, that is, the rapist and his characteristics—in your mind. The smell is acting as a trigger for the feelings you're experiencing.

With each episode of re-experiencing the rape, you may find that you strive even harder to push the feelings away, bury them in effect, to relieve the pain. This cycle acts as a catalyst for more intense symptoms.

Smells, tastes, noises, even something as innocuous as a color, can all serve as triggers for the rape. A trigger is anything that makes you remember or relive the rape in your mind.

Taking Control of Your Triggers

Take several breaths and remind yourself that you're no longer in danger. You're safe here in this time and place, and better yet, take steps to continue to be safe. Be proud of the progress that you're making in taking control of one of your symptoms.

Evaluate your feelings surrounding the trigger once you have gained control of yourself once again and determine what you need to do to anticipate them in the future. What can you learn from this trigger having taken place? Have yo learned that a particular color or sound prompted the trigger?

Identifying your triggers is the first step to coping with them; next you must find a way that's effective for you to not only work with them but to find a way to lessen their impact on your life.

Try to stop what you're doing, if only for a moment, to determine your feelings. Many times we're deep into a feeling before we consciously realize we're upset. Give a name to the feeling or emotion.

"I don't want to talk about it; what's the point?"

✍ A Personal View

I thought I was over my rape—I really did—until a friend of mine was raped. It was highly publicized and in the paper for a number of weeks as it was committed by a serial rapist. This was my closest friend of six years and yet I found myself avoiding her and was sick about it. When she needed me most, I wasn't there. I was really in torment over wanting to be there for her but not able to face her, so I saw a social worker that my husband and I had seen a couple of times.

At first I didn't bring up the fact that I'd been raped a number of years ago. As I said, I thought I was over it. I began to see though, through her questioning of my discomfort being with my friend, that I wasn't 'over it' at all—if there's any such thing. I learned that I resented the fact that no one was there to help me when I suffered through the months after my rape.

What I came to realize was that I gradually began to think of myself as unworthy, in a sense, of getting the kind of help that seemed to be available to my friend. While I didn't like what I learned about myself, it was important for me to realize how I felt and that it was my responsibility and my right to get help for myself as needed. My friend and I became even closer following my confession to her of my own rape, which she hadn't known about previously. —Sue, 28

I thought about this a number of times when I first started therapy. My therapist insisted that it was a good idea and I see the value—now, looking back. He gently moved me in the direction of telling him, even while I was avoiding it. I was moving around my problem though, not tackling it, and that was the fact that it had affected me more than I thought.

My fear was becoming "bigger". My anxiety, more intense. I was saying words that had no meaning, until we started discussing the rape. Of course, tears flowed. I screamed. I swore. But that was what was necessary for me to get better. —Lucy, 34

✚ A Clinical View

The Definition of Avoidance

You are remembering and reliving the rape and it's effect on you, a great deal of your time anyway. With the more formalized approach to resolving your issues that therapy will provide, or with your own self-study, you will begin to see the value of expressing your feelings about the rape.

You are avoiding emotions surrounding rape—a very useful, if you examine the behavior—method of avoiding pain. There is a difference, though between having successfully moved beyond a traumatic experience and continuing to avoid the emotions surrounding it. Avoidance of our emotions eventually leads, in many cases, to behavior that is unacceptable and painful to us.

The road to recovery is circuitous not linear, and you'll see that there are times when you just need to retreat as a turtle in its shell—take this time to take care of yourself; change takes place very slowly and occurs when you least expect it.

Taking Control of Avoidance

It's scary to feel the pain associated with rape. Sometimes it's overwhelmingly sad, depressing, terrifying, fearful—all at the same time and we wonder if we're ever going to feel the same as we did before the rape. You may feel that if you let your emotions out, if you allow yourself to really *feel*, you're not going to be able to stop—that you will slip down and be overcome by those feelings.

There are no magic pills we can take to get well; we must all walk the path of recovery in our own time. Coping with avoidance is not easy. Remnants from the rape can creep into many different facets of life. You will know when it's right for you to start feeling and sharing aspects of the rape. Try on a small scale to venture inside yourself. Find a safe, supportive place to begin.

"Why don't I feel like doing anything anymore?"

✍ A Personal View

The first time I knew something was wrong with my wife, Sandy, was when she lost interest in our home project. We had been in the middle of a large home renovation for about two months when she was raped on her campus. It was devastating for us but she seemed to move past everything quite well. Of course the renovation was put on hold for a couple of months while she recuperated and we went through the criminal proceedings but she kept telling me she was anxious to get back to it.

Finally, after seven months of procrastinating, she admitted that she just didn't care anymore. That scared me more than anything—that she just didn't care. It was an important turning point for us though. If I hadn't been aware of how much she enjoyed this project before the rape, I never would have seen the difference between "before" and "after." Needless to say, we sought help immediately. —Steve, 34

I try to explain to Steve how I feel: I'm all cried out—I can't even feel anything anymore. I don't feel sadness, anger, happiness—I just don't feel anything. You would think it would bring a kind of freedom, but it doesn't. The emptiness is unrelenting and I so envy those people who can feel something—anything. I want to feel rage against the man who raped me. Full-force, powerful rage so that I can get all of this out of me and move on. But I just don't feel anything anymore.—Sandy, 31

✚ A Clinical View

The Definition of Emotional Numbing

Emotional numbing is defined as a loss of interest in your family, friends, work, and social life; a symptom that's often terribly upsetting to a rape victim.

You're probably very familiar with the feeling and can even predict when you're going to slide into it. You may become confused and what some women describe as "fuzzy."

We're not used to not feeling anything; so something, as Sandy described above, would be better than nothing but the feelings of rage and anger are so frighteningly real, we're sometimes afraid of what we might do with those feelings—who we might become.

The seeming ease at which you seemed to cease feeling may be disturbing as well, but you must remember that this is a normal response to a very abnormal event and is a way in which you are coping. Remember, feeling something is not the same as acting on it.

Taking Control of Emotional Numbing

Try to define just one of the emotions that may be contributing to your inability to concentrate. In other words, is your "zoning out" a mechanism for avoiding anger, resentment, or rage? Perhaps it's more fearful for you to express these intense feelings than it is to simply allow yourself to feel nothing at all.

1. Resolve to write at least a paragraph in your journal whenever you experience that "zoning out" feeling. Pinpoint at least one emotion that may be beneath the surface.

2. Identify one song that makes you *feel* something positive. Perhaps it's the song that was playing when you met your husband, or the song that you've both identified as "your song." Maybe it's the song that was playing at a concert that you attended. Play that song when you're feeling emotionally empty.

"Why can't I concentrate anymore?"

✍ A Personal View

Meetings were becoming impossible for me to sit through. When people spoke with me, I just seemed to zone out. I really felt as if I were slipping out of myself. I used to be so focused and self-assured about what should be done next. I was sexually assaulted by a co-worker, which made working even more difficult for me.

I changed jobs, I even changed careers, but still that feeling of 'none of this is even worth it anymore' seemed to just suffocate me. I decided I needed to get more information about what I was feeling and immersed myself in books relating to rape. I decided that for me the first step would be to develop focus—in all things. I knew that some kind of action was better than none and started using skills that I'd learned in graduate school.

First I needed to decide what unfinished business the rape still held for me. I examined the effects that the rape had on my relationships—friends, family, romantic—I examined its effect on my health, my business—everything. And I made a list of specific activities I had to undertake to resolve this unfinished business. I needed a sense of closure to this time in my life. I had a list of goals now to work on that made my focus all the more strong. —Allison, 26

✚ A Clinical View

The Inability to Concentrate

The inability to concentrate is often the need to escape thought—to be free of the sadness and pain that surrounds you and seems so all-encompassing. When we have surgery, we're given a specific timetable that we can expect to recover—unfortunately recovery from rape is far less definitive.

Developing Focus

1. Develop awareness of your feelings. The more specific you are in defining your feelings, the more precise you can be in determining your goals.

2. Develop a list of unfinished business that you may be experiencing from the rape. What effect has the rape had on your emotional life, on your relationships, on your career and schooling? Perhaps you were raped on your campus and left school due to disturbing trigger reactions. If you abandoned the pursuit of a dream career for a job you aren't happy in, an inability to concentrate would not be unexpected. Developing this list is extremely useful in helping you focus.

3. Develop a second list to help you determine your benefits for resolving this particular piece of unfinished business. What will you gain from, for example, returning to school for your degree? This helps define the motivation necessary to help you with concentration.

4. Dedicate a Day-Timer® for the exclusive use of your goals pertaining to the recovery of this symptom. It needn't be fancy, just a small one for this exclusive use.

5. Perform the mechanical steps of writing down very short-term goals—weekly or even daily. The discipline of focusing on one task to completion serves to increase your confidence in completing larger tasks.

"Why do I jump out of my skin at the slightest noise?"

✍ A Personal View

I seemed to leap out of my skin at the slightest noise—anything made me jump. I was on edge all the time. I learned, with the help of my therapist, that it was because I still didn't have a feeling of safety, even two years after the rape.

Mine was a stranger rape where he quite literally dragged me off the street from behind. I didn't see him coming up behind me, so as a consequence, I began sitting with my back against the wall—I needed to sit in a position of control so that I wasn't surprised. This is impossible to do in 'real' life, so my therapist suggested a self-defense course.

I was scared to death during the real-life re-enactments, but I persisted. The repeated occurrence of someone being behind me as the rapist had been and then learning to control the situation through skills I developed and listening to my intuition gave me more confidence. I'm more cognizant of my surroundings—more aware, but in a positive way.—Anna, 28

✚ A Clinical View

The Definition of Hyperarousal

Hyperarousal symptoms can include difficulty sleeping, irritability and sudden outbursts of anger and rage, difficulty concentrating, and an exaggerated startle response, such as being jumpy as described above. These symptoms all point to a lack of feeling safe within your environment and the very real effort of your body attempting to avoid re-victimization.

The amygdala (we have two, one in each hemisphere of our brain) is just one of three structures that comprise the limbic system, the system of the brain responsible for emotions. In a simplistic sense, its role is to control major emotions, such as love, friendship, rage, aggression, as well as acting as the center for identification of danger. It's responsible for our fight-or-flight mechanism, responsible for the feelings we have when we hear footsteps behind us when we're walking alone.

Taking Control of Your Hyperarousal

Increasing your sense of security and safety in your environment is paramount, a challenge for many people, let alone victims of rape. There are very real, practical things you can do to feel safe in your environment: Self-defense courses, security systems in your home, neighborhood watch programs, and general safety precautions during your daily life. Relaxation techniques and employing music to help calm you are two very good ways to alleviate the symptoms of hyperarousal.

Do what you must to make yourself feel safe. Explore the circumstances surrounding the rape: Were you raped on campus and feel a move into an apartment or home off campus will help you feel more safe? Perhaps a roommate would make you feel safer. Were you raped while jogging alone? Forming a jogging club or resolving to go jogging only when a friend is available will enhance your feelings of safety.

"My doctor has diagnosed me as having anxiety attacks; what are they?"

✍ A Personal View

My panic attack—actually my first panic attack—happened one afternoon while I was grocery shopping. I felt as if I were having a heart attack. My pulse was racing. My hands were clammy. I felt dizzy and was frightened that I'd pass out. My daughter, who was three at the time, kept tugging on my jacket and I could hear her calling for her mommy over and over. I wanted to run but couldn't move my feet; they stayed glued to the floor until finally I was able to pick up one foot—then the other. I left my shopping cart where it was, scooped up my daughter and sat in my car sobbing.

I made an appointment with my doctor that afternoon and after running numerous tests, she diagnosed my symptoms as a panic attack. I started therapy later that month and learned how to handle the panic attacks and, though they still occur, I'm aware of things I can do to ease the anxiety.—Joan, 32

✚ A Clinical View

The Definition of Panic Disorders

Panic disorders are a physiological effect of the rape and are common, but that makes them no less terrifying. Panic attacks are one of those responses that leave the rape victim terrified.

Most of the time, these panic attacks occur in places that are entirely safe and have no correlation to the location of the rape, such as a supermarket or in your car. While there may be no direct correlation to location however, there may be some aspect of the situation you're in that makes you re-live an emotion during the rape, such as stuck in traffic, not in control.

One difficulty in experiencing panic attacks is that they may lead you to worry that you will have another or will lose control, have a heart attack, etc. Panic or anxiety attacks can be treated with a combination of medication and therapy. You may experience a number of the symptoms below:

- Pounding heart or fast pulse
- Shortness of breath
- Nausea and stomach discomfort
- Tightness around the upper chest and neck
- Dizziness, feeling of lightheadedness, fainting
- Detachment from your own body

Taking Control of Your Panic Disorder

Relaxation tapes and exercises are both excellent means to alleviate panic attacks. Once you've been diagnosed with a panic attack, you'll have had the experience and will be able to learn the warning signs of one occurring to lessen your symptoms.

Exercise is also an effective way to release tension in an effort to avoid a panic attack. I suggest that my clients select two or three activities (preferably social) they really enjoy to vary their physical activities. Join a bowling league, take dancing lessons, join a softball team. These are all excellent ways for us to make physical activity fun.

Resources for Your Emotional Healing

☎ General Resources

American Board of Sleep Medicine, The
Phone: (507) 287-9819

American Counseling Association
Phone: (703) 823-9800

American Psychological Association
Phone: (800) 374-2721

Anxiety Disorders Association of America
Phone: (301) 231-9350

Association for Humanistic Psychology
Phone: (510) 769-6495

Association for the Study of Dreams, The
Phone: (209) 724-0889

Campus Outreach Services
Phone: (610) 989-0651

Center for Women's Policy Studies
Phone: (202) 872-1770

DC Rape Crisis Center
Phone: (202) 232-0789

International Society for Traumatic Stress Studies
Phone: (847) 480-9028

National Anxiety Foundation
Phone: (606) 272-7166

National Clearinghouse For Alcohol and Drug Information
Phone: (800) 729-6686

National Crime Prevention Council
Phone: (202) 466-6272

National Criminal Justice Reference Service (NCJRS)
Phone: (800) 851-3420

National Institute of Mental Health (NIMH)
NIMH Public Inquiries
Phone: (301) 443-4513

NIMH Anxiety Disorders Education Program
NIMH Public Inquiries
Phone: (301) 443-4513

PTSD Alliance
Phone: (877) 507-PTSD

Rape Crisis Center of Central Massachusetts
Phone: (508) 799-5700

Safe Campuses Now
Phone: (706) 354-1115

SafePlace of Austin
Phone: (512) 267-SAFE

Security On Campus, Inc.
Phone: (610) 768-9330

Sexual Assault & Trauma Resource Center of Rhode Island
Phone: (401) 421-4100

Sidran Traumatic Stress Foundation
Phone: (410) 825-8888

South Carolina Coalition Against Domestic Violence and Sexual Assault
Phone: (800) 260-9293

⌐ Internet Resources

About.com Guide to Panic and Anxiety Disorder
    www.panicdisorder.about.com

American Board of Sleep Medicine, The
    www.absm.org

American Counseling Association
    www.counseling.org

American Psychology Association
    www.helping.apa.org

Anxiety Coach, The
    www.anxietycoach.com

Anxiety Disorders Association of America, The
    www.adaa.org

Anxiety Panic Internet Resource, The
www.algy.com/anxiety

Association for Humanistic Psychology
www.ahpweb.org

Association for the Study of Dreams, The
www.asdreams.org

AtHealth.com "Dreams and Nightmares"
www.athealth.com

Campus Outreach Services (COS)
www.campusoutreachservices.com

DC Rape Crisis Center
www.dcrcc.org

Department of Justice, Drug Enforcement Administration
www.usdoj.gov/dea/pubs/rohypnol/rohypnol.htm

Dr. John Grohol's Mental Health Page
www.psychcentral.com

Gift from Within
www.sourcemaine.com/gift

International Society for Traumatic Stress Studies, The
www.istss.org

Kelly Bulkeley, Ph.D.
www.kellybulkeley.com

Mental Health Forum
www.mentalhealthchannel.net

Mental Health Net
www.mentalhelp.net

Mental Health Sanctuary
www.mhsanctuary.com/ptsd

National Anxiety Foundation
www.lexington-on-line.com/naf.html

National Clearinghouse for Alcohol and Drug Information, The
www.health.org

National Criminal Justice Reference Service
www.ncjrs.org

National Institute of Mental Health
www.nimh.nih.gov/anxiety/ptsdfacts.cfm

National Institute of Mental Health PTSD Information
www.nimh.nih.gov/anxiety/anxiety/ptsd/ptsdinfo.htm

Nightmare Treatment Center
www.nightmaretreatment.com

NIMH Anxiety Disorders Education Program
www.nimh.nih.gov/anxiety

Office of Crime Victim Services
www.ojp.usdoj.gov/ovc/help/welcome.html

PTSD Alliance
www.PTSDAlliance.org

Rape Crisis Center of Central Massachusetts
www.rapecrisiscenter.org

SafePlace of Austin
www.austin-safeplace.org

Security on Campus, Inc.
www.campussafety.org

Sexual Assault & Trauma Resource Center of Rhode Island
www.satrc.org

Sidran Traumatic Stress Foundation
www.sidran.org

Social Phobia/Social Anxiety Association (SP/SAA), The
www.socialphobia.org

South Carolina Coalition Against Domestic Violence and Sexual Assault
www.sccadvasa.org

Texas Department of Public Safety
www.txdps.state.tx.us

Trauma Information Pages (Dr. David Baldwin, Ph.D.)
www.trauma-pages.com

Tulsa, Oklahoma Rape Crisis & Education Center
www.callrape.com

Women's Centers & Offices at American Colleges & Universities
www.uic.edu/depts/owa/womens_centers.html

Yahoo! Anxiety Groups Online
www.groups.yahoo.com/search?query=anxiety

Yahoo! Panic Disorder Groups Online
www.groups.yahoo.com/search?query=panic

📖 Book Resources

After a Sexual Assault
By Dane County Rape Crisis Center

After Silence: Rape and My Journey Back
By Nancy Venable Raine

Against Our Will: Men, Women and Rape
By Susan Brownmiller

Anxiety, Phobias, and Panic: A Step-by-Step Program for Regaining Control of Your Life
By Reneau Z. Peurifay

Attention and Avoidance: Strategies in Coping With Aversiveness
By Heinz Walter Krohne (Editor)

Avoiding Rape On and Off Campus
By Carol Pritchard

A Woman's Guide to Personal Safety
By Janee Harteau, Holly Keegel

Before College Book for Women: Protecting Yourself from Campus Crime
By Donna L. Betancourt

Before He Takes You Out: The Safe Dating Guide for the 90s
By Scott Lindquist

Campus Gang Rape: Party Games?
By Julie K. Ehrhart, Bernice R. Sandler

Case for Taking the Date Out of Rape, The
By Aileen McColgan

Changing Character: Short-Term Anxiety-Regulating Psychotherapy for Restructuring Defenses, Affects, and Attachment
By Leigh McCullough Vaillant

Concentration: A Guide to Mental Mastery
By Mouni Sadhu

Concentration: An Approach to Meditation
By Ernest Wood

Concentration and Meditation
By Christmas Humphreys

Coping With Date and Acquaintance Rape
By Andrea Parrot, Ph.D.

Date and Acquaintance Rape
By Robin Warshaw

Dreams and Nightmares: The New Theory on the Origin and Meaning of Dreams
By Ernest Hartmann, M.D.

Emotional Alchemy: How the Mind Can Heal the Heart
By Tara Bennett-Goleman

Exploring the World of Lucid Dreaming
By Stephen LaBerge

Fraternity Gang Rape: Sex, Brotherhood, and Privilege on Campus
By Peggy Reeves Sanday

Getting Through the Day: Strategies for Adults Hurt As Children
By Nancy J. Napier

Healing the Trauma of Abuse: A Woman's Workbook
By Mary Ellen Copeland, Maxine Harris

I Can't Get Over It: A Handbook for Trauma Survivors
By Aphrodite Matsakis, Ph.D.

If You Are Raped: What Every Woman Needs to Know
By Kathryn M. Johnson, Ph.D.

In Coping with Trauma: A Guide to Self-Understanding
By Jon Allen

I Never Called It Rape: The Ms. Report on Recognizing, Fighting, and Surviving Date and Acquaintance Rape
By Robin Warshaw

Inner World of Trauma, The: Archetypal Defenses of the Personal Spirit
By Donald Kalsched

It's Not All in Your Head
By S.B. Swedo, H.L. Leonard

Mastery of Your Anxiety and Worry
By Michelle Craske

Nightmare Help: A Guide for Adults and Children
By Ann Sayre Wiseman

Nightmares: How to Make Sense of Your Darkest Dreams
By Alex Lukeman, Ph.D.

Nightmare: The Psychology and Biology of Terrifying Dreams, The
By Ernest Hartmann

Other Side of Silence, The: Women Tell About Their Experiences With Date Rape
By Christine Carter

Outgrowing the Pain: A Book for and About Adults Abused as Children
By Eliana Gil, Ph.D.

Overcoming Panic, Anxiety, & Phobias: New Strategies to Free Yourself from Worry and Fear
By Shirley Babior, Carol Goldman

Post Traumatic Stress Disorder Sourcebook, The: A Guide to Healing, Recovery and Growth
By Glenn R. Schiraldi

Post-Traumatic Stress Disorder: The Victim's Guide to Healing and Recovery
By Raymond Flannery

Rape on Campus
By Bruno Leone (Editor)

Real World Safety for Women
By Christine Schlattner, Michael Linehan

Recovering from Rape
By Linda E. Ledray

Self-Defense for Women
By Elizabeth Parnell

Sexual Assault on Campus: The Problem and the Solution
By Carol Bohmer, Andrea Parrot

Sexual Assault on the College Campus: The Role of Male Peer Support
By Martin D. Schwartz (Editor), Walter S. Dekeseredy

Sexual Assault: Will I Ever Feel Okay Again?
By Kay Scott

Sex Without Consent: Rape and Sexual Coersion in America
By Merrill Smith (Editor)

Shyness & Social Anxiety Workbook, The: Proven Techniques for Overcoming Your Fears
By Martin M. Antony, Richard P. Swinson

Sky is Falling, The: Understanding and Coping with Phobias, Panic, and Obsessive-Compulsive Disorders
    By Raeann Dumont, Aaron T. Beck

Sleep Well, Sleep Deep
    By Alex Lukeman, Ph.D.

Start Where You Are: A Guide to Compassionate Living
    By Pema Chodron

Still Loved By The Sun: A Rape Survivor's Journal
    By Migael Scherer

Straight Talk About Date Rape
    By Susan Mufson, Rachel Kranz

Telling: A Memoir of Rape and Recovery
    By Patricia Weaver

The Power of Focus
    By Jack Canfield, Mark Victor Hansen, Les Hewitt

Total Awareness: A Woman's Safety Book
    By Beth Laur, Darren Laur

Trauma and Dreams
    By Deidre Barrett

Trauma and Recovery
    By Judith Herman, M.D.

Triumph Over Fear: A Book of Help and Hope for People With Anxiety, Panic Attacks, and Phobias
    By Jerilyn Ross, Rosalynn Carter

What Your Dreams Can Teach You
    By Alex Lukeman, Ph.D.

Your Weapon Within: How to Lower the Risk of Sexual Assault
    By William G. Nelson

2

Spiritual Healing

For the purpose of this book and its role in your recovery from rape, I've defined "spiritual healing" as that which encourages your healing. We begin with becoming educated on the facts of rape, the stages that you move through in your recovery, and an overview of professionals who can assist you in your goals. I recognize that professional therapy is not possible in all cases, or even preferable to some, so I've included a section on self-directed recovery.

- Learning about and coping with the facts of rape
- An overview of the categories of rapists
- Becoming educated
- Man's capacity to rape
- An overview of the criminal aspects of rape

"I want to understand. Is this helpful?"

✍ A Personal View

As a rape victim I felt the need to understand, as completely as possible, the effect that the rape had on me, but at the same time I was frightened that the more I read, the more I learned—and the more I learned, the more frightened I might become.

Can anyone really understand all the intricacies of an evil mind? The most difficult part of learning about rape was learning about the different categories of rapists. I had a hard time comprehending that there were four different types of rapists: Power-Reassurance, Power-Assertive, Anger-Retalitory, and Anger-Excitation. When I learned that the man who raped me fit the profile of an Anger-Excitation rapist I was devastated, not because it was something I didn't know but because there are so many men who fit this profile that they've put a name to it. It's shameful.

My education, though, into the facts of rape have gone far beyond categories of rapists. I've learned that the symptoms that my mind and body experienced following the rape were not unusual, in fact, they were to be expected. With that knowledge came the responsibility to work on my recovery. I've come a long way, but I've got a long way to go.—Anonymous, 33

How does one integrate such a monumental event as a rape into their life? I had an extremely difficult time—I learned the facts and I know that was to be the first step for me.

At first I took a very critical, very logical view. I had a number of symptoms that I needed to address and I was going through therapy but it just wasn't working for me fast enough. The symptoms just kept holding on—until I began reading about other women's experiences with rape. What a relief to learn how well people had come through their experiences.

I began going to a support group at the same time as therapy in order to learn more about how others had handled the issues that were just coming up for me. —Sandy, 24

✦ A Clinical View

Learning the Facts of Rape

You owe it to yourself to become educated about your rape. This is a significant event that's taken place in your life and you must know what to expect from your body, your psyche, your mind. You must be aware of what you need to do to heal.

While there are specifics that are vital for you to learn, such as the symptoms of PTSD and therapies that might be beneficial, the law and how it pertains to you as a rape victim, and sexual recovery, there is also one very important source of information for you: Other rape victims. I wholeheartedly encourage reading others' experiences and ways in which they have survived, and thrived.

Man's Capacity to Rape

Every man has the tool to rape—a penis—thus every man is physically capable, yet, every man does not have the cruel intent to rape. Men are as capable of compassion and empathy as women and to classify all men as potential rapists is doing them, and yourself, a disservice. Rape is an abhorrent crime to every man with whom I've spoken.

"What kind of man could do this?"

✍ A Personal View

It was probably two years or so into my therapy that I stopped asking myself, and my therapist, this question. I'll save you a lot of time and energy and answer this question directly: A cold-blooded murderer of a person's soul.

If one is fortunate, they survive the rape physically and without too many injuries, but the rapist is a murderer nonetheless—of one's trust—of innocence—of self-esteem—of security. —June, 31

I'd read the different "descriptions" of rapists. I became knowledgeable about their motives and behaviors. Did it help me to read that my rapist would be classified "sadistic" and learn more of his motivations? I'm not certain. Actually I felt sadness that there were so many rapists in the first place that they could be classified. The problem that I struggle with is that a rapist may not look at all different than any other man on the street. How are we ever to know who the "bad" guys are? Still, to put one's head in the sand is not good, either. —Susie, 41

✚ A Clinical View

Rape is an act of aggression, not sexual desire. Unfortunately, you can't tell whether a man is a rapist by looking at him, making it all the more important to be attuned to your intuition. Sexual aggressors can come in all shapes and sizes and can be strangers, acquaintances, friends, dates, and even husbands.

While some women feel a need to analyze their rape and rapist, others want to know only how to get on with their lives. There is no right or wrong in wanting to know this information; it's a personal decision.

The one thing to remember—always—is that the rape was not your fault.

Major Categories of Rapists

Power-Reassurance
This rapist generally rapes women in his own age range and likes to take something of the victim with him, such as a scarf or a glove. He often exhibits stalking or Peeping Tom tendencies.

Power-Assertive
This rapist often takes his victim into isolated areas, leaving her in the area. He would likely con women, such as those stranded by the side of the road, or hitch-hiking, to get into the car. Often his rapes are related to his drug and alcohol use.

Anger-Retaliatory
This rapist is extremely angry at women, striking out at women who perhaps remind him of someone, such as his mother. These women have committed (imaginary) wrongs against him and he will punish them using his penis as the weapon. Far more anger is inflicted against the victim than is necessary; this type of rapist has been shown to hit women with their fists, generally in their stomach.

Anger-Excitation
Aggression is eroticized for this type of rapist and as a result he causes intense suffering and torture during the rape, growing more sexually excited inflicting intensifying pain on his victim. He is typically a stranger and his attack is vicious as well as sexually and verbally hostile and angry. Restraint is common and injuries are sexual in nature as is the use of drugs or alcohol during the attack.

"Can I have this person charged with a crime?"

✍ A Personal View

Monetary damages alone can't make you whole or make the pain go away. It can, however, help to rebuild your life. I was in a very depressed mood for such a long time after my criminal trial which, due to a lack of evidence, was dismissed.

I'd waited so long for the trial—I can't count the number of sleepless nights I had—when finally the verdict came. I was beside myself. Totally powerless. Here this man, a co-worker had raped me when we were away at a conference and I could do nothing.

His attorney put that shadow of doubt in the minds of the jurors that perhaps it was consensual. My husband knew differently and also knew that I'd feel a sense of power over my situation if I was able to win a civil lawsuit against him. He was right—and I won. It allowed me to go to private therapy that my insurance didn't cover, but the rest of it I donated to a women's group.

The fight of the cases brought against this man were exhausting, going over the same details again and again. I'm just not certain I'd have the energy again. He took more from me than money could ever repay.—Jane, 41

✚ A Clinical View

Your Legal Rights

You may file a civil lawsuit against your perpetrator, no matter what the outcome of the criminal trial. In a civil lawsuit, the justice system doesn't determine guilt or innocence; rather the courts determine whether the perpetrator is liable for injuries you sustained during the crime. If the perpetrator is found to be liable, he may be required to pay monetary damages to the victim. Contact your local rape crisis center for assistance in moving through the legal system.

The National Crime Victim Bar Association provides referrals of local attorneys. Interview several prior to selecting one; most cases are handled on a contingency basis (your attorney is paid only if a money settlement is awarded) necessitating a retainer agreement.

Various costs may have to be borne by you regardless of the outcome of the case; so be sure that you understand all aspects of this contract prior to signing.

Resolve to be as communicative as possible regarding the details of the crime. This is difficult but is necessary for your attorney to do as thorough a job as possible. You may want to take someone along with you, such as your husband or partner, a friend, or your rape victim advocate. Try to schedule your appointment for later in the day and treat yourself to a nice dinner. You've accomplished quite a large task and should reward yourself for having taken this step.

Be prepared with as much of the following documentation as possible.

- A copy of the police report if filed
- Any information possible about the rapist
- Information about a third party who may be liable for the crime, i.e., a university if the rape occurred on campus
- Information relating to your physical, emotional, and pyschological injuries
- Medical treatment, location, and provider information
- Amount of time lost from work (your own as well as your spouse)
- Money recovered from insurance polices, crime victim compensation programs, and any other restitution

"The rape didn't affect me; I can't change anything so why bother thinking about it?"

✍ A Personal View

But you can change it.

The only thing we can't change is the past—but our future is in our hands. It's true that you can't change the fact that you were raped, but you can change behaviors that may be holding you back because of that rape. You can change emotions that leave you feeling as if it happened yesterday. You can wake up feeling different about yourself tomorrow.

Don't allow the rapist to take any more away from you than he already has. I come from a family of pilots—everyone in our family flew, anyplace, anytime. Pilots deal in reality and most live by the saying "A good crash is one you walk away from." I started thinking about this in terms of my own rape: I walked away from it. This is surviving. Many women didn't get this opportunity and were killed by their rapist. They didn't get the gift of being able to wake up the next day.

When I absorbed the meaning of having "walked away," even with extensive injuries, emotional and physical, I have another chance. My rape is the crash that I walked away from. —Teresa, 44

✚ A Clinical View

The Definition of Denial

We engage in denial when we refuse to admit that we're in an unhealthy situation. It's a defense mechanism that we all use at one point or another.

Denial allows us to cope with the way in which the rape has affected us. "It was no big deal—I'm over it."

If we look closely at your question it appears that what you're trying to do is forget what happened, to escape the feelings that are present, and normal, following rape. This defense mechanism may work for a time, but the energy that it takes to bury feelings is enormous.

The effects of the rape are still there and may present themselves in your self-image, your relationships with your friends and family, your work or school. These feelings need to be unearthed and discussed with either a therapist or someone you trust.

The problem is exacerbated by the fact that we can't only bury bad feelings; good feelings become buried as well. Soon we're feeling as if we have no emotions at all; that we're simply incapable of feeling anything. We've successfully buried all feelings.

The risk of this happening is great and comes at a great expense to you; every moment that you have following your rape is a moment of opportunity to change.

Taking Control of Your Denial

While it may not seem like it, this question signifies your desire to change. You are in the first stage of recovery from your rape, that is, you are becoming aware of the after-effects of the rape and its effect on you. And further, you *can* change the behaviors, emotions, and thoughts that may be troubling you following your rape. Therapy is extremely helpful in helping to recognize and overcome denial.

"How could God let this happen to me?"

✍ A Personal View

It's hard for me to express how angry I was at God for allowing the rape to occur. I recognize this now as illogical thinking, but having spent a lifetime of loving God and living as a Catholic I looked at the rape as a personal indictment against me from God.

During the rape I had cried out to him for help and later turned my back on Him as I felt he had done to me.

This anger was important in my recovery, as personally painful as it was. This was a spiritual journey that I had no intent on making but now that I have I'm stronger in my faith. I've learned that my rape was an affront to God as it was to me.—Kate, 44

✝ A Clinical View

The Definition of Anger

The question you're asking may indicate anger—at God, at the heavens, at the forces that allowed this rape to occur. There is a sense of disbelief. We've read about rape but this is personal.

The feeling of isolation, of having been singled out and of having been abandoned by God is one that many women experience. When we experience rape we are angry and feel cheated out of losing the person we might have been. You know anger. That intense emotion that makes your heart pound and energy increase.

But a rape is much like a death has occurred—the death of our innocence, of our trust, of the person we were "before." The anger you feel is expected and wholly normal. You have every right to feel angry; you were violated and hurt. Your anger may be directed at your friends, family, at the criminal justice system, even at other women who have not been raped.

It's a normal response to act your anger out in aggressive ways. You may find yourself surprised at your rage and anger and may find yourself thinking of ways to revenge the rape—of having the same form of torture inflicted on the rapist that he inflicted on you. This is NOT unusual and doesn't make you a bad person; it's an expected, normal response to the rape.

In fact, our anger and rage become a problem only when it affects the quality of our personal and work relationships and we act out on the anger.

Taking Control of Your Anger

Expressing your needs in an assertive, rather than aggressive way, is a healthy means to controlling your anger. You're not being irrational; you've been hurt emotionally and psychologically, perhaps even physically, and these feelings and emotions should be expressed to whomever you feel comfortable.

"What if I'd been more careful; maybe this wouldn't have happened?"

✍ A Personal View

The "what if" question; I've asked myself this question to the point of exhaustion. Facing the fact that I had a serious drinking problem and that I couldn't remember who I was with or what I'd been doing was a turning point for me but was one that was slow in coming. In a twisted way, being raped might have saved me life
—Janna, 42

✚ A Clinical View

The Definition of Bargaining

Bargaining can be characterized as "what if" thinking: "What if I'd been at home instead of out?" "What if I hadn't worn a short skirt?" "What if I hadn't talked to the guy?" Bargaining is an irrational, almost excessive amount of self-blaming for the rape.

Taking Control of the Bargaining Stage of Recovery

There are two assumptions that are made in the bargaining process: 1) that you hold some responsibility for what happened, and 2) that since you hold responsibility for what happened, you must be punished.

Regarding the first assumption: By engaging in the constant, exhausting "what if" questioning of yourself, you're assuming you had some type of responsibility for the rape. You did not. Not if you wore a short skirt. Not if you were drunk. Not even if you were flirting.

While some of these behaviors may not be in your best interest, you didn't ask for nor did you deserve to be raped. Wearing a short skirt doesn't give license to any man on the street to rape you, nor does it say you're easy; it says that you like to wear short skirts.

Regarding the second assumption: You're gaining nothing in your recovery process by continuing to punish yourself. If you believe that your behavior contributed to your rape, resolve to stop that behavior.

Perhaps you feel that your guard was down because you had too much to drink. Solutions might include resolving to limit your number of drinks allowing you to remain in control and going out with trusted friends who can help watch out for you (and you for them).

If you're unsure whether your behavior contributed to your rape, consider again your best friend: If she had behaved just as you did prior to your rape, would you criticize her? Would you have held her responsible for what happened? If you truly would hold her responsible (for instance, she had a tendency to drink to excess) would you help her find the help she needed or would you just keep punishing her?

The point is to translate the compassion and empathy you have for your best friend to yourself. As you would say to her, stop punishing yourself immediately; it serves no purpose.

"The world seems dead to me. Why am I so depressed?"

✍ A Personal View

Depression is so painful, so all-encompassing, that all I wanted to do was stay in bed. I say "was," but in reality I still suffer from depression. Less often, but there are days when it's amazingly overpowering for me.

Emotionally, I felt a sense of failure. Not in my abilities, but in my ability to cope with life in general. Individual tasks I could accomplish really well, but when it came to just handling life, I felt as if I were unable. Everyone around me seemed so "able."

My therapist noticed it first: He brought up the fact that I just sit and stare every now and then during our sessions. I just seem to "zone out" but it truly seemed that anything I had to say was inadequate for how I felt and so I said nothing. The world seemed dead to me as well.

How could the rest of the world continue after what had happened? I'm certain that this is what grief is. In fact, that's exactly how I felt, as if I had died. Or more accurately the person I was, the person I'd hoped to be, no longer existed. What was I to do now? —Shana, 30

I spoke with my therapist about medication—I'd heard so many success stories but he discouraged me from beginning to use it because it may mask feelings and emotions relating to the rape. Emotions that needed to be acknowledged, discussed, and processed.

But I'll tell you at the time, it felt unfair to me that he had asked me to continue to suffer as others were happily going about their business, having taken their "happy pill" for what I considered to be far less severe depression.

I came to realize my thinking was flawed on several levels: It wasn't my place to determine how "severe" one person's depression was as compared to mine and anti-depressants aren't "happy pills."

But more importantly I'd displaced the feeling of unfairness onto my therapist for not prescribing something I thought was in my best interest, instead of where it belonged and that was the unfairness I felt for having been singled out for the rape. That was unfair—and that's what I had to accept.

Had I taken the antidepressants as I'd wanted to, I'm uncertain whether I'd have developed that insight. In retrospect, he was correct. It was difficult—it was hell sometimes—but I made progress in my recovery.—Anonymous, 44

✚ A Clinical View

The Definition of Depression

Depression is a medical illness, not a "mood." No one is immune to depression—regardless of race, gender, income level, or profession. We all are susceptible and we've all heard how accomplished people, such as Vincent Van Gogh, Mark Twain, Winston Churchill, and Abraham Lincoln suffered with depression. A stigma remains, which may prevent sufferers from getting the help they need.

Taking Control of Your Depression

It's important for you to know that depression is treatable and that early treatment can be very successful helping alleviate even the most distressing symptoms, such as thoughts of death and suicide. Mental health resources are available to provide both medication and therapy. I would suggest a combination of the two if medication is prescribed. It does little good to simply alleviate the symptoms of depression without discussing your core issues at the same time.

Negative self-thinking can be detrimental to your mental health and often results in depression. Stopping these negative thoughts immediately upon becoming aware of them can be of great benefit in coping with your depression, a skill that can be learned and improved upon. Negative thoughts include: Self-blame and self-criticism, having a negative opinion of yourself, and having a negative feeling about your future.

"How can I learn to accept what happened?"

✍ A Personal View

I believe this stage of my recovery was by far the hardest.

I couldn't seem to be able to accept the fact that I'd never be the same; that I would always have a memory of the rape. I felt that no memories at all would be better than the ones I had.

Actually, how I finally gained acceptance was just by becoming exhausted. I felt as if I were working so hard to forget or to wish away what had happened until one moment in time that I realized it would be less painful to accept what had happened and move on than to continually struggle to make it right.

So, I took three days and just sank down into myself. I took out a journal that my therapist suggested I keep during my therapy and really read the words I'd written. I mean, really absorbed them. I saw a pattern that I'd developed. I denigrated myself in nearly every session—"I'm so stupid to have ...", "I'm so unrealistic ...", on and on.

After four years of therapy, it just appeared as if I were whining with no realization of the facts—no insight. The continual denigrating of myself was serving no useful purpose.

I suppose I employed "tough love" thinking. The rape wasn't my fault. There was nothing I was ever going to do about it. It was as if a light went on in my head: Accept it. Period. No magic. I went into my next session ready to work. I told my therapist that it was time to move on.

I feel like I'm working hard at becoming the person I want to be and have put the rape into proper perspective: It was a traumatic, awful experience, one that I don't want to repeat, but it's over now. Time to move on. —Teddi, 44

✦ A Clinical View

The Definition of Acceptance

Acceptance is the final stage of healing. It's being able to say to yourself that, yes, I was raped, but I can continue. I can learn about myself and what it takes to survive. I know what I need to do to take care of myself. I know how to meet my needs and wants.

Learning Acceptance

There are truths about acceptance: You'll reach this stage at your own time; there is no timetable that I can give you. You'll reach this stage with a greater appreciation for your courage to survive a horribly traumatic experience and for your ability to examine your fears. You'll reach this stage secure in your ability to judge when and who is best to provide you with the support you need to thrive and you'll reach this stage having known yourself better than you ever have—and better than most people get to know themselves.

You've been through trial by fire. You've walked through hell and survived and when you look back on your life in five years, or ten years, you'll be astounded at your courage and survival skills. You'll also be proud of yourself. You've won—not the rapist.

"What short-term help is there for rape recovery?"

✍ A Personal View

I'm not certain I could have gotten through the physical examination and then the court case without my advocate from the rape crisis center that was contacted. She was there for me every moment that I needed her, and even more important, she let me know what to expect at every step.

For instance, I didn't realize that during a rape exam that my pubic hair would be combed through for evidence, then plucked from the root. Had she not told me what to expect, the exam would have been much more uncomfortable, both physically and emotionally. She even stayed with me in the hospital.—Megan, 22

✛ A Clinical View

Professionals with differing sets of skills and areas of expertise exist for both your short-term and long-term goals. Whether the rape happened twenty minutes or twenty years ago, you may be feeling anxiety and discomfort and need immediate relief.

I know that the task of searching for help is arduous but you're worth the time and effort this search takes. The simple act of recognizing your need for help and finding it makes you stronger and more confident in your ability to take care of yourself. Professionals specially trained to work with rape victims in the crisis phase include:

Rape Crisis Centers

Your local rape crisis center has advocates available on staff to accompany you to the hospital and provide you with the information necessary to get you through the crisis stage of your rape.

Your advocate will also accompany you to the police station or be present during the inverviews, provide you with reporting procedures, information about HIV and pregnancy testing, sexually transmitted diseases, and provide counseling and referrals for all your needs, both immediate and long-term.

To call your rape crisis center a short-term resource is truly not giving them their due; rape advocates may spend months of time and a great deal of energy in assisting a rape victim with their needs.

Sexual Assault Response Teams

S.A.R.T. teams include nurse examiners, law enforcement, campus and rape crisis center personnel who have been specially trained to provide a comprehensive, community-based approach for the treatment of rape victims and the prosecution of the perpetrator. This approach is designed to alleviate the length of time required of the victim while being interviewed multiple times.

Sexual Assault Nurse Examiners

S.A.N.E. nurses are registered nurses that have been trained to provide specialized, comprehensive care following a sexual assault. They conduct forensic exams developed to collect and preserve evidence, provide expert witness testimony, and most importantly provide compassion and empathy at a time when you are in most need.

"What can I expect in terms of help in this crisis phase?"

✍ A Personal View

Your short-term care is critical. Rape is such an intrusive, terrifying thing to go through that you shouldn't be alone. For a while you will feel disoriented, angry, isolated—you'll go through a number of emotions during the first thirty days.

My life was a blur; no one is prepared, I'm sure, for the amount of time and energy it takes to recover from rape. I couldn't have worked my way through the system without an advocate helping me; making appointments, talking to my husband and me together so that we could make plans.

I suppose it's like a life-altering illness in that it comes out of the blue and turns your world upside down. I remember the first time we went out to a restaurant after the rape—probably two weeks later—and feeling as if I'd accomplished something amazing. I looked around me and the world hadn't changed—the same waitresses were there, the same items were on the menu, the same function of picking up a fork and chewing. Yet everything had changed in my world.

Without utilizing the short-term help I had to get me through the routine of every day, I'm afraid I may have been in much worse shape. This is why I, as an advocate now myself, encourage women to seek help immediately. —Angelica, 41

✛ A Clinical View

The sooner you receive help in this crisis phase, the less likely your chance for long-term issues. There are a number of services available to you as a rape victim; please, even though it's a difficult time for you and may be against your independent nature, allow others to help you.

Phases in Crisis Intervention

Forensic Examination

The first phase is a forensic examination, often called a "rape kit." A nurse or doctor (please ask your rape advocate if a S.A.N.E. nurse is available) will collect the necessary evidence and conduct an internal examination.

Swabs will be collected of secretions left behind from the mouth, vagina, and anal area (if these areas were involved). Samples of your hair and pubic hair will be removed from the root and the pubic hair will be combed for hair and secretions. Photographs will be taken to record any injuries and your clothes will be held as evidence. A report will be taken if you decide to report the rape.

Again, please ask your rape advocate if a Sexual Assault Response Team (S.A.R.T.) is available.

Because of the collaborative efforts of the team, the reporting process is more streamlined and repeat interviews are kept to an absolute minimum. Your rape advocate is specially trained to provide an overall assessment of your medical, physical, and mental health needs and provide information and referral to same.

Also, she can supply you with information and assistance in providing for your personal safety.

Assessment Phase

The second phase is an assessment of your immediate emotional needs to determine how your life has been affected by the rape; a recovery plan is developed so that healing may begin.

Re-Normalization Phase

The third phase involves re-normalization of your life so that healing may continue. Your rape advocate remains by your side to help you interact with the criminal justice system and various agencies.

"What long-term help is there for rape recovery?"

✍ A Personal View

Following my rape I knew I desperately had to see someone, but had no idea how to go about finding that someone with whom I could share my innermost thoughts and feelings. Being a logical person though, I started to research who might best meet my needs. I ended up seeing a psychiatrist for medication and a psychologist for therapy. I'm fortunate to have found both of the professionals that I did. —JoAnne, 44

✚ A Clinical View

As I've mentioned previously, the very act of being aware of your need for professional help speaks volumes about your motivation to recover. Professional therapists include the following:

Licensed Clinical Social Workers (LCSWs)

Social workers are mental health professionals who hold bachelors, masters, or doctoral degrees in social work. They practice in a wide variety of settings, including private practice, and are trained to address numerous issues. The national membership organization for Licensed Clinical Social Workers is the National Association of Social Workers.

Marriage and Family Therapists (MFTs)

Marriage and Family Therapists are mental health professionals trained in psychotherapy and family systems. They are trained to diagnose and treat mental and emotional disorders and work primarily with couples and families. The national membership organization for Marriage and Family Therapists is the American Association for Marriage and Family Therapy.

Psychologists

Psychologists hold a doctoral degree in psychology from an APA-accredited university or professional school who have been trained in the study of mind and behavior from the function of the brain to life development issues. The national membership organization for psychologists is the American Psychological Association.

Psychiatrists

Psychiatrists are physicians who have completed an additional four years of residency training in psychiatry following medical school, with many psychiatrists undergoing additional training in specialty areas. Medical training allows the psychiatrist to understand the relationship between emotional and physical illness and appropriately form a treatment plan and is the only mental health professional with the ability to prescribe medication. The national membership organization for psychiatrists is the American Psychiatric Association.

"How can I find a therapist?"

✍ A Personal View

I interviewed three therapists before finding one with whom I could work and re-learn trust. Past the mechanics of credentials and such, I believe the most important aspect was the rapport we had initially. I knew there was something in that first meeting to build on that I didn't feel with the other two therapists. Chemistry.
—Anna Marie, 30

✦ A Clinical View

Trauma Specialists

The International Society for Traumatic Stress Studies (ISTSS) members include psychiatrists, psychologists, social workers, marriage and family therapists, nurses, counselors, and researchers among other disciplines.

Locating a Therapist

1. Obtain referrals for three therapists from the professional organizations listed at the end of this chapter, a local rape crisis center, or RAINN.

2. Interview the therapists with a 10 to 15-minute phone call to provide them with an overview of your symptoms and goals. Obtain the following information on each therapist in order to help you decide whether to make an appointment for an initial consultation:

   - His background, training, and credentials.
   - His particular method of therapy and experience and success in treating clients with your symptoms.

3. Following your phone interview or initial consultation, reflect on the following to help you select your therapist:

   - Most importantly, did you have a rapport with the therapist? Is he someone you feel you could grow to trust? Were you comfortable speaking with him about your symptoms?
   - Did he seem to understand the issues and concerns that you brought him?
   - Did he seem interested in your issues, willing to listen, and accepting of your situation?

"What types of therapy are available for rape?"

✍ A Personal View

I researched this at length prior to starting therapy. What was available? What would work best for me? I think the area of psychology and psychiatry are so foreign to lay people that we simply don't know where to start.

And what about the type of therapy? I'd read a number of curriculum vitae for psychologists, psychiatrists, LCSWs, MFTs, everyone—and began getting more confused than ever. One spoke of behavioral therapy; one cognitive; still another both cognitive-behavioral.

Finally in reading about all the various types I decided on cognitive/behavioral, a very logical straightforward method. I knew that my negative thinking about myself in terms of the rape, and if I'm honest, even before, was playing a huge part in my staying "stuck." I couldn't seem to understand how others could be, well, so easy on themselves. I'd always played by the rules, done a good job, stayed focused but it was a struggle—nothing I seemed to do was good enough. And this was me talking to me.

My therapist assured me that changing those negative thoughts, thoughts that were holding me back in effect, had to go. He gave me a great deal of homework and I feel as if I made good progress. He helped me focus on my unwanted behavior, then tie that into how my thoughts had produced that behavior. I didn't want to spend 15 years in therapy—this was an excellent therapeutic method for me. —Sherry, 39

✚ A Clinical View

Behavioral Therapy

A behavioral therapist assists you in identifying and changing unwanted behaviors through the use of rewards, desensitization and reinforcement.

Biomedical Therapy

In a biomedical therapy plan, medication is used in combination with psychotherapy for emotional disorders. A psychiatrist is the only mental health professional who can prescribe medication and may be the provider of psychotherapy as well, or work in conjunction with your therapist.

Cognitive Therapy

A cognitive therapist assists you in identifying and correcting distorted thinking that leads to your unwanted behaviors, in short, the therapist helps you change the way you think.

Cognitive/Behavioral Therapy

A behavioral/cognitive therapist utilizes both the behavioral and cognitive method of therapy and is generally short-term in length. A very active type of therapy, the behavioral/cognitive therapist will rely heavily on homework and reading assignments in advancing the desired results of therapy.

Interpersonal Psychotherapy

A psychotherapist utilizing direct one-on-one conversations to assist you in identifying and resolving your issues through insight. Behavioral changes are the goal of psychotherapy.

Psychoanalysis

A psychoanalyst assists you in identifying past issues that may have a direct effect on your current behaviorial and emotional issues. This can be an intense form of therapy with a number of meetings with the psychoanalyst.

"Someone has suggested art therapy; would that help?"

✍ A Personal View

I see pain—anger—hurt—in the form of colors and shapes. I undertook a form of "art therapy," I suppose you could say, on my own. I have an undergraduate degree in Art History but have never used it.

I'm employed in a corporate setting where I never use the painting and drawing abilities that I've developed through years of study. Following a pretty vicious rape by an acquaintance, I found that nothing gave me solace.

So, one day when cleaning out the closet, I came across my oils. I remember the day exactly: Overcast and rainy, I set my easel up and just put brush to canvas. All the anger and rage came out ... expressed in colors and shapes. The more I painted, the less angry my images became and, as a result, the less angry I became.

I started looking for a therapist who specializes in art therapy and have since found peace in a way I hadn't been able to find.—Toni, 32

✚ A Clinical View

Art therapy is a means of expression through traditional forms of art media, such as painting, drawing or photography, to name a few. The intent, when used in therapy, is to allow the expression of feelings and conflicts through these means.

Art therapy allows the client and therapist to explore behavior and problem-solving abilities and can be undertaken informally through your own study or with a therapist with a specialization in art therapy.

How to Locate an Art Therapist

1. Obtain referrals for three therapists from the American Art Therapy Association, Inc. (AATA), the association granting certifications to art therapists. Information on how to reach the AATA can be found at the end of this chapter.

2. Interview the therapists with a 10 to 15-minute phone call to provide them with an overview of your symptoms and goals. Obtain the following information on each therapist in order to help you decide whether to make an appointment for an initial consultation:

   - His background, training, and credentials. A graduate degree in psychology or social work, along with further education and training in art therapy, is recommended.

   - His particular method of therapy and experience and success in treating clients with your symptoms.

3. Following your phone interview or initial consultation, reflect on the following to help you select your therapist:

   - Most importantly, did you have a rapport with the therapist? Is he someone you feel you could grow to trust? Were you comfortable speaking with him about your symptoms?

   - Did he seem to understand the issues and concerns that you brought him?

   - Did he seem interested in your issues, willing to listen, and accepting of your situation?

"What is EMDR? Would this type of therapy help me?"

✍ A Personal View

I was frightened when my therapist suggested EMDR—Eye Movement Desensitization and Reprocessing—for several reasons: First, it was an unknown. He told me that I'd be thinking of certain aspects of the rape, something that was completely uncomfortable for me at the time, and that we'd try to re-direct my thoughts in effect. Second, and I suppose this has to do with other issues that arose, I felt an abandonment by him.

He assured me that he'd be with me at all times when his colleague would be performing the EMDR therapy, but I felt that he was introducing another person into our relationship. The information that I'd shared with him was so intensely personal and I wasn't ready to share that, or him, with any other person, and certainly not within that hour.

I grudgingly accepted the offer and could not have been happier that I did so. He was true to his word and stayed with me every moment that his colleague was there.

She spoke with me for several sessions, gaining my trust and confidence, prior to starting the EMDR-specific activity. It was different for me, speaking with a woman while undergoing therapy with a man. She showed great sensitivity in determining from my records exactly the symptoms to work on. Nothing extraneous. No time wasted, yet I didn't have the feeling I was being rushed.

In any event, the therapy worked wonderfully. Her method of tapping—admittedly I'm simplifying her process greatly—while she helped me recall certain instances during the rape—worked. I simply couldn't think of the re-direction of thoughts and the rape at the same time. Just couldn't do it. In short order, the intense emotions of the rape became replaced somehow. Amazing.—Eleanor, 33

✚ A Clinical View

The Definition of EMDR

EMDR is a relatively new form of therapy used for alleviating symptoms of PTSD. In admittedly simplistic terms, in EMDR (Eye Movement Desensitization and Reprocessing) therapy, the therapist guides you as you recall thoughts and emotions that are currently causing you discomfort, allowing you to re-experience them in the safety of his or her presence.

As the disturbing feelings are exposed, the therapist re-directs your eye movement and as a result, releases the accompanying emotions.

How to Locate an EMDR-Trained Therapist

In my experience, referrals to EMDR therapy are from a present therapist who often consults with the EMDR-trained therapist and stays with the client in the room while undergoing EMDR. If this is not the case, obtain referrals from the EMDR Institute and follow the guide for locating a therapist seen in this chapter.

Following your initial consultation review the following. If you feel as if you can't work with the therapist that your original therapist has referred, don't hesitate to tell him; your needs during recovery are paramount:

- Was the therapist someone you felt you could grow to trust? Were you comfortable in his office?
- Did he seem to understand the issues and concerns that you brought him?
- Did he seem interested in your issues and willing to listen?
- Were you able to establish a rapport?

"Should I go to group therapy?"

✍ A Personal View

This is a personal decision, of course, and I can only relate that which has worked for me. I needed intense, one-on-one therapy in order to discuss what I felt were very personal issues. I could not have related the detail of the rape with a group of people.

Now of course, I see the benefit of relating, in detail, the pain of rape so that others might understand, however when in therapy I needed the empathy and compassion that only my therapist could offer. I felt that a group might be in their own level of pain.

Does this mean that I would never suggest group therapy? No. In many cases it's very helpful to share with others who are in a similar situation. The fact remains that my therapist never experienced rape and had I been in a support group, they would have understood through shorthand many of the emotions I was experiencing.

On the other hand, it was important for me to find my voice and be able to express myself to someone such as my therapist who hadn't experienced the feelings firsthand.—Susan, 33

I went through several groups before I found one that was good for me. While I got a great deal out of my sessions with my therapist I had other concerns that I didn't want to address with him, due to time constraints.

So, my initial attempt to find a group therapist was through my crisis center. I wasn't completely happy with the group therapist they referred: She wasn't strong enough in laying down the rules that I felt needed to be established.

For example, she didn't request that people attending make a minimum commitment of time and pandered to several of the people in that they could come and go as they pleased, yet there seemed to be more rules for the rest of the people attending.—Toni, 38

✦ A Clinical View

The Definition of Group Therapy

Group therapy is a selection of a number of people (approximately six to eight) with similar issues, selected by a therapist, who might benefit both from intervention from a professional as well as interaction from the group. Interpersonal relationships are the focus in group therapy.

How to Find the Right Group

Finding the right therapy group is as important as finding a personal therapist. If you're currently seeing a therapist, it's important to speak with him to discuss the benefits you might derive from group therapy and request a referral.

Carefully consider the qualifications of the therapist leading the group as professional certification is available from the American Group Psychotherapy Association.

Mental health professionals, such as psychologists, psychiatrists, licensed clinical social works, and marriage and family counselors receive highly specialized training that results in certification and must attend continuing education credits.

"Would a support group be better for me?"

✍ A Personal View

Support therapy can be very beneficial if the group is compatible. I've been in a group therapy setting run by a therapist as well as several support groups for adult rape victims. During the group, one learns from modeling by the therapist whereas support groups count on the similarity of experiencing for drawing the group together.

I had a devastating experience in a group setting that I felt needn't have happened when one of the members, a male, verbally attacked me. I'm shy and it takes me a great deal of time to open up. He misinterpreted that aspect of my personality as being "stuck-up" for lack of a better word and took the entire hour to chastise me. In retrospect his behavior shouldn't have been tolerated by either the therapist leading the group, the other group members, or me.

The group must be a place of safety and trust for all the members and this wasn't the case. While I was hoping to work on the after-effects of the rape, this experience set me back. I learned that for myself, a support group of other rape victims— women only—offered greater protection for me and for my (at the time) seriously wounded self-confidence.

Another option for support groups is the Internet, however one must be extremely careful not to give personal information, such as address, etc. for you really don't know who's on the other side. I would rely on support groups run by agencies or well-known therapists for an extra measure of security.—Madelyn, 24

✛ A Clinical View

The Definition of a Support Group

Support groups differ from group therapy in that support groups are typically led by a layperson, not a therapist. An example of an exception to this is support groups led by rape crisis centers that have a professional counselor or rape advocate to facilitate support groups.

The benefits of a support group are numerous, including sharing information on therapy treatments, professional resources, and legal information with those who have experienced sexual assault.

Support groups can be extremely effective, others damaging, in terms of your recovery. I recognize the contradictory nature of this statement, however just as in any form of therapy, the success of your recovery in a support group lies in the abilities of the leader and the compatibility of the group members. Trust your intuition; if you feel the support group that you have selected is not meeting your needs, search for another.

How to Find the Right Support Group

1. Obtain referrals from your therapist or your local rape crisis center.

2. Speak with the facilitator running the support group to determine the following:

   - The focus of the support group: Is it information and referral-based or sharing of personal experience? How would the focus of the group work in tandem with your ongoing therapy? Would it meet your needs if you are not in therapy?

   - The group dynamic: How large is the group? Is it intimate? Is there time to share with the group on a weekly basis if need be to obtain emotional support? Is family or your spouse invited to attend and receive support?

   - Frequency of meetings and meeting times

   - Location of the group

   - Size of the group

3. Interview the support group leader as you would in the selection of a therapist found earlier in this chapter.

"What's expected of me if I start therapy?"

✍ A Personal View

Time. Honesty with your feelings and emotions. Trust (though that builds over time). Patience—lots of patience. Goals, and the willingness to share them with your therapist. The ability to realize that all things change.

It's the hardest work you'll probably ever do but the most worthwhile. I learned things about myself that went far beyond what happened during my rape. I was adopted, and while I thought that had nothing—less than nothing—to do with my rape, I was mistaken.

My therapist became a mother figure to me and provided me with a comfort and acceptance that was sorely lacking in my life. She was everything I'd hoped my biological mother would be and when it came time to end therapy all the same abandonment issues that I'd been struggling with my whole life returned.

I started experiencing PTSD symptoms—flashbacks, nightmares—after months of being free of them. I didn't want her to "leave" me and the symptoms were my desire (unconsciously) for her to stay with me. Before therapy I never could have experienced the insight that I did. I'd have felt the feelings, been confused as I have been with other significant relationships in my past, and pushed her away before she could "leave." This was a tremendous break-through for me—the key to a life-long puzzle.

You are the person after the rape that you were before. You have the same foibles. The same fears. The same emotions. But the upside is that you have a strength you probably never knew you possessed. You have your intelligence. You have your character and your resolve.

You have all that it takes to recover from rape; you just need a teacher, a guide you can count on to lead you out of that dark forest.—Callie, 37

✚ A Clinical View

What You Can Expect from Your Therapist

A therapist has several duties: To educate you and to help you gain insight into your behaviors and actions so that you may live more fully and realize your potential. I understand your concern regarding expectations that may be required of you, however I believe it's also important to know what you may expect from your therapist.

You're investing your time and energy and are to be congratulated for taking this step; selecting a therapist that you can work with comfortably will serve to make you more self-confident in your ability to make decisions and take action that is in your best interest.

Your therapist will assess you for Post Traumatic Stress Disorder (PTSD) and other relevant problems, such as substance abuse, depression, self-injury, and obsessive compulsive disorder (OCD) and formulate a treatment plan.

Your therapist may determine that medication would be of help, in addition to your therapy, and refer you to a psychiatrist or medical doctor for evaluation. A combination of medication and therapy shouldn't be viewed as less effective; he may be taking into account other symptoms that may be alleviated and allow you to progress more quickly.

You can expect confidentiality from your therapist and a person whom you can trust. You must feel safe in his presence and believe at all times, through his actions and words, that he has your best interest in mind. You can expect that he will never do anything to compromise your recovery. You can expect trust to grow in both your relationship with your therapist and in yourself. You can expect to work hard on your recovery; you can expect to be challenged into new ways of thinking and behaving. You can expect your therapist to model these behaviors with you. You can expect to be confused and angry and hurt and sad— all of the emotions that one experiences when recovering from rape—and you can expect all of these emotions to be acceptable within the confines of your therapist's office. You can expect to be accepted.

The road to recovery is not linear. I know it's difficult to find the patience necessary to continue working, but recovery is an obtainable goal.

"I don't want to go to therapy. Is there anything I can do?"

✍ A Personal View

I'm not a "therapy" type of person. I haven't shared my rape with anyone, not my husband, not my family, not a therapist—I didn't even report it to the police.

The rape was so overwhelming to me in terms of what I could accept that I retreated completely. I knew I was in serious trouble but the act of picking up the phone was impossible. I tried a number of different times to tell my husband what happened but the words wouldn't leave my mouth.

So I developed my own plan for healing from the rape. I read everything I could get my hands on. Memoirs of women who had been raped, rape recovery books written by lay people and therapists, and even textbooks professionally written by therapists for therapists. Every book held something—some nugget for me to hold onto in helping my recovery. Also I took up journal writing, which was immensely helpful. I committed to paper all that I so desperately wanted to tell someone.

I'll never tell anyone about the rape. It's my own experience and I just know no one, not even my husband will know about it—ever. But I'm eternally grateful to the many writers who have put their story on paper. They helped me more than they'll ever know. I know I'm not alone. —Lana, 32

My rape occurred a number of years ago when encouragement to share one's experiences was frowned upon, but I had the lifelong habit of writing in a journal. I believe it saved my life. I was able to commit to paper that which I couldn't speak out loud. It became even more of a friend and confidante than in years prior.

An added benefit: I was able to "rehearse" in effect, what I said to my husband and family when telling them what happened. The rape occurred just prior to my marriage and I never told my husband. I regretted that, and was able to direct some of those feelings into my writing. —Sue, 54

✚ A Clinical View

Journal Writing

A journal is an excellent idea—I encourage it wholeheartedly. Expressing your feelings and thoughts is vital to recovering from rape and is an excellent way to record and reassess your behavior.

If you aren't ready at this particular point in time to speak with your family, friends, or a professional, or in tandem with your therapy, a journal can be invaluable. You will likely recognize that much of your insight occurs while writing.

Self-Directed Study

Self-directed study is for those of us who are solitary creatures—we keep our pain inside and find our own way. Self-directed study makes recovery possible if you are uncomfortable with undertaking formal therapy.

Support Groups

Support groups can be a very effective means of working on your recovery, either on its own or in conjunction with one-on-one psychotherapy. Sharing both information and personal experiences can be beneficial in terms of your emotional symptoms. The support system that a group can provide can be invaluable as can sharing resource and referral information in terms of time and energy.

Resources for Your Spiritual Healing

☎ General Resources

Alaska Network on Domestic Violence and Sexual Assault
Phone: (800) 478-1090

American Art Therapy Association, Inc., The
Phone: (888) 290-0878

American Association for Marriage and Family Therapy (AAMFT)
Phone: (202) 452-0109

American Group Psychotherapy Association
Phone: (877) 668-2472

American Psychiatric Association (APA)
Phone: (888) 357-7924

American Psychological Association (APA)
Phone: (800) 964-2000

Association for Advancement of Behavior Therapy
Phone: (212) 647-1890

Association of Traumatic Stress Specialists
Phone: (803) 781-0017

Brazos County Rape Crisis Center in Bryan
(979) 731-1000

California Coalition Against Sexual Assault
Phone: (916) 446-2520

Center for Mental Health Services (CMHS), The
Knowledge Exchange Network (KEN)
Phone: (800) 789-2647

EMDR Institute, Inc.
Phone: (831) 372-3900

EMDRIA (EMDR International Association)
Phone: (512) 451-5200

Indiana Coalition Against Sexual Assault
Phone: (800) 691-2272

Kentucky Association of Sexual Assault Programs, Inc.
Phone: (502) 226-2704

King County Sexual Assault Resource Center
Phone: (425) 226-5062

Louisiana Foundation Against Sexual Assault
Phone: (985) 345-5995

Michigan Coalition Against Domestic & Sexual Violence
Phone: (517) 347-7000

Minnesota Coalition Against Sexual Assault
Phone: (800) 964-8847

National Association of Social Workers (NASW)
Phone: (202) 408-8600

National Center for Victims of Crime, The
Phone: (800) FYI-CALL

National Crime Victim Bar Association, The
(Referral service to local attorneys specializing in victim-related litigation)
Phone: (703) 276-0960

National Depressive and Manic Depressive Association
Phone: (800) 826-3632

National Institute of Mental Health
Phone: (301) 443-4513

National Institutes of Health—Depression Information
Phone: (800) 421-4211

National Organization for Victim Assistance
Phone: (800) try-nova

New York State Coalition Against Sexual Assault
Phone: (518) 482-4222 phone

Northern California Art Therapy Association
Phone: (415) 522-3915

Office for Victims of Crime Resource Center
Phone: (800) 627-6872

Rape, Abuse & Incest National Network (RAINN)
Phone: (800) 656-HOPE

Rape Treatment Center (RTC)
Phone: (310) 319-4000

Self-Help Network of Kansas
Phone: (316) 978-3843

Standing Together Against Rape (Anchorage, AK)
Phone: (907) 276-7279

SupportWorks
Phone: (704) 331-9500

Tennessee Coalition Against Domestic and Sexual Violence
Phone: (615) 386-9406

University of Minnesota
Phone: (800) 779-8636

Wisconsin Coalition Against Sexual Assault
Phone: (608) 257-1516

⌐ Internet Resources

Alaska Network on Domestic Violence and Sexual Assault
www.andvsa.org

American Advancement of Behavior Therapy
www.aabt.org

American Art Therapy Association, Inc., The
www.arttherapy.org

American Association for Marriage and Family Therapy
www.aamft.org

American Group Psychotherapy Association
www.groupsinc.org

American Psychiatric Association
www.psych.org

American Psychological Association
www.helping.apa.org

American Self-Help Clearinghouse
www.cmhc.com/selfhelp

Association of Traumatic Stress Specialists, The
www.atss-hq.com

Aviva Gold: Painting from the Source
www.avivagold.com

California Coalition Against Sexual Assault
www.calcasa.org

Center for Mental Health Services (CMHS)
Knowledge Exchange Network (KEN), The
    www.mentalhealth.org

eGroups Online Support Groups for Anxiety
    www.egroups.com/search?query=anxiety

eGroups Online Support Groups for Panic Disorder
    www.egroups.com/search?query=panic%20disorder

EMDR Institute, Inc.
    www.emdr.com

EMDRIA Institute, Inc.
    www.emdria.org

Florida Council Against Sexual Violence
    www.fcasv.org

Gift from Within
    www.sourcemaine.com

Health Journals
    www.healthjourneys.com

Indiana Coalitions Against Sexual Assault
    www.incasa.org

Julian Center, The
    www.juliancenter.org

Kentucky Association of Sexual Assault Programs, Inc.
    www.kasap.org

King County Sexual Assault Resource Center
    www.kcsarc.org

Louisiana Foundation Against Sexual Assault
    www.lafasa.org

Mental Health Sanctuary
    www.mhsanctuary.com

Mental Health Sanctuary Trauma Wellness Workshop Online
    www.mhsanctuary.com/traumaworkshop

Michigan Coalition Against Domestic and Sexual Violence
    www.mcadsv.org

MINCAVA (Minnesota Center Against Violence and Abuse Clearinghouse)
www.mincava.umn.edu

Minnesota Coalition Against Sexual Assault
www.mncasa.org

National Association for Social Workers
www.naswdc.org

National Association of Cognitive-Behavioral Therapists
www.nacbt.org

National Center for Victims of Crime, The
www.ncvc.org

National Crime Victims Bar Association
www.victimbar.org

National Depressive and Manic Depressive Association
www.ndmda.org

National District Attorneys Association
www.ndaa-apri.org

National Mental Health Consumers' Self-Help Clearinghouse
www.libertynet.org/~mha/cl_house.html

National Organization for Victim Assistance
www.try-nova.org

New York State Coalition Against Sexual Assault
www.nyscasa.org

Northern California Art Therapy Association
www.norcata.com

Partnership Against Violence
www.pavnet.org

Psych Central
www.psychcentral.com/grohol.htm

Rape, Abuse & Incest National Network
www.rainn.org

SelfHelp Magazine
www.shpm.com/articles/trauma/index.shtml

Self-Help Network of Kansas/Wichita State University
www.wsupsy.psy.twsu.edu/shnok

Self Improvement Online
www.selfgrowth.com

Sounds True
www.soundstrue.com

Standing Together Against Rape
www.star.ak.org

Support-Group.com
www.support-group.com

SupportWorks
www.supportworks.org

Survivors Art Foundation
www.survivorsartfoundation.org

Tennessee Coalition Against Domestic and Sexual Violence
www.tcadsv.citysearch.com

The Rape Treatment Center (RTC)/Santa Monica-UCLA Medical Center
www.911rape.org

TherapistFinder
www.TherapistFinder.net

Wisconsin Coalition Against Sexual Assault
www.wcasa.org

WritingtheJourney.com
www.writingthejourney.com/exercises/

Yahoo! Online Support Group for PTSD
www.groups.yahoo.com/search?query=ptsd

📖 Book Resources

Aftermath of Rape, The
By T.W. McCahill, L.D. Meyer, A.M. Fischman

Aftermath: Survive and Overcome Trauma
By Mariann Hybels-Steer

Aftermath: Violence and the Remaining of a Self
By Susan J. Brison

After Silence: Rape and My Journey Back
By Nancy Venable Raine

A Guide to Psychotherapy
By Gerald Amada, Ph.D.

A Mood Apart: The Thinker's Guide to Emotion and Its Disorders
By Peter C. Whybrow

Anatomy of Motive, The:
By John Douglas, Mark Olshaker

Anger Kills
By Redford Williams, M.D., Virginia Williams, Ph.D.

Anger: The Misunderstood Emotion
By Carol Tavris

Angry Self: A Comprehensive Approach to Anger Management, The
By Miriam M. Gottlieb, Ph.D.

A Path Through Loss: A Guide to Writing Your Healing and Growth
By Nancy C. Reeves

Art and Healing: Using Expressive Art to Heal Your Body, Mind, and Spirit
By Barbara Ganim, Michael Samuels, Mary Rockwood Lane (Foreword)

Art as Medicine
By Shaun McNiff

Art Is a Way of Knowing
By Pat B. Allen

Art Therapy Sourcebook, The
By Cathy A. Malchiodi

Art Therapy with Sexual Abuse Survivors
By Stephanie Brooke

Asserting Yourself
By Sharon Bower, Gordon H. Bower

A Voice of Her Own: Women and the Journal Writing Journey
By Marlene A. Schiwy, Marion Woodman

A Woman's Journey to God: Finding the Feminine Path
By Joan Borysenko, Ph.D.

Bird by Bird: Some Instructions on Writing and Life
By Anne Lamott

Calm and Confident: Overcome Stress and Anxiety With EMDR
By Mark Grant

Choosing an Online Therapist: A Step-By-Step Guide to Finding Professional Help on the Web
    By Gary S. Stofle

Cognitive Therapy and the Emotional Disorders
    By Aaron T. Beck

Cognitive Therapy: Basics and Beyond
    By Judith S. Beck

Conquering the Beast Within: How I Fought Depression and Won. . .and How You Can, Too
    By Cait Irwin

Coping With Survivors and Surviving
    By Julie Skinner

Coping With Trauma: A Guide to Self-Understanding
    By Jon G. Allen, Ph.D.

Creative Connection: Expressive Arts As Healing
    By Natalie Rogers

Diary Of A Rape Victim: Breaking the Silence to Break Free
    By Phillis Van Godwin

Effective Support Groups
    By James E. Miller

Embracing Your Inner Critic: Turning self-criticism into a Creative Asset
    By Hal and Sidra Stone

EMDR in the Treatment of Adults Abused As Children
    By Laurel Parnell, Ph.D.

EMDR: The Breakthrough Therapy for Overcoming Anxiety, Stress, and Trauma
    By Francine Shapiro, Margot Silk Forrest

Emotional Brain, The: The Mysterious Underpinnings of Emotional Life
    By Joseph LeDoux

Emotional Healing at Warp Speed: The Power of EMDR
    By David Grand

Emotional Intelligence: Why It Can Matter More Than IQ for Health and Lifelong Achievement
    By Daniel Goleman

Error: Emotion, Reason and the Human Brain
    By Antonio R. Damasio

Evil That Men Do, The: FBI Profiler Roy Hazelwood's Journey into the Minds of Sexual Predators
By Stephen G. Michaud, Roy Hazelwood

Feeling Good Handbook, The
By David Burns

Finding the Energy to Heal: How EMDR, Hypnosis, TFT, Imagery, and Body-Focused Therapy Can Help Resolve Health Problems
By Maggie Phillips

Fire in the Soul: A New Psychology of Spiritual Optimism
By Joan Borysenko, Ph.D.

Flow: The Psychology of Optimal Experience
By Mihaly Csikszentmihaly

For Your Own Good: Hidden Cruelty in Childrearing and the Roots of Violence
By Alice Miller, Ph.D.

Freedom from Fear Forever
By Dr. James V. Durlacher, Roger J. Callahan, Guy McGill

Free of the Shadows: Recovering from Sexual Violence
By Caren Adams, Jennifer Fay

Group Therapy Experience, The: From Theory to Practice
By Louis R. Ormont

Helping Crime Victims: Research, Policy, and Practice
By Albert R. Roberts

Honoring Differences: Cultural Issues in the Treatment of Trauma and Loss
By Kathleen Nader, D.S.W., Nancy Dubrow, Ph.D., B. Hudnall Stamm, Ph.D. (Editors)

How to Choose a Psychotherapist
By The American Psychological Association

How to Choose a Therapist
By Sidran Foundation

How to Think Straight About Psychology
By Keith E. Stanovich

If You Are Raped: What Every Woman Needs to Know
By Kathryn M. Johnson

Intimate Partner Violence : Societal, Medical, Legal, and Individual Responses
By Sana Loue

It's Not As Bad As It Seems: A Thinking Straight Approach to Happiness
By Dr. Ed Nottingham

It's Not Personal! A Guide to Anger Management
By Alice J. Katz

Journey to Wholeness: Healing from the Trauma of Rape
By Vicki Aranow, Monique Lang

Learned Optimism: How to Change Your Mind and Your Life
By Martin Seligman

Learning to Love Yourself: A Guide to Becoming Centered
By Gay Hendricks

Learning to Love Yourself Workbook, The
By Gay Hendricks

Life After Trauma
By Dean Rosenbloom, Mary Beth Watkins

Lovingkindness
By Sharon Salzberg

Malignant Sadness: The Anatomy of Depression
By Lewis Wolpert

Managing Traumatic Stress Through Art: Drawing From the Center
By Barry M. Cohen, Mary-Michola Barnes, Anita B. Rankin

Meeting at the Crossroads
By Wisconsin Department of Health and Family Services, Bureau of Community Mental Health

Mindhunter
By John Douglas, Mark Olshaker

Men Who Rape
By Nicholas A. Groth

No Fairy Godmother, No Magic Wands: The Healing Process After Rape
By Judy H. Katz

No Safe Haven: Male Violence Against Women At Home, At Work, and In the Community
By Mary P. Koss

On the Edge of Darkness: Conversations About Conquering Depression
By Kathy Cronkite

On Wings of Light: Meditations for Awakening to the Source
By Joan Borysenko, Ph.D.

Our Guys: The Glen Ridge Rape and Secret Life of the Perfect Suburb
By Bernard Lefkowitz

Overcoming Anger and Irritability: A Self-Help Guide Using Cognitive Behavioral Techniques (Overcoming Series)
By William Davies

Overcoming Depression
By Demitri and Janice Paplos

Pain Control With EMDR
By Mark Grant

Painting from the Source: Awakening the Artist's Soul in Everyone
By Aviva Gold

Portable Therapist, The
By Susanna McMahon, Ph.D.

Protecting Confidentiality of Victim-Counselor Communications
By National Center on Women and Family Law

Quest for Respect: A Healing Guide for Survivors of Rape
By Linda Braswell

Rape Crisis Intervention Handbook: A Guide for Victim Care
By Sharon McCombie

Rape: The Misunderstood Crime
By Julie A. Allison, Lawrence S. Wrightsman

Reach for the Rainbow: Advanced Healing for Survivors of Sexual Abuse
By Lynne D. Finney, J.D., M.S.W.

Real Rape: How the Legal System Victimizes Women Who Say No
By Susan Estrich

Rebuilding Shattered Lives: The Responsible Treatment of Complex Post-Traumatic and Dissociative Disorders
By James A. Chu, M.D.

Recovering from Rape
By Linda Ledray

Recovering from the Losses of Life
By H. Norman Wright

Rising to the Dawn: A Rape Survivor's Journey into Healing
By Laverne C. Williams

Self-Help Handouts for Survivors and Support Groups
By Wisconsin Coalition Against Sexual Assault

Self-Help Sourcebook, The: Your Guide to Community & Online Support
By Barbara J. White, Edward J. Madara (Editors)

Self-Respect & Sexual Assault
By Jeanett Mauro-Cochrane

Sexual Violence: Our War Against Rape
By Linda A. Fairstein

Sexual Violence: The Unmentionable Sin
By Marie Marshall Fortune

Speaking of Sadness: Depression, Disconnection, and the Meanings of Illness
By David Karp

Starting/Running Support Groups
By Buz Overbeck, Joanie Overbeck

Stopping Rape: Successful Survival Strategies
By Pauline B. Bart, Patricia H. O'Brien

Strategies for the Treatment and Prevention of Sexual Assault
By The American Medical Association

Support Group Sourcebook, The: What They Are, How You Can Find One, and How They Can Help You
By Linda L. Klein

Surviving Sexual Assault
By Rochel Grossman, Joan Sutherland

Surviving the Silence: Black Women's Stories of Rape
By Charlotte Pierce-Baker

Survivor Personality: Why Some People are Stronger, Smarter, and More Skillful at Handling Life's Difficulties ... and How You Can Be Too, The
By Al Siebert, Ph.D.

Taking Back My Life
By Nancy Ziegenmeyer

The Rape Victim: Clinical and Community Interventions
By Mary P. Koss

Transforming a Rape Culture
By Emilie Buchwald, Martha Roth, Pamela Fletcher (Editors)

Trauma Recovery and Empowerment: A Clinician's Guide for Working with Women in Groups
By Maxine Harris, Ph.D.

Understanding Violence Against Women
By Nancy A. Crowell, Ann W. Burgess (Editors)

Victims of Crime: Issues, Programs, and Policy
By Robert Jerin

Victim's Rights: Opportunities for Action
By The National Victim Center, 1989

Violence Against Women: There is No Typical Victim
By Catherine Walters

Voices of the Survivors
By Patricia Eastel

Where I Stopped: Remembering Rape at Thirteen
By Martha Ramsey

Women's Legal Guide: A Comprehensive Guide to Legal Issues Affecting Every Woman
By Barbara R. Hauser

3

Physical Healing

Your physical health is paramount for your healing and rape can have far reaching effects on your health; it's vitally important that you enlist professionals who will assist you in returning to your previous health or become even healthier than you were previously.

"I'm nervous about my next OB/GYN appointment. What can I do?"

✍ A Personal View

My first gynecological exam following the rape was filled with apprehension. A gynecological exam even without the experience of rape is sometimes difficult because you're in a position wherein you have little control. You're on your back, with your feet up, a (virtual) stranger is inserting things inside you. And generally it's a male.

I did come up with some ideas though that served to make my experience a little more palatable. First, I made the appointment with my gynecologist—a male doctor that I'd been seeing for about seven years—for first thing in the morning. That way I knew I wouldn't be waiting if he got backed up throughout the day. Waiting means anxiety—something you don't need.

And I requested that I be able to see him for 15 minutes longer than the regular appointment so that we might have a consultation prior to the exam. I wanted to see him in his office, with my clothes on and my feet on the floor. This would be the first time since the rape that someone touched me and I wanted it to be on my terms.

Second, immediately after making the appointment I dropped off a copy of the report that the examining doctor at the hospital had prepared after the rape. I asked his nurse to add it to my file and requested that my doctor read it prior to our appointment.

Third, I made a list of my injuries at the time and how I was feeling now. I was very succinct. I knew I'd be nervous and didn't want to miss anything.

Fourth, I took the remainder of the day off from work and did exactly what I wanted—I had an early lunch with a friend, went shopping for a couple of hours and then went to a movie and dinner with my boyfriend. This was a pretty big deal for me and I was proud of the way I went about it.

You must take care of yourself and taking care of your physical injuries is of utmost importance.—Janice, 33

✚ A Clinical View

What Happens During a Gynecological Exam

What happens during a gynecological exam is a mystery to most of us. Whether or not you received injuries during your sexual assault, it's important that your OB/GYN know that you were raped.

You may have been treated by a physician in a hospital or may not have been treated at all, however, your own physician is in the best position for determining your follow-up care.

In addition, knowing what to expect allows you to be prepared for the physical sensations you will feel in various phases of the pelvic exam. Informative guides on gynecological exams can be found on the Internet sites in the following resource section. In addition to a breast exam, a very brief overview of the pelvic exam includes:

The External Genital Exam

A visual examination of the vulva and opening of the vagina; abnormalities, rashes, cysts, genital warts, etc. are noted.

The Speculum Exam

A speculum is inserted to facilitate examination of the cervix; abnormalities are noted; and testing for STDs is performed as is a Pap Test.

The Bimanual Exam

One or two gloved, lubricated fingers are inserted into the vagina while your physician presses down on the lower abdomen to feel the internal organs. Size, shape, tenderness, pain, swelling and enlargement of organs is noted.

Rectovaginal Exam

A gloved finger is inserted into the rectum to locate possible tumors and check the condition of the muscles.

"Should I be tested for AIDS?"

✍ A Personal View

It's important to be tested for HIV immediately. Ask your therapist, HMO, or rape crisis center for a referral to a testing center.

I was impressed by the manner in which I was treated. An appointment was made for the very afternoon I called with a registered nurse specially trained in counseling patients pre and post HIV testing. She was fantastic and put my mind at ease immediately. She told me what the test measured, what the results would mean, follow-up testing requirements and asked about my risk factor.

When the counselor learned that I was there following a rape, she spent an additional 45 minutes simply talking to me. She set up an appointment for two days later and asked that I return. She cried along with me when she told me it was negative as I assume she does with other patients on the too-frequent times she tells others that their tests are positive.

She was an angel—even though she has a terribly difficult job she did it with grace and compassion.—Karen, 28

✚ A Clinical View

HIV Testing

It's of utmost importance to locate a confidential testing facility that has trained, professional counselors on staff to provide pre-test counseling. I understand the emotional difficulty of considering having contracted HIV as a result of the sexual assault, however it's important to be tested as soon as possible in order to establish a baseline.

Request an appointment in any case once the results are known. It is very important that you not be contacted simply by phone call or worse, through the mail. It's best if the appointment for the follow-up is made when you are there for the test. The counselor can be invaluable in sorting out the myriad of feelings with sexual assault. And be honest, she is there to help you.

"I'm terrified that I'm going to become pregnant from the rape. What can I do?"

✍ A Personal View

I became pregnant as the result of a rape. Devastating. How could one life be turned upside down so completely? I'm a devout Catholic and I struggled greatly with my decision to have the child. While I would never presume to tell someone what to after such a horrendous ordeal, I have moments of self-doubt. I really do.
—Kerrie, 38

I was referred to a clinic and went the following day after the rape. I elected to take emergency contraceptives, which eliminated any chance of pregnancy. I often wonder how I would have dealt with this had I been married and there was even the slightest chance that I was pregnant. I would have had to seriously consider what to do if there was even the slightest chance of my aborting a child my husband and I had created. I suppose I'm lucky in that I never faced that. Still, my heart aches for women in that situation. It's amazing to me how much pain can be absorbed by the human soul.—Annalynn, 26

✚ A Clinical View

Your Risk of Pregnancy

Your risk of pregnancy from unprotected sex can vary based upon your menstrual cycle and is difficult to predict. Emergency contraceptives, also called "morning after" pills reduce the risk of pregnancy; however, they do not prevent sexually transmitted diseases (STDs). This method of contraception can be started immediately after the sexual assault and has a 72-hour window, although it should be started as soon as possible. Alternatively an IUD (the copper-T intrauterine device) may be inserted within five days following the rape.

Coping with Pregnancy Following a Rape

According to the CDC, the adult pregnancy rate associated with rape is estimated to be 4.7%, suggesting a possibility of 32,101 rape-related pregnancies annually, based upon U.S. Census figures.

It's devastating to learn that you are pregnant from rape, but you have choices. As a woman you are aware, no doubt, of the importance of making a decision in a timely manner; and this is a decision only you can make. Your choices include:

- Continuing with the pregnancy and keeping the baby
- Continuing with the pregnancy and placing the baby for adoption
- Terminating the pregnancy

"I think I may be developing an eating disorder; how can I stop this?"

✍ A Personal View

I was looking in a mirror one day, probably about four months after the rape. I was shocked! I hadn't even looked at my body since the rape because I felt dirty—used. I just didn't want to see myself, almost like an accident victim who knows her face has been injured but doesn't want to look at it.

I'd never seen my body in such awful shape. I was thin—emaciated. I looked as if my skin was just hanging off my bones. I'd been wearing large sweaters and pants lately, but what I didn't realize, I suppose I'd been in denial, was that I was trying to hide what I was doing to myself. I'd successfully hidden it from my boyfriend, although he kept asking me why I wasn't eating and trying to tell me that my skin looked gray.

I began seeing a therapist right away and talking about the fact that I was devastated by the rape and the part my body played. I'd always been proud of my figure and men looked at me but I started thinking all men were just thinking about raping me.

I'm eating and making progress, a day at a time, but I tell my therapist I just don't want to look good enough to rape. I know I have a long way to go.
—Melina, 30

✛ A Clinical View

It's extremely difficult to simply stop an eating disorder. The intricacies of eating disorders of women who have been raped are very complex and the reasons they develop following rape, numerous. For example, a woman who develops anorexia may be attempting to gain control over her body to compensate for the lack of control she had during the rape.

A woman who develops bulimia may be attempting to alleviate the pain and intense emotion of having been raped by forcing the food down. A woman who develops bulimia of a purging type may be attempting to release these intense emotions. And finally, a woman who compulsively overeats may be attempting to change her body in order to avoid future rapes. In her mind she may believe that it was her body that invited the rape. An overview of three eating disorders appears below:

Anorexia

- An inability to maintain a body weight that's consistent with other women your age, build, and height
- An overwhelming fear of becoming overweight, regardless of your present shape or weight
- An inability to evaluate your own physical appearance
- You must have missed three consecutive menstrual cycles to be diagnosed with anorexia

Bulimia (Purging and Non-Purging Type)

- Engaging in recurrent episodes of binge eating at least twice a month for three months
- An inability to stop eating or to tell how much is being eaten
- Engaging in excessive exercise
- Inducing vomiting—purging type
- Misusing laxatives, enemas, and medication—purging type

Compulsive Overeating

- Compulsive eating for reasons other than hunger
- Experiencing shame and guilt about compulsive overeating

215

"Why do I want to hurt myself?"

✍ A Personal View

Shortly after my rape, I began cutting myself. First, it was little tiny scratches with a knife. Later, it became really frightening as I started making bigger and bigger cuts that were taking longer to heal, so much so that I had to start wearing long-sleeved blouses and sweaters.

My pain over the rape was just too big; I couldn't contain my emotions. I felt that my emotions couldn't hurt any worse, so I had to make my body hurt. It was the only way I knew how to cope with the rape.

My therapist and I worked out a way in which I could stop cutting myself: As soon as that incredible urge to cut myself appeared, I would try to stop what I was doing and wait 30 minutes. I was to sit down and do deep breathing and relaxation exercises for a full five minutes. I sat on a chair with my feet flat on the floor and breathed three breaths deeply, from my abdomen. I had to work on becoming aware of my feelings. Next, I was to put a mark on the spot I wanted to cut.

This seems so simplistic but it worked for me. The awareness really was the first step. I haven't cut myself in months and am optimistic; but I take one day at a time.—Rochelle, 25

✦ A Clinical View

Also known as self-injury and cutting, self-mutilation is more common in rape victims than one would think. Those who partake in self-mutilation do it in order to feel something—anything, to cope with powerful feelings and emotions, and to punish oneself for being "bad" as is often the result of shame and guilt.

Self-mutilation is a deliberate act but one typically not designed to commit suicide and is usually moderate in nature, but the point is still to hurt oneself. Acts of self-mutilation include cutting, pinching, and burning oneself.

Taking Control of the Urge to Hurt Yourself

1. Develop an awareness of how you're feeling: Sad? Angry? Frustrated? Resolve to write in your journal prior to every moment that you feel you'd like to harm yourself. Pick up a pen and write for at least five minutes, then ten, then twenty, until the feelings become less intense. Try to share these feelings with your husband, partner, support system, or therapist.

2. Reward yourself each time you're able to avoid hurting yourself. Perhaps you're feeling alone: Write that down on a piece of paper and put it in a jar. After each time that you're able to ride that wave that comes over you before you hurt yourself, replace that piece of paper with something that you'd really like to have, perhaps a book or piece of art—and then buy it within a short amount of time, say perhaps five days. Again, the point is to reward yourself for the courage to work on something tremendously difficult for you.

3. Distract yourself with some other pursuits to avoid harming yourself. The urge for pain can sometimes be alleviated by acts that cause sharp, physical sensations but no lasting damage, such as: Snapping a rubber band on your wrist or crushing ice between your hands. Other techniques that satisfy this craving include: Writing on your hand with a red pen or punching a soft, stuffed pillow.

4. After the wave to injure yourself has passed, release some of that energy by pampering yourself with something that you like to do: Listen to music, watch a funny movie, or take a soothing bath. These are all immediate activities that serve to reward you.

"I feel disconnected from my body; why don't I 'work' sexually anymore?"

✍ A Personal View

I felt after the rape that I didn't "work" sexually anymore as well. I felt like my body was no longer mine. There was a moment during my rape that I've tried to explain to my therapist: I'm out of my body—away up in a corner and looking at myself. Removed. Almost as if I've died and I'm looking down at my body. How frightening. How truly bizarre and frightening.

Well, I feel the same thing about my body, particularly when I'm making love with my husband. I feel like I'm one large head with no body until I look in the mirror and see the rest of me. I've been working with this in therapy—feeling my body again—but it's truly disconcerting.

For me something as simple as keeping my eyes open while I'm making love helps me feel connected.—Deanna, 26

✛ A Clinical View

You're experiencing feelings of dissociation from your body and as a result, feel as if you're not sexual any longer. The goal is to re-integrate those parts of your-self that are unreachable for you and while this is a sexual concern, the dissociation is also a physiological effect of the rape and so appears in this section.

The Definition of Dissociation

The experience of dissociation from one's body is very normal in a person who has been sexually assaulted. When faced with severe psychological trauma, our minds separate from the events we're experiencing in order to protect us from the intense, emotional pain.

Dissociation can be defined as a lack of connection in your sense of identity, your feelings, your thoughts—even your memories. We experience feelings of losing touch in a very mild way when we're, for example, daydreaming.

You needn't suffer one more moment from sexual dysfunction. Help is avail-able. Female sexual dysfunction is a term commonly used for a number of different disorders and is differentiated from disinterest in sexual relations.

"What can I do to feel safe again?"

✍ A Personal View

I'd wanted to attend a self-defense class for some time. The school I chose specialized in classes for women; actual, everyday situations in which a woman could find herself. I spoke with my therapist first, did my research, and even went to a course so that I could see how the instructors and students interacted.

I liked what I saw—I went to one of the programs in which the instructor—typically a male—is in a large padded "head." I felt, certainly, momentary panic several times when it came my turn to be "attacked" but I suffered no flashbacks, thankfully.

I do feel safer having taken the course, perhaps also because it integrates safety with assertiveness; the "NO!" instruction was especially helpful. I think that because the attack during class was quite close to my own rape (from behind) I feel better prepared should anything happen again. God forbid.—Carrie, 25

✚ A Clinical View

Self-Defense Courses

Learning self-defense is an excellent way to feel more in control over your environment. A great deal of success has been reported by actual survivors who were able to put into practice the safety strategies, and assertiveness and awareness skills that are taught in these courses. A number of women have reported that they've been able to escape violent attacks as a direct result of the skills they've learned.

How to Find a Self-Defense Course

1. Research self-defense courses being offered; a number have excellent web sites or seek a referral from your local rape crisis center.

2. Review the courses being offered. Courses range from beginning to intermediate to advanced and some offer additional subjects, such as successfully fending off a gang attack and attackers with weapons. In addition, some offer individual self-defense training.

3. Determine if the course fits into your time and money schedule.

4. Once you narrow down several programs, speak with the director or instructor to give them additional background regarding your rape. You want someone skilled in working with sexual assault victims. Be sure the instructor is aware of the symptoms you're currently experiencing so that if you should have a flashback or other difficulty, they can be there to help.

5. Speak with your therapist, particularly if you're suffering from symptoms currently.

6. Observe a class session and speak with students afterward to see how they're doing.

7. Determine whether you're more comfortable with a male or female instructor. Male instructors are becoming more prevalent based on the type of self-defense course being offered, however some rape victims are more comfortable with females in an all-women course.

8. Determine if you feel safe and trusting of the instructors.

Resources for Your Physical Healing

☎ General Resources

American Association of Suicidology
Phone: (202) 237-2280 / (800)-SUICIDE (784-2433)

BAMM/IMPACT Self-Defense
Phone: (800) 77-FIGHT

Capital City Model Mugging/IMPACT
Phone: (916) 636-8580

Centers for Disease Control—National HIV/AIDS Hotline
American Social Health Association
Phone: (800) 342-AIDS

Association for Pre- & Perinatal Psychology and Health
Phone: (707) 857-4041

Eating Disorders Awareness and Prevention, Inc.
Phone: (206) 382-3587

Healthy Within, Inc.
Phone: (858) 622-0221

International Association of Eating Disorders Professionals
Phone: (602) 934-3024

International Society for the Study of Dissociation, The
Phone: (847) 480-0899

Marriage & Family Health Center, The
Phone: (303) 670-2630

Martial Hearts, Inc.
Phone: (770) 640-6986

Masters and Johnson
Phone: (636) 532-9772

National Association of Anorexia Nervosa and Associated Disorders (ANAD)
Phone: (847) 831-3438

National Woman's Health Information Center, The
Phone: (800) 994-WOMAN / (800) 994-9662

Overeaters Anonymous
Phone: (505) 891-2664

PREPARE, INC.
Phone: (800) 345-5425

Rape Assistance and Awareness Program (RAAP) of Denver
Phone: (303) 329-9922

SAFE Alternatives (Residential program for self-injurers)
Phone: (800) DONTCUT / (800) 366-8288)

⌐⊕ Internet Resources

About.com Women's Health
www.womenshealth.about.com

American Association of Suicidology
www.suicidology.org

Association for Pre- and Perinatal Psychology and Health
www.birthpsychology.com

BAMM/IMPACT Self-Defense
www.bamm.org

Body Positive
www.bodypositive.com

Capital City Model Mugging
www.ccmmselfdefense.org

Dyspareunia Website
www.dyspareunia.org

Eating Disorders Awareness and Prevention, Inc.
www.edap.org

Healthy Within, Inc.
www.healthywithin.com

International Association of Eating Disorders Professionals
www.iaedp.com

International Society for the Study of Dissociation, The
www.issd.org

Marriage and Family Health Center, The
www.passionatemarriage.com

Martial Hearts, Inc.
www.martialhearts.com

Masters and Johnson
www.mastersandjohnson.com

National Association of Anorexia Nervosa and Associated Disorders
www.anad.org

National Women's Health Information Center
www.4woman.gov

OB/GYN.net's Women's Pavilion
www.obgyn.net

Overeaters Anonymous
www.overeatersanonymous.org

PREPARE, Inc.
www.prepareinc.com

Rape Assistance and Awareness Program (RAAP) of Denver
www.raap.org

SAFE Alternatives
www.selfinjury.com

Yahoo! Anorexia Support Group List
www.groups.yahoo.com/search?query=anorexia

Yahoo! Bulimia Support Group List
www.groups.yahoo.com/search?query=bulimia

Yahoo! Compulsive Overeating Support Group List
www.groups.yahoo.com/search?query=overeating

📖 Book Resources

Adoption Healing—A Path to Recovery
By Joe Soll

Allies in Healing: When the Person You Love Was Sexually Abused as a Child
By Laura Davis

Beauty Bites Beast: Awakening the Warrior Within Women and Girls
By Ellen Snortland

Beyond the Darkness
By Cynthia Kubetin, James Mallory

Birthmothers: Women Who Have Relinquished Babies for Adoption Tell Their Stories
    By Merry Bloch Jones

Bodily Harm: The Breakthrough Treatment Program for the Self-Injurer
    By Karen Conterio, Wendy Lader

Body Betrayed, The: A Deeper Understanding of Women, Eating Disorders, and Treatment
    By Kathryn J. Zerbe, M.D.

Bodylove: Learning to Like Our Looks and Ourselves
    By Rita Freedman, Ph.D.

Color Atlas of Sexual Assault
    By Diana K. Faugno, Patty C. Seneski

Compassion and Self-Hate: An Alternative to Despair
    By Theodore Isaac Rubin

Death Wishes? The Understanding and Management of Deliberate Self-Harm
    By H. Morgan

Everything You Always Wanted to Ask Your Gynecologist
    By Scott Thornton, M.D., Kathleen Schramm, M.D.

Exploding the Myth of Self-Defense: A Survival Guide for Every Woman
    By Judith Fein, Ph.D.

For Each Other: Sharing Sexual Intimacy
    By Lonnie Barbach, Ph.D.

For Women Only: A Revolutionary Guide to Overcoming Sexual Dysfunction and Reclaiming Your Sex Life
    By Jennifer Berman, M.D., Laura Berman, Ph.D.

Full Catastrophe Living: Using the Wisdom of Your Body and Mind to Face Stress, Pain, and Illness
    By Jon Kabat-Zinn

Ghosts in the Bedroom
    By Ken Graber

Gift of Fear, The: Survival Signs that Protect Us From Violence
    By Gavin DeBecker

Gurze Books Eating Disorders Recourse Catalogue (Very extensive catalogue)
    www.gurze.com or www.bulimia.com

Healing Choice, The: Your Guide to Emotional Recovery After an Abortion
By Candace De Puy, Ph.D., Dana Dovitch, Ph.D.

Her Wits About Her: Self-Defense Success Stories by Women
By Denise Caignon, Gail Groves

HIV and AIDS: Testing, Screening, and Confidentiality
By Rebecca Bennett, Charles A. Erin (Editors)

How Good People Make Tough Choices: Resolving the Dilemmas of Ethical Living
By Rushworth M. Kidder

I Hate You-Don't Leave Me!
By Jerold Kreisman, Hal Straus

In Good Conscience: A Practical, Emotional, and Spiritual Guide to Deciding Whether to Have an Abortion
By Anna Runkle

More Harm Than Help: The Ramifications for Rape Survivors of Mandatory HIV Testing of Rapists
By Lisa Bowleg

Ordinary Women, Extraordinary Sex: Every Woman's Guide to Pleasure and Beyond
By Sandra Scantling, Sue Browder

Passionate Marriage: Love, Sex, and Intimacy in Emotionally Committed Relationships
By David Schnarch, Ph.D.

Peace After Abortion
By Ava Torre-Bueno

Saying Goodbye to a Baby: Birthparents Guide to Loss and Grief in Adoption
By Patricia Roles

Self-Therapy for Sex Problems
By Daniel Steele

Sexual Assault: A Manual for Emergency Care
By Patricia A. Hargest, Robi Findley, R.N.

Testing for HIV: What Your Lab Results Mean
By N. L. Gifford (Editor)

The Third Choice: A Woman's Guide to Placing a Child for Adoption
By Leslie Foge, Gail Mosconi

Violence and Abuse: Implications for Women's Health
   By S.B. Plichta

Women's Sexuality Across the Life Span: Challenging Myths, Creating Meanings
   By Judith Daniluk

4

Sexual Healing

You may remember that one of my goals in writing this book was to provide you with information on reclaiming and savoring your sexuality as a woman after having been raped. You deserve to be free to receive loving touches without the pain of past memories. I believe that our ability to experience sexuality is one of the greatest gifts bestowed on women and this exquisite gift shouldn't be diminished in any way because of the rape you experienced.

I'd like to say something about the time it takes to recover from rape. It's difficult, if not impossible, to estimate how long your own recovery will take, making it vital that your partner be informed as to your needs and desires, sexual and otherwise, without imposing his own. One of the most devastating things that a rape victim can hear is, "Aren't you over it yet?"

Therefore, keep him involved in your recovery: Consider attending therapy sessions together, discuss the possibility of sex counseling in addition to psychotherapy, and gather information, such as articles and books, that will help him understand your feelings. I've also received very positive feedback from men who have attended support groups for intimate partners of rape victims. Again, it's vital that you both recognize that this is a temporary situation and both of you need to work at the recovery process.

"How can I feel sensual again?"

✍ A Personal View

I don't feel sensual anymore. I used to get dressed up; hair—makeup. And I used to like to go out with a friend a couple of nights a week. I always felt sensual and like I looked my best. Since the rape I haven't had the desire to get dressed up at all. Actually I wear baggy jeans and large sweaters if you want to know the truth.

My therapist suggested I begin by masturbating. I'd never done it prior to my rape but I was having real difficulty feeling sexual again with my husband. I was scared to death of—I'm not sure what. But I found that I would get to a certain point and then have to stop. I felt sexual to begin with, but as soon as my husband touched my breasts and genitals, I'd become rigid. My therapist suggested masturbating to become reacquainted with being touched. It took me several more sessions to get up the nerve to tell her that I'd never masturbated before.

She suggested several good books and it took a good deal of "practice" for me, but I found that it re-awakened something inside me that I thought I'd lost. Very slowly, I replaced my husband's hands with mine. It has served to bring us closer than we were before.—Kaye, 31

✚ A Clinical View

Your sensuality prior to the rape may feel lost to you; as if it's a feeling that others may be fortunate to feel, but something that you'll never experience again.

Please recognize that this is a temporary state of being. Your emotional symptoms and any injuries you may have must take precedence at this time, which allows you time to work on the issues regarding your sexuality.

Enhancing Your Sensuality

There are a number of ways to enhance your feeling of sensuality and becoming ready again to make love:

Masturbation

Many women feel that masturbation has been an integral part to their feeling sensual again following rape. If it's something you enjoyed prior to your rape, there's no reason to avoid it now. It's safe, you're under no pressure, and it's with someone you know—and trust.

Awareness of your feelings as you become aroused, as you feel the warm rush of excitement that moves from your toes through your sexual organs may help to communicate your needs to your partner and teach both of you new ways to relate.

As you experience orgasm you may have an overwhelming feeling of letting go, of experiencing a lack of control. That's a good thing. That's what your body was designed to do—experience intense pleasure. When masturbating you can let go all you wish while remaining completely safe.

Sexual Education

There are a number of books and videos that can help you begin feeling more sensual, a number of which have been produced by sex educators and sex therapists who specialize in enhancing intimacy between couples.

The value of professionally written and produced videos cannot be overstated. In the privacy of your own home, you can view detailed techniques and skills in a very sensitive setting.

"I just don't feel like having sex anymore; I'm at the end of my rope; should I see a sex therapist?"

✍ A Personal View

My husband and I had always had a wonderful sex life—until I was raped. I just didn't want to do anything anymore. I felt as if the rapist saw my sexuality—my "femaleness"—and that the very fact that I was a sexual human being put me in danger. It put me in a position where I might have been killed. I wanted to avoid looking sexual, feeling sexual, at all costs. I found it impossible though to try to come across as asexual in public and then flip a switch and become a sexual partner again to my husband.

My husband asked our regular therapist whether we should go for sex counseling. I was shocked that he'd noticed how bad it had become but I was grateful that he had asked.

In seeing a specialist I learned that my symptoms were to be expected. Her therapy was action-oriented and we made progress almost immediately.

In retrospect, I would have preferred for my regular therapist to ask us about our sexual relations sooner. I've learned that reclaiming one's sexuality after rape is a major issue but no one brought it up—it made me feel as if I shouldn't either. One of the things I didn't "get" while in therapy was the fact that my therapist let me lead. I'd suggest that you bring up issues as soon as they arise. Don't let them lie hoping things will get better. You're paying for your therapist's time and expertise. Use it.—Nancy, 33

✚ A Clinical View

Primary ISD (Inhibited Sexual Desire) is often seen in victims of rape and is defined as an absence of sexual fantasies and desire for sexual activity. Secondary Inhibited Sexual Desire (ISD) is most commonly the cause of relationship issues.*

Sex Therapists

Sex therapists are mental health professionals who have additional training in human sexuality and who are interested in promoting healthy sexual behavior in their clients.

The national membership organization for sex therapists is the American Association of Sex Educators, Counselors, and Therapists (AASECT).

Locating a Sex Therapist

1. Obtain referrals for three therapists from AASECT, listed at the end of this chapter.

2. Interview the therapists with a 10 to 15-minute phone call to provide them with an overview of your symptoms and goals. Obtain the following information on each therapist in order to help you decide whether to make an appointment for an initial consultation:

   ■ His background, training, and credentials. A graduate degree in psychology or social work, along with further education and training in human sexuality, is recommended.

   ■ His particular method of therapy and experience and success in treating clients with your symptoms.

3. Following your phone interview or initial consultation, reflect on the following to select your therapist:

   ■ Most importantly, did you have a rapport with the therapist? Is he someone you feel you could grow to trust?

   ■ Did he seem to understand the issues and concerns that you brought him?

Reprinted with permission from the Diagnostic and Statistical Manual of Mental Disorders, Fourth Edition, Text Revision. Copyright 2000 American Psychiatric Association.

"Certain positions are very difficult for me emotionally; what can I do?"

✍ A Personal View

I experienced something very similar. I wasn't aware of the correlation between the rape and my discomfort during sex with my husband but at times I felt frightened, at times I felt almost angry.

I was sodomized during the rape and while my husband and I don't do that, we used to have a little play thing we did—he'd turn me over and bite my back. I used to love it but after the rape, turning me over was impossible. There were times when I'd go into fits of giggles, which was really perplexing because when I thought about it, nothing of course was funny, but it was a safe way to get my husband to stop without hurting his feelings. Other times, I'd get this panicky feeling—almost as if I was being pinned down against my will.

Of course had I just said something to my husband he would have turned me over and let me up, but my own embarrassment made this discomfort go on much longer than necessary. I finally said something to my therapist because it was getting really ridiculous not being able to enjoy something that was so intimate and pleasurable to both of us. I had to take about four months to work up my courage because I was shy in speaking with him about this, but once I uncovered that it was a reminder of the emotions I experienced during the rape—a trigger if you will—I was able to communicate that to my husband.

He was shocked that I'd been so uncomfortable for so long but it reinforced for me the importance in speaking with him immediately if things bother me. My husband didn't even make the connection between what happened during the rape and the play things that we do—it's so important to communicate.—Amy, 29

✚ A Clinical View

There are several reasons why certain positions may make you emotionally uncomfortable: You may be engaging in positions that reminded you of the rape, or you may feel a lack of control during lovemaking.

Positions That Remind You of the Rape

It's likely that certain positions remind you of aspects of the rape, however you needn't suffer any longer. There are any number of exciting, fulfilling positions in which you and your partner can engage, however first you must determine which positions cause the most distress.

Think back to the last time you made love and section off your different activities into foreplay and intercourse. Jot down a short note about what took place during foreplay: Any distress here? Were you lying on your side or on your back? Did your husband turn you over at all? What was your first sign of discomfort? Did it stop you cold or could you continue? Were you able to continue making love?

Try to isolate the position or act or moment, if possible, where things became uncomfortable. Awareness is the key. If this is a position you previously enjoyed, desensitization exercises will allow you to return to them. Otherwise, use this opportunity to explore other positions in your lovemaking. Several excellent book and video resources follow.

A Sense of Being Out of Control

I know the effects of rape present constant challenges, and I know it's tiring sometimes to have to continually be reminded of it in some form—even while making love. But, you're a sexual human being and deserving of a fabulous sex life. A sense of being out of control is not unusual following rape—you were most definitely not in control.

Selecting positions where you do have a sense of power is very attainable; the most obvious being that you are on top. If this is not something you engaged in previously, consider this an opportunity to learn something new, if you're comfortable. The most important thing is to remember that there may be times, even further into your recovery, that you need that sense of control. Take the opportunity to build intimacy whenever you can and communicate your needs to your partner.

"I feel so guilty—I responded sexually during the rape. What's wrong with me?"

✍ A Personal View

For the longest period of time, I felt disgusted at myself for having responded in a sexual way during the rape. I was much more difficult on myself than the rapist. I felt that in some way I must have wanted what happened to me but that couldn't have been further from the truth.

It took a number of months of therapy to realize that my response was a biological result to the situation, not a conscious desire on my part to be raped.
—Anna, 23

✚ A Clinical View

Your Sexual Responses

It's important to realize that if you responded during the rape, you are not at fault. Your sexual organs worked as they were designed and nothing more. You responded to physical stimulation, not the person delivering it. You may also be confused as to how you could feel so frightened, yet feel sexual. It's important to understand the physiology of sexual arousal, a subject that's further discussed.

What you are struggling with is common—a number of women report that they either became lubricated or had an orgasm during their rape. This means only that they are sexual human beings, not that they enjoyed it. The guilt and shame that are produced from this aspect of the rape must be addressed.

Our senses are heightened by tactile stimulation; sexual response is heightened by stimulation in the areas of the abdomen, lower extremities and buttocks as stimulation is provided to the same two nerve plexuses.

Of particular interest in terms of trauma is the role of the amygdala, which is associated with fear and pleasure, and the hippocampus, which is associated with rage, sexual arousal, and memory.

Knowing the function of these systems allows us further understanding as to why we may experience sexual arousal during rape. You were stimulated and worked in the way in which you were designed. Nothing more.

If you responded sexually during the rape, you may be feeling a degree of guilt and shame. Resolve to stop this thought process immediately; there is no beneficial result to feeling guilt over your rape. You did nothing wrong.

You, I, everyone you see on the street is a sexual being. Your clitoris does not have a brain but an exquisitely designed set of nerve endings that respond when touched.

Thoughts such as: "If I wasn't wearing that dress . . . If only I hadn't had so much to drink . . . If only I hadn't been alone with him . . ." are statements of guilt—of a particular act you did or did not do. But wearing that dress, drinking that drink, being alone with a man, doesn't give someone license to rape you.

A thought such as: "I'm a bad person because this happened to me . . ." is a statement of shame—it attacks the person that you are. It's longer-lasting and more toxic than guilt and must be addressed.

"How can I tell my husband I'm ready to make love again?"

✍ A Personal View

My therapist and I spent a number of sessions on how to go about approaching the subject of making love again.

I found that the direct approach usually works for me in my normal "everyday" life, but frankly, I was unwilling to face the rejection that I feared if my husband didn't want me. I was in a fragile state at the time but needed to feel like a woman again and return to our sex life.

For me, at the time of my therapy though, an indirect approach worked best: I made reservations at a bed and breakfast that we went to when we were first married and made sure all the things necessary for a wonderful weekend were arranged. And we had the weekend I'd hoped for.

Later I told my husband of my initial fear of his rejection. He put my mind at ease but during our discussion I discovered numerous other issues: Fear of my own reaction was even more heightened. Would having him on top of me remind me of the rape? Would I have a flashback and how would that affect him? How would I feel about being touched? Would I be able to have an orgasm again? A number of questions for which I would have no answer until we were finally in front of each other, making love.

Thankfully, everything did go well for us and I didn't have a flashback. Our discussion that evening lasted into the night and was a breakthrough for us—even more than I had hoped—and was more precious to me than the weekend had been.

Looking back, I wished I'd been more direct and simply told him what I wanted. It allowed us to start talking. Had I to do it over again I would have brought up my fears keeping our discussion on the real issues instead of falling back on the fear of being rejected. It would have benefited us both more.—Carol, 32

✚ A Clinical View

There are only two ways that your partner will know that you are ready to make love to him again: To tell him or to show him.

How do you typically communicate outside the bedroom? How do you typically approach lovemaking? Do you initiate or does your husband? We're the same people after the rape as before—but with a history now of rape, and that brings a new way in which we have to relate to the world—marriage included.

If lack of communication or intimacy was an issue for you in your marriage before the rape, it may be intensified. However, a life-altering experience, such as rape, forces us to look at the world differently; remember, you've been through an extremely stressful situation and in a very real way may have felt as if you would not survive the rape. This oftentimes demonstrates how fragile—and fleeting life is.

Communicating Your Needs

Communicating your needs and wants is imperative to your marriage. There may be a number of reasons that you don't feel comfortable with communicating your needs to your husband, particularly following the rape.

It's helpful to realize the layers of communication we all engage in daily: First, we share general information, the least intimate of our communication. This we share with strangers, family, and our spouse as well. At the other end of the spectrum, sharing our fears and concerns, our most intimate hopes and desires—that which is closest to our hearts—is typically reserved for our spouse. Our needs go unmet when we stay within the confines of lower-level communicating with our spouse, but we have the opportunity to enhance our communication skills every day.

Creating Intimacy

It's very likely that your husband may be allowing you to approach the subject when you feel you're ready. His sensitivity should be acknowledged. Perhaps you feel unsure how the two of you will feel making love the first time following the rape; however, if you're feeling ready, be secure in your feelings that this is the right time for you. Create an atmosphere in which you know he'll respond; perhaps a weekend away for just the two of you.

"I cringe when touched; what can I do?"

✍ A Personal View

I understand completely. I used to cringe as well, every time my husband came near me. I didn't think he noticed and I tried to get back to "normal" but little by little he touched me less. I couldn't articulate that what he was doing—touching my arm, stroking my face, caressing my breast—was killing me inside. My mind had replaced even gentle, loving touches with horrible images of a man I didn't know doing things that were unspeakable. I was out of my mind with worry that he would leave me; we just grew further and further apart.

I happened to notice a magazine on massage in a bookstore one day and picked it up. There was an article on the necessity of touch—not only the touch of lovers, but of a mother's touch. It's that basic, our need for touch. Reading on, I learned that studies have been done that have shown that babies who have been caressed develop differently than those who don't. Our need for touch is primal and basic. I became engrossed in learning about massage and bought several books that taught me how to touch—and be touched—by my husband in ways that we hadn't ever experienced.

It's as if we broke through a wall when we began learning about and giving each other these loving massages and we started opening up in other ways. I'm not certain whether I could have gone to a massage therapist—it didn't even occur to me that I could learn so much without having seen that magazine. Words are great teachers.—Rhonda, 27

✚ A Clinical View

The Necessity of Touch

For women who have been raped, even the slightest touch can trigger memories of the assault. Our logical mind may understand that we're not in a dangerous situation, but the body doesn't forget the assault, the terror, the fear, and so it reacts.

The physiology of our response to touch is intricate and complex and while the following is a simplistic view it nonetheless addresses how touch affects our trauma symptoms. It's also important to recognize that your senses may lead you to become aroused, which is perfectly normal.

The Physiology of Touch

The Central Nervous System

As previously mentioned, our senses are heightened by tactile stimulation. Sexual responses are generated from this sensory response as stimulation is generated by the central nervous system. Sexual response can be heightened by stimulation in the area of the abdomen, lower extremities and buttocks as stimulation is provided to the same two nerve plexuses.

The Parasympathetic and Sympathetic Systems (The Automatic Nervous System)

The parasympathetic system and sympathetic systems control regulatory activities such as heartbeat, digestive, urinary, and reproductive systems. The sympathetic system functions during times of great stress and is responsible for our "flight or fight" reaction, while the parasympathetic system is responsible for our rest and digestion and controls our functioning during normal conditions. These two systems oppose each other to achieve equilibrium. During massage, our parasympathetic control is induced and relaxation and possible sexual response results.

The Hypothalamus, the Amygdala, and the Hippocampus (The Limbic System)

The hypothalamus, the amygdala, and the hippocampus control our emotions and, it is thought, our memory. Of particular interest in terms of trauma is the role of the amygdala, which is associated with fear and pleasure, and the hippocampus, which is associated with rage, sexual arousal, and memory. Knowing the function of these systems allows us further understanding as to why we may experience sexual arousal during massage and at the same time experience intense emotional reactions.

"How can I find a massage therapist who will understand my history?"

✍ A Personal View

Finding a massage therapist that you can trust is as important, I think, as finding a psychotherapist. I interviewed six massage therapists before selecting a woman I liked.

I pre-qualified each massage therapist as belonging to the AMTA. This is important as they have ethical and professional standards. I was up front with all those that I spoke with about my history and paid close attention to their reaction. If they were taken aback, they weren't for me. My role is not to be their on-the-job training for treating trauma victims. If they remained open, I asked about their experience in providing services to women who have been raped. We went on to discuss their success with clients with this history and their success rates. Although several I think were very qualified, it came down to the rapport that I felt with the one I chose.

My first visit was difficult but we worked through it and I continue to go still— it's an excellent way to retrain your body after the rape because the body does remember. —Leah, 39

✚ A Clinical View

Trauma is remembered in the body, making re-learning the benefits of touch an integral part of your healing from the rape. We need the soothing touch of a lover, not only while engaged in intercourse, but in everyday life.

Massage therapists and bodywork specialists are becoming more attuned to, and developing protocol for, the application of massage techniques for trauma victims.

The sensitivity shown by these professionals can facilitate healing. Triggers of memories of the sexual assault, hypervigilance while being touched, extreme sensations, the release of memories, flashbacks, numbing, and dissociation, are but a small number of symptoms for which the massage professional must be aware and prepared.

Touch has been used against us once—or in some cases, many times—and it's sometimes a difficult, lengthy process to regain trust. However, the benefits of massage therapy are numerous, including relieving stress and tension, improving posture, and strengthening the immune system. In addition, massage increases the connection and awareness between mind and body and allows for calmer thinking.

A safe, cohesive treatment plan is the goal for bodywork that you may be considering and for that reason, I can't stress enough the importance of selecting a therapist trained in working with victims of sexual assault. For more detailed information, I've developed a comprehensive method for interviewing massage therapists on my Web site at: www.RapeRecovery.com. If you don't have access to the Internet, please send a self-addressed, stamped envelope to my address and I will send you this information.

The American Massage Therapy Association and the Associated Bodywork & Massage Professionals are two organizations that require high moral and ethical standards from their members.

"I have chronic pain from the rape; can you help?"

✍ A Personal View

Chronic pain can be debilitating, not only during sex but in getting through the day. My lower back was hurt during a sexual assault and robbery. The man threw me on the ground and actually jumped up and down on my pelvis before raping me. Nothing was broken but I was bruised and miserable for months. Sitting, standing, walking—it was all difficult and I had to stop all exercising.

My gynecologist could find nothing wrong but severe bruising and told me I'd have to just have patience and wait to heal. The pain was horrible but the fact that he told me I'd have to take time was just unacceptable so I tried some alternative healing techniques, such as acupuncture.

I learned about a pain management course offered by my HMO that I took. I looked forward to getting on top of the pain—if you're in chronic pain you know what I mean by on top. You know that spot where you can keep yourself before the pain overwhelms you. They taught a number of different strategies but I was unprepared for the first several sessions. I actually, because of the positioning on the floor in which you do the exercises, had several flashbacks. I was able to stay coherent and spoke with the doctor leading the group. He encouraged me to work with it and stayed at my side during the class, helping me remain in the here-and-now.

The class was invaluable and allowed me to get through the remaining months before the pain started to subside.—Martha, 43

✚ A Clinical View

The Definition of Chronic Pain

Chronic pain is pain that continues a month or more past the usual recovery period for a particular illness or injury. It may be intermittent or continuous and extend over a period of months or years. Pain that lasts this amount of time most assuredly takes a toll on your emotional and physical health.

In addition to the economics of being unable to work and continue with your daily activities, sexual life, and exercise, pain takes a frustrating turn in that it's difficult to explain the extent and intensity of your pain to your physician and family. Pain is an intensely personal experience and can't be seen on x-rays or through lab results.

Coping with Chronic Pain

It's felt that the stages of grief that a person works through, denial, anger, bargaining, grief, and acceptance, can be applied to coping with chronic pain as well. While all these stages must be worked through when we're faced with a challenge such as chronic pain, it's important to remember that recovery is circuitous, not linear.

Defining Your Pain

Try to use descriptors when explaining your pain:

- Throbbing, aching, burning, stinging?
- Intermittent or constant?
- What precedes the pain? Where is it located? Does it travel or stay localized?
- Where is the pain and how long have you had it?
- How has the pain affected your life physically? Emotionally?

Pain Management

A number of pain management techniques are available as are classes, alternative medicine, and music for recovery. Please consult the resources at the end of this chapter.

"I have a permanent disability from the rape; can you help?"

✍ A Personal View

My disability from the rape was enough to stop me at one time. In fact, I felt like dying. Nothing could return me to "normal"—I had to learn a different kind of normal; my kind.

I'll be honest, I went through a period of severe self-pity. The kind that makes your stomach burn and makes you so angry you'd like to punch someone. The only problem is the "someone" I wanted to punch was never found. I knew that I had to re-direct my energy or I was going to die from anger and hurt.

Hearing about other people bravely carrying on after being hurt didn't give me solace or even encouragement, it just made me feel more impotent, as if something was missing from me that I didn't have the ability to "rise above" like other people did.

My disability didn't hurt any longer—it was just there—but I took a long look at myself and asked myself if I wanted a life like this. Could I see myself at 65, 70, 75 and see myself without a husband? Without a sexual life? Or was I as entitled as anyone to all the joys that a lover brings? I decided that I was worth it. It was a conscious, fully aware decision. I was—am—worth all that life has to offer. It didn't happen overnight but it's a year and half later and I'm engaged and looking very forward to my honeymoon.

There are tremendous sexual aids for people with disabilities and I've researched all of it. I've learned what makes me feel sensual again and in the process am looking forward to my sexual life with my husband-to-be.—Pat, 26

✚ A Clinical View

I'm terribly sorry that you're suffering a disability as the result of a rape. As you are well aware it takes great courage to continue following this devastating crime. In addition to the emotional healing that you must live through, your physical and sexual concerns must be addressed. A number of resources exist for women with disabilities; you needn't suffer alone a moment longer.

Coping with a Permanent Disability

Because this issue is so highly specialized, and so very important to your emotional and sexual health, I feel very strongly that you be aware of the information available. In a break from the traditional format of this book, I'd like to provide an overview of an excellent resource for your review.

Dr. Mitchell Tepper, Ph.D., M.P.H. is the Founder and President of the Sexual Health Network and SexualHealth.com. On his site, www.sexualhealth.com, Dr. Tepper brings together sexual health experts who address a variety of sexual issues. While the site is extremely valuable for this reason alone, Dr. Tepper in addition provides comprehensive information on sexuality and disability issues, such as:

Adjusting and Adapting, Back Pain, and Body Image, along with Current Research Studies.

"I'm ashamed to take off my clothes because of my scars; how do I feel comfortable again being naked?"

✍ A Personal View (External Scarring)

The scars from my rape could have stopped me cold from going out. I have a large gash from a knife along the side of my cheek—horrible to look at every day and I can't wait to put on my makeup but even that doesn't hide it completely.

Every time I look in the mirror, I'm reminded of the moment when I saw a shiny object coming toward me. I didn't feel any pain at first, I just brought my hand up and blood gushed out.

I couldn't keep thinking about that every day so I decided to try therapy for the scar; to change my physical self was easier than living with the images. The scar therapy that worked the best restored the soft texture to my skin and lightened the redness of the scar remarkably.—Nicki, 26

✚ A Clinical View

External Scar Therapy

Scars can be devastating to our self-esteem, however there are a number of new products that help reduce the visibility and color inherent in scars. New scar therapy products work to soften and smooth the scar, which returns the skin to a more natural texture and color, is safe for sensitive skin, and works on old and new scars alike. Products such as Scar Therapy from Curad have shown to provide tremendous results with external scarring.

"I've been in a great deal of pain and my doctor says I might have scarring from the rape; what can I do?"

✍ A Personal View (Internal Scarring)

It's important that you be checked immediately for scar tissue surrounding the repro-
ductive organs. I found that the infertility I was experiencing was due to the rapist
inserting something that caused injuries.

My doctor wasn't aware of the rape but when I learned there was scar tissue, I
felt I should tell him about my history. He said that he suspected there were a
number of women with scarring from injuries suffered during sexual assaults but
because it's not often talked about, the information doesn't get the exposure it
deserves.

There's help available—I had surgery for removal of some large areas of scar
tissue, then massage therapy that helped relieve the pain and stretch the muscles sur-
rounding the organs. I have a beautiful baby girl now thanks to resolving
this.—Betty, 32

✚ A Clinical View

Internal Scar Therapy

Scarring is formed by trauma, illness, or surgery to tissues that have become inflamed. The tissues shrink, causing restriction in movement and adhesions form which persist after healing.

Pain from internal scarring and adhesions can be treated surgically, however it is felt that pain can also be greatly reduced through the use of deep tissue massage to the affected areas by mobilizing the scar tissue and stretching the connective tissue. This gentle stretching is done over an extended period of time.

Select either a physical therapist or massage therapist specializing in deep muscle tissue therapy and who has advanced training in pelvic and abdominal regions. Share your history of sexual assault with the therapist so that she can be mindful of triggers that may arise.

"My OB/GYN wants to test me for STDs; what are they?"

✍ A Personal View

Ssexually transmitted diseases (STDs) can be devastating. This is a personal plea: Please don't hesitate to be tested. It's imperative that you begin treatment immediately if you or your doctor believe you may have contracted an STD.

A close relative contracted syphilis during a sexual assault and was never tested for STDs. She suffered grave neurological consequences and was hospitalized for the remainder of her tragically short life. This need not have happened to her—please, if you suspect that there's any hint that you may be infected, please see your doctor or visit a clinic immediately.—Teddi, 44

✚ A Clinical View

Sexually transmitted diseases (STDs) are infections spread by secretions or fluids from the skin and mucosal surfaces of the genitals. Common STDs are chlaymydia, gonorrhea, syphilis, and herpes simplex virus (HSV-2).

Symptoms are as follows:

Chlaymydia

- NOTE: Chylaymydia can lead to infertility; it's imperative that you be tested following your rape
- Diagnosed with a culture
- Vaginal discharge and lower abdominal pain in women
- Penile discharge and burning upon urination in men

Gonorrhea

- Diagnosed with a culture
- Vaginal discharge and lower abdominal pain in women
- Penile discharge and burning upon urination in men

Syphilis

- Diagnosed with a blood test
- Painless genital ulcers in early stages
- Rash, sore joints, swollen lymph nodes and neurological damage in later stages

Herpes Simplex Virus

- Painful skin ulcers on genitalia of both sexes and in the vagina in women
- Fever and swollen lymph glands in groin (typically found in the first occurrence of herpes)
- Ulcers (in subsequence occurrences of herpes)

"My doctor diagnosed vaginismus; what is it and what can I do about it?"

✍ A Personal View

Vaginismus is intense vaginal muscle spasms when something is inserted. My diagnosis of vaginismus provided a temporary sense of relief—finally the intense pain I felt when my husband and I started making love again following the rape was given a name.

Still, my relief was short-lived. Now that I knew what I had, I had to work on the cure. I had intense muscle spasms as soon as my husband's penis came anywhere near me. We were patient for a while, feeling that it was a just a matter of time for me to relax, trying primarily relaxation massages. I was growing more and more impatient though because I'd told my husband, and truly did believe, that after intense therapy and a long period of time since the rape, I was ready to make love again.

But my body was belying the fact and even I began questioning myself. I asked my therapist for a referral to a sex therapist thinking that perhaps I had some underlying remnants from my rape that I hadn't resolved. She suggested a vaginal dilator, told me the results I might expect and then referred me back to my OB/GYN for a prescription and instruction in its use and regular appointments for follow-up.

It was extremely helpful to see the sex therapist as well, as we worked out more issues.

I was able to make love with my husband after only three weeks on this therapy but continued using the dilators for another year and a half.—Cherie, 32

I was able to make love with my husband after only three weeks on this therapy but continued using the dilators for another year and a half.—Cherie, 32

✚ A Clinical View

The Definition of Vaginismus

Vaginismus is a muscle spasm that occurs in the outer third of the vagina, often triggered by the anticipation of pain, making insertion of any object difficult.

It's important to realize that not only women who have been assaulted suffer from vaginismus. Because other disorders may be the underlying cause of vaginismus, it's important that all other disorders be ruled out by your gynecologist and if he's unaware of your sexual assault it's important to share this information with him.

I know it's difficult to divulge information such as this if your physician isn't aware of your history, however in this case it's important that he be able to refer you to someone who can help you with this specialized problem.

Coping with Vaginismus

Vaginismus can be very successfully treated, once diagnosed. A sex therapist is often the professional to use in guiding you during your recovery.

The goal is for the muscles surrounding the vagina to become less tense by inserting, first a small object, then increasing the size. Fingers and vaginal dilators are used to slowly condition the vaginal muscles to relax during penetration.

Because vaginismus has been found to be so prevalent in sexual assault victims it is often suggested that you combine treatment for vaginismus with psychotherapy in order to resolve any lingering symptoms from the rape. I'd like to stress that undertaking psychotherapy and considering a sex therapist for this type of work does not mean that the vaginismus is "in your head." Vaginismus is a physical disorder that can be treated; select a sex therapist specially trained to work with rape victims in conjunction with your therapy.

Use this opportunity to learn more about your body and how you respond to your partner. Prior to using the vaginal dilator, take a hot bath for 15 to 30 minutes in order to relax your muscles. Engage your partner in the use of the vaginal dilator, using liberal amounts of lubricants. The act of helping you overcome vaginismus can be a goal for both of you to share and can enhance your intimacy.

Resources for Your Sexual Healing

☎ General Resources

American Massage Therapy Association
Phone (847) 864-0123

American Pain Society
Phone: (847) 375-4715

American Physical Therapy Association (Scar Therapy)
Phone: (703) 684-2782

Americans with Disabilities (Department of Justice)
Phone: (800) 514-0301 (voice) or (800) 514-0383 (TTY)

Associated Bodywork & Massage Professionals
Phone: (800) 458-2267

California Association of Marriage and Family Therapists
Phone: (858) 292-2638

Center for Creative Growth
Phone: (510) 527-2100

Center for Research on Women with Disabilities (CROWD)
Phone: (800) 44-CROWD

Consortium for Citizens with Disabilities, The
Phone: (202) 785-3388

Kinsey Institute, The
Phone: (812) 855-7686

National Foundation for the Treatment of Pain, The
Phone: (831) 655-8812

Trager Institute, The
Phone: (216) 896-9383

Women's Therapy Center
Phone: (516) 576-1118

🖱 Internet Resources

1001 Ways To Be Romantic
    www.1001waystoberomantic.com/home.html

AfraidtoAsk.com
    www.afraidtoask.com/std.html

American Association of Sex Educators, Counselors, and Therapists
www.aasect.org

American Massage Therapy Association
www.amtamassage.org

American Medical Women's Association
www.amwa-doc.org

American Pain Foundation
www.painfoundation.org

American Pain Society
www.ampainsoc.org

American Physical Therapy Association
www.apt.org

Americans With Disabilities (Department of Justice)
www.usdoj.gov/crt/ada/adahoml.htm

Associated Bodywork & Massage Professionals
www.abmp.com

Association of Reproductive Health Professionals
www.arhp.org

A Woman's Touch
www.a-womans-touch.com

California Association of Marriage and Family Therapists
www.camft.org

Center for Creative Growth
www.creativegrowth.com

Center for Research on Women with Disabilities
www.bcm.tmc.edu/crowd

Clear Passage Therapist
www.clearpassage.com

Curad
www.curad.com/scar_main.asp

Dr. Glazer's Vulvodynia.com
www.vulvodynia.com

Eve's Garden
www.evesgarden.com

Good Vibrations
www.goodvibes.com

HealthyPlace.com
www.healthyplace.com

Kinsey Institute, The
www.indiana.edu/~kinsey

National Foundation for the Treatment of Pain, The
www.paincare.org

Pain.com
www.pain.com

SexualHealth.com
www.sexualhealth.com

Sexuality.org
www.sexuality.org

Sinclair Intimacy Institute
www.intimacyinstitute.com

The Consortium for Citizens with Disabilities
www.c-c-d.org

Thrive Online
www.thriveonline.oxygen.com/sex/ourbodies/ourbodies.sexuality6.html

Trager Institute, The
www.trager.com

WebMD
www.my.webmd.com

Wendy Maltz, MSW
www.healthysex.com

Women's Therapy Center
www.womentc.com

📖 Book & Pamphlet Resources

1998 Guidelines for Treatment of Sexually Transmitted Diseases
By Centers for Disease Control

An Easy Guide to Loving Carefully for Men and Women
By Lyn McKee, Winifred Kempton, Lynn Stiggall-Muccigrosso

A Woman's Guide to Overcoming Sexual Fear and Pain
   By Aurelie Jones Goodwin; Marc E. Agronin, M.D.

Becoming Orgasmic: A Sexual and Personal Growth Program for Women
   By Julia Heiman, Joseph Lopiccolo

Best Sex You'll Ever Have, The: 101 Exciting Positions for Ecstatic Sexual Fulfillment
   By Richard Emerson

Book of Massage: The Complete Step-By-Step Guide to Eastern and Western Techniques
   By Lucy Lidell

Choices: Sex in the Age of STDs
   By Jeffery A. Nevid

Color Atlas and Synopsis of Sexually Transmitted Diseases
   By H. Hunter Hansfield, M.D.

Compassionate Touch: The Body's Role in Emotional Healing and Recovery
   By Clyde W. Ford

Culture of Shame
   By Andrew P. Morrison

Dance of Intimacy, The: A Woman's Guide to Courageous Acts of Change in Key Relationships
   By Harriet Lerner

Discover Your Sensual Potential: A Woman's Guide to Guaranteed Satisfaction
   By Barbara Keesling

Erotic Passions: A Guide to Orgasmic Massage, Sensual Bathing, Oral Pleasuring, and Ancient Sexual Positions
   By Kenneth Ray Stubbs

Fear of Intimacy
   By Robert W. Firestone, Joyce Catlett

For Yourself: The Fulfillment of Female Sexuality
   By Lonnie Barbach, Ph.D.

Good Hands: Massage Techniques for Total Health
   By Robert Bahr

Good Marriage, The: How and Why Love Lasts
   By Judith S. Wallerstein, Sandra Blakeslee

Reflexology for Women: Restore Harmony and Balance Through Precise Massaging Techniques
By Nicola M. Hall

Romantic Massage
By Randy Nikola

Secret Sexual Positions: Ancient Techniques for Modern Lovers
By Kenneth Ray Stubbs

Self-Therapy for Sex Problems
By Daniel Steele

Sensual Sex: Arousing Your Sense and Deepening the Passion in Your Relationship
By Beverly Engel, Ph.D.

Sexual Healing Journey, The: A Guide for Survivors of Sexual Abuse
By Wendy Maltz, MSW

Sexuality and Chronic Illness
By Leslie R. Schover, Soren Buus Jensen

Sexually Transmitted Diseases: A Physician Tells You What You Need to Know
By Lisa Marr

Sexual Positions: Games Lovers Play
By Rosie Hughes

Sexual Positions (The Joy of Sex Series)
By Alex Comfort

Shame and Guilt: Masters of Disguise
By Jane Middelton-Moz

SUPER MASSAGE Simple Techniques for Instant Relaxation
By Gordon Inkeles, Sigga Bjornsson

Tappan's Handbook of Healing Massage Techniques: Classic, Holistic, And Emerging Methods
By Frances M. Tappan, Patricia J. Benjamin

To See Differently
By Dr. Susan Trout

Trauma and Recovery
By Judith Lewis Herman, M.D.

Truth About Love, The: The Highs, the Lows, and How You Can Make It Last Forever
By Patricia Love

Two Sides of Love, The: What Strengthens Affection, Closeness and Lasting Commitment
By Gary Smalley, John T. Trent

Understanding and Letting Go of Guilt
By Lucy Freeman, Herbert S. Strean

Understanding Your Referral to a Sex Therapist
By Robert W. Birch

Use of Massage in Facilitating Holistic Health: Physical and Mental Effects, the Nature of Massage and the Techniques for Application
By Robert Henley Woody

Vaginismus
By Linda Valins

When a Woman's Body Says No to Sex: Understanding and Overcoming Vaginismus
By Linda Valins

Why Do I Feel Guilty When I've Done Nothing Wrong?
By Ty C. Colber

Why People Don't Heal and How They Can
By Carolyn Myss, Ph.D.

Women With Physical Disabilities: Achieving and Maintaining Health and Well-Being
By Danuta M. Krotoski, Margaret A. Nosek

▦ Video Resources

Better Sex Video Series
Partners in Healing
By Wendy Maltz, MSW

Passionate Marriage™: Keeping Love and Intimacy Alive in Committed Relationships
By David Schnarch, Ph.D.

Relearning Touch
By Wendy Maltz, MSW

The Great Sex Series
By Dr. Frank Sommers, Pathway Productions, P.O. Box 1033, Station F, Toronto, Ontario M4Y 2T7, (416) 922-4506

5

Family & Friends

Following her rape, you are the most important person to your wife, your lover, your daughter, your mother, your friend. You hold an important key to how she will recover from this most intrusive crime that's been committed against her. Ask her what she needs at this time, and then provide it.

Go easy on yourself as well. This is a difficult situation for any relationship, one that no one should have to face; I'm truly sorry that you must walk this road.

"My wife is in so much pain and all I feel is rage; what can I do to help her—and myself?"

✍ A Personal View

I understand completely the feelings of rage. I can't even tell you how angry I am over my wife's rape. I see red sometimes—I actually see red. It's the most difficult thing in the world to sit and watch her have a nightmare or flashback and feel completely impotent to help. I hold her when she wakes up crying but all I want to do is break the neck of the guy who raped her.

And when I do say something to her I only make it worse so I keep it inside. I know I can do nothing to help her. I realized that I had to have some other outlet for this rage—I was only adding to her pain.

I went into therapy myself. I see her therapist with her once every other week and then I see him on my own every week. It's made a tremendous difference being able to speak frankly with someone—other than my wife—about my fantasies of what I'd like to do to this guy. And it helps to speak with a male therapist, I think, because he knows where I'm coming from.

I know I'd never do anything physical to another human being—and certainly nothing that would put my wife or myself in jeopardy, but it's a great release to be able to get this stuff off my chest. Your wife has enough to deal with; it's important to you and to her to find another outlet for your rage.—Ray, 33

My husband assumed I wanted to be alone. I'm not certain why he thought that, but in retrospect, I realize that we never really talked about the rape. He never asked me what I wanted, and I never told him. The last thing I wanted was to be left alone. —Catherine, 28

I have to admit that I want my wife, Catherine, to be better. I want her the way she was—funny, spontaneous, loving. She seems like a different person and I don't know what to do. I know I seem shallow and impatient but I'm at the end of my ability to handle what she's going through. —Mike, 46

✛ A Clinical View

Her Time Frame for Recovery

Unfortunately, there is no timetable for the recovery of rape. She may be "better" in a month; certainly some of her more acute systems may have subsided. She may be "better" in a year. The problem is, no one can tell. She's going to have to heal at her rate, based on the person that she is.

What You Can Do To Help

Be compassionate and empathetic to what she's been through. Compassion can be defined as literally suffering with another and feeling sorrow over their misfortune. What she's been through is a horrible event; there are no shortcuts to healing from rape and she'll face it in her own time. Be patient.

It's perfectly natural to want to "fix" the situation. Men in particular are doers and feel that *some* action should be taken. Listen to her without judging. Encourage her to talk to you and to a therapist or mental health provider. The sooner she forms a relationship of trust with a therapist and they begin work on her issues of anger, guilt, shame, and loss, the less likely long-term symptoms will develop. Encourage her to write or engage in some sort of creative outlet to express her feelings.

"Would therapy be effective in helping my wife get better? Should I go?"

✍ A Personal View

It's important for you to ask your wife what she would like. She's going through a lot herself now and she may feel that she needs to take care of your feelings too. She needs to be listened to, to be respected, and to know that she wasn't at fault. At all costs, she needs to know that.

Has she been in therapy on her own for long? Has she said that she'd like you there? I'd ask her first, and tell her you'd be happy to go and then if after a couple of sessions she'd like you to stop coming for awhile, don't be hurt or angry at her.

This happened with my wife and I thought it might be best to have a couple more sessions with her therapist to discuss my feelings after I stopped, so that they didn't spill over onto her. It's a difficult situation you both need to find your way with.—Mark, 34

✛ A Clinical View

Therapy may help your wife immensely. It's important that she be in control of the decision-making process regarding selection of a therapist, however she would probably appreciate your assistance in locating a list of therapists and narrowing down choices.

How to Help Her Locate a Therapist

Suggest that your wife read Chapter 2 of this book, which provides an overview of therapy, different types of therapists, and how to locate a therapist. She may be particularly upset (and this is to be expected) if she is still within a month of the rape and may find it difficult to make decisions.

If this is the case, but she does express a desire to move forward or if she asks for your help, obtain referrals from the professional organizations provided herein or a local rape crisis center.

1. Interview the therapists with a 10 to 15-minute phone call to provide them with an overview of your symptoms and goals. Obtain the following information on each therapist in order to help you and your wife decide whether to make an appointment for an initial consultation:

   - His background, training, and credentials.
   - His particular method of therapy and experience and success in treating clients with your wife's symptoms.

2. Following your phone interview or initial consultation, take the time to speak with your wife and reflect on the following to help her select her therapist:

   - Most importantly, did she experience good rapport with the therapist? Is he someone she feels she can grow to trust? Was she comfortable speaking with him about her symptoms?
   - Did he seem to understand the issues and concerns that she brought him?
   - Was he open to the two of you attending therapy as a couple (if this is something she wishes to do)? Did he have suggestions or recommendations for simultaneous individual counseling for either of you?

"I blame myself for not protecting my wife; does she?"

🔊 A Personal View

I can relate very well to your feelings. I'm not certain who I was more angry with—the man who raped my wife or myself for not being there to protect her.

I can't tell you the sleepless nights I had just going over and over and over in my mind what he did to her and blaming myself for being away on a business trip.

We talked this over a number of times and while she said she didn't blame me, I did. It's my duty as a husband—I know that sounds almost medieval—to protect my wife. I had failed her. I'm a person who likes to take action though, as I suspect lots of guys are, and it wasn't good enough for her to just say no, no, no—she wasn't blaming me and that everything was okay. I started by having an alarm system put in our house—then I put into place a Neighborhood Watch program.

Lastly, I started taking self-defense courses with her so that if I wasn't around she could have a fighting chance. I have to tell you—this attack scared me to death. I'd do anything to protect my wife and keep it from happening again.—Tom, 44

✛ A Clinical View

Over-Protectiveness Following Your Wife's Rape

Only another man can know how you feel after your wife's rape, however it's not unusual to be overly protective. We live in today's society based on a set of rules and one of the rules that most of us prescribe to is that a husband takes care of his wife. The need to fulfill the role of protector is one which you seem to take very seriously, however you were not to blame in any way, shape, or form for her rape. It's natural to want to exact revenge, find the rapist and serve your own justice; however, while those feelings are normal, your wife needs your support and guidance at this time, not to feel as if she must take care of your feelings as well as her own.

Helping Her Learn to Protect Herself

It's important that you take constructive steps to help your wife learn how to protect herself. This can include some of the following suggestions:

1. Ask her if she would like to take self-defense classes, either on her own or with you. I'd suggest going together as a couple, if she's amenable, as it allows you both time to process this event in your life and provides a sense of togetherness; you're working together to protect her.

2. Discuss issues of safety with your wife; along with your options. Concentrate first on the location and time your wife was raped. Did the rape occur in your home during the day? Perhaps a security alarm would provide you both with a measure of security.

3. Discuss forming a neighborhood watch program with your wife. Police departments typically have Crime Prevention Divisions that are happy to help you establish the particulars of a program such as this.

4. Discuss your feelings with your therapist if you're currently in therapy, or perhaps a friend or support group. Your feeling of being to blame should be processed and resolved so that you can both move past this extremely difficult period. Again, I think it's important to talk with another man about these issues for support and perspective.

5. Help her gain control over her life, first in small ways, then in larger, more signifiant ways. Encourage her to do things that will help her gain confidence in her decisions.

"My sister is in serious denial about her eating disorder; what can I do to help her?"

✍ A Personal View

My sister also had real difficult following her rape. She just stopped eating. She said that she just didn't feel like eating anymore—it's as if all her pain, all her anger, was turned right back onto herself. She suffered so much—it was difficult even being around her.

I tried to speak with her about it, tried all the things that I'd read that you should do to try and get anorexics to see themselves as they really are in order for them to get help. Nothing worked.

Finally she fainted and was hospitalized, first to return her to some semblance of health and then admitted to an in-patient program. She's eating now and gaining weight but she's in out-patient therapy working on her feelings from the rape.

She'd always had high goals for herself—a perfectionist in a way—and since learning about anorexia it doesn't surprise me that this is how the feelings about the rape have manifested. In her mind she was no longer "perfect"—she was damaged. She couldn't have been more wrong. Her family and friends love her more than she will ever realize and would do anything to have kept this from happening.

I could have done more to learn the facts and try to get professional help sooner. Don't wait—it could mean her life. —Jay, 31

✚ A Clinical View

You don't specify the type of eating disorder that your sister is suffering from; however, whether anorexia, bulimia, or compulsive overeating, an eating disorder can be extremely difficult on the entire family.

The intricacies of an eating disorder of a woman who has been raped are very complex and the reasons they develop following rape, numerous. For example, a woman who develops anorexia may be attempting to gain control over her body to compensate for the lack of control she had during the rape.

A woman who develops bulimia may be attempting to alleviate the pain and intense emotion of having been raped by forcing the food down. A woman who develops bulimia of a purging type may be attempting to release these intense emotions.

And finally, a woman who compulsively overeats may be attempting to change her body in order to avoid future rapes. In her mind she may believe that it was her body that invited the rape.

"I suspect that my daughter is deliberately hurting herself; I'm afraid for her. What can I do?"

✍ A Personal View

You must become educated about your daughter's problem now. I discovered my daughter's "cutting" ritual one evening after she fell asleep on the couch. She was in therapy for sexual assault that went on for a long period of time that neither her father nor I were aware of and we thought she was doing well. She was returning to her self—she was always a great girl, worked hard, and she has a wonderful personality and several close friends she began seeing again.

I was covering her with a blanket that evening after she fell asleep watching television and her arm dropped over the edge. Her sweater caught and exposed her arms. I was devastated. Shocked. In total disbelief—I'd had no knowledge of what was going on in my own home. I didn't say anything that evening but stayed up all evening researching self-injury. I knew I had to get help for her fast and called her therapist early the next morning.

I've read everything I can find on self-injury and know why she's doing it. At least for her it's out in the open to us and to her therapist so that we're all working together to help her. There are a number of good books and support groups for you as a parent—become educated now. Don't judge her—take action. —Doris, 50

✚ A Clinical View

It's distressing to learn that your daughter may be engaging in self-injury behaviors, however the fact that you've noticed alarming evidence of her problem means that you'll be able to help her now.

The Definition of Self-Injury

Also known as self-harm and cutting, self-mutilation is more common in rape victims than one would think. Those who partake in self-mutilation do it in order to feel something—anything, to cope with powerful feelings and emotions, and to punish oneself for being "bad," which is often the result of shame and guilt.

Self-mutilation is a deliberate act but one typically not designed to commit suicide and is usually moderate, but the point is still to hurt oneself. Acts of self-mutilation include cutting, pinching, and burning oneself. Ways that your daughter can learn to cope with self-injury can be found in "Physical Healing." Help her locate a therapist if she's at all amenable.

Resources for Family & Friends

☎ General Resources

American Anorexia/Bulimia Association, Inc. (AABA)
Phone: (212) 575-6200

American Association for Marriage and Family Therapy
Phone: (202) 452-0109

American Psychological Association
Phone: (800) 964-2000

Association of Traumatic Stress Specialists
Phone: (803) 781-0017

BAMM/IMPACT Self-Defense
Phone: (800) 77-FIGHT

Capital City Model Mugging/IMPACT
Phone: (916) 636-8580

Eating Disorders Awareness and Prevention, Inc. (EDAP)
Phone: (206) 382-3587

Eating Disorders Coalition
Phone: (202) 543-3842

Full Circle @ Cross Train Concepts
Phone: (206) 782-2199

IMPACT Personal Safety, Inc.
Phone: (800) 345-5425

Overeaters Anonymous
Phone: (505) 891-2664

PREPARE, INC.
Phone: (800) 442-7273

⊕ Internet Resources

AAMFT Couples Therapy with Traumatized Partners
www.aamft.org

American Anorexia/Bulimia Association, Inc. (AABA)
www.aabainc.org/familyfriends/index.html

Association of Traumatic Stress Specialists, The
www.atss-hq.com

BAMM/IMPACT Self-Defense
www.bamm.org

Eating Disorders Awareness and Prevention, Inc. (EDAP)
www.edap.org

Eating Disorders Coalition
www.eatingdisorderscoalition.org

Madison Institute of Medicine, Inc.
www.factsforhealth.org

Martial Hearts, Inc.
www.martialhearts.com

Overeaters Anonymous
www.overeatersanonymous.org

Pittsburgh Action Against Rape
www.paar.net

PREPARE, Inc.
www.prepareinc.com

RelationshipWeb.com
www.relationshipweb.com

Secondary Survivors
www.latebloomerpublishing.com/secondary_survivors.htm

Self Injury Site: A Healing Touch
www.healthyplace.com/Communities/Self_Injury/healingtouch

TherapistFinder
www.TherapistFinder.net

📖 Book Resources

After Sexual Assault: How Can I Help? A Guide for Friends and Family
By Shelley Sandow, Women's Services

A Guide to Psychotherapy
By Gerald Amada, Ph.D.

A Life Without Fear
By Laura Martin

Anorexia Nervosa: A Guide for Suffers and Their Families
  By R.L. Palmer

Beauty Bites Beast: Awakening the Warrior Within Women and Girls
  By Ellen Snortland

Beyond Sympathy: What to Say and Do for Someone Suffering an Injury, Illness or Loss
  By Janice Harris Lord, Eugene D. Wheeler (Editor)

Beyond the Darkness
  By C. Kubetin, J.D. Mallory

Bodily Harm: The Breakthrough Treatment Program for the Self-Injurer
  By Karen Conterio; Wendy Lader, Ph.D.; Jennifer Bloom

Bulimia: A Guide for Family and Friends
  By Roberta Trattner Sherman, Ron A. Thompson, Robert Trattner Sherman

Choosing an Online Therapist: A Step-By-Step Guide to Finding Professional Help on the Web
  By Gary S. Stofle

Death Wishes? The Understanding and Management of Deliberate Self-Harm
  By H. Morgan

Exploding the Myth of Self-Defense: A Survival Guide for Every Woman
  By Judith Fein, Ph.D.

Father Hunger: Fathers, Daughters, and Food
  By Margo Maine

Freedom from Fear Forever
  By Dr. James V. Durlacher, Roger J. Callahan, Guy McGill

Free of the Shadows: Recovering From Sexual Violence
  By Caren Adams, Jennifer Fay

Gift of Fear, The: Survival Signs that Protect Us From Violence
  By Gavin DeBecker

Her Wits About Her: Self-Defense Success Stories by Women
  By Denise Caignon, Gail Groves

If She is Raped: A Book for Husbands, Fathers, and Male Friends
  By Alan W. McEvoy, Jeff B. Brookings

I Hate You—Don't Leave Me!
  By J. Kreisman, H. Straus

Like Mother, Like Daughter: How Women are Influenced by Their Mother's Relationship with Food and How to Break the Pattern
By Debra Waterhouse

Lovers and Survivors: A Partner's Guide to Living With and Loving a Sexual Abuse Survivor
By S. Yvette de Beixedon, Ph.D.

Partners in Healing: A Handbook for Partners of Rape Survivors
By Teri Platt

Portable Therapist, The
By Susanna McMahon

Recovery: How to Survive Sexual Assault for Women, Men, Teenagers, and Their Friends and Families
By Helen Benedict

Stopping Rape: A Challenge For Men
By Rus Ervin Funk

Surviving an Eating Disorder: New Perspectives and Strategies for Family and Friends
By Michele Siegel, Judith Brisman, Margot Weinshel

Trust After Trauma: A Guide to Relationships for Survivors and Those Who Love Them
By Aphrodite Matsakis, Ph.D.

When You Are the Partner of a Rape or Incest Survivor: A Workbook for You
By Robert Barry Levine

⊙⊙ Video Resources

Partners Surviving: My Partner Was Sexually Abused
By Partners in Video

Section III

Resources

Great care has been taken in selecting the following resources, however please be aware that the information provided is simply a guide. Please visit my Web site at RapeRecovery.com for updates.

☎ General Resources

Art Therapy

American Art Therapy Association, Inc., The
Phone: (888) 290-0878

Northern California Art Therapy Association
Phone: (415) 522-3915

Campus Rape

Campus Outreach Services
Phone: (610) 989-0651

Safe Campuses Now
Phone: (706) 354-1115

Security On Campus, Inc.
Phone: (610) 768-9330

Chronic Pain

American Pain Society
Phone: (847) 375-4715

National Foundation for the Treatment of Pain, The
Phone: (831) 655-8812

National Woman's Health Information Center, The
Phone: (800) 994-WOMAN / (800) 994-9662

Criminal Justice

National Center for Victims of Crime, The
Phone: (800) FYI-CALL

National Crime Victim Bar Association, The
Phone: (703) 276-0960

National Organization for Victim Assistance, The
Phone: (800) TRY-NOVA

Office for Victims of Crime Resource Center
Phone: (800) 627-6872

Date Rape Drugs

DC Rape Crisis Center
Phone: (202) 232-0789

National Clearinghouse For Alcohol and Drug Information
Phone: (800) 729-6686

Texas Department of Public Safety
Phone: (512) 424-2000

Depression

National Depressive and Manic Depressive Association
Phone: (800) 826-3632

National Institutes of Health (Depression Information)
Phone: (800) 421-4211

National Institute of Mental Health
Phone: (301) 443-4513

Disabilities

Americans with Disabilities
Phone: (800) 514-0301 (voice) / (800) 514-0383 (TTY)

Center for Research on Women with Disabilities (CROWD)
Phone: (800) 44-CROWD

Consortium for Citizens with Disabilities, The
Phone: (202) 785-3388

Dissociation

International Society for the Study of Dissociation, The
Phone: (847) 480-0899

Dreams and Nightmares

American Board of Sleep Medicine, The
Phone: (507) 287-9819

Association for the Study of Dreams, The
Phone: (209) 724-0889

Eating Disorders

Healthy Within, Inc.
Phone: (858) 622-0221

International Association of Eating Disorders Professionals
Phone: (602) 934-3024

Overeaters Anonymous
Phone: (505) 891-2664

EMDR Therapy Resources

EMDR Institute, Inc.
Phone: (831) 372-3900

EMDRIA (EMDR International Association)
Phone: (512) 451-5200

Group Therapy

American Group Psychotherapy Association
Phone: (877) 668-2472

King County Sexual Assault Resource Center
Phone: (425) 226-5062

Intimacy

American Association for Marriage and Family Therapy
Phone: (202) 452-0109

California Association of Marriage and Family Therapists
Phone: (858) 292-2638

Sinclair Intimacy Institute
Phone: (800) 955-0888

Massage Therapy

American Massage Therapy Association
Phone: (888) 843-2682

Associated Bodywork & Massage Professionals
Phone: (800) 458-2267

Trager Institute, The
Phone: (216) 896-9383

Medical Information

Centers for Disease Control - National HIV/AIDS Hotline
Phone: (800) 342-AIDS

National Center for Victims of Crime, The
Phone: (202) 467-8700

National Health Information Center
Phone: (800) 336-4797

National Institutes of Health AIDS Treatment
Phone: (888) 826-9438

National Woman's Health Information Center, The
Phone: (800) 994-WOMAN or (800) 994-9662

National Women's Health Network
Phone: (202) 628-7814

National Women's Resource Center
Phone: (800) 354-8824

Panic Disorders

Anxiety Disorders Association of America
Phone: (301) 231-9350

National Anxiety Foundation
Phone: (606) 272-7166

NIMH Anxiety Disorders Education Program
NIMH Public Inquiries
Phone: (301) 443-4513

Pregnancy

Association for Pre- & Perinatal Psychology and Health
Phone: (707) 857-4041

Rape Crisis Intervention

RAINN (Rape Abuse and Incest National Network)
Phone: (800) 656-HOPE (4673)

Rape Treatment Center (Santa Monica, CA)
Phone: (310) 319-4000

University of Minnesota
Phone: (800) 779-8636

Rape-Related Pregnancy

Association for Pre- & Perinatal Psychology and Health
Phone: (707) 857-4041

Rape Assistance and Awareness Program (RAAP) of Denver
Phone: (303) 329-9922

Rape Trauma

Alaska Network on Domestic Violence and Sexual Assault
Phone: (800) 478-1090

American Counseling Association
Phone: (703) 823-9800

American Psychological Association
Phone: (800) 374-2721

Brazos County Rape Crisis Center (Bryan, Texas)
Phone: (979) 731-1000

California Coalition Against Sexual Assault
Phone: (916) 446-2520

Center for Mental Health Services (CMHS)
Phone: (800)-789-2647

Center for Women's Policy Studies
Phone: (202) 872-1770

Indiana Coalition Against Sexual Assault
Phone: (800) 691-2272

International Society for Traumatic Stress Studies
Phone: (847) 480-9028

Kentucky Association of Sexual Assault Programs, Inc.
Phone: (502) 226-2704

Louisiana Foundation Against Sexual Assault
Phone: (985) 345-5995

National Institute of Mental Health
Phone: (301) 443-4513

National Organization for Victim Assistance
Phone: (202) 232-6682

PTSD Alliance
Phone: (877) 507-PTSD

Rape, Abuse & Incest National Network (RAINN)
Phone: (800) 656-HOPE

Rape Crisis Center of Central Massachusetts
Phone: (508) 799-5700

SafePlace of Austin
Phone: (512) 267-SAFE

Sexual Assault & Trauma Resource Center of Rhode Island
Phone: (401) 421-4100

Sidran Traumatic Stress Foundation
Phone: (410) 825-8888

South Carolina Coalition Against Domestic Violence and Sexual Assault
Phone: (800) 260-9293

Standing Together Against Rape (Anchorage, AK)
Phone: (907) 276-7279

Wisconsin Coalition Against Sexual Assault
Phone: (608) 257-1516

Scar Therapy

American Physical Therapy Association
Phone: (703) 684-2782

Self Defense

BAMM/IMPACT Self-Defense
Phone: (800) 77-FIGHT

Capital City Model Mugging
Phone: (916) 636-8580

Martial Hearts
Phone: (770) 640-6986

PREPARE, INC.
Phone: (800) 345-5425

Self-Harm

American Association of Suicidology
Phone: (202) 237-2280 / (800) SUICIDE (784-2433)

SAFE Alternatives (Residential program for self-injurers)
Phone: (800) DONTCUT / (800) 366-8288

Self-Help

Brazos County Rape Crisis Center (Bryan, Texas)
Phone: (979) 731-1000

Self-Help Network of Kansas
Phone: (316) 978-3843

Sexual Dysfunction

Marriage & Family Health Center, The
Phone: (303) 670-2630

Masters and Johnson
Phone: (636) 532-9772

Sexuality

American Association for Sex Educators, Counselors & Therapists
Phone: (319) 895-6203

Kinsey Institute, The
Phone: (812) 855-7686

Masters and Johnson
Phone: (636) 532-9772

Sinclair Intimacy Institute
Phone: (800) 955-0888, ext. 8NET2

Sexually Transmitted Diseases

American Medical Women's Association
Phone: (703) 838-0500

Association of Reproductive Health Professionals
Phone: (202) 466-3825

National STD Hotline
Phone: (800) 227-8922

Substance Abuse

Cocaine Anonymous
Phone: (800) 347-8998

National Clearinghouse for Alcohol and Drug Information
Phone: (800) 729-6686

National Cocaine Hotline
Phone: (800) 262-2463

Support Groups

Self-Help Network of Kansas
Phone: (316) 978-3843

Therapy

American Association for Marriage and Family Therapy
Phone: (202) 452-0109

American Association of Sex Educators, Counselors, and Therapists
Phone: (319) 895-8407

American Counseling Association
Phone: (703) 823-9800

American Psychological Association
Phone: (800) 964-2000

Association for Advancement of Behavior Therapy
Phone: (212) 647-1890

Association for Humanistic Psychology
Phone: (510) 769-6495

California Association of Marriage and Family Therapists
Phone: (858) 292-2638

Center for Mental Health Services (CMHS)
Phone: (800)-789-2647

International Association of Traumatic Stress Specialists
Phone: (803) 781-0017

Vaginismus

Center for Sexual and Marital Health
Phone: (732) 235-4273

Women's Therapy Center (Santa Monica, CA)
Phone: (516) 576-1118

📖 Book Resources

Art Therapy

Art and Healing: Using Expressive Art to Heal Your Body, Mind, and Spirit
By Barbara Ganim, Michael Samuels, Mary Rockwood Lane

Art as Medicine
By Shaun McNiff

Art Is a Way of Knowing
By Pat B. Allen

Art Therapy Sourcebook, The
By Cathy A. Malchiodi

Art Therapy with Sexual Abuse Survivors
By Stephanie Brooke

Creative Connection: Expressive Arts As Healing
By Natalie Rogers

Managing Traumatic Stress Through Art: Drawing From the Center
By Barry M. Cohen, Mary-Michola Barnes, Anita B. Rankin

Painting from the Source: Awakening the Artist's Soul in Everyone
By Aviva Gold

Campus Rape

Avoiding Rape On and Off Campus
By Carol Pritchard

Before College Book for Women: Protecting Yourself from Campus Crime
By Donna L. Betancourt

Campus Gang Rape: Party Games?
By J. Ehrhart

Fraternity Gang Rape: Sex, Brotherhood, and Privilege on Campus
By Peggy Reeves Sanday

Rape on Campus
By Bruno Leone (Editor)

Sexual Assault on Campus: The Problem and the Solution
By Carol Bohmer, Andrea Parrot

Sexual Assault on the College Campus: The Role of Male Peer Support
By Martin D. Schwartz (Editor), Walter S. Dekeseredy

Chronic Pain

How to Live Between Office Visits
By Bernie S. Siegel, M.D.

Living With Chronic Pain One Day at a Time
By Mark Allen Zabawa

Mastering Chronic Pain: A Professional's Guide to Behavioral Treatment
By Robert N. Jamison, Ph.D.

Mayo Clinic on Chronic Pain
By David W. Swanson (Editor)

Pain Free: A Revolutionary Method for Stopping Chronic Pain
By Pete Egoscue

Sexuality and Chronic Illness
By Leslie R. Schover, Soren Buus Jensen

To See Differently
By Dr. Susan Trout

Your Pain Is Real: Free Yourself from Chronic Pain With Breakthrough Medical Treatments
By Dr. Emile Hiesiger

Why People Don't Heal and How they Can
By Carolyn Myss, Ph.D.

Criminal Justice

Real Rape: How the Legal System Victimizes Women Who Say No
By Susan Estrich

Stopping Rape: Successful Survival Strategies
By Pauline B. Bart, Patricia H. O'Brien

Strategies for the Treatment and Prevention of Sexual Assault
By The American Medical Association

Victim's Rights: Opportunities for Action
By The National Victim Center

Women's Legal Guide: A Comprehensive Guide to Legal Issues Affecting Every Woman
By Barbara R. Hauser

Date Rape

Before He Takes You Out: The Safe Dating Guide for the 90s
By Scott Lindquist

Case for Taking the Date Out of Rape, The
By Aileen McColgan

Coping With Date and Acquaintance Rape
By Andrea Parrot

Date and Acquaintance Rape
By Gustav Mark Gedatus, Ph.D.

Date Rape
By Ruth Goring

Date Rape: A Hot Issue
By Kathleen Winkler

Date Rape and Consent
By Mark Cowling

Date Rape Drugs
By Clare Tattersall

Date Rape Prevention Book, The: The Essential Guide for Girls and Women
By Scott Lindquist

Drugs and Date Rape
By Maryann Miller

Everything You Need to Know About Date Rape
By Frances Shuker-Haines

Guide to Coping With Date Rape and Acquaintance Rape
By Andrea Parrot, Ph.D.

I Never Called It Rape: The Ms. Report on Recognizing, Fighting, and Surviving Date and Acquaintance Rape
By Robin Warshaw

Man to Man When Your Partner Says No: Pressured Sex and Date Rape
By Scott Johnson

Other Side of Silence, The: Women Tell About Their Experiences With Date Rape
By Christine Carter

Straight Talk About Date Rape
By Susan Mufson, Rachel Kranz

Depression

A Mood Apart: The Thinker's Guide to Emotion and Its Disorders
By Peter C. Whybrow

Beast, The: A Journey Through Depression
By Tracy Thompson

Blue Day Book, The: A Lesson in Cheering Yourself Up
By Bradley Trevor Greive

Call Me Anna: The Autobiography of Patty Duke
By Patty Duke, Kenneth Turan

Compassion and Self-Hate: An Alternative to Despair
By Theodore Isaac Rubin

Conquering the Beast Within: How I Fought Depression and Won . . . and How You Can, Too
By Cait Irwin

Depression Workbook, The: A Guide for Living with Depression and Manic Depression
By Mary Ellen Copeland

Feeling Good Handbook, The
By David Burns

It's Not As Bad As It Seems: A Thinking Straight Approach to Happiness
By Ed Nottingham, Ph.D.

Malignant Sadness: The Anatomy of Depression
By Lewis Wolpert

Moodswing
By Ronald R. Fieve

On the Edge of Darkness: Conversations About Conquering Depression
By Kathy Cronkite

Overcoming Depression
By Demitri and Janice Paplos

Speaking of Sadness: Depression, Disconnection, and the Meanings of Illness
By David Karp

Undercurrents: A Life Beneath the Surface
By Martha Manning

Undoing Depression: What Therapy Doesn't Teach You and Medication Can't Give You
By Richard O'Connor

When Words Are Not Enough: The Women's Prescription for Depression and Anxiety
By Valerie D. Raskin, M.D.

Willow Weep for Me, A Black Woman's Journey Through Depression: A Memoir
By Meri Nana-Ama Dumquah

You Are Not Alone: Words of Experience and Hope for the Journey Through Depression
By Julia Thorne, Larry Rothstein

Disabilities and Chronic Pain

An Easy Guide to Loving Carefully for Men and Women
By Lyn McKee, Winifred Kempton, Lynn Stiggall-Muccigrosso

Choices: A Sexual Assault Prevention Workbook for Persons with Physical Disabilities
By Ellen Shaman, Seattle Rape Relief

Choices: A Sexual Assault Prevention Workbook for Persons with Visual Impairments
By Ellen Shaman, Seattle Rape Relief

Illustrated Guide to Better Sex for People with Chronic Pain, The
By Robert W. Rothrock, Gabriella D'Amore

Preventing Sexual Abuse of Persons with Disabilities
By The Minnesota Program for Victims of Sexual Assault

Price Against Prejudice: Transforming Attitudes to Disability
By Jenny Morris

Providing Counseling and Advocacy for Disabled Persons Who Have Been Sexually Abused: A Training Manual for Staff and Volunteers
By Ellen Shaman, Yvette Parr, Seattle Rape Relief

Sex and Back Pain: Advice on Restoring Comfortable Sex Lost to Back Pain
By Lauren Andrew Hebert

Sexual Assault and Persons with Disabilities
By Darlys Vander Beek, Julie Biernat, Brian Clapham

Sexual Concerns When Illness or Disability Strikes
By Carol L. Sandowski, MSW

Sexuality and Sexual Assault: A Disabled Perspective
By Virginia W. Stuart, Charles K. Stuart

Teach Training Manual: Sexual Abuse of Persons with Disabilities: Techniques for Planning and Implementing a Self-Protection Program
By Seattle Rape Relief Disabilities Project

Women with Disabilities: Essays in Psychology, Culture and Politics
By Michelle Fine, Adrienne Asch

Dreams and Nightmares

A Little Course in Dreams: A Basic Handbook of Jungian Dreamwork
By Kelly Bulkeley

Committee of Sleep: How Artists, Scientists, and Athletes Use Dreams for Creative Problem-Solving — And How You Can Too
By Robert Bosnak

Conscious Dreaming
By Robert Moss

Control your Dreams
By Patricia Garfield

Creative Dreaming
By Eugene T. Gendlin

Dreamgates: An Explorer's Guide to the Worlds of Soul, Imagination, and Life Beyond Death
By Robert Moss

Dream Reader: Contemporary Approaches to the Understanding of Dreams
By Jeremy Taylor

Dreams
By Morton Kelsey

Dreams and Dreaming
By Gayle Delaney

Dreams and Nightmares: The New Theory on the Origin and Meaning of Dreams
By Ernest Hartmann, M.D.

Dreams and Spiritual Growth: A Christian Approach to Dreamworld
By Alan B. Siegel

Dreams That Can Change Your Life
By Anthony Shafton

Dreamtime & Dreamwork
By Robert Moss

Dreamwork for the Soul: A Spiritual Guide to Dream Interpretation
By Ernest Hartmann, M.D.

Exploring the World of Lucid Dreaming
By Stephen LaBarge

Families and the Interpretation of Dreams
By G. Constable

Interpretation of Dreams, The
By Jayne Gackenback, Jane Bosveld

Let your Body Interpret your Dreams
By Rosemary Guiley

Night & Day: Use the Power of Your Dreams to Transform Your Life
By Patricia Maybruck

Nightmares: How to Make Sense of Your Darkest Dreams
By Alex Lukeman, Ph.D.

Nightmare: The Psychology and Biology of Terrifying
By C.G. Jung

Our Dreaming Mind
By Lillie Weiss

Practical Dreaming: Awakening the Power of Dreams in Your Life
By Lillie Weiss

Pregnancy & Dreams
By Henry Reed

Sleep Well, Sleep Deep
By Alex Lukeman, Ph.D.

Trauma and Dreams
By Deidre Barrett

What Your Dreams Can Teach You
By Alex Lukeman, Ph.D.

Wilderness of Dreams, The
By Edward Bruce Bynum

Eating Disorders (Anorexia and Bulimia)

A Hunger So Wide and So Deep
By Becky Thompson

Am I Thin Enough Yet? The Cult of Thinness and the Commercialization of Identity
By Sharlene Hesse-Biber

Anatomy of Anorexia
By Steven Levenkron

Anorexia : A Guide to Recovery
By Lindsey Hall, Monika Ostroff

A Skeleton in the Closet: Remembering My Spirit
By B. Sarabura (Editor)

Best Little Girl in the World, The
By Steven Levenkron

Bitter Ice: A Memoir of Love, Food, and Obsession
By Barbara Kent Lawrence

Bulimia: A Guide to Recovery Understanding & Overcoming the Binge-Purge Syndrome
By Lindsey Hall, Leigh Cohn

Bulimarexia: The Binge/Purge Cycle
By Marlen Boskind-White

Bulimia Nervosa & Binge-Eating: A Guide to Recovery
By Peter J. Cook

But I'm Not a Bad Person
By Lauren M. Traer

Never Too Thin
By Eva Szekely

One Size Does Not Fit All
By Beverly Naidus

Owl Was a Baker's Daughter
By Marion Woodman

Real Gorgeous: The Truth About Body and Beauty
By Kaz Cooke

Secret Language of Eating Disorders, The
By Peggy Claude-Pierre

Stick Figure: A Diary of My Former Self
By Lori Gottlieb

Treating and Overcoming Anorexia Nervosa
By Steven Levenkron

Wasted: A Memoir of Anorexia and Bulimia
By Marya Hornbacher

Eating Disorders (Compulsive Overeating)

Anatomy of a Food Addiction
By Anne Katherine

Beyond Feast or Famine: Daily Affirmations for Compulsive Eaters
By Susan Ward, M.S.W.

Breaking Free from Compulsive Eating
By Geneen Roth

Chocolate Is My Kryptonite: Feeding Your Feelings How to Survive the Forces of Food
By Matthew S. Keene

Eating Disorders and Obesity: A Comprehensive Handbook
By Kelly D. Brownell, Christopher G. Fairburn

Fat and Furious: Women and Food Obsession
By Judi Hollis, Ph.D.

Fat Is a Family Affair
By Judi Hollis, Ph.D.

Feeding the Hungry Heart - The Experience of Compulsive Eating
By Geneen Roth

Full Lives: Women Who Have Freed Themselves from Food & Weight Obsession
By Lindsey Hall

Hunger Within, The: A Twelve-Week Self-Guided Journey from Compulsive Eating to Recovery
By Marilyn Migliore, Philip Ross (Contributor)

I Wish I Were Thin, I Wish I Were Fat: The Real Reasons We Overeat and What We Can Do About It
By Michelle Joy Levine

Losing Your Pounds of Pain: Breaking the Link Between Abuse, Stress, and Overeating
By Doreen Virtue

Overcoming Overeating
By Jane R. Hirschmann, Carol H. Munter

Weigh Down Diet
By Gwen Shamblin

When You Eat at the Refrigerator, Pull Up a Chair: 50 Ways to Feel Thin, Gorgeous, and Happy (When You Feel Anything But)
By Geneen Roth, Anne Lamott

Zen of Eating, The: Ancient Answers to Modern Weight Problems
By Ronna Kabatznick

EMDR

Calm and Confident: Overcome Stress and Anxiety With EMDR
By Mark Grant

EMDR in the Treatment of Adults Abused As Children
By Laurel Parnell, Ph.D.

EMDR: The Breakthrough Therapy for Overcoming Anxiety, Stress, and Trauma
By Francine Shapiro, Margot Silk Forrest

Emotional Healing at Warp Speed: The Power of EMDR
By David Grand

Finding the Energy to Heal: How EMDR, Hypnosis, TFT, Imagery, and Body-Focused Therapy Can Help Resolve Health Problems
By Maggie Phillips

Pain Control With EMDR
By Mark Grant

Small Wonders: Healing Childhood Trauma with EMDR
By Joan Lovett

Transforming Trauma: EMDR: The Revolutionary New Therapy for Freeing the Mind, Clearing the Body, and Opening the Heart
By Laurel Parnell, Ph.D.

Group Therapy

Group Therapy Experience, The: From Theory to Practice
  By Louis R. Ormont

Trauma Recovery and Empowerment: A Clinician's Guide for Working with Women in Groups
  By Maxine Harris, Ph.D.

Intimacy

Compassionate Touch: The Body's Role in Emotional Healing and Recovery
  By Clyde W. Ford

Dance of Intimacy, The: A Woman's Guide to Courageous Acts of Change in Key Relationships
  By Harriet Lerner

Fear of Intimacy
  By Robert W. Firestone, Joyce Catlett

Human Significance of Skin, The
  By Ashley Montagu

In the Meantime: Finding Yourself and the Love You Want
  By Iyanla Vanzant

Passionate Marriage: Love, Sex, and Intimacy in Emotionally Committed Relationships
  By David Schnarch, Ph.D.

Romantic Massage
  By Randy Nikola

Sensual Sex: Arousing Your Senses and Deepening the Passion in Your Relationship
  By Beverly Engel, Ph.D.

Trauma and Recovery
  By Judith Lewis Herman, M.D.

Truth About Love, The: The Highs, the Lows, and How You Can Make It Last Forever
  By Patricia Love

Two Sides of Love, The: What Strengthens Affection, Closeness and Lasting Commitment
  By Gary Smalley, John T. Trent

Journal Writing

A Garden of Thoughts: My Affirmation Journal
  By Louise L. Hay

A Path Through Loss: A Guide to Writing Your Healing and Growth
  By Nancy C. Reeves

A Voice of Her Own: Women and the Journal Writing Journey
By Marlene A. Schiwy, Marion Woodman

Bird by Bird: Some Instructions on Writing and Life
By Anne Lamott

Book of Myself, The: A Do-It-Yourself Autobiography in 201 Questions
By Carl Marshall

Book of Self-Acquaintance, The
By Margaret Tiberio

Coping With Trauma: A Guide to Self-Understanding
By Jon G. Allen, Ph.D.

Creative Journal: The Art of Finding Yourself
By Lucia Capacchione

I'm a Princess, I Don't Do Dishes: A Wish Journal
By Ellen Edith

Journal to the Soul: The Art of Sacred Journal Keeping
By Rose Offner

Life After Trauma
By Dean Rosenbloo, Mary Beth Williams, Barbara Watkins

Recovery of Your Inner Child
By Lucia Capacchione

Soul Catcher: A Journal to Help You Become Who You Really Are
By Kathy Eldon, Amy Eldon

Tao Te Ching Journal
By Stephen Mitchell (Translator)

Things That Tick Me Off! A Guided Journal
By Joan Mazza, M.S.

Way of the Journal, The: A Journal Therapy Workbook for Healing
By Kathleen Adams

What Do You Dream? Daily Journal & Inspiration to Live Your Dreams
By Belma Johnson

Woman's Book of Changes: A Notebook Journal
By Ilene Segalove, Felice Willat

Massage

Ayurvedic Massage: Traditional Indian Techniques for Balancing Body and Mind
By Harish Johari

Book of Massage: The Complete Step-By-Step Guide to Eastern and Western Techniques
By Lucy Lidell

Good Hands: Massage Techniques for Total Health
By Robert Bahr

Handbook of Chinese Massage: Tui Na Techniques to Awaken Body and Mind
By Maria Mercati

Healing With Pressure Point Therapy: Simple, Effective Techniques for Massaging Away More Than 100 Common Ailments
By Jack Forem, Steve Shimer

Joy of Reflexology, The: Healing Techniques for the Hands & Feet to Reduce Stress & Reclaim Health
By Ann Gillanders

Massage Basics: A Guide to Swedish, Shiatsu, and Reflexology Techniques
By Mark Beck, Shelley Hess, Erica Miller

Reflexology for Women: Restore Harmony and Balance Through Precise Massaging Techniques
By Nicola M. Hall

Self-Healing Reiki: Freeing the Symbols, Attunements, and Techniques
By Barbara Emerson

Spinal Manipulation Made Simple: A Manual of Soft Tissue Techniques
By Jeffrey Maitland

SUPER MASSAGE Simple Techniques for Instant Relaxation
By Gordon Inkeles, Sigga Bjornsson

Tappan's Handbook Of Healing Massage Techniques: Classic, Holistic, And Emerging Methods
By Frances M. Tappan

Use of Massage in Facilitating Holistic Health: Physical and Mental Effects, the Nature of Massage and the Techniques for Application
By Robert Henley Woody

Medical Information

Color Atlas of Sexual Assault
By Diana K. Faugno, Patty C. Senseshi

Everything You Always Wanted to Ask Your Gynecologist
By R. Scott Thornton, M.D.; Kathleen Schramm, M.D.

Full Catastrophe Living: Using the Wisdom of Your Body and Mind to Face Stress, Pain, and Illness
By Jon Kabat-Zinn

Sexual Assault: A Manual for Emergency Care
By Patricia A. Hargest, Robi Findley, R.N.

Violence and Abuse: Implications for Women's Health
By S.B. Plichta

Medical Information and HIV

HIV and AIDS: Testing, Screening, and Confidentiality
By Rebecca Bennett, Charles A. Erin (Editors)

More Harm Than Help: The Ramifications for Rape Survivors of Mandatory HIV Testing of Rapists
By Lisa Bowleg

Testing for HIV: What Your Lab Results Mean
By N. L. Gifford (Editor)

Panic Disorders

Anxiety, Phobias and Panic: A Step-by-Step Program for Regaining Control of Your Life
By Reneau Z. Penrifoy

It's Not All in Your Head
By S.B. Swedo, H.L. Leonard

Mastery of Your Anxiety and Worry
By Michelle Craske

Overcoming Panic, Anxiety, & Phobias: New Strategies to Free Yourself from Worry and Fear
By Shirley Babior, Carol Goldman

Sky is Falling, The: Understanding and Coping With Phobias, Panic, and Obsessive-Compulsive Disorders
Raeann Dumont, Aaron T. Beck

Trauma and Recovery
By Judith Herman, M.D.

Triumph Over Fear: A Book of Help and Hope for People with Anxiety, Panic Attacks, and Phobias
By Jerilyn Ross, Rosalynn Carter

Rape Crisis Intervention

Aftermath of Rape, The
By T.W. McCahill, L.D. Meyer, A.M. Fischman

Coping With Survivors and Surviving
By Julie Skinner

Helping Crime Victims: Research, Policy, and Practice
By Albert R. Roberts

Rape Crisis Intervention Handbook: A Guide for Victim Care
By Sharon McCombie

Rape Victim, The
By E. Hilberman

Rape, The: Misunderstood Crime
By Julie A. Allison, Lawrence S. Wrightsman

Rape Victim, The: Clinical and Community Interventions
By Mary Koss, Mary Harvey

Victims of Crime: Issues, Programs, and Policy
By Robert Jerin

Rape-Related Pregnancy and Abortion

Peace After Abortion
By Ava Torre-Bueno

Rape-Related Pregnancy and Adoption

Adoption Healing — A Path to Recovery
By Joe Soll

Birthmothers: Women Who Have Relinquished Babies for Adoption Tell Their Stories
By Merry Bloch Jones

Saying Goodbye to a Baby: Birthparents Guide to Loss and Grief in Adoption
By Patricia Roles

Third Choice, The: A Woman's Guide to Placing a Child for Adoption
By Leslie Foge, Gail Mosconi

Rape-Related Pregnancy and Decision Making

How Good People Make Tough Choices: Resolving the Dilemmas of Ethical Living
By Rushworth M. Kidder

In Good Conscience: A Practical, Emotional, and Spiritual Guide to Deciding Whether to Have an Abortion
By Anna Runkle

Rape Trauma

Aftermath: Survive and Overcome Trauma
By Mariann Hybels-Steer

After Silence: Rape and My Journey Back
By Nancy Venable Raine

Diary Of A Rape Victim: Breaking the Silence to Break Free
By Phillis Van Godwin

Embracing Your Inner Critic: Turrning Self-Criticism Into a Creative Asset
By Hal Stone, Sidra Stone

Free of the Shadows: Recovering from Sexual Violence
By Caren Adams, Jennifer Fay

301

If You Are Raped: What Every Woman Needs to Know
  By Kathryn M. Johnson

Journey to Wholeness: Healing from the Trauma of Rape
  By Vicki Aranow, Monique Lang

Learning to Love Yourself: A Guide to Becoming Centered
  By Gay Hendricks

Learning to Love Yourself Workbook, The
  By Gay Hendricks

No Fairy Godmother, No Magic Wands: The Healing Process After Rape
  By Judy H. Katz

Quest for Respect: A Healing Guide for Survivors of Rape
  By Linda Braswell

Recovering from Rape
  By Linda Ledray

Recovering from the Losses of Life
  By H. Norman Wright

Rising to the Dawn: A Rape Survivor's Journey into Healing
  By Laverne C. Williams

Self-Respect & Sexual Assault
  By Jeanett Mauro-Cochrane

Surviving Sexual Assault
  By Rochel Grossman, Joan Sutherland

Trust After Trauma: A Guide to Relationships for Survivors and Those Who Love Them
  By Aphrodite Matsakis, Ph.D.

Voices of the Survivors
  By Patricia Eastel

Rape Trauma (Anger Symptoms)

Anger Kills
  By Redford Williams M.D.; Virginia Williams, Ph.D.

Anger: The Misunderstood Emotion
  By Carol Tavris

Angry Self, The: A Comprehensive Approach to Anger Management
  By Miriam M. Gottlieb, Ph.D.

Asserting Yourself
  By Sharon Bower, Gordon H. Bower

If You Are Raped: What Every Woman Needs to Know
  By Kathryn M. Johnson

It's Not Personal! A Guide to Anger Management
By Alice J. Katz

Overcoming Anger and Irritability: A Self-Help Guide Using Cognitive Behavioral Techniques (Overcoming Series)
By William Davies

Quest for Respect: A Healing Guide for Survivors of Rape
By Linda Braswell

Rape Trauma (Avoidance Symptoms)

Attention and Avoidance: Strategies in Coping With Aversiveness
By Heinz Walter Krohne (Editor)

Changing Character: Short-Term Anxiety-Regulating Psychotherapy for Restructuring Defenses, Affects, and Attachment
By Leigh McCullough Vaillant

Inner World of Trauma, The: Archetypal Defenses of the Personal Spirit
By Donald Kalsched

Shyness & Social Anxiety Workbook, The: Proven Techniques for Overcoming Your Fears
By Martin M. Antony, Richard P. Swinson

Rape Trauma (Guilt and Shame)

Culture of Shame
By Andrew P. Morrison

Healing the Shame That Binds You
By John Bradshaw

Many Faces of Shame, The
By Donald L. Nathanson

Pride, Shame, and Guilt: Emotions of Self-Assessment
By Gabriele Taylor

Shame and Guilt: Characteristics of the Dependency Cycle
By Ernest Kurtz

Understanding and Letting Go of Guilt
By Lucy Freeman, Herbert S. Strean

Why Do I Feel Guilty When I've Done Nothing Wrong?
By Ty C. Colber

Rape Trauma (Inability to Concentrate)

Concentration: A Guide to Mental Mastery
By Mouni Sadhu

Concentration: An Approach to Meditation
By Ernest Wood

Concentration and Meditation
By Christmas Humphreys

Emotional Alchemy: How the Mind Can Heal the Heart
By Tara Bennett-Goleman

Getting Through the Day: Srategies for Adults Hurt as Children
By Nancy J. Napier

Improve Your Concentration
By Robert Griswold

Outgrowing the Pain: A Book for and About Adults Abused as Children
By Eliana Gil, Ph.D.

Post Traumatic Stress Disorder Sourcebook: A Guide to Healing, Recovery and Growth
By Glen R. Schiraldi

Power of Focus, The
By Jack Canfield, Mark Victor Hansen, Les Hewitt

Start Where You Are: A Guide to Compassionate Living
By Pema Chodron

Still Loved by the Sun: A Rape Survivor's Journal
By Migall Scherer

Safety and Self-Defense

A Woman's Guide to Personal Safety
By Jamee Harteau, Holly Keegel

Chalice And The Blade, The
By Diane Eisler, David Loye

Female Experience, The: An American Documentary
By Gerda Lerner (Editor)

Gift of Fear
By Gavin De Becker

How to Protect Yourself from Crime
By Ira A. Lipman

Real World Safety For Women
By Christine Schlatter, Michael Linehan

Self Defense: Steps To Success
By Joan Nelson

Sexual Assault: How To Defend Yourself
By Dan Lena, Marie Howard

Stopping Rape: Successful Survival Strategies
By Pauline B. Bert, Patricia H. O'Brien

Strategies for the Treatment and Prevention of Sexual Assault
By The American Medical Association

Strong On Defense
By Sanford Strong

Total Awareness: A Woman's Safety Book
By Beth Laur, Darre Laur

Whoever Fights Monsters
By Robert Ressler, Tom Shachtman

Women's Self-Defense: A Complete Guide to Assault Prevention
By R. Hill, J. Iten Sutherland, P. Giggans, the Los Angeles Commission on
Assaults Against Women

Self-Harm

A Bright Red Scream: Self-Mutilation and the Language of Pain
By Marilee Strong

Beyond the Darkness
By Cynthia Kubetin, James Mallory

Bodies under Siege: Self-Mutilation and Body Modification in Culture and Psychiatry
By Armando R. Favazza

Coping with Self-Mutilation
By Alicia Clarke, Carolyn Simpson

Coping with Self-Mutilation
By Jordan Lee

Crosses
By Shelley Stoehr

Cut
By Patty McCormick

Cutting: Understanding and Overcoming Self-Mutilation
By Steven Levenkron

Everything You Need to Know about Self-Mutilation: A Helping Book for Teens Who Hurt Themselves
By Gina Ng

Healing the Hurt Within: Understand and Relieve the Suffering Behind Self-Destructive Behaviour
By Jan Sutton

Luckiest Girl in the World, The
By Steven Levenkron

Mutilating the Body: Identity in Blood and Ink
By Kim Hewitt

305

Scarred Soul, The: Understanding and Ending Self-Inflicted Violence
By Tracy Alderman, Ph.D.

Self-Mutilation and Art Therapy: Violent Creation
By Diana Milia

Skin Game
By Caroline Kettlewell

Stop Obsessing: How to Overcome Your Obsessions and Compulsions
By E.B. Foa, R. Wilson

Understanding Self-Injury: A Workbook For Adults
By Kristy Trautmann, B.S.; Robin Connors, Ph.D.

Women and Self-Harm: Understanding, Coping and Healing from Self-Mutilation
By Gerrilyn Smith, Dee Cox, Jacqui Saradjian

Women Living with Self-Injury
By Jane Wegscheider

Women Who Hurt Themselves: A Book of Hope and Understanding
By Dusty Miller, Ed.D.

Self-Help

Appetites: On the Search for True Nourishment
By Geneen Roth

Art of the Inner Meal: Eating As a Spiritual Path
By Donald Altman

Creating Love: The Next Great Stage of Growth
By John Bradshaw

Dance Naked in Your Living Room: Handling Stress and Finding Joy
By Rebecca Ruggles Radcliffe

Desperately Seeking Self: An Inner Guidebook for People With Eating Problems
By Viola Fodor

Don't Diet, Live-It!
By Marsea Marcus, Andre LoBue

Emotional Weight: Change Your Relationship With Food by Changing Your Relationship With Yourself
By Colleen A. Sundermeyer, Ph.D.

Exacting Beauty: Theory, Assessment, and Treatment of Body Image Disturbance
By J. Kevin Thompson, Leslie J. Heinberg, Madeline N. Altabe, Stacey Tantleff-Dunn

French Toast for Breakfast: Declaring Peace With Emotional Eating
By Mary Anne Cohen

Getting Better Bit(E) by Bit(E): A Survival Kit for Sufferers of Bulimia Nervosa and Binge Eating Disorders
By Ulrike Schmidt, Janet Treasure

Good Girls Don't Eat Dessert: Changing Your Relationship to Food and Sex
By Rosalyn Meadow, Lillie Weiss

Homecoming: Reclaiming and Championing Your Inner Child (Book and Audio Cassette)
By John Bradshaw

Hope, Help, and Healing for Eating Disorders: A New Approach to Treating Anorexia, Bulimia, and Overeating
By Gregory L. Jantz

Intuitive Eating: A Recovery Book for the Chronic Dieter: Rediscover the Pleasures of Eating and Rebuild Your Body Image
By Evelyn Tribole, Elyse Resch

It's Not About Food: Change Your Mind; Change Your Life; End Your Obsession With Food and Weight
By Carol Emery Normandi, Laurelee Roark

Making Peace With Food
By Susan Kano

Somebody to Love: A Guide to Loving the Body You Have
By Leslea Newman

Stabilize the Level of Sugar in Your Blood
By Kathleen DesMaisons, Ph.D.

Thin Veils
By Anne Hanson

Transforming Body Image: Love the Body You Have
By Marcia Germaine Hutchinson

When Food is Love
By Geneen Roth

Why Weight: A Guide to Ending Compulsive Eating
By Geneen Roth

Sexual Dysfunction

Allies in Healing: When the Person You Love Was Sexually Abused As a Child
By Laura Davis

For Each Other: Sharing Sexual Intimacy
By Lonnie Barbach, Ph.D.

For Women Only: A Revolutionary Guide to Overcoming Sexual Dysfunction and Reclaiming Your Sex Life
By Jennifer Berman M.D., Laura Berman, Ph.D.

Ghosts in the Bedroom
By Ken Graber

Ordinary Women, Extraordinary Sex: Every Woman's Guide to Pleasure and Beyond
By Sandra Scantling, Sue Browder

Passionate Marriage: Love, Sex, and Intimacy in Emotionally Committed Relationships
By David Schnarch, Ph.D.

Self-Therapy for Sex Problems
By Daniel Steele

Women's Sexuality Across the Life Span: Challenging Myths, Creating Meanings
By Judith Daniluk

Sexuality

Becoming Orgasmic: A Sexual and Personal Growth Program for Women
By Julia Heiman, Joseph Lopiccolo

Discover Your Sensual Potential: A Woman's Guide to Guaranteed Satisfaction
By Barbara Keesling

Family Guide to Sex and Relationships, The
By Richard Walker, Ph.D.

For Yourself: The Fulfillment of Female Sexuality
By Lonnie Barbach, Ph.D.

Good Marriage, The: How and Why Love Lasts
By Judith S. Wallerstein, Sandra Blakeslee

Passionate Marriage: Keeping Love, Sex, and Intimacy in Emotionally Committed Relationships
By David Schnarch, Ph.D.

Private Thoughts: Exploring the Power of Women's Sexual Fantasies
By Wendy Maltz MSW, Suzie Boss

Self-Therapy for Sex Problems
By Daniel Steele

Sexual Healing Journey, The: A Guide for Survivors of Sexual Abuse
By Wendy Maltz, MSW

Understanding Your Referral to a Sex Therapist
By Robert W. Birch, Ph.D.

Women, Sex, and Desire: Exploring Your Sexuality at Every Stage of Life
By Elizabeth Davis

Sexually Transmitted Diseases

1998 Guidelines for Treatment of Sexually Transmitted Diseases
  By Centers for Disease Control

Choices: Sex in the Age of STDs
  By Jeffery A. Nevid

Color Atlas and Synopsis of Sexually Transmitted Diseases
  By Hansfield Hunter, M.D.

Sexually Transmitted Diseases: A Physician Tells You What You Need to Know
  By Lisa Marr

Sexual Positions

Best Sex You'll Ever Have, The: 101 Exciting Positions for Ecstatic Sexual Fulfillment
  By Richard Emerson

Erotic Passions: A Guide to Orgasmic Massage, Sensual Bathing, Oral Pleasuring, and Ancient Sexual Positions
  By Kenneth Ray Stubbs, Ph.D.

Kama Sutra of Sexual Positions: The Tantric Art of Love
  By Kenneth Ray Stubbs, Ph.D.

Secret Sexual Positions: Ancient Techniques for Modern Lovers
  By Kenneth Ray Stubbs, Ph.D.

Sexual Positions: Games Lovers Play
  By Rosie Hughes

Sexual Positions (The Joy of Sex Series)
  By Alex Comfort

Spirituality

Affirmations for the Inner Child
  By Rokelle Lerner

Affirmations: Your Passport to Happiness
  By Anne Marie, Lee Pulos

Affirmations for Artists
  By Eric Maisel

A Woman's Journey to God: Finding the Feminine Path
  By Joan Borysenko, Ph.D.

Facing Life's Challenges: Daily Meditations for Overcoming Depression, Grief, and 'the Blues'
  By Amy E. Dean

Fire in the Soul: A New Psychology of Spiritual Optimism
  By Joan Borysenko, Ph.D.

I Believe in Me
By Connie Bowen

I Turn to the Light
By Connie Bowen

Pocketful of Miracles
By Joan Borysenko, Ph.D.

Today I Will Do One Thing: Daily Readings for Awareness and Hope for Those of Us With Addiction and Emotional or Psychiatric Illness
By Tim T. McIndoo, James Jennings

Substance Abuse

Love First: Intervention for Alcoholism and Drug Addiction
By Jeff Jay, Debra Jay

Many Roads, One Journey: Moving Beyond the 12-Steps
By Charlotte Davis Kasl

Personality: Understanding the Addictive Process and Compulsive Behavior
By Craig Nakken

Support Groups

Self-Help Handouts for Survivors and Support Groups
By Wisconsin Coalition Against Sexual Assault

Self-Help Sourcebook, The: Your Guide to Community & Online Support
By Barbara J. White, Edward J. Madara (Editors)

Therapists (Selecting)

Guidelines for Choosing a Behavior Therapist
By The Association for Advancement of Behavior Therapy

How to Choose a Psychotherapist
By The American Psychological Association

How to Choose a Therapist
By Sidran Foundation

Seeking Help for Life's Challenges: What is Counseling?
By The American Counseling Association

Therapy

A Guide to Psychotherapy
By Gerald Amada, Ph.D.

Cognitive Therapy and the Emotional Disorders
By Aaron T. Beck

Cognitive Therapy: Basics and Beyond
By Judith S. Beck

Emotional Brain, The: The Mysterious Underpinnings of Emotional Life
By Joseph LeDoux

Emotional Intelligence: Why It Can Matter More Than IQ for Character, Health and Lifelong Achievement
By Daniel Goleman

Error: Emotion, Reason and the Human Brain
By Antonio R. Damasio

Flow: The Psychology of Optimal Experience
By Mihaly Csikszentmihaly

Freedom of Fear Forever
By Dr. James V. Durlacher, Roger J. Callahan, Guy McGill

How to Think Straight About Psychology
By Keith E. Stanovich

Learned Optimism: How to Change Your Mind and Your Life
By Martin Seligman

Lovingkindness
By Sharon Salzberg

Managing Social Anxiety: A Cognitive-Behavioral Therapy Approach
By Debra A. Hope, Richard G. Juster

Mental Health Care: What to Look For, What to Ask
By The Center for Mental Health Services (CMHS)

Mind Over Mood: A Cognitive Therapy Treatment Manual for Clients
By Dennis Greenberger, Christine A. Padesky

Opening Up: The Healing Power of Expressing Emotions
By James W. Pennebaker

Overcoming Shyness and Social Phobia: A Step-by-Step Guide
By Ronald M. Rapee

Portable Therapist, The
By Susanna McMahon, Ph.D.

Rebuilding Shattered Lives: The Responsible Treatment of Complex Post-Traumatic and Dissociative Disorders
By James A. Chu, M.D.

Surviving the Silence: Black Women's Stories of Rape
By Charlotte Pierce-Baker

Survivor Personality, The: Why Some People are Stronger, Smarter, and More Skillful at Handling Life's Difficulties ... and How You Can Be Too
By Al Siebert, Ph.D.

Taking Back My Life
By Nancy Ziegenmeyer

Wanting What You Have: A Self-Discovery Workbook
By Timothy Miller

What You Can Change and What You Can't: Complete Guide to Successful Self-Improvement, The
By Martin Seligman

Where I Stopped: Remembering Rape at Thirteen
By Martha Ramsey

Vaginismus

A Woman's Guide to Overcoming Sexual Fear and Pain
By Aurelie Jones Goodwin, Marc E. Agronin, M.D.

Vaginismus
By Linda Valins

When a Woman's Body Says No to Sex: Understanding and Overcoming Vaginismus
By Linda Valins

Violence

Aftermath: Violence and the Remaking of a Self
By Susan J. Brison

Anatomy of Motive, The
By John Douglas, Mark Olshaker

Evil That Men Do, The: FBI Profiler Roy Hazelwood's Journey into the Minds of Sexual Predators
By Stephen G. Michaud, Roy Hazelwood

For Your Own Good: Hidden Cruelty in Childrearing and the Roots of Violence
By Alice Miller, Ph.D.

Intimate Partner Violence: Societal, Medical, Legal, and Individual Responses
By Sana Loue

Mindhunter
By John Douglas, Mark Olshaker

No Safe Haven: Male Violence Against Women At Home, At Work, and In the Community
By Mary P. Koss

Our Guys: The Glen Ridge Rape and Secret Life of the Perfect Suburb
By Bernard Lefkowitz

Rape Victim, The: Clinical and Community Interventions
By Mary P. Koss

Reach for the Rainbow: Advanced Healing for Survivors of Sexual Abuse
By Lynne D. Finney, J.D., MSW

Sexual Violence: Our War Against Rape
By Linda A. Fairstein

Sexual Violence: The Unmentionable Sin
By Marie Marshall Fortune

Transforming a Rape Culture
By Emilie Buchwald, Martha Roth, Pamela Fletcher (Editors)

Understanding Violence Against Women
By Nancy A. Crowell, Ann W. Burgess (Editors)

Violence Against Women: There is No Typical Victim
By Catherine Walters

📼 Audio & Video Resources

Please visit my Web site at www.RapeRecovery.com for more information on ordering the following audio and videotapes.

Disabilities

Sexual Abuse Prevention: 5 Safety Rules for Persons Who are Handicapped
  By Magic Lantern Communication

Dreams and Nightmares

Dream Gates: A Journey into Active Dreaming
  By Stephan L. LaBerge

Health Journey: Healing and the Mind
  By Bill Moyers

Sexual Assault

Sexual Abuse Prevention: 5 Safety Rules for Persons Who are Handicapped
  By Magic Lantern Communication

Sexuality

Better Sex Advanced Techniques Series - Dr. Sandra Scantling's Ordinary Couples, Extraordinary Sex
  By Sinclair Intimacy Institute

Problems of Sexual Desire: Who Really Wants to Want?
  By David Schnarch, Ph.D.

Substance Abuse

Numbing the Pain: Substance Abuse and Psychological Trauma
  By Cavalcade Productions

⌁ Internet Resources

12 Step Cyber Café
www.12steps.org
1001 Ways To Be Romantic
www.1001waystoberomantic.com

A
About.com Guide to Panic and Anxiety Disorder
www.panicdisorder.about.com
About.com Guide to Women's Health
www.womenshealth.about.com
Addictions
www.habitsmart.com
Addiction Search
www.addictionsearch.com
AfraidtoAsk.com
www.afraidtoask.com/std.html
Alabama Coalition Against Rape
www.acar.org
Alcoholics Anonymous
www.recovery.org
American Association for Marriage and Family Therapy
www.aamft.org
American Association of Sex Educators, Counselors, and Therapists
www.aasect.org
American Association of Suicidology
www.suicidology.org
American Board of Sleep Medicine
www.absm.org
American College of Obstetricians and Gynecologists
www.acog.org
American Counseling Association
www.counseling.org
American Group Psychotherapy Association
www.groupsinc.org
American Pain Foundation
www.painfoundation.org
American Pain Society
www.ampainsoc.org
American Physical Therapy Association
www.apta.org

American Psychiatric Association
www.psych.org

American Psychological Association
www.helping.apa.org

Americans With Disabilities (Department of Justice)
www.usdoj.gov/crt/ada/adahoml.htm

Anxiety Coach, The
www.anxietycoach.com

Anxiety Disorders Association of America
www.adaa.org

Anxiety Disorders Caregiver Site
www.pacificcoast.net/~kstrong

Association for Advancement of Behavior Therapy
www.aabt.org

Association for Pre- and Perinatal Psychotherapy and Health
www.birthpsychology.com

Association for the Study of Dreams, The
www.asdreams.org

Association of Traumatic Stress Specialists
www.atss-hq.com

AtHealth.com
www.athealth.com

Aviva Gold: Painting from the Source
www.avivagold.com

A Woman's Touch
www.a-womans-touch.com

B

Behavioral Health World for Professionals and their Clients/Patients
www.bhworld.com

Birth Psychology
www.birthpsychology.com

Body Positive
www.bodypositive.com

Brazos County (Texas) Rape Crisis Center, Inc. (BCRCC)
rapecrisis.txcyber.com

C

California Association of Marriage and Family Therapists
www.camft.org

California Coalition Against Sexual Assault
www.calcasa.org

Campus Outreach Services (COS)
www.campusoutreachservices.com

Capital City Model Mugging
www.ccmmselfdefense.org

Center for Mental Health Services (CMHS)
www.mentalhealth.org

Center for Research on Women with Disabilities
www.bcm.tmc.edu/crowd

Clear Passage Therapist
www.clearpassage.com

Cocaine Anonymous
www.ca.org

Connecticut Sexual Assault Crisis Services, Inc. (CONNSACS)
www.connsacs.org

Consortium for Citizens with Disabilities, The
www.c-c-d.org

Curad.com/scar
main.asp

D

David Baldwin's (Ph.D.) Trauma Information Pages
www.trauma-pages.com

Department of Justice, Drug Enforcement Administration
www.usdoj.gov/dea/pubs/rohypnol/rohypnol.htm

DiscoveryHealth.com
www.health.discovery.com

Dr. John Grohol's Mental Health Page
www.psychcentral.com

Dr. Glazer's Vulvodynia.com
www.vulvodynia.com

Dyspareunia Website
www.dyspareunia.org

E

Eating Disorder Recovery
www.joannapoppink.com

Eating Disorder Referral and Information Center
www.edreferral.com

Eating Disorders Awareness and Prevention, Inc.
www.edap.org

Eating Disorders in a Disordered Culture
www.eating.ucdavis.edu

Eating Peacefully
www.power-nutrition.com

EMDR Institute, Inc.
www.emdr.com

G

Grant Me The Serenity
www.open-mind.org

Gurze Books Eating Disorders Recourse
www.gurze.com or www.bulimia.com

H
HealthyPlace.com
www.healthyplace.com
Healthy Within, Inc.
www.healthywithin.com
Hunger Pains
www.nisa.net/~lee/main.html

I
IMPACC USA
www.impaccusa.com
International Association of Eating Disorders Professionals
www.iaedp.com
International Society for the Study of Dissociation, The
www.issd.org
International Society for Traumatic Stress Studies
www.istss.org
Internet Directory of Therapists
www.psychology.com/therapy.htm
Intervention Center
www.intervention.com

J
Joan Borysenko, Ph.D.
www.joanborysenko.com
Julian Center, The
www.juliancenter.org

K
Kelly Bulkeley, Ph.D.
www.kellybulkeley.com
King County Sexual Assault Resource Center
www.kcsarc.org
Kinsey Institute, The
www.indiana.edu/~kinsey

L
Learning Publications, Inc.
www.learningpublications.com
Love First: Intervention for Alcoholism and Drug
www.lovefirst.net

M
Marriage and Family Health Center, The
www.passionatemarriage.com

Martial Hearts
www.martialhearts.com

Mental Health Forum
www.mentalhealthchannel.net

Mental Health Net
www.mentalhelp.net/selfhelp

Mental Health Sanctuary
www.mhsanctuary.com

N
National Anxiety Foundation
www.lexington-on-line.com

National Association for Social Workers
www.naswdc.org

National Association of Anorexia Nervosa and Associated Disorders
www.anad.org

National Association of Cognitive-Behavioral Therapists
www.nacht.org

National Center for Victims of Crime, The
www.ncvc.org

National Clearinghouse for Alcohol and Drug Information, The
www.health.org

National Clearinghouse on Marital and Date Rape
www.members.aol.com/ncmdr

National Crime Prevention Council
www.ncpc.org/10yth3.htm

National Crime Victim Bar Association
www.victimbar.org

National Criminal Justice Reference Service
www.ncjrs.org

National Depressive and Manic Depressive Association
www.ndmda.org

National District Attorneys Association
www.ndaa-apri.org

National Crime Victims Center, The
www.musc.edu/cvc

National Institute of Mental Health
www.nimh.nih.gov

National Organization for Victim Assistance, The
www.try-nova.org

National Women's Health Information Center
www.4woman.gov

New York Coalition Against Sexual Assault
www.nyscasa.org
Nightmare Treatment Center
www.nightmaretreatment.com
NIMH Anxiety Disorders Education Program
www.nimh.nih.gov/anxiety

O
OBGYN.net's Women's Pavilion
www.obgyn.net
Overeaters Anonymous
www.overeatersanonymous.org

P
Pain.com
www.pain.com
Partnership Against Violence
www.pavnet.org
Pennsylvania's University Center for Excellence
www.temple.edu/inst_disabilities
Pittsburgh Action Against Rape
www.paar.net
Prepare, Inc.
www.prepareinc.com
Psych Central
www.psychcentral.com/grohol.htm
PTSD Alliance
www.PTSDAlliance.com

R
Rape Assistance and Awareness Program of Denver
www.raap.org
Rape Crisis Center of Massachusetts
www.rapecrisiscenter.org
Recovery USA
www.RecoveryUSA.net
RelationshipWeb.com
www.relationshipweb.com

S
SAFE Alternatives
www.selfinjury.com
Scars.com
www.scars.com.au/pages/scarTherapy.html

Security on Campus, Inc.
www.campussafety.org

SelfHelp Magazine
www.shpm.com

Self-Help Network of Kansas
www.selfhelpnetwork.edu

Self Improvement Online
www.selfgrowth.com

SexualHealth.com
www.sexualhealth.com

Sinclair Intimacy Institute
www.bettersex.com or www.intimacyinstitute.com

Sidran Foundation and Press, The
www.sidran.org

Sinclair Intimacy Institute
www.intimacyinstitute.com

South Carolina Coalition Against Domestic Violence & Sexual Assault
www.sccadvasa.org

Standing Together Against Rape
www.STAR.AK.org

SupportWorks
www.supportworks.org

Survivors Art Foundation
www.survivorsartfoundation.org

T
Texas Dept. of Public Safety
www.txdps.state.tx.us

TherapistFinder
www.TherapistFinder.net

Thrive Online
www.thriveonline.oxygen.com

Tulsa, Oklahoma Rape Crisis & Education Center
www.callrape.com

W
Wendy Maltz, MSW
www.healthysex.com

Wisconsin Coalition Against Sexual Assault
www.wcasa.org

Women's Centers & Offices at American Colleges & Universities
www.uic.edu/depts/owa/womens_centers.html

WritingtheJourney.com
www.writingthejourney.com

Writers Resource Center
www.poewar.com

Y

Yahoo! Anorexia Support Group List
www.groups.yahoo.com/search?query=anorexia
Yahoo! Anxiety Groups Online
www.groups.yahoo.com/search?query=anxiety
Yahoo! Bulimia Support Group List
www.groups.yahoo.com/search?query=bulimia
Yahoo! Compulsive Overeating Support Group List
www.groups.yahoo.com/search?query=overeating
Yahoo! Dissociative Disorders Support Group
www.groups.yahoo.com
Yahoo! Panic Disorder Groups Online
www.groups.yahoo.com/search?query=panic
Yahoo! Online Support Group for PTSD
www.groups.yahoo.com/search?query=ptsd

State Sexual Assault Coalition

ALABAMA
Alabama Coalition Against Rape
Phone: (888) 725-RAPE (7273)
Web site: www.acar.org

ALASKA
Alaska Network on Domestic Violence and Sexual Assault
Phone: (907) 586-3650
Web site: www.andvsa.org

ARIZONA
Arizona Sexual Assault Network
Phone: (602) 254-2466
Web site: www.azsan.org

ARKANSAS
Arkansas Coalition Against Violence to Women and Children
Phone: (800) 269-4668

CALIFORNIA
California Coalition Against Sexual Assault
Phone: (916) 446-2520
Web site: www.calcasa.org

COLORADO
Colorado Coalition Against Sexual Assault (CCASA)
Phone: (303) 861-7033
Web site: www.ccasa.org

CONNECTICUT
Connecticut Sexual Assault Crisis Services, Inc.
Phone: (860) 282-9881
Web site: www.ccasa.org

DELAWARE
Coordinating Council Against Sexual Assault in Delaware (CCASAD)
Phone: (302) 761-9800

FLORIDA
Florida Council Against Sexual Violence
Phone: (850) 297-2000
Web site: www.fcasv.org

GEORGIA
Network to End Sexual Assault
Phone: (404) 377-1429
Web site: www.gnesa.com

HAWAII
Hawaii Coalition for the Prevention of Sexual Assault
Phone: (808) 733-9038
Web site: www.fhsd.health.state.hi.us

IDAHO
Idaho Coalition Against Sexual & Domestic Violence
Phone: (208) 384-0419

ILLINOIS
Illinois Coalition Against Sexual Assault (ICASA)
Phone: (217) 753-4117

INDIANA
Indiana Coalition Against Sexual Assault, Inc. (INCASA)
Phone: (317) 423-0233
Web site: www.incasa.org

IOWA
Iowa Coalition Against Sexual Assault (Iowa CASA)
Phone: (515) 244-7424

KANSAS
Kansas Coalition Against Sexual and Domestic Violence (KCSDV)
Phone: (800) 400-8864

KENTUCKY
Kentucky Association of Sexual Assault Programs, Inc.
Phone: (502) 226-2704
Web site: www.kasap.org

LOUISIANA
Louisiana Foundation Against Sexual Assault (LaFASA)
Phone: (985) 345-5995
Web site: www.lafasa.org

MAINE
Maine Coalition Against Sexual Assault
Phone: (207) 626-0034

MARYLAND
Maryland Coalition Against Sexual Assault
Phone: (410) 974-4507
Web site: www.mcasa.org

MASSACHUSETTS
Jane Doe Inc., Massachusetts Coalition Against Sexual Assault and Domestic Violence
Phone: (617) 248-0922

MICHIGAN
Michigan Coalition Against Domestic & Sexual Violence
Phone: (517) 347-7000
Web site: www.mcadsv.org

MINNESOTA
Minnesota Coalition Against Sexual Assault
Phone: (612) 313-2797
Web site: www.janedoe.org

MISSISSIPPI
Mississippi Coalition Against Sexual Assault
Phone: (601) 987-9011

MISSOURI
Missouri Coalition Against Sexual Assault
Phone: (816) 931-4527

MONTANA
Coalition Against Domestic and Sexual Violence
Phone: (406) 443-7794
Web site: www.mt.net\~mcadsv

NEBRASKA
Nebraska Domestic Violence & Sexual Assault Coalition (NDVSAC)
Phone: (402) 476-6256
Web site: www.ndvsac.org

NEVADA
Nevada Coalition Against Sexual Violence
Phone: (702) 914-6878

NEW HAMPSHIRE
New Hampshire Coalition Against Domestic and Sexual Violence
Phone: (800) 735-2964
Web site: www.nhcadsv.org

NEW JERSEY
New Jersey Coalition Against Sexual Assault (NJCASA)
Phone: (609) 631-4450
Web site: www.njcasa.org

NEW MEXICO
New Mexico Coalition of Sexual Assault Programs, Inc.
Phone: (505) 883-8020
Web site: www.swcp.com\nmcsaas

NEW YORK
New York State Coalition Against Sexual Assault (NYSCASA, Inc.)
Phone: (518) 482-4222
Web site: www.nyscasa.org

NORTH CAROLINA
North Carolina Coalition Against Sexual Assault (NCCASA)
Phone: (919) 676-7611
Web site: www.nccasa.org

NORTH DAKOTA
North Dakota Council on Abused Women's Services - Coalition Against
Sexual Assault in ND
Phone: (800) 472-2911

OHIO
Ohio Coalition on Sexual Assault (OCOSA)
Phone 614-268-3322

OKLAHOMA
Oklahoma Coalition Against Domestic Violence and Sexual Assault
Phone: (405) 848-1815

OREGON
Oregon Coalition Against Domestic and Sexual Violence (OCADSV)
Phone: (800) OCADSV-2 or (800) 622-3782
Web site: www.ocadsv.com

PENNSYLVANIA
Pennsylvania Coalition Against Rape (PCAR)
Phone: (800) 692-7445
Web site: www.pcar.org

RHODE ISLAND
Rhode Island Coalition Against Sexual Assault
Phone: (401) 421-4100
Web site: www.satrc.org

SOUTH CAROLINA
South Carolina Coalition Against Domestic Violence & Sexual Assault
Phone: (800) 260-9293
Web site: www.sccadvasa.org

SOUTH DAKOTA
South Dakota Coalition Against Domestic Violence and Sexual Abuse
Phone: (605) 964-7233

TENNESSEE
Tennessee Coalition Against Domestic and Sexual Violence
Phone: (800) 289-9018
Web site: www.tcadsv.citysearch.com

TEXAS
Texas Association Against Sexual Assault (TAASA)
Phone: (512) 474-8161
Web site: www.taasa.org

UTAH
Coalition of Advocates for Utah Survivors' Empowerment (CAUSE)
Phone: (801) 322-1500

VERMONT
Vermont Network Against Domestic Violence and Sexual Assault
Phone: (800) 489-7273

VIRGINIA
Virginians Aligned Against Sexual Assault (VAASA)
Phone: (804) 979-9002
Web site: www.vaasa.org

WASHINGTON
Washington Coalition of Sexual Assault Programs
Phone: (360) 754-7583
Web site: www.wcsap.org

WEST VIRGINIA
West Virginia Foundation for Rape Information & Services
Phone: (304) 366-9500
Web site: www.fris.org

WISCONSIN
Wisconsin Coalition Against Sexual Assault (WCASA)
Phone: (608) 257-1516
Web site: www.wcasa.org

WYOMING
Wyoming Coalition Against Domestic Violence & Sexual Assault
Phone: (307) 235-2814
Web site: www.wcadvsa.vcn.com

Research-Based Methods
of Reading
Instruction

Grades K–3

Sharon Vaughn
Sylvia Linan-Thompson

Association for Supervision and Curriculum Development ~ ~ ~ Alexandria, Virginia USA

Association for Supervision and Curriculum Development
1703 N. Beauregard St. • Alexandria, VA 22311-1714 USA
Phone: 800-933-2723 or 703-578-9600 • Fax: 703-575-5400
Web site: http://www.ascd.org • E-mail: member@ascd.org
Author guidelines: www.ascd.org/write

Gene R. Carter, *Executive Director;* Nancy Modrak, *Director of Publishing;* Julie Houtz, *Director of Book Editing & Production;* Ernesto Yermoli, *Project Manager;* Georgia McDonald, *Senior Graphic Designer;* Valerie Sprague and Keith Demmons, *Desktop Publishing Specialists;* Tracey Franklin, *Production Manager*

Paperback ISBN: 0-87120-946-7 ASCD product #104134 List Price: $23.95 ($18.95 ASCD member price, direct from ASCD only) s8/04

e-books ($23.95): netLibrary ISBN 1-4166-0068-X ebrary ISBN 1-4166-0069-8; Retail PDF ISBN 1-4166-0221-6

Also available as an e-book through ebrary, netLibrary, and many online booksellers (see Books in Print for the ISBNs).

Library of Congress Cataloging-in-Publication Data
Vaughn, Sharon, 1952–
   Research-based methods of reading instruction, grades K–3 / Sharon Vaughn and Sylvia
Linan-Thompson.
       p.   cm.
   Includes bibliographical references and index.
   ISBN 0-87120-946-7 (alk. paper)
 1. Reading (Primary)—United States.   I. Linan-Thompson, Sylvia, 1959–   II. Title.

   LB1525.V34   2004
   372.41—dc22

                                                                                            2004009794

11   10   09   08   07   12   11   10   9   8   7   6   5

Research-Based Methods of Reading Instruction

Grades K–3

♦   ♦   ♦

This book is dedicated to the late

H. E. Hartfelder, a man of great integrity and foresight;

his daughter Patricia; and Patricia's husband,

Porky Haberman. As the H. E. Hartfelder/Southland

Corporation Regents Chair at the University of Texas

at Austin, I wish to express my sincere appreciation

for the outstanding support that Pat and Porky

have provided to teachers.

H. E. Hartfelder loved education and educators

and passed that devotion on to his daughter

and son-in-law, who have been involved in educational

events on the University of Texas campus and

in public schools throughout Texas.

♦   ♦   ♦

Acknowledgments

WE HAVE MANY PEOPLE TO THANK FOR CONTRIBUTING TO OUR LEARNING ABOUT early reading and the types of activities that influence teaching and student success.

First, we would like to thank each other. Having worked together on several intervention studies aimed at improving reading outcomes for students, we have learned the value of partnering, sharing, supporting, and depending on each other.

Second, we would like to thank our colleagues. We work with the most talented, exciting, interesting, thoughtful, hardworking, and knowledgeable team anywhere: Meaghan Edmonds, Ae-hwa Kim, Michael Krezmien, Pam Bell Morris, Kim Rodriguez, Shari Sharboneau, Martha Smith, and Jeanne Wanzek.

Next, we would like to thank the teachers and principals who have partnered with us on our many reading projects: Marty Hougen, Bernard Blanchard, Sandra Dowdy, Joyce Bannerot, Jean McInnis, Steve Ogle, Candace Phillips, Bertha Arellano, and Berta Hernandez.

We would also like to recognize Paulette Jackson for her assistance with manuscript preparation, as well as the tutors, too many to list, who worked with us on the intervention studies. We greatly appreciate the support given us by the Dean of Education's office at the University of Texas at Austin, specifically Dean Manuel Justiz and Associate Dean Marilyn Kameen.

Lastly, we would like to acknowledge the contribution of Mark Goldberg. Simply stated, he is the most careful, thoughtful, interesting, and motivating colleague and editor imaginable. We were motivated to complete our chapters so we could meet with Mark to get his feedback, in large part due to his interest in what we were writing. He even tried our activities with his grandchildren, and told us how they worked. Perhaps most valuable about Mark is his genuine enthusiasm for improving education. As a former principal and teacher, he recognizes that teachers are the central and most important link to student success—and, thus, the future of our society.

◆   ◆   ◆

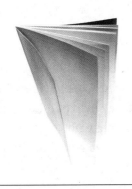

Introduction

THIS BOOK IS DESIGNED TO SHOW TEACHERS WHAT WE HAVE LEARNED FROM science-based reading research, and how they can best use that research to teach initial reading effectively. It is also designed to provide dozens of classroom activities that promote reading, drawn from practices that have been successful in actual classrooms and are based on solid research. The material in this book can be used with all students regardless of any special issues or needs, including those with dyslexia, at-risk for reading problems, or who simply require additional instruction to become successful readers.

Who benefits from scientifically based approaches to reading? Everyone! Recent National Assessment of Educational Progress (NAEP) reports state that as many as 38 percent of all 4th graders cannot read well enough to comprehend a simple children's book (2003). Without science-based approaches to reading, students with reading or language difficulties, attention or learning problems, a specific disability related to reading, and limited proficiency in English also risk being left behind.

Many students will learn to read as long as teachers use a substantial and consistent approach. We can optimize learning for students by using approaches that are validated by research. This book provides teachers and administrators with the essential elements of proven reading methods, and with classroom lessons for teaching them. The essential elements identified in this book—phonemic awareness, phonics/word study, fluency, vocabulary, and comprehension—and the corresponding classroom activities relate both to Reading First and to the No Child Left Behind Act of 2001.

Chapter 1 makes the case for using scientific research in the teaching of reading. Chapters 2–6 are devoted to different essential elements, and include clear definitions of the elements, suggestions for teaching them, several sample lessons, and annotated bibliographies useful for classroom teachers. These chapters are organized around questions, followed by a long section of classroom activities. For example, Chapter 2 is divided into the following sections:

- What Is Phonemic Awareness?
- Why Should I Teach Phonemic Awareness?
- What Are the Phonemic Awareness Skills That Students Should Know?
- How Do I Teach Phonemic Awareness?

- What Are Some Useful Classroom Phonemic Awareness Activities?

Chapter 7 closes the book with an overview of how to put the ideas presented to use in the classroom. Some may wish to read Chapter 7 before reading anything else, as it may help put the other chapters in perspective, though not everything will be fully understood until the rest of the book is read.

We intend this book to provide readers with a comprehensive introduction to the case for the scientific teaching of reading, and with enough material to proceed with their own substantial program.

1

Why Science Matters

SUPPOSE THAT WHEN DR. JONAS SALK PERFECTED THE POLIO VACCINE AND published the results, the medical community had not paid attention. After all, most of their patients did not contract polio, and they were accustomed to treating those who did with time-honored methods, such as iron lungs.

"New vaccines are not the way we approach things," these physicians might have said. "We really believe in the iron lung philosophy. Besides, staying well and getting well are natural processes, and we have faith that our patients will improve if given the right hospital environment."

Is this an absurd scenario? Yes. Scientific research has been the accepted method for establishing the medical procedures that revolutionized healthcare in the last century. Do we have rigorous, science-based research that could guide our decision-making in education? Yes, but the implications of the research have not been fully recognized, agreed upon, or implemented in the classroom.

Why not? For one thing, the medical profession matured and turned to scientific procedures at a much earlier date than did education. Also, results in education are much harder to observe. Being unable to breathe is much more obvious (and elicits much more sympathy) than being unable to read or compute. In general, medical interventions take effect much more rapidly and appear more dramatic than those in education. But most important, medical procedures are chosen and administered by practitioners trained at a professional level unmatched by many other fields. The fact that educators are not trained to a similar level makes it even more important that we use principles of scientific research to form the body of knowledge that serves as

3

a basis for our classroom methods, and we must present these methods in an understandable, straightforward way.

How a Scientific Approach Helps Practicing Teachers

A science-based approach can reduce the influence of politicians, parents, school board members, and others and increase the influence of reading experts and teachers. As Walberg notes:

> Educators are deluged by a huge amount of opinion and advocacy. Much of it is poorly conceived, ill written, and biased. Little is based on the findings of rigorous inquiry. For this reason, education has not made the fact-based productivity strides enjoyed by other professions and industries. (1998, p. ix)

Opinions on nonpedagogical matters such as salary schedules or bond issues should be valued, but educational materials and methods should be based in scientific research (to the extent possible).

It is not unusual to find teachers, principals, or members of school boards or state departments of education who have made important decisions that run counter to research findings. For example, Harris Cooper, a social psychologist, became a member of the school board in a district with a population of approximately 100,000. He soon realized that most school board members have dual roles as both advocates and accommodators:

> Decision makers who are advocates on an issue would be tempted to ignore research or use it

as a weapon, perhaps culling through the literature to find studies that supported their position while ignoring the conflicting literature. On the other hand, decision makers who view themselves as accommodators on an issue might have been more likely to want to know "what the research says." However, I can now see how, on occasion, accommodators might be motivated to actively avoid research findings. (1996, p. 30)

The above comments show that research is not always used in the way research scientists would hope or expect. Chall (2000) points out that the problem is not that pertinent research is nonexistent, but that its implications have not been recognized, agreed on, or implemented widely. It is crucial that administrators, teachers, and board members appreciate the value of scientific research in education.

What Is Science?

You probably have had many experiences with science, and not all of them positive. You may remember science classes where you were taught principles and reasons for these principles, or conducted experiments and interpreted the findings or memorized answers. Mostly, when you took science classes you were trying to understand a well-documented system of knowledge in a particular area. We define science as the development of an objective, consistent, documented system of knowledge based on rigorous, systematic observations that lead to hypotheses that are then tested and refined (Vaughn & Dammann, 2001). The scientific process conflicts with other approaches in that its goal is to publicly distribute the resulting information.

Why should you value science in education? Because techniques derived from scientific methods are *useful*. They get things done. In education, getting things done means students are better educated, more knowledgeable, more capable, and more informed citizens.

Not all educational undertakings require specific quantifiable results. Some, like the presentation of a humorous play, aim toward producing experiences, and some kinds of art are produced simply to express their creator's feelings. But if your mission is pragmatic, such as teaching reading, or science, math, the applicability of the scientific approach is indisputable.

There may be no organized human activities that are totally free of bias, political stands, or points-of-view based on wishful thinking or even noble intentions, but science stands out as being as free of these influences as possible. Still, educators sometimes resist scientific approaches that they feel may control or otherwise inhibit them. To counter this point-of-view, Stanovich (2000) points out that:

> What science actually accomplishes with its conception of publicly verifiable knowledge is the democratization of knowledge, an outcome that frees practitioners and researchers from slavish dependence on authority; and it is subjective, personalized views of knowledge that degrade the human intellect by creating conditions in which it is inevitably subjugated to an elite whose "personal" knowledge is not accessible to all. (p. 402)

When teachers develop an understanding of scientific findings related to education, it gives them a powerful means to justify decisions and gain independence from the more traditional roles in which they have been cast, as well as a means to resist political pressures.

Are there alternatives to using science as the basis of our methods? It is apparent that our methods are not all based on science right now. What alternatives can there possibly be?

Folklore

Folklore is transmitted by word-of-mouth, as anecdotes, tales, and so-called facts are passed, sometimes with distortions, from one generation to the next. Though often composed of superstitions, folklore embraces a wide range of information. Folklore may be important for supporting school spirit and traditions, but it is an unreliable basis for teaching and learning.

Not all folklore in education is bad; though most of it is unproven, some of it is based on practice. Folklore can be a way of telling stories about previous principals and how they behaved or treated teachers. These stories can serve as ways of bringing the community of teachers together and remembering shared experiences. However, folklore can also be harmful by misleading educators to believe that the findings of educational research merely state the obvious and could be figured out by any good educator without conducting a study. Of course, 100 years of research in medicine, psychology, and education have taught us that the obvious is not always true.

Craft

Craft is a goal-oriented body of knowledge developed through trial and error, and is a more acceptable basis for knowledge than folklore. It is also far more compatible with science. Craft has been used to develop knowledge throughout human history; in fact, some of the great accomplishments of the past, such as the cathedrals of Europe, the circumnavigation of the globe, and some medical practices, were developed from craft-based knowledge. Though science often has its beginnings in craft, craft is not as rigorous, systematic, objective, or well documented as science—craft cannot claim the confidence, generality, or pertinence that science-based approaches can.

We can see the inefficiency of craft by comparing the growth of knowledge in the three centuries that the scientific method has been in existence to the thousands of years during which craft reigned alone. For example, though craft was helpful for centuries in Japan in the building of earthquake-resistant structures, rigorous scientific testing has extended that ability dramatically in the last 50 years.

As indicated above, science and craft are not mutually exclusive. Several of the attributes of the scientific approach were introduced at various times into the culture of craft. With time, scientific approaches were introduced into craft-based fields such as architecture, where they were used to develop and confirm technical aspects of the work. In medicine, the beneficial effects of various pharmaceuticals came to be tested and evaluated scientifically, leading to a systematic and growing body of knowledge that gives us effective methods and techniques in which we can have confidence. Because of this, participants in these areas come to be viewed as professionals. As Carnine (1999) notes:

> A mature profession…is characterized by a shift from judgments of individual experts to judgments constrained by quantified data that can be inspected by a broad audience, less emphasis on personal trust and more on objectivity, and a greater role for standardized measures and procedures informed by scientific investigations that use control groups. (p. 9)

Education: Craft or Science?

Like many other disciplines, education has developed largely as a craft, though substantial science-based research has been established in many areas. The basis exists for education to build on this foundation and, following the example of its successful predecessors, embrace the scientific approach in order to develop into an effective and mature profession. Education is now poised to make the shift that medicine has already accomplished: that is, to a profession largely based on scientific evidence. "Until education becomes the kind of profession that reveres evidence," notes Carnine, "we should not be surprised to find its experts dispensing unproven methods, endlessly flitting from one fad to another" (1999, p. 3).

Our experience working with teachers in classrooms across the United States shows they are eager to learn and use effective instructional practices. Teachers want to make a difference. They want the quality of their students' lives to be improved because of their experience in their classroom. We are convinced that if teachers start on the road to effective research-based reading practices with their students, they will go a long way toward accomplishing these goals.

Annotated Bibliography

American Federation of Teachers (June, 1999). *Teaching reading is rocket science: What expert teachers of reading should know and be able to do.* Washington, DC: Author.

This document describes why preventing reading failure is a top priority for education. It describes the difficulty of learning how to teach reading, and asserts that many teachers are unprepared to assure that students are able to read words and obtain meaning from print. The document also presents a curriculum for teacher preparation and professional development in reading, and can be obtained from the American Federation of Teachers, 555 New Jersey Avenue NW, Washington, DC 20001-2079. (Ask for Item No. 372.)

Web Sites That Teach

http://www.nifl.gov.

The National Institute for Literacy (NIFL) is an independent federal organization that supports the development of high-quality state, regional, and national literacy services so that all Americans can develop the literacy skills they need. NIFL administers the Partnership for Reading and other programs that promote child and adult literacy.

http://www.nationalreadingpanel.org.

In 2000, the National Reading Panel issued a report entitled *Teaching Children to Read*, which provides meta-analyses of studies conducted in such critical areas of reading as phonemic awareness, phonics, and fluency. This Web site provides information on how to obtain a full copy of that report.

http://www.getreadytoread.org.

This Web site targets childcare workers and provides information about a "constellation of care" to encourage early literacy. Also included on the site are skill-building activities, frequently asked questions about building early literacy skills, information on programs and resources, training alerts, and research information.

2 | Phonemic Awareness

CHILDREN WHO ENTER SCHOOL WITH PHONEMIC AWARENESS HAVE A VERY HIGH likelihood of learning to read successfully. Children who lack phonemic awareness have a great deal of difficulty learning to read. Obviously, children who come without phonemic awareness need to develop it! The question is not if but how. (Cunningham, 1999, p. 69)

This chapter provides an overview of phonemic awareness: what it is, how to assess it, and how to design instructional activities to promote it. Instructional classroom activities are provided to guide teachers and parents in the use of phonemic awareness skills with children.

What Is Phonemic Awareness?

Phonemic awareness, the most complex part of a phonological awareness continuum that includes rhyming and segmenting words and sentences, is the ability to identify the *phonemes* (smallest identifiable units of sound) of spoken language, and how they can be separated (pulled apart or segmented), blended (put back together), and manipulated (added, deleted, and substituted). You may have learned that a phoneme is the smallest sound in spoken language that makes a difference in words. For the purpose of reading instruction, a phoneme is a single sound that maps to one or more printed letters. For example, the word *sat* has three phonemes: /s/, /a/, and /t/. While there is no break between the sound segments, we can tell that there are three phonemes because we can compare *sat* to the word *pat*, where the initial /p/ sound is substituted for the /s/ sound; to the word *Sam*, where the final /m/ sound is substituted for the /t/ sound; and to the word *sit*, where the medial /i/ sound is substituted for the /a/ sound. Children learn to read more easily when they are aware of these phonemes.

In some words, letters combine to produce a single sound, as with the /sh/ in the word *shrimp*. We would say that there are five phonemes in shrimp: /sh/, /r/, /i/, /m/, and /p/. In the word *check*, we would say that there are three: /ch/, /e/, and /ck/. It is not always easy for young children to determine how many sounds a word has, but there are many activities to help them understand and manipulate the sounds in words. These activities, several of which are provided at the end of this chapter, are fun and teach children to understand that words are made up of many sounds.

Why Should I Teach Phonemic Awareness?

> Children who begin school with little phonological awareness have trouble acquiring alphabetic coding skill and thus have difficulty recognizing words. (Stanovich, 2000, p. 393)

More than 52 peer-reviewed experimental studies reveal that there are significant positive benefits from explicit instruction in phonemic awareness, especially when combined with instruction in letter names (National Reading Panel [NRP], 2000). Phonemic awareness influences outcomes in word recognition and comprehension, as well as spelling, for all students except those with established learning disabilities.

As kindergarten teacher Margaret Fischer told us:

> Learning to hear the sounds in words, manipulate these sounds, and segment them is essential for my students. I practice these activities 15–20 minutes a day with all of my students to assure that they have the building blocks of phonemic awareness to improve their success as readers. I understand that the benefits are not just improved phonemic awareness but that my students will be able to more readily read words and understand what they read. Also important is that I am teaching them how to listen to sounds so that as they spell and write they become more accurate.

Fischer understands what the research has proven: preschoolers and kindergarteners who are provided phonemic awareness training become better readers (Ball & Blachman, 1991; Lundberg, Frost, & Peterson, 1998). In fact, one of the best predictors of how well students will learn to read during their first two years of school is phonemic awareness (Learning First Alliance, 2000; NRP, 2000). Students who have difficulty learning to read in the early grades are often unable to do activities related to phonemic awareness, and those with poor phonemic awareness skills at the end of their kindergarten year are more likely to become poor readers than those with well-developed phonemic awareness skills (Adams, 1990; Pressley, 1998; Stanovich, 1986).

Explicit instruction in phonemic awareness benefits most beginning readers, including those with reading difficulties and English language learners. Some teachers have the mistaken idea that phonemic awareness instruction is only for students with severe reading disabilities. Others are uncertain whether calling attention to sounds in language is helpful to English-as-a-second-language (ESL) students.

The National Reading Panel report (2000) indicates that phonemic awareness helps students with disabilities, students with reading difficulties, very young students (preschoolers), kindergarteners, 1st graders, students from a range of socioeconomic groups, and ESL students. Furthermore, since phonemic awareness can be taught in a relatively brief amount of time each day (15 minutes) and throughout the school day, time should not be a constraint in providing appropriate training to beginning readers.

What Are the Phonemic Awareness Skills That Students Should Know?

Fortunately, phonemic awareness can be developed through instruction, with clear benefits to subsequent acquisition of reading skills. (Pressley, 1998, p. 104)

Segmenting words into phonemes and blending phonemes into words contribute more to learning to read and spell well than any of the other phonological awareness skills (NRP, 2000). Words can be divided into sound units such as syllables, onset-rime, or phonemes. Words that can be divided into onset-rime are one-syllable words. "Onset" refers to the consonant or consonants before the vowel, and "rime" refers to the vowel and every sound that follows it. For example, in the word *can*, /c/ is the onset, and /an/ is the rime. In *scratch*, the onset is /scr/ and the rime is /atch/. Words of any length can be divided into phonemes or individual sounds. The greater the number of sounds in a word, the more difficult the word is to segment.

Figure 2.1 provides an overview of the critical skills and activities that are part of the phonological awareness spectrum.

Though it might be tempting to teach all of the phonological awareness skills at once or to skip around among them, it is better to focus on teaching one or two skills at a time, perhaps for a week, especially at the phoneme level (Ehri, Nunes, & Willows, 2001). Segmenting words into onset-rime and rhyming are considered warm-up skills, and you should shift instruction to segmenting and blending at the phoneme level as quickly as possible.

According to Ehri and colleagues (2001), kindergarten students benefit from phonemic awareness instruction more than students who receive their first lessons in phonemic awareness in 1st or 2nd grade. Of course, 1st and 2nd grade teachers should teach phonemic awareness to students who have trouble with the concept. In addition, some skills are more appropriate for students in different stages of acquiring phonemic awareness. For example, kindergarten teachers might begin the school year teaching students to manipulate larger sound units in words, segment words into syllables, and blend syllables into words. By the beginning of the second half of kindergarten, they should start teaching how to segment words into phonemes and blend phonemes into words.

FIGURE 2.1 ➤ **Overview of Phonological Awareness Skills and Activities**

Discriminating. Students listen to determine if two words begin or end with the same sound.

Counting. Students clap the number of words in a sentence, syllables in a word (*cowboy, carrot*), sounds in a word (*me, jump*).

Rhyming. Students create word families with rhyming words (*all, call, fall, ball*).

Alliteration. Students create tongue twisters (*Sally's silly shoe sank slowly in the slime*).

Blending. Students say the sounds in a word and then "say them fast" while the teacher combines blocks or letters to demonstrate blending.

Segmenting. Students say the word and then say each syllable or sound (*inside* is /in/ /side/ or /i/ /n/ /s/ /i/ /d/).

Manipulating. Deleting, adding, and substituting sounds and syllables.

- **Deleting.** Students listen to words and then say them without the first syllable (*baseball* becomes *ball*), or sound (*bat* becomes *at*).

- **Adding.** Students listen to words and add syllables (to *come* add /ing/), or sounds (add the /s/ sound to the beginning of /un/).

- **Substituting.** Students listen and change sounds (change /r/ in *run* to /b/ to make *bun*).

Source: Adapted from Bos and Vaughn (2002).

(First grade students who lack phonemic awareness, or who read fewer than 20 words per minute, should also learn these skills.) This instruction should not take the place of teaching phonics and other reading components.

How Do I Teach Phonemic Awareness?

Effects of PA training on reading lasted well beyond the end of training. PA instruction produced positive effects on both word reading and pseudo word reading, indicating that it helps children decode novel words as well as remember how to read familiar words. (NRP, 2000, pp. 2–5)

When considering how to teach phonemic awareness, there are several important questions to consider:

- Do my students need phonemic awareness instruction?
- What phonemic awareness instruction would they most benefit from?
- How much time should I spend teaching phonemic awareness?

- What if several students are not making progress in phonemic awareness?

These questions can be addressed via progress monitoring (see below). However, as a rule of thumb, kindergarten or 1st grade students who can read more than 20 words per minute accurately rarely need additional instruction in phonemic awareness.

Progress Monitoring

The first step in determining how and what to teach is to use a progress monitoring system to identify which phonemes the student knows and does not know. A good system will allow teachers to determine which of the three critical aspects of phonemic awareness—deleting, segmenting, and blending—are problematic. Progress monitoring helps teachers identify students who are at-risk of failing to acquire phonological awareness skills, and helps monitor their progress during instruction. Effective systems should both guide instruction and be predictive of later reading ability.

The following tests can be useful guidelines as you make decisions about the measures you will use to monitor student progress in phonemic awareness (Chard & Dickson, 1999).

Test of Phonological Awareness (TOPA; Torgesen & Bryant, 1994). The TOPA is a test of students' awareness of sounds in words for grades K–2. It can be administered in groups or individually. The aim of the test is to identify students at-risk for reading difficulties or to detect phonological deficits in those already experiencing reading difficulties. The kindergarten version consists of two subtests. First, students are asked to mark pictures (multiple choice) that begin with the same sound as a target word. Then they must choose pictures that begin with a different sound. The elementary version consists of the same two subtests, except students are asked to focus on ending sounds. The TOPA is nationally normed and includes standard scores and percentiles. Group administration time is approximately 15–20 minutes.

Comprehensive Test of Phonological Processing (CTOPP; Wagner, Torgesen, & Rasholte, 1999). The CTOPP is an individually administered test that assesses three areas: phonological awareness, phonological memory, and rapid-naming ability. The first version of the test is for ages five and six (kindergarteners and 1st graders), and a second version is for ages 7–24. The phonological awareness subtests consist of blending sounds in words (/c/ /a/ /t/ = cat), deleting parts of words (*baseball* without base = *ball*), and matching words with similar beginning or ending sounds (students choose pictures that start or end with the same sound as a target word). Phonological memory subtests include recall of a series of digits and repetition of nonwords (*blit*). Rapid-naming tests are timed and consist of naming colors and objects (for 5- and 6-year-olds), or naming digits and letters (for 7-year-olds and up). The core subtests take approximately 30 minutes to administer; supplemental subtests are also included to allow for more specific assessment of student strengths and weaknesses. The CTOPP is nationally normed and includes standard scores and percentiles.

Yopp-Singer Test of Phoneme Segmentation (Yopp, 1995). Students are asked to segment each phoneme separately from a list of 22 presented words, receiving credit if they say all of the sounds in the word correctly. For example, if students were asked to identify the phonemes in the word *fit*, they would receive no credit for identifying the first phoneme correctly if they missed the following two phonemes. Students receive feedback after each response: for correct responses, they are told that they were right; for incorrect responses, the test administrator tells them the correct response. Like most phonemic awareness measures, this one is administered individually to children.

Phoneme Segmentation Fluency (Dynamic Indicators of Basic Early Literacy Skills [DIBELS]; Kaminski & Good, 1996). There are 18 parts of this test, with 24 words of up to five phonemes in each part. This test is also individually administered; unlike the Yopp-Singer Test, it is timed. Students are given 60 seconds to get as many phonemes correct as possible, receiving points for each correct phoneme even if the entire word is not correct. Students are not provided corrective feedback for errors.

When selecting good screening measures for your students, consider whether they

- Allow you to predict with accuracy students who will later have difficulties in reading,
- Help you to differentiate current high, average, and low performers,
- Tell you what phonemic awareness skills you need to teach, and

- Have multiple forms, or are designed so that you can administer them more than once a year.

If the test provides all of the above, the measure will serve you well as a teacher.

Instructional Factors

After you identify what your students know about phonemic awareness, you are ready to begin planning for instruction. Be sure that the instruction you provide is systematic and explicit—obvious, visible, and with goals that are easily determined by anyone listening. Lessons should be highly focused and well sequenced. They should allow time for the teacher to model, for students to respond individually and in groups, and for the teacher to determine which students are making progress and which need additional support. All of this can be done in 15 to 20 minutes a day. Figure 2.2 provides guidelines for teaching phonetic awareness.

While many activities will be oral, training is most beneficial when it is combined with connecting sounds to letters (Bradley & Bryant, 1985; Share, 1995). You should provide many opportunities for students to write the letters that represent the sounds that they hear. Whenever possible, teach students these skills in small groups of four to six students. Students who are taught in small groups transfer their phonemic awareness skills to reading and spelling better than those who receive whole-class instruction or one-to-one instruction (Ehri et al., 2001).

FIGURE 2.2 ➤ **Guidelines for Teaching Phonemic Awareness**

- Determine the phonemic awareness skills the students in your class have and need to learn. Provide group activities that address the needs of most or all of the students. Provide small group activities to address the specific needs of selected students.

- Based on each student's level of development, identify the tasks that need to be mastered.

- Model each activity, demonstrating what you want students to do and how you want them to do it. Then provide students with an opportunity to practice the task. For example, "Watch me, I'm going to say each of the sounds in the word *mast* separately, then I'm going to put them together and say the word. Watch my lips and fingers: /m/, /a/, /s/, /t/ (put one finger up for each sound until four fingers are up), *mast*. Now do it with me, "*mast*: /m/ /a/ /s/ /t/." Watch to be sure students hold up one finger for each sound.

- Use manipulatives, body movements, or fingers to make the auditory or oral tasks more visible. For example, "Watch me, I'm going to take one step sideways each time I say a sound in the word *cap*. /c/, /a/, /p/ (teacher takes one step for each sound). Now you stand up. After I say a word, you say the sounds with me and take one step sideways for each sound in the word." Teachers can use Elkonin boxes to move markers or write letters, or have students clap or use their fingers to signal the phoneme. (see p. 23)

- Proceed from less to more difficult tasks, considering:

  ○ Identifying syllables and separating onset and rime are easier than blending and segmenting phonemes.

  ○ Segmenting and blending phonemes in the initial position is easier than blending phonemes in the final or medial position.

  ○ Segmenting and blending words with two phonemes is easier than blending three phonemes. Three phonemes are easier to segment and blend than four phonemes.

- Provide positive and corrective feedback and many opportunities for practice and review. Allow students to answer together in a group and give students opportunities to respond individually.

Source: Adapted from information provided in Bos and Vaughn (2002) and Smith, Simmons, and Kame'enui (1998).

The two most important aspects of phonemic awareness are segmenting and blending (NRP, 2000). Activities for involving students in segmenting sounds and then blending them together can use both real words and nonsense words. Students can use letters to manipulate phonemes and apply their knowledge of segmenting and blending when they read and write new words. When oral blending and segmenting are paired with letters, you can explicitly teach the alphabetic principle (Goswami, 2000; Greaney, Tunmer, & Chapman, 1997). The alphabetic principle is the establishment of a correspondence between a phoneme and a written symbol.

The following activities involve students in segmenting sounds:

- "Say the first sound in *sit*."
- "Say each sound separately in *mop*."
- "Say *fast* without the /t/ sound."

These activities involve students in blending sounds:

- "Say *an*. Put /c/ in front of /an/. Say the word."
- "I'm going to say some sounds. You put the sounds together to make a word. Listen: /i/ . . . /t/. Say the word."
- "Put the /d/ sound at the end of *san*. Say the word."

These activities involve students in both segmenting and blending sounds:

- "I'm going to say some sounds. You put the sounds together to make a word. Listen: /m/, /a/, /d/." After students say *mad* say, "Now say each sound separately in the word *mad*, and count the sounds on your fingers: /m/, /a/, /d/."
- "I'm going to say a word. You tell me the first sound in the word. Listen: *bat*. Now, change the /b/ to /s/. Say the new word."
- "I'm going to say some sounds that make a word. You put them together, and think of the word in your head. Don't say the word

aloud. When I call on you, tell me each of the sounds in the word. Listen: /f/, /i/, /sh/."
- "Say the sounds in fish." After students say /f/, /i/, /sh/ say, "Now say it the fast way."

The following activities can help students link the sounds of language to print:

- "I'm going to say some sounds that make a word. You tell me the word. Listen: /p/, /o/, /t/. What is the word? Yes, the word is *pot*. Now write the first sound in *pot*. Now write the last sound in *pot*."
- "I'm going to say some sounds that make a word. After I say the sounds, put them together and say the word. Listen: /s/, /l/, /i/, /t/. What is the word? Yes, the word is *slit*. Now say the word *slit* without the /s/ sound."
- "I'm going to say four sounds separately. Write each sound after I say it. Listen: /f/, /i/, /s/, /t/. Now, say the word."
- "I'm going to say the last part of a word. You write a letter that could be added to the beginning to make a new word. Listen: *am*. Write a letter at the beginning to make a new word." Rapidly call on individual students to say their new word. If students say a nonword, say, "That is a make-believe word."
- "I'm going to say a sound. You write a word that begins with that sound. Listen: /m/."
- Provide each student with a small dry erase board. Use a large dry erase board to model. Say, "I'm going to write each letter that represents the sound I say. Watch me." Say, "/s/." (Write *s* on the board.) "/t/." (Write *t* on the board.) "/e/." (Write *e* on the board.) "/p/."

(Write *p* on the board.) "Now, what word is /s/ /t/ /e/ /p/? Yes, that's right; it is *step*. Now, I will say some sounds and I want you to write the letter that represents each sound. Then tell me the word."

- Provide each student with a small dry erase board. Use a large dry erase board to model. Say, "I'm going to write each letter that represents the sound I say. Watch me." Say, "/s/." (Write *s* on the board.) "/p/." (Write *p* on the board.) "/i/." (Write *i* on the board.) "/n/." (Write *n* on the board.) "Now, what is that word? Yes, it is *spin*. Now write *spin* without the /s/ sound."

Teachers who have difficulty identifying, segmenting, and blending speech sounds at a level required for explicit instruction may be more willing to teach the critical elements of phonemic awareness if they have the confidence and skills needed to provide instruction. Teachers who have had little experience with phonemic awareness need time to rehearse the skills needed to manipulate language sounds for instructional purposes. It may be useful for them to further understand the system of speech sounds that make up English and contribute to reading; while there are 26 letters in the alphabet, there are between 40 and 44 speech sounds, depending on how linguists differentiate the sounds. A good source for information on sounds is the Neuhaus Education Center at the W. Oscar Neuhaus Memorial Foundation (4433 Bissonnet, Bellaire, Texas 77401-3233; Web site: http://www.neuhaus.org).

Remember, phonemic awareness activities should be fun to teach and fun for students to practice and learn. They can occur throughout the day and are particularly good to use as transitions from one activity to the next, or when you have a few minutes before lunch or recess. Build a repertoire of phonemic awareness activities that you can use whenever you have transition time or a few spare minutes in your classroom.

What Are Some Useful Classroom Phonemic Awareness Activities?

The following activities are appropriate for all students in the second semester of kindergarten, 1st grade students weak in phonemic awareness, and any students who read fewer than 20 words per minute. (Working with the larger sound units in words is typically more appropriate for students in the first semester of kindergarten.)

Syllable Split

Objective: Given a compound word, two-syllable word, or three-syllable word, students will separate the word into syllables.

Materials: Word list for teacher (see Figure 2.3).

Sequence: Compound words, two-syllable words, three-syllable words, words with more than three syllables.

1. For compound words, tell students that some words are two words put together to make one word. These are called compound words. Tell them a compound word and ask them to tell you the two words that were put together to create it.

2. For words of two or more syllables, tell students that words can be separated into syllables or parts and that each syllable contains a vowel.

3. Model the task by separating words into parts or syllables.

4. Have students segment words with you. For example, "The word is *football*. Say the parts with me: *foot ball*." Ask them to do several examples with you to demonstrate that they do the task correctly. If a student makes a mistake, have all the students watch you model it correctly and repeat the word with you.

5. Ask students to separate a compound word or two-syllable word. Have students respond as a group, then call on individual students.

6. Once all students have performed the task correctly, give them new words to demonstrate that they have mastered the skill.

Variation: Use student names for syllables.

Scaffolds: Students use chips, tiles, or their fingers to help them keep track of syllables. Tell students how many syllables each word has.

Challenge: Use words with three or more syllables.

Deleting Syllables

Objective: Given a compound word, one-syllable word, or two-syllable word, students will delete one part or syllable and say the new word.

Materials: Word list for teacher (see Figure 2.3).

Sequence: Compound words, two-syllable words, three-syllable words, words with more than three syllables.

1. For compound words, tell students that some words are two words put together to make one word. Tell them a compound word, then ask them to take away part of the word and say the word that is left. For words with two or more syllables, tell students that words can be separated into syllables or parts. Tell them to take away one syllable and say the syllable that is left.

2. Model the task by saying the word, saying the part you will leave off, and saying the new word. For example, "The word is *baseball*. I will take away *base*. The new word is *ball*."

3. Model by having students do it with you. For example, "Say *daytime*." (You and the students say *daytime* together.) "Take away *day*." (Students do this in their heads and do not say anything.) "Say the new word with me." (Students say the new word with you.) "*Time*." Have students do several examples with you to be sure they can do the task correctly before moving on. If students make a mistake, stop and model the example for the

FIGURE 2.3 ➤ **Word Types for Use in Activities**

Compound Words			
sunshine	cowboy	bookcase	seesaw
baseball	cupcake	inside	cowgirl
someplace	outside	shoeshine	oatmeal
steamship	sometime	himself	daytime
cardboard	airplane	eyelash	playmate
football	herself	doorbell	upset
homework	housework	applesauce	bobcat
armpit	popcorn	spaceship	shapeless
birthday	highway	hallway	myself
wristwatch	withdraw	doorknob	knothole
snowplow	somehow	handbook	snowball
bullfrog	cartwheel	ladybug	bulldog
backyard	bathtub	toothbrush	haystack

Two-Syllable Words				
bubble	mister	candy	person	rabbit
cartoon	funny	daddy	garden	barber
window	paper	magic	after	little
dentist	monkey	kitten	chicken	napkin
bashful	kettle	butter	mistake	empty
April	July	August	yellow	purple
needle	apple	teacher	student	buddy
spider	bamboo	panda	magnet	attic

(continued)

FIGURE 2.3 ➤ Word Types for Use in Activities—*cont.*

Two-Syllable Words				
eager	baker	invite	jolly	rusted
happen	lazy	baby	ladle	crayon
whisper	reply	quickly	nylon	zero
maybe	payment	away	purchase	hundred
thousand	compass	almost	walnut	fallen
author	country	glasses	number	problem
breakfast	vibrate	children	older	explain

Three-Syllable Words				
peppermint	carpenter	wonderful	buttermilk	understand
fisherman	forgetful	important	mistaken	September
valentine	October	November	December	excitement
Saturday	family	example	gasoline	capitol
rapidly	consider	property	popular	woodpecker
grandmother	vacation	potato	volcano	umbrella
magazine	hyena	energy	babysit	ladybug
handwriting	however	parachute	beautiful	rollerskate
microscope	telephone	museum	photograph	alphabet
neighborhood	employer	animal	different	gentleman
elephant	Indian	referee	dangerous	wonderful

(continued)

FIGURE 2.3 ➤ **Word Types for Use in Activities—*cont.***

Two-Phoneme Words				
go	see	Jay	sigh	on
no	knee	tie	say	me
bay	mow	rye	is	hi
each	my	ill	off	ate
oak	ease	ice	so	odd
aim	ace	up	age	he
day	an	may	new	eat
egg	we	by	ache	own
pie	it	zoo	be	if
ash	ape	low	us	ray

Three-Phoneme Words				
man	dip	hop	men	sup
tip	bit	ran	bat	sun
ten	fit	mop	bed	cup
fun	can	hit	top	let
fed	pup	fat	fit	pop
chop	less	Dan	bug	sit
big	shop	Ben	fan	dug
dim	sun	shop	pen	pan
back	mug	web	wit	end
dash	and	fade	sash	hide
bite	fish	bone	date	joke

(continued)

FIGURE 2.3 ➤ **Word Types for Use in Activities—*cont.***

Three-Phoneme Words				
beat	nice	rush	math	lock
cane	shot	cape	seek	chat
beef	bus	bake	cuff	rice
poke	seen	home	light	cave
came	tone	feet	kite	side
cage	late	soak	act	slow

Four-Phoneme Words (CVCC)*				
best	told	list	rent	fault
fact	mind	sold	cent	lunch
vast	task	pest	dance	bench
mist	kind	must	test	help
bend	past	lent	pant	rest
wind	gold	chant	lend	gift
band	mild	sent	last	cold
mend	fast	hand	yelp	lift
mask	bold	sift	cast	land
send	wild	sand	dust	milk
child	west	silk	lint	wisp
cast	since	went	bind	jump
find	pact	budge	bump	mold
just	shift	cinch	nest	lump

* "C" = consonant and "V" = vowel.

(continued)

FIGURE 2.3 ➤ **Word Types for Use in Activities—*cont.***

Four-Phoneme Words (CCVC)				
crab	bleach	step	tribe	slid
plug	price	bled	fried	spill
flies	drab	cluck	bread	slight
green	brick	fluff	fled	fright
blade	preach	sniff	brim	skin
pride	stuck	flab	speech	flight
sleet	grade	broke	smack	slime
fries	broom	plead	sled	spoon
slide	sneak	flop	grab	still
track	creek	bright	stop	cream
click	spade	please	skies	slope
bleed	glide	stage	sped	crack
played	speak	stick	blot	press
spoke	braid	grim	steal	black
club	steam	gloom	snail	plus
sweet	brim	plop	snub	dress

Note: Special recognition to Shirley Dickson for her contribution to word types and phonemic awareness ideas.

whole group, and have them repeat the word and task with you.

4. Ask students to say a word, leave part off in their heads, and say the new word. Have students respond as a group, then call on individual students. For example,

"Say *cowboy*." (Students say *cowboy*.) "Take away *cow*." (Give students a few seconds.) "Say the new word." (Students say *boy*.)

5. After students perform the task correctly, continue giving them new words.

Variation: Use student names, take away the last word part or syllable.

Scaffold: Students use chips, tiles, or their fingers to help keep track of syllables, covering up the one that represents the word part that is being taken away.

Challenge: Use words with three or more syllables.

Jumping Syllables

Objective: Given a two-syllable word or three-syllable word, students will identify the syllables and then manipulate them to form pseudo-words.

Materials: Word list for teacher (see Figure 2.3).

Sequence: Two-syllable words, three-syllable words.

1. Review with students that words can be separated into syllables and that every syllable contains a vowel.
2. Model the task by separating two or three two-syllable words into syllables.
3. Ask students to separate several two-syllable words into syllables.
4. Tell students that now they will make syllables jump from the beginning of the word to the end to form new silly words.
5. Model by separating two-syllable words into syllables and then moving the first syllable to the end. For example, "Listen to the word I'm saying: *mistake*. Let's count the parts or syllables in *mistake*:

mis-take. Yes, there are two syllables. What is the first syllable? *mis*. What is the second syllable? *take*. Now I'm going to jump the first syllable *mis* and put it at the end of the second syllable, and say a silly word: *takemis*. Yes, *takemis* is a silly word. Now you try it."
6. Give students a practice word, and ask them to identify the syllables, move the first syllable to the end, and say the new word.
7. Once students master jumping two-syllable words, advance to jumping three-syllable words, and jumping around the first, second, or third syllable.

Scaffolds: Use manipulatives such as chips or tiles to help students visualize what they are doing; use compound words.

Challenges: Use words that have more than two syllables. Move the middle syllable to the beginning or end.

Note: This activity was adapted from the University of Texas Center for Reading and Language Arts (2001a).

Elkonin Boxes

Preparation: Elkonin (1973) boxes are boxes drawn together in a horizontal line, like this:

They can be drawn on a piece of paper or on an index card. Laminating the paper or index cards help them to last longer. One box represents one sound. For words with three phonemes, students have three boxes connected together; for words with four phonemes, students have four boxes. For each sound, students can put a marker into a box, touch the box, move a letter into the box, or write the letter(s) for the sound in the box. For kindergarten students, it helps to put a green dot or a picture in the first box to reinforce that print moves from left to right.

Objective: Given a word, students will segment it into phonemes.

Materials: Word list for the teacher (see Figure 2.3); Elkonin boxes and chips for the students. The number of boxes in a row matches the number of phonemes in the given word.

Sequence: Two-phoneme words, CVC words, CVCC words, CCVCC words (C = consonant and V = vowel).

1. Tell students that words can be divided into sounds.
2. Model the task by segmenting a word into phonemes and moving a chip into a box after you say each sound. For example, "The word is *Go*. What are the sounds? /g/" (move a chip into the first box) "/o/" (move a chip into the second box).
3. Have students segment several words with you. See that students move a chip into a box for each sound, and listen to determine that they say the right sounds. If a student makes a mistake, stop and have all the students watch you model, then have them segment the word and move

chips with you. Continue having students do the task with you until they are fairly successful.

4. Tell the students a word. Have students segment it into phonemes (sounds) and respond as a group. Call on individual students to be sure they are segmenting correctly. If any student makes a mistake, stop and have all the students watch you model, then have them segment the word and move chips with you. Continue with new words, having students respond without your modeling.
5. Once students have mastered segmenting two-phoneme words, advance to three-, four-, and five-phoneme words.

Variations:

- Use a puppet. Tell students the puppet's name is "/M/ /a/ /t/ *Matt*" or any other segmented one-syllable name, and that he only understands slow talk. Tell students a word the fast way, then ask them to tell the puppet the word in the slow (segmented) way.
- After students learn the sound for a letter, use that letter in place of a chip. See that students place the letter in the corresponding box. As students learn more letter-sound correspondences, use letters instead of chips. Limit the number of letters students can choose from so that you do not lose instructional time for teaching segmenting.

Scaffolds:

- Stretch the word to help students identify the phonemes.

- Tell students how many phonemes the word has.
- If students are having difficulty identifying phonemes in CVC words even with prompts, do the activity at the onset/rime level.

Challenges: Use words with blends and digraphs, or with more than one syllable.

Note: Adapted from Elkonin (1973).

M&M Phonemes

Objective: Given a word, students will segment it into phonemes.

Materials: M&M candies (or colored chips); word list for the teacher (see Figure 2.3).

Sequence: Phonemes in CVC words, one-syllable words, phonemes in longer words.

1. Tell students that words can be separated into phonemes or sounds.
2. Model the task by segmenting a CVC word into phonemes and moving an M&M from a pile into line as you say each phoneme.
3. Distribute M&Ms.
4. Model by having students do one or two words with you. Say the word, then with the students move an M&M into line as you say each phoneme. Watch and listen to the students; if a student makes a mistake, stop the group, model, and have the group repeat the task with you.

5. Give students a CVC word and ask them to segment it, moving an M&M into line each time they say a sound in the word.
6. See that each student performs the task correctly. If a student makes a mistake, stop the group, model for the group, have the group segment the word with you, and continue to the next word.
7. After all students have mastered segmenting CVC words, advance to segmenting longer words.

Variations: Use Skittles or another hard candy. Use chips, tiles, or counters instead of candy.

Scaffolds:
- Stretch the word to help students identify the phonemes.
- Tell students how many phonemes the word has.
- If students are having difficulty identifying phonemes in CVC words even with prompts, do the activity at the onset/rime level.

Challenges: Use words with blends and digraphs. Use words with more than one syllable.

What Did I Say?

Objective: When given a segmented word, students will blend the sounds and identify the word.

Materials: Word list for teacher (see Figure 2.3).

Sequence: CVC words, two-syllable words, words with blends and digraphs.

1. Tell students to listen carefully to the sounds you say, and then tell you the word.
2. Model the task by blending phonemes into words. For example, say "/s/ /a/ /t/. What word is that? Yes, the word is *sat*." If students have difficulty hearing the sounds and blending sounds into words, stretch the sounds. If students still have difficulty, stretch the first sound (the onset) and say the last two sounds (the rime) as a syllable (/s/ /at/).
3. Have students do several words with you. For example, "/c/ /a/ /n/. Say the word with me: *can*."
4. Give students two or three words to blend. Determine whether students are performing the task correctly by asking each student to blend sounds into a word.
5. After all students are performing the task correctly, continue giving them words for a short time.

Variation: Let students provide the words.
Scaffolds:
- Extend each sound. For example: /mmmm/ aaaa/t/.
- Extend the first sound (onset) /m/ and say the last two sounds (rime) as one syllable, /at/.
- Give students chips. Model the task by lining the chips up in a row, but apart from each other. Move the first chip into the second chip and into the third chip as students blend the sounds together. Have students use the chips as they blend words.

- Use the Elkonin boxes. Have students touch the first box and slide a finger across the boxes as they blend the sounds together to make a word.

Challenges: Use words that are longer but only have a few sounds, such as tough or might. Use words with blends, digraphs, and vowel blends.

Do the Phoneme Shuffle

Objective: Given a word and directions to substitute a phoneme, students will substitute phonemes in words.
Materials: Word list for teacher (see Figure 2.3).
Sequence: Substitute phonemes in the initial position, final position, medial position, all three positions.

1. Review with students that words are made up of phonemes or sounds.
2. Tell students that they will be changing one phoneme or sound in a word to create a different word.
3. Model the task by changing the phoneme in the initial position of two or three words. For example, "The word is *hat*. I change the /h/ to /b/ and I get *bat*. Now you do it. The word is *sit*. Change the /s/ to /l/. What do you get? That's right, *lit*."
4. Give students two or three practice words. See that they are performing the task correctly before moving on to changing the phoneme at the end of the word.

5. Changing sounds at the end of the word is more difficult that at the beginning of the word. Model by changing the phoneme in the final position of two or three words. For example, "Listen to the sounds and tell me the word. /f/ /a/ /t/. That's right, the word is *fat*. Now drop the /t/ sound. What do you get? That's right, you get *fa*. Now add /n/ to the end of *fa*. What word do you get? That's right, you get *fan*."

6. After all students have performed the task correctly, continue giving them words from the word list for a short time.

Scaffold: Use manipulatives such as plastic chips or tokens that students can see and move with each sound. These will also help students see how sounds are removed.

Variation: After students learn a few letter-sound correspondences, use a word list with the learned letter sounds. Give each student a plastic bag containing four or five of the learned letter sounds. (e.g., /a/, /m/, /t/, /s/, and /f/). Ask students to put the letters in a row at the top of their desks. Say, "Move the first sound you hear so it is in front of you: *mat*." (Students move the /m/ in front of them.) Say, "Now change the /m/ to /s/." (Students move the /m/ back and move the /s/ in front of them.) Say, "What is the new word?" (Students say, "*sat*.")

Challenge: Substitute phonemes in all three positions and use longer words.

Note: Adapted from the University of Texas Center for Reading and Language Arts (2001a).

Smiley Face Phonemes

Objective: Given a word, students will determine whether or not the target sound is present in the beginning, middle, or end of the word as identified by the teacher.

Materials: Word list for teacher (see Figure 2.3); smiley face stickers.

Sequence: Sounds in the initial position, ending position, medial position, all three positions.

1. Give students one smiley face sticker each and ask them to place the sticker on their thumbs.

2. Review with students that words are made up of phonemes or sounds.

3. Tell students to listen for a specific sound at the beginning of the word. If they hear the sound, they should show the smiley face; if they do not, they should lay their hand on the table.

4. Model the task by using some words that meet the criteria and some that do not.

5. Give students two or three practice words to determine that they are performing the task correctly.

6. After all students have performed the task correctly, continue giving them words from the word list for a short time.

Variation: Give each student a card with "yes" written on one side and "no" on the other, or red and green slips of paper to hold up.

Scaffold: Emphasize the target sound by elongating the sound as you say it. Elongate the sound in the target position.

Challenge: Have students listen for words that have similar sounds, such as words with /e/ and

/i/. Other similar-sounding letter pairs include /b/ and /d/, /m/ and /n/, and /ch/ and /sh/.

Note: Adapted from the University of Texas Center for Reading and Language Arts (2001a).

Which Word Is Different?

Objective: Given three words, students will identify the one that has a different vowel sound.

Materials: Word list for teacher (see Figure 2.3).

Sequence: Words with the target sound in the initial position, words with the target sound in the middle position.

1. Tell students that you will say three words and they will identify the one that has a different vowel sound.
2. Model the task. For example, "Listen carefully to each of these three words. Listen for the vowel sound at the beginning of the word. Tell me the word that is different from the others. Listen: *am, an, it.* Which word begins with a different sound?" Stretch the vowels if you need to.
3. Give students two or three sets of words to ensure they can complete the task.
4. After all students have performed the task correctly, continue giving them sets of words from the word list for a short time.

Variation: Use minimal pairs that aren't vowels, such as /ch/ and /sh/.

Scaffold: Use words with two distinct vowel sounds /a/ and /i/.

Challenge: Use words with similar vowel sounds in the middle position.

◆   ◆   ◆

Annotated Bibliography

Adams, M. J., Foorman, B. R., Lundberg, I., & Beeler, T. (1998). *Phonemic awareness in young children: A classroom curriculum.* Baltimore: Paul H. Brookes Publishing.

This book provides phonological and phonemic awareness activities geared primarily to kindergarteners, 1st grade students, and some older students with special needs. The introduction provides a brief description of phonemic awareness and its importance, and is followed by a sequence of activities. These activities are detailed enough to help teachers provide instruction in the classroom, and each includes an extensive wordlist. The book also contains group-administered assessments, suggested grade level sequences, and resources for materials and rhyming stories.

Blachman, B. A., Ball, E. W., Black, R., & Tangel, D. M. (2000). *Road to the code: A phonological awareness program for young children.* Baltimore: Paul H. Brookes Publishing.

This book presents an activity-based program designed for kindergarteners and 1st graders struggling to learn to read, and includes an introduction with information about phonological awareness as well as guidelines for getting started with the lessons. The remainder of the book contains scripted phonological awareness lessons and guidelines for teaching them. Each lesson includes: activities where words are segmented with manipulatives, activities that teach letter names and sounds, and practice activities for reinforcing various phonological awareness skills. The book also contains reproducible pictures and cards needed to complete the activities.

O'Connor, R. E., Notari-Syverson, A., & Vadasy, P. F. (1998). *Ladders to Literacy*. Baltimore: Paul H. Brookes Publishing.

This activity book is intended for kindergarten students, and includes lessons for instructing students on print awareness, phonological awareness, and oral language. The authors indicate activities that are appropriate for the beginning, middle, and end of the year. Teachers are encouraged to use activities that fit their classroom routines and units studied. Each lesson contains a written objective for the teacher and an outline of targeted skills. After each activity, specific instructions for providing further support at three different levels—high demand/low support, medium demand/medium support, and low demand/high support—are provided to help teachers adjust the amount and type of support given as needed.

Torgesen, J. K., & Mathes, P. G. (2000). *A basic guide to understanding, assessing, and teaching phonological awareness*. Austin: Pro-Ed.

Phonological awareness and its importance, as well as specifics related to assessment and instruction, are described. The book is organized into three sections. The first section describes phonological awareness and gives teachers benchmarks of normally developing phonological awareness in conjunction with general information regarding the role of instruction in the development of phonological awareness. The second section provides information on assessing phonological awareness and gives detailed descriptions of eight published assessments available for teacher use. The third section provides information regarding instruction in phonological awareness and presents detailed descriptions of 12 published programs in phonological awareness available for teacher use.

Web Sites That Teach

http://www.ldresources.com/readwrite/readingtolearn
.html.

Provides an overview of learning to read with an emphasis on phonological awareness and word identification.

http://www.ldonline.org/ld_indepth/reading/
teaching_children_to_read.html.

Provides specific information on phonemic awareness, alphabetic principle, and phonics.

http://www.ldonline.org/ld_indepth/
teaching_techniques/cld_hownow.html.

Provides phonemic awareness activities for collaborative classrooms.

http://www.texasreading.org.

This Web site from the University of Texas at Austin's Center for Reading and Language Arts provides numerous resources and links for reading instruction, including phonological awareness.

http://www.Ericec.org/digests/3540.htm.

Provides information on phonological awareness.

http://www.pbskids.org/lions.

This PBS Web site for the show *Between the Lions* contains information and activities for beginning reading with emphasis on phonological awareness and phonics.

3

Phonics and Word Study

THIS CHAPTER PROVIDES AN OVERVIEW OF PHONICS AND WORD STUDY: WHAT IT is, how to assess it, the sequence of skills, and how to design instructional activities. The chapter also includes instructional classroom activities to guide teachers and parents and an annotated bibliography.

What Is Phonics and Word Study Instruction?

To learn to read and spell using phonics, children have to learn the relationship between letters (graphemes) and sounds (phonemes), and then remember the exact letter patterns and sequences that represent various speech sounds (Moats, 2000). Other terms for phonics include letter-sound correspondences, letter-sound relationships, and sound-symbol associations. There are several forms of phonics instruction, including synthetic, analytic, embedded, spelling-based, and analogy-based phonics. The National Reading Panel (2000) reports that the various forms of phonics instruction vary in 13 important ways, depending on the size of the unit, the pace of instruction, and the precise elements of the learning activities. Because word study is based on the stages of spelling, this chapter describes an explicit approach to phonics instruction that includes a range of skills, from alphabetic knowledge to reading in decodable books.

Given the differences and similarities available across instructional approaches, how will you know if the program you are using is effective? To read successfully—to read independently and construct meaning from text—beginning readers need to be able to identify words automatically and have an effective strategy for decoding unknown words (Bos & Vaughn, 2002; NRP, 2000; Snow, Burns, & Griffin, 1998). To reach this point, students have to learn the relationships between 44 speech sounds and more than 100 spellings used to represent them (Blevins, 1998; Bos & Vaughn, 2002). They then have to apply this knowledge to reading both known and unknown words, in isolation as well as in context, and learn to read irregular words.

An effective phonics program follows a defined sequence and includes direct teaching of a set of letter-sound relationships. Each instructional set includes sound-spelling relationships of both consonants and vowels. Sequencing helps students to learn the relationship between letters and sounds, and to use that knowledge to blend the sounds in order to read words, and to segregate the sounds in order to write words, even before they have learned all the letter-sound correspondences. Effective programs also include books and stories that contain a lot of words for children to decode using letter- sound relationships, and provide children with opportunities to spell words and write their own stories using letter-sound relationships (Blevins, 1998; Center for the Improvement of Early Reading Achievment [CIERA], 2001; NRP, 2000; Texas Education Agency [TEA], 2000).

Phonics instruction provides key knowledge and skills needed for beginning reading. However, phonics should not be the entire reading program, but should be integrated with other elements such as language activities, story time, and small group tutoring, to create a balanced reading program. While two years of phonics is sufficient for most students, other students may require more instruction. Use assessment information to adapt phonics programs to meet the needs of individual students (NRP, 2000). Most important, starting early is key. As Stahl (2001) notes, "Early and systematic instruction in phonics seems to lead to better achievement in reading than later and less systematic instruction" (p. 333). Adams (2001) points out that to learn to read, "all students must know the letters of the alphabet, understand their linguistic significance (phonemic awareness), and learn the logic and conventions governing their use (phonics); and . . . ensuring students' grasp of these basics must be a serious goal of any responsible program of beginning reading instruction" (pp. 67–68).

Why Should I Teach Phonics and Word Study?

The goals of phonics and word study instruction are to teach children that there are systematic relationships between letters and sounds, that written words are composed of letter patterns representing the sounds of spoken words, that recognizing words quickly and accurately is a way of obtaining meaning from them, and that they can blend sounds to read words and segment words into sounds to spell (Adams, 1990; Chard & Osborn, 1999; NRP, 2000). Gough and Tumner (1986) identify two basic processes necessary for learning to read: learning to convert letters into recognizable words, and comprehending the meaning of print. The first process can be taught through phonics and can lead to students comprehending the meaning of text.

The combination of deficient decoding skills and difficult material results in unrewarding early reading experiences that lead to less involvement with reading activities (Cunningham & Stanovich, 1998). On the other hand, systematic and explicit phonics instruction improves children's word recognition, spelling, and reading comprehension, and is most effective when it begins in kindergarten or 1st grade (CIERA, 2001; NRP, 2000).

What Elements Should I Include in My Phonics and Word Study Instruction?

The crucial elements of phonics and word study are: phonological and phonemic awareness, print awareness, alphabetic knowledge, alphabetic principle, decoding, reading practice with decodable text, irregular or high-frequency words, and reading fluency. How much time you spend on each of these elements will depend on the age and level of your students. As children participate in phonics and word study activities, their understanding of the conventions that govern language will increase. The elements do not have to be taught sequentially; for example, kindergarteners benefit from learning prerequisite skills for strong word recognition, the communicative function of print, alphabetic knowledge, phonemic awareness, and the alphabetic principle (Chard, Simmons, & Kame'enui, 1998). As students master

the skills, they can use them to decode and spell regular words and practice reading decodable text. Most students who have had effective phonics instruction can read quickly and easily, and have an effective decoding strategy for reading unknown words.

Print Awareness

Print awareness is the ability to understand that

- Written language is related to oral language and carries messages,
- Speech can be written down and read,
- What is written can be spoken,
- The length of a spoken word is usually related to the length of the written word,
- Print is read from left to right,
- The structures of written language are different from those of spoken language, and
- There is a difference between words and nonwords.

Students with print awareness can usually read some signs and logos (Blevins, 1998; Reutzel & Cooter, 1999; TEA, 2000). This awareness of the forms and functions of printed language is a reliable predictor of future reading achievement.

Children develop print awareness when they have opportunities to hear books and participate in read-aloud activities. To help them develop this awareness, you can reinforce the forms and functions of print found on classroom signs, labels, posters, calendars, etc.; explain print conventions such as print directionality, word boundaries, capital letters, and end punctuation;

and emphasize book awareness and handling. Listening to and reading predictable, patterned stories and books helps students practice what they are learning (Reutzel & Cooter, 1999; TEA, 2000). These kinds of books help model the concepts of print and conventions, as well as oral reading fluency and expression. Students should read the same predictable and patterned stories repeatedly, and the stories should include the use of context and picture clues and repeating language patterns (Bos & Vaughn, 2002).

Alphabetic Knowledge

Alphabetic knowledge, also known as alphabet recognition, involves knowing the shapes, names, and sounds of letters and progresses from letter names to shapes to sounds. Children should recognize and name letters quickly and accurately (Adams, 1990). Knowledge of letter names is strongly related to the ability to remember the shapes of written words, treat words as sequences of letters, and develop the alphabetic principle (the association of letters with their corresponding sounds). Students who cannot name certain letters are likely to have trouble mapping sounds to their corresponding letters; those who already know something about written letters tend to be more interested and able to learn more about the letters (Chard & Osborn, 1999).

Most children can identify an average of 14 letters when they enter kindergarten (Hiebert & Sawyer, 1984); others do not know any. These children need planned instruction that allows them to see, play with, and compare letters. Specifically, activities should use a sequence of letter

introduction that can be adjusted to each student's needs—some might learn several letters each week, whereas others may only learn one. Teachers should include games, songs, and other activities that help children identify letters, learn uppercase and lowercase forms, and point out differences and similarities among the letters. Teachers should also plan writing activities that encourage children to practice writing the letters they are learning and to experiment with and manipulate letters to make words and messages (Blevins, 1998; TEA, 2000).

The Alphabetic Principle

The alphabetic principle refers to the systematic relationship between sounds and letters. Children who understand that the sequence of letters in written words represents the sequence of sounds in spoken words and who know letter-sound correspondences can use this knowledge to decode both familiar and unfamiliar regular words (Bos & Vaughn, 2002; Ehri, 1991; TEA, 2000). Children who understand the alphabetic principle can translate the letters and patterns of written words into speech sounds automatically.

Effective alphabetic principle instruction should be planned and sequenced. To achieve this goal, adopt the following practices:

- Teach letter-sound correspondences explicitly and in isolation initially, then provide multiple opportunities daily to practice using this new knowledge to read and write;
- Provide practice opportunities with both new and previously taught sound-letter relationships;

- Give your students opportunities to apply their knowledge of letter-sound relationships to reading phonetically spelled words that are familiar in meaning (TEA, 2000).

Once you start phonics and word study instruction, some students will begin to make connections between letters and sounds on their own, but many will need explicit instruction to learn all the necessary letter-sound correspondences.

Decoding and Reading Practice with Decodable Text

Decoding is the process of reading letters or letter patterns in a word to determine the meaning of the word; for students, it is a strategy for reading unknown words. Once children develop this skill, they can apply it to reading words automatically and effortlessly. This allows them to focus on getting meaning from what they read (NRP, 2000; TEA, 2000). Students should begin by working with word families, spelling patterns, and onsets and rimes. As they become more sophisticated readers, they will need more advanced decoding strategies that focus on structural analysis: the ability to understand parts of words in order to understand the words as a whole. These parts of words include:

- **Inflectional endings.** Meaningful word parts (morphemes) that indicate tense, number, person, or gender when added to base words (*-ed, -es*).
- **Prefixes.** Word parts at the beginning of base words (*pre-, in-, un-*).

- **Suffixes.** Word parts at the end of base words (*-ful, -ly*).

More advanced students can use structural analysis to identify word parts and multisyllabic words. In addition, structural analysis teaches students about letter combinations and derivatives (words with the same root or base words)—knowledge they can use to segment multisyllabic words into decodable parts to determine their meaning (Henry, 1997). Teaching students about affixes in particular helps them learn that some word parts are common across words.

When teaching structural analysis, teachers should teach meanings along with recognition, and model how to look for word parts. Structural analysis will increase the number of words students can easily decode. Consider the following:

- The most common affixes in the primary grades are *re-, un-, con-, -ness, -ful,* and *-ion*;
- The prefixes *un-, re-, in-, im-, ir-, il-,* and *dis-* are used in 58 percent of all prefixed words; and
- Three inflectional endings, *-s/-es, -ed,* and *–ing*, are found in 65 percent of words that have inflectional endings and suffixes (White, Sowell, & Yanagihara, 1989).

Effective programs allow students to use their knowledge of sound-letter correspondences to practice decoding words both in isolation and in context. The use of decodable text provides teachers with the opportunity to model how to blend and segment sounds, sound out unknown words, and use onset rimes or word chunks to decode words. Students should practice these skills early on, as well as recognize less predictable words by sight as whole words and practice reading words and phrases independently. Students should then learn about letter sounds and simple spelling patterns, and to fluently and independently read words, sentences, and connected text (Bos & Vaughn, 2002).

Decoding lessons should include discussions about the text, to promote comprehension and reinforce the idea that the purpose of reading is to get meaning (TEA, 2000). Decodable books allow students to practice new skills, but teachers should gradually introduce books and stories that are less controlled so that they can extend those skills further.

Irregular Words

Not all words can be read through decoding. For example, in irregular words, some or all of the letters do not represent their most commonly used sound (for example, the vowel sound in *from* is not the usual sound for a short o). Students should encounter some of these words in texts for beginning readers, and will need to identify them by sight or automatically. To help students learn these words, teachers should introduce them in a reasonable order, and cumulatively review the ones that have been taught.

Sound-letter correspondences are important components in beginning reading instruction; rather than teach them in isolation, teachers should coordinate them to reinforce and extend student learning. Daily, integrated lessons that include explicit introductions to letter-sound relationships and opportunities to blend sounds, build and practice spelling words, and read

words and decodable texts will enhance the beginning reading experience (Blevins, 1998).

How Can I Teach Phonics and Word Study?

> By emphasizing all of the processes that contribute to growth in reading, teachers will have the best chance of making every child a reader. (National Reading Panel, 2000, p. 92)

Once your students meet the prerequisite conditions for word recognition, print awareness, alphabetic knowledge, and phonemic awareness, you can begin teaching them about the four subprocesses essential to teaching phonics and word study: letter-sound knowledge or alphabetic understanding; regular word reading; irregular word reading; and reading in decodable text.

Letter-Sound Knowledge

Letter-sound knowledge—also known as alphabetic understanding—helps students understand that the letters or clusters of letters that make up words represent separate spoken sounds, and that to read a word they must first identify the most common sound of each letter, then blend the sounds together. Figure 3.1 provides the most frequent spellings of the 44 English sounds, as well as keywords to guide pronunciation. It is important to teach the most common sound for each letter first.

Though teachers often teach one letter a week, introducing letter sounds in alphabetical order limits the number of words the students can form, thus limiting their ability to practice using the alphabetic

FIGURE 3.1 ➤ **Guide to Pronunciation of English Sounds**

Sound	Key Word	Most Frequent Spelling	Other Spellings
/ĭ/	it	i (66 percent of the time)	y
/t/	tip	t (97 percent of the time)	tt, ed
/p/	pig	p (96 percent of the time)	pp
/n/	nose	n (97 percent of the time)	nn, kn, gn
/s/	see	s (73 percent of the time)	c, ss
/ă/	at	a (96 percent of the time)	ae
/l/	lip	l (91 percent of the time)	ll
/d/	did	d (98 percent of the time)	dd, ed
/f/	fly	f (78 percent of the time)	ff, ph, lf
/h/	him	h (98 percent of the time)	wh
/g/	get	g (88 percent of the time)	gg, gh
/ŏ/	on	o (79 percent of the time)	aw, augh, ough
/k/	kit	c (73 percent of the time)	cc, k, ck, lk, q
/m/	man	m (94 percent of the time)	mm
/r/	rat	r (97 percent of the time)	rr, wr
/b/	bin	b (97 percent of the time)	bb
/ĕ/	elm	e (91 percent of the time)	ea, e_e
/y/	yet	y (44 percent of the time)	i
/j/	jar	g (88 percent of the time)	j, dg
/u/	us	u (86 percent of the time)	o, ou
/w/	wet	w (92 percent of the time)	u
/v/	vet	v (99.5 percent of the time)	f (of)

(continued)

FIGURE 3.1 ➤ **Guide to Pronunciation of English Sounds—*cont.***

Sound	Key Word	Most Frequent Spelling	Other Spellings
/z/	zoom	z (23 percent of the time)	zz, s
/th/	that	th (100 percent of the time)	– –
/ch/	chill	ch (55 percent of the time)	t
/sh/	shop	sh (26 percent of the time)	ti, ssi, s, si, sci
/zh/	sure	si (49 percent of the time)	s, ss, z
/hw/	wheel	wh (100 percent of the time)	– –
/ng/	song	n (41 percent of the time)	ng
/oi/	boil	oi (62 percent of the time)	oy
/ou/	house	ou (56 percent of the time)	ow
/o͝o/	soon	oo (38 percent of the time)	u, o, ou, u_e, ew, ue
/o͝o/	book	oo (31 percent of the time)	u, ou, o, ould
/ā/	aim	a (45 percent of the time)	a_e, ai, ay, ea
/ē/	ear	e (70 percent of the time)	y, ea, ee, ie, e_e, ey, i, ei
/ī/	ice	i_e (37 percent of the time)	i, igh, y, ie, y_e
/ō/	oat	o (73 percent of the time)	o_e, ow, oa, oe
/yo͞o/	use	u (69 percent of the time)	u_e, ew, ue
/th/	the	th (100 percent of the time)	– –
/ô/	ball	o	a, au, aw, ough, augh
/û/	bird	er (40 percent of the time)	ir, ur
/ä/	car	a (89 percent of the time)	aw, aa, ah
/a/	alarm	a (24 percent of the time)	e, i, o, u
/â/	chair	a (29 percent of the time)	are, air

Source: Adapted from Blevins (1998), pp. 43 and 90.

principle to read and write. A better strategy is to teach letter-sound associations that can be combined to make words that children can read and understand. The combination of a vowel and a few consonants—for example, /m/, /s/, /a/, /t/—allows children to form several words. Teachers should begin by teaching sounds that are easy to articulate. Continuous sounds, such as /m/ and /s/, are easy to say and hear because the sounds can be held without distortion, whereas stop sounds, such as /p/ and /b/, are easily distorted. It is not practical to teach all the letters with continuous sounds before any with stop sounds, because some stop sounds appear often in books for beginning readers. If a student is having trouble, teachers should focus on letter-sound relationships that are easier to pronounce.

During initial instruction, teachers should separate confusing letter-sound associations, such as letters that are visually or aurally similar, and determine that students have mastered one before teaching the next. Visually similar letters can differ in the vertical direction of their extensions (b/p, d/q), their left-right orientation (b/d, p/q), and their top-bottom orientation (w/m, u/n) (Blevins, 1998). Aurally similar letters include /b/, /p/, and /d/. As with visually similar letters, aurally similar ones should be separated to help students learn each as a distinct sound.

The following is a common sequence for introducing letter-sound correspondences:

1. Initial consonants (*m, n, t, s, p*)
2. Short vowel and consonant combinations (*-at, -in, -ot*)
3. Blends (*bl, dr, st*)
4. Digraphs (*th, sh, ph*)
5. Long vowels (*eat, oat*)
6. Final e (*-ake, -ute, -ime*)
7. Variant vowels and dipthongs (*-oi, -ou*)
8. Silent letters and inflectional endings (*kn, wr, gn, -es, -s*) (Blevins, 1998)

The number of letter-sound correspondences teachers introduce each week will vary based on the students, but two per week should be adequate for most. Teachers should remember to select letter-sound relationships that will allow the students to form words.

Here is a basic lesson for introducing letter-sound correspondences once students have learned letter names and forms:

1. Hold up a letter card and tell students the sound. Say, "This letter is *A*. The sound for *A* is /a/."
2. Ask students to tell you the name and then the sound. Be sure they know the difference between the two.
3. Ask students to write the letter as they say the sound.

If students at the beginning of first grade know none or only a few letter names, teachers should teach both the letter names and sounds simultaneously.

Regular Word Reading

Once children know three or four letter-sound associations, teachers should begin regular word reading and building activities. For example, students who have learned the letter-sound correspondences for *i, t, p, n,* and *s* can begin applying them to reading words such as *it, in, pit, pin, sit, sip,* and *tip.* Teaching them the short sound for *a* can more than double the number of words they can read and write.

Students need opportunities to practice regular word reading. Once they learn enough letter-sound correspondences to form words, teachers should integrate regular word reading into the instruction. Here is a basic regular word reading lesson that teaches students to blend sounds:

1. Sound out words without stopping between sounds. Use words with letters that begin with continuous sounds, like *sit,* to make this step easier.
2. After students sound out the word, ask them to first read each sound without stopping ("ssssiiit"), and then to say the whole word fast.
3. Teach students to sound words silently first before sounding them aloud.

The following are general guidelines for planning and teaching regular word reading:

- During initial instruction, begin with short vowel–consonant and consonant–short vowel–consonant words (*it* to *sit* and *pit, in* to *pin* and *tin*) before moving on to patterns that include blends and digraphs (CCVC [*stop*], CVCC [*mast*], CVCE [*bike*], and CCVCC [*truck*]). Progress from simple to more complex sound spellings.

- Teach consonant sounds (/b/, /m/, /s/) before blends (*br, cl, sn*) or digraphs (*sh, ch*).
- Teach short vowel sounds, then long vowel sounds, then variant vowels (*ea, oa*) and dipthongs (*oi, oy*).
- Select words that end with stop sounds.
- Select words that are familiar to students and that they are likely to encounter in their reading. (Blevins, 1998; Chard & Osborn, 1999)

Students who are taught to apply their letter-sound knowledge and given opportunities to do so will be able to read and write sentences even before learning all the letter-sound correspondences.

Since about a quarter of the most frequently used words in children's writing and texts are irregular (Moats, 2000), they should learn to read irregular as well as regular words. Figure 3.2 includes a list of irregular words; because students can't apply their knowledge of letter-sound relationships to these words, they will have to learn them as whole words.

Here are some guidelines for teaching irregular words:

- Select and teach words that appear frequently in stories and informational texts.
- The number of words taught in each lesson will depend on the student.
- Teach new irregular words before they appear in a story. Discuss the words and any special features, and point out parts of the words that are regular.
- Review previously taught words on a daily basis.

- Provide students with opportunities to use the words in their reading and writing activities. (Blevins, 1998; Chard & Osborn, 1999)

Reading in Decodable Text

Learning letter-sound relationships in isolation is necessary, but not enough. Students must know how to apply their knowledge to reading text. They should begin by reading decodable text comprised largely of words containing previously taught letter-sound relationships and gradually move to less controlled text as their ability and confidence grow. Because most decodable texts contain irregular words, be sure to teach these in advance if students do not know them. Once the class has read a book as a group, teachers should provide opportunities for the students to reread the text. Many publishers have decodable book series, and 1st grade basal programs often include decodable texts. Figure 3.3 provides a list of decodable book series for teachers. (For specific letter-sound relationship lessons, see the instructional activities section of this chapter.)

Progress Monitoring

Monitoring student progress helps teachers plan instruction and alerts them if students are falling behind. Teachers can use the information gleaned from monitoring to group students for instruction and modify the pace of instruction based on the skill level of students in each group. Student progress in every area can be monitored informally. For example, to assess student knowledge of letter-sound relationships, teachers might maintain a list of letter-sound associations that the students have already mastered; about once every two weeks, they can ask the students to identify the sounds of letters on the list, or to give the letter name of a given sound. Teachers can also give students a letter dictation—provide a letter name or sound and have the students write the corresponding letter.

FIGURE 3.2 ➤ **Thirty Irregular Words for Beginning Readers**

the	you	said	his	people
to	they	were	do	know
was	would	are	some	your
of	there	because	as	mother
is	one	what	could	who
two	too	should	put	whose

Source: Adapted from Moats (2000), p. 189.

FIGURE 3.3 ➤ **Decodable Book Series**

Publisher	Series Name	Contact Information
McGraw-Hill	Lippincott Phonics Easy Readers	Phone: 1-800-442-9685; Web site: http://www.mhschool.com
Scholastic, Inc.	Scholastic Phonics	Phone: 1-800-724-6527; Web site: http://www.scholastic.com
SRA/McGraw-Hill	SRA Phonics	Phone: 1-888-772-4543; Web site: http://www.sra4kids.com
Steck-Vaughn	Phonics Readers Phonics Readers Plus	Phone: 1-800-531-5015; Web site: http://www.steck-vaughn.com
Sundance Publishing	Sundance Phonics Readers	Phone: 1-800-343-8204; Web site: http://www.sundancepub.com

Teachers should monitor regular and irregular words separately, but can use the same process for each type of word. To monitor word reading in isolation, teachers should ask students to read a set of familiar words and see if the students can read them automatically. In most instances, it will take the students fewer than three seconds to read the word. Teachers can also keep a record of the words students miss repeatedly while reading connected text.

Instructional Activities

Note: Each lesson title in the following activites indicates whether the activity is an introduction to a new skill or element or a follow-up practice lesson.

Basic Lesson in Letter-Sound Knowledge: Name That Letter/ Say That Sound

Objective. Students will identify letter names and letter sounds.

Materials. Uppercase and lowercase letters.

Sequence. Begin by introducing one vowel and three or four consonants, adding new letters as students master them.

1. Tell students they will be learning the names and sounds of letters so they can begin to form words.
2. Model the task. Show students the first letter and say, "This is *A*." Then ask, "What letter is this?"

3. Repeat with each letter.
4. Show each letter to students and ask them as a group to name it.
5. After the group names each letter, ask the students to name letters individually, going from student to student as quickly as possible.
6. Repeat steps 2–5 using letter sounds.

Scaffolds. Use one vowel and two consonants; use only lowercase or uppercase letters.

Challenge. Show students a letter. Tell them to listen carefully to directions since they will sometimes be asked to name the letter, and other times to name the sound.

Follow-Up Lesson in Letter-Sound Knowledge: Which Letter Am I?

Objective. Given a letter sound, students will write the letter that makes that sound.

Materials. White boards, markers, erasers.

Sequence. Begin by introducing one vowel and three or four consonants, adding new letters as students master them.

1. After reviewing the letters they've learned, tell students that you will say a letter sound or name, and they will write the corresponding letter as they say the sound.
2. Model the task for the students. Say a letter sound, writing the letter as you do so.
3. Give students a sound and monitor them as they write the corresponding letter.
4. If students write the incorrect letter, show them the correct one. Ask them to say the sound and write the letter slowly as they do so.

5. Say the sound or name of the next letter.
6. Once all students have performed the task correctly, continue giving them letter names or sounds.

Variation. Ask students to write the letter as many times as they can in 10 seconds while saying the sound.

Scaffold. Give students either letter names or sounds.

Follow-Up Lesson in Letter-Sound Knowledge: Slap Cards

Objective. Students will identify letter names or sounds.

Materials. Uppercase and lowercase letters on index cards.

Sequence. Begin by introducing one vowel and three or four consonants, adding new letters as students master them.

1. Tell students whether they will be practicing naming letters or saying letter sounds.
2. Review letter cards.
3. After students have named each letter or identified each sound as a group, ask them to do the same individually.
4. Ask each student to place a card on a pile in the center of a table and say the name of the letter on the card. When a student places a vowel on the pile, all the students slap the pile of cards. The student whose hand is on the bottom takes the pile.
5. Pass out an equal number of cards to each student. Choose a student to start the game.

6. Play until one of the students is out of cards or time is up.

Variations. Use regular or irregular words.

Note: This activity was adapted from the University of Texas Center for Reading and Language Arts (2001a).

Basic Lesson in Regular Word Reading: Read the Word

Objective. Given a regular word, students will read it.

Materials. Word cards using words from the following list:

- VC: *in, at, am, it, up, ox*
- CVC: *mat, hop, cut, sit, pin, can, ten, get, not, cup, cut, tap, red, him, cob, run, gum, ham, mad, hid, dip, box, bug, big*
- CCVC: *stop, flap, snap, trip*
- CVCC: *mast, jump, bunk, fall, hand, will, bend, rock, told, dash, back, duck*
- CVC silent E: *bike, take, joke, made, time, more, cape, kite, five, name*
- CCVCC: *truck, sport, blast, small*

Sequence.
1. Tell students they will be reading new words.
2. Tell students that when shown a word card, they will first sound out each letter-sound and then read the word fast.
3. Show students a word card. Model the task by saying each sound continuously as you point to each letter ("*iiiinnnn*").

4. After sounding out the word, read the word fast ("*in*").
5. Show a word and ask the students to say each sound. Determine that all students have said each sound correctly. If a student makes an error, review the correct letter-sound correspondence and repeat.
6. Once students have sounded out the word, ask them to read it fast. If a student reads the word incorrectly, ask him or her to sound it out first and then read the word fast.
7. Continue with the remaining word cards.

Scaffolds.
- Review the individual letter-sound correspondences that appear in the words shown.
- Students point to each sound as they pronounce it, and sweep their fingers under the word when reading it fast.
- Students use letter tiles, pulling down each tile as they say the sound and sweeping a finger under the tiles when they say the word fast.

Follow-Up Lesson in Regular Word Reading: And the Word Is . . .

Objective. Students will read words containing rime patterns.

Materials. One set of cards containing previously studied onsets, and oneset containing previously studied rimes.

Sequence.
- Onsets:
  1. Single letters
  2. Blends (*bl, fl, sn, st*)

3. Digraphs (*gr, br*)
- Rimes:
  1. VC: -an, -ap, -at, -aw, -in, -ip, -ir, -op, -or, -ug, -it, -an, -et, -ot, -up, -ut
  2. VCE: -ake, -ale, -ame, -ate, -ice, -ide, -ine, -ore, -oke, -ade, -ike, -ime
  3. VVC: -ail, -ain, -eat, -eek, -een, -oot, -eed, -eep, -ait, -eet, -eem, -oot, -oop
  4. VCC: -ack, -ank, -ash, -ell, -est, -ick, -ill, -ing, -ink, -ock, -unk, -ump, -uck
- All:
  1. Review the onset and rime cards.
  2. Place the two sets of cards face down in the middle of the table.
  3. Explain to the students that they will pick the top card from each pile, put the two together, and read the word.
  4. Model the activity.
  5. Ask each student to take a turn. If all students do the activity correctly, have them take turns picking cards and reading the words. After reading a word, each student should say whether it is real or made-up.

Scaffolds.
- Limit the number of rimes used. Use rimes with the same vowels, such as *-at* or *-an*.
- Limit the number of onsets used.
- Ask all students to read each word formed.

Follow-Up Lesson in Regular Word Reading: Tic-Tac-Read

Objective. Students will read previously taught regular words.

Materials. A laminated tic-tac-toe board for each pair of students, word cards with regular

words, and ten plastic counters, half in one color and the other half in another color.

Sequence.
1. Give each pair of students a game board, a matching set of cards, and counters.
2. Explain how to play the game.
3. In each pair, one student picks a word card from the stack and reads it. The other student decides if the word was read correctly. If it was, the first student places his or her counter on the board. If it was not, the second student reads the word correctly and places his or her counter on the board.
4. Students continue playing until one student in the pair has three counters in a row or all the spaces are filled.

Variation. Fill the squares with irregular words.

Challenge. Impose a time limit for reading the word.

Note: This activity was adapted from the University of Texas Center for Reading and Language Arts (2001a).

Basic Lesson for Irregular Word Reading: What's the Word?

Objective. Given irregular words, students will read them.

Materials. Three to five word cards, a pocket chart, a notebook that has each page marked with one letter of the alphabet, and pencils.

Sequence. Begin with the most common irregular words.

1. Tell students they will be learning words that do not follow the letter-sound correspondences they already know, so they'll have to learn these words as a whole.
2. Show students the first word card and read the word. Ask them to repeat the word in unison.
3. Spell the word as you point to each letter, then ask the students to spell the word in unison.
4. Ask the students to read the word again and write it in their notebooks.
5. Monitor the students to determine that they spelled the words correctly.
6. Place the word card in the pocket chart.
7. Follow steps two to six with the other words.
8. Review the words taught. Point to each word card in the pocket chart and ask the students to read it in unison. Then ask individual students to read the word.

Variation. Use words from a text that students will be reading.

Follow-Up Lesson in Irregular Word Reading: Irregular Word Road Race

Objective. Students will read irregular words that have been previously taught.

Materials. For each student: a game board (see Figure 3.4), word cards matched to the game board, and a chip or game piece.

Sequence.

1. Explain the game to students. Tell them to place a chip in the start box, read the word in the first box, and then read each word card aloud until finding the card with the word that matches the word in the first box. Next, they will move the chip into the box containing the word. Tell them to repeat the process with the word in the next box on the board, and to continue to the end of the board. (Note that cards are not discarded but are placed back in the pile.)
2. Model for students.
3. Give each student a game board, a set of cards, and a chip. Remind students to read each card in the set aloud.
4. Monitor students to determine mastery of the skill.

Variations. Fill the squares with regular words or specific onset-rime patterns. For kindergarten students and struggling 1st graders, fill each square with a letter, and ask students to provide either the name or sound.

Scaffolds. Pair students with more able partners and ask them to take turns reading the word cards; limit the number of words.

Challenge. Impose a time limit for reading the word.

Note: This activity was adapted from the University of Texas Center for Reading and Language Arts (2001a).

Basic Lesson in Structural Analysis: Let's Add Word Parts

Objective. Students will understand that affixes change the meanings of words.

FIGURE 3.4 ➤ Sample Game Board

what	they
too	would
who	know
people	said
could	because
one	were
was	two
you	mother
Start	**Finish**

Source: Adapted from the University of Texas Center for Reading and Language Arts (2001a), p. 17.

Materials. Chart paper, a marker, and a list of root words students can read and give the meaning.

Sequence. Most common prefixes and suffixes, less common prefixes and suffixes.

1. Tell students that adding parts to a word will change its meaning. Tell them that prefixes appear at the beginning of a word, and they will learn the meaning of the prefix, then add it to root words.
2. Write a prefix on the chart paper. Read the prefix and tell students its meaning.
3. Ask students to read the prefix and say what it means.
4. Write a root word on the chart paper. Ask students to read the word and say what it means. If students do not know the meaning, provide it.
5. Write the root word with the prefix. Ask students to read the word.
6. Model how to determine the meaning of the new word. For example, say, "The new word is *unhappy*. *un-* means 'not' and *happy* means 'with joy,' so unhappy means 'not happy' or 'without joy.'"
7. Provide additional root words and ask students to read and define the prefix, read the root word, read the word with prefix added, and define the new word.
8. Repeat steps 2–7 using the second prefix.

Variation. Use suffixes.

Scaffold. Limit the number of prefixes introduced.

Note: This activity was adapted from the University of Texas Center for Reading and Language Arts (2002b).

Follow-Up Lesson in Structural Analysis: Make a New Word

Objective. Students will add previously taught prefixes or suffixes to a root word, and will give the meaning of the new word.

Materials. Three to four cards with root words written on them per student and 1 x 1.5-inch sticky notes with a prefix or suffix written on each.

Sequence. Most common prefixes and suffixes, less common prefixes and suffixes.

1. Tell students they will review the meaning of prefixes and suffixes they have learned and practice reading words with prefixes and suffixes.

2. Review the prefixes and suffixes written on the sticky notes. Ask students to read them in unison and provide the meaning for each.

3. Ask students to read the root words in unison, then give each of them three to five root word cards.

4. Tell students you will pick an affix from the pile, and each of them will add that affix to his or her root word card before reading the new word and saying what it means.

5. If students have trouble providing the meaning of a word, ask them the meaning of the affix, then the meaning of the root word. If the students still cannot provide the meaning, model the task. For example, say, "'*un*- means 'not,' and *happy* means 'with joy,' so *unhappy* means 'not happy' or 'without joy.'"

6. Repeat with the other affixes.

Scaffolds. Limit the number of affixes used; use only prefixes or suffixes.

Note: This activity was adapted from the University of Texas Center for Reading and Language Arts (2002b).

✦   ✦   ✦

Annotated Bibliography

Bear, D. R., Templeton, S., Ivernizzi, M., & Johnston, F. (1996). *Words their way: Word study for phonics, vocabulary, and spelling*. Des Moines, IA: Prentice-Hall, Inc.

This book provides an approach to word study instruction based on developmental stages of spelling. The text includes a discussion of the basis for the approach, instructions for assessing students prior to beginning instruction, and activities for students in each of the stages of development.

Blevins, W. (1998). *Phonics from A to Z: A practical guide*. New York: Scholastic Professional Books.

This guide provides a wealth of information for teachers in a practical, easy-to-read format. The book begins with a brief description of phonics, followed by activities, lists, and teaching guidelines for alphabet recognition, phonemic awareness, letter-sound correspondences, and regular and irregular word reading.

✦   ✦   ✦

Web Sites That Teach

http://reading.uoregon.edu/big_ideas/au.php.

This Web site includes a definition of alphabetic principle, research findings on phonics, a discussion of the importance of phonics, and instructions on how to sequence phonics skills in grades K–3.

http://reading.uoregon.edu/instruction/instruc_ap.php.

This Web site provides information on critical phonics skills and features of phonics instruction.

http://www.texasreading.org/tcrla/publications/primary/primary_phonics.htm.

This Web site allows readers to download a professional development guide on phonics and decoding instruction that includes strategies and instructional materials.

http://www.nifl.gov/partnershipforreading/publications/reading_first1phonics.html.

This Web site provides an introduction to phonics instruction, including science-based findings and a discussion of different instructional approaches.

http://www.ed.gov/offices/oese/sasa/rb/slide009.html.

This Web site provides a discussion of phonics instruction, including research findings, different instructional approaches, and cautions about the process.

http://www.nrrf.org/aboutphonics.htm.

This Web site introduces science-based phonics instruction and contains links to several papers, as well as a list of phonics product companies.

http://www.ldonline.org/ld_indepth/reading/ldrp_chard_guidelines.html.

This Web site includes an article on effective phonics and word recognition instruction for students with reading disabilities.

http://doe.state.in.us/publications/phonics.html#anchor 3978700.

This Web site allows readers to download a "Phonics Tool Kit" booklet and includes video clips that explain the kit. The booklet provides reading strategies (including phonics) and contains practical tips for teachers.

4 | Fluency

DO YOU HAVE STUDENTS WHO CAN READ WORDS, BUT DO SO VERY SLOWLY? THIS IS how Marci, a 2nd grade student, reads words on a list provided by her teacher:

/b/, /b/, /ba/, /bat/
/s/, /s/, /it/, /sit/
/mmmm/, /u/, /s/, /t/, /must/

Rather than read each word quickly, Marci slowly sounds out most of the letters. She eventually combines the sounds accurately to say a word, but the process is very slow. When Marci reads connected text, it is painful to listen to her labor over the sounds, unable to read the words quickly by sight. Her teacher realizes that if she does not become a more automatic reader, her motivation to read will be reduced, and her reading comprehension will be negatively affected.

Marci has a problem with reading fluency. She is unable to read words quickly enough to be a fluent reader who interacts with text. Fluent readers are able to read words quickly, automatically, and accurately so that they can focus on the meaning of text, whether it's a word list, a sentence, or some other passage. Marci's difficulty with rapid word reading will affect her ability to understand and interpret text. For this reason, she would benefit from fluency instruction.

Let's listen in on a 3rd grade student, Juan, who also has difficulty with fluency. As we listen to him read a 3rd grade–level passage aloud to a partner, we note that he reads about 50 words per minute and makes about 20 errors. Juan has trouble with the two main aspects of fluency: speed and accuracy. As we move Juan to less difficult text, we find that he can read a beginning 2nd grade–level passage at the same rate while making only three errors. This is a much more acceptable reading level for Juan, but he is still reading too slowly; he needs additional instruction in fluency to improve his reading speed.

Lalika is a kindergarten student who has been learning the names of letters. It is April, and all of her classmates know the names of at least 20 letters. Lalika knows the names of about 12, and it often takes her several seconds to name the letter once she sees it. Sometimes she needs to look up at the alphabet and recite it in order to remember the name of a letter. Like Marci and Juan, Lalika has difficulties with fluency. She knows the names of some letters, but they do not come to her automatically. She has the same problem with sounds: it takes her a second or more to think of a sound before she can name it.

Fluency is an essential element of reading for K–3 students. It is not something that only 2nd and 3rd grade teachers need to be concerned about. Fluency develops over time and from the beginning stages of reading. This chapter addresses fluency instruction: what it is, why it is important, how to teach it, and how to use progress monitoring to determine which students would benefit from additional fluency instruction. Instructional activities are provided to help teachers and parents teach fluency skills to students.

What Is Fluency Instruction?

Fluency is the accurate and rapid naming or reading of letters, sounds, words, sentences, or passages. When students can perform reading and reading-related tasks quickly and accurately, they are on the path to fluency, an essential element of comprehension and mature reading.

To become fluent, students need to learn to decode words rapidly and accurately, in isolation as well as in connected text, and to increase reading speed while maintaining accuracy. Teachers need to

- Provide students with opportunities for repeated oral reading that includes support and feedback from teachers, peers, and parents;
- Determine students' reading levels, and ensure that texts are matched to them; and
- Apply systematic practices in classrooms to instruct and monitor student progress.

Why Should I Provide Fluency Instruction?

If children do not acquire good word reading skills early in elementary school, they will be cut off from the rich knowledge sources available in print, and this may be particularly unfortunate for children who are already weak in general verbal knowledge and ability. (Torgesen, 2000, p. 58)

A recent National Assessment of Educational Progress (NAEP) report on reading ability revealed that 44 percent of U.S. 4th graders had low fluency (2003). Students who struggle with fluency also struggle with text comprehension; they focus so much on decoding words that they pay less attention to understanding what they read.

Perfetti (1977, 1985) suggests that slow word reading interferes with automaticity, and thus impairs reading comprehension. Research indicates that students who have reading difficulties have significant problems with fluency and continue to be slow readers into adolescence and adulthood (Shaywitz & Shaywitz, 1996; Stanovich, 1986; Torgesen, Wagner, & Rashotte, 1994).

Fluency instruction may be the missing element in reading instruction for most teachers, because most of us learned to teach reading with a focus on accuracy and comprehension; few of us were taught how to teach students to read quickly and automatically. However, we have learned that fluency is an essential element that bridges the gap between word recognition and comprehension. Though some students will learn to read accurately, quickly, and with prosody (good expression) with little direct instruction from teachers, many will require practice and support from peers and teachers to improve their fluency and make reading a more valued activity.

It is natural for beginning students to read slowly and laboriously at first. As they rehearse passages, they will get more and more comfortable reading words quickly.

How Can I Teach Fluency?

In practice, a high number of words read correctly per minute, when placed in the proper developmental perspective, indicates efficient word-level processing, a robust vocabulary knowledge base, and meaningful comprehension of the text. In contrast, a low (fluency) rate suggests inefficient word recognition skills, a lean or impoverished vocabulary, and faulty text comprehension skills. (Kame'enui & Simmons, 2001, p. 208)

According to the No Child Left Behind (NCLB) Act, "no research evidence is available to confirm that instructional time spent on silent, independent reading with minimal guidance and feedback improves reading fluency and overall reading achievement" (2001, p. 13). Providing students with extensive time to read without implementing practices that improve fluency is thus unlikely to improve readers' speed and accuracy. However, this does not mean that extensive opportunities to read before and after school, during free time, at home, and whenever else possible are not excellent strategies for promoting reading and improving knowledge, vocabulary, and interest.

Students should read the following level of texts during fluency activities, depending on their skill level:

- **Independent-level text.** Students can read easily, making fewer than five mistakes for every 100 words (95 percent correct).

- **Instructional-level text.** Students typically make fewer than 10 mistakes for every 100 words (90 percent correct).
- **Frustration-level text.** Students make more than 10 mistakes for every 100 words (89 percent correct or less).

When students engage in fluency activities alone or with peers, they should work with independent-level text; when they work with tutors or other knowledgeable adults, instructional-level text may provide a greater challenge. Students should not be engaged in fluency activities with frustration-level text.

When selecting text, consider whether it's the first time the student has read the text. For the purpose of improving fluency, students should read and reread text that they have already read, since their goal is to improve accuracy and speed.

First through 3rd graders should spend approximately 20 minutes each day on fluency-related activities. These activities include model reading and rereading or choral reading, paired reading with a student or adult, and tape-recorded reading. At least once every two weeks, teachers should time students reading a passage they have not read before, and the students should graph the numbers of words that they read in a minute.

What Practices Can I Use to Teach Fluency Explicitly?

Regardless of how book difficulty is determined, it is critical that all children in a classroom, including the least able readers, have easy "fingertip" access to books that they can read accurately, fluently, with good comprehension....Easy reading material develops fluency and provides practice in using good reading strategies. (Allington & Cunningham, 2002, p. 57)

The following reading and rereading exercises can improve fluency:

Reading With a Model Reader. The model reader can be the teacher, the teacher's assistant, a trained volunteer adult, or an older student. The model reader reads the passage first, then the student reads it. Next, the student reads the passage again as quickly and accurately as he or she can without speed-reading. The model reader and the student can ask each other questions about what they have read, or they can summarize the key points they've read. The amount of time the model reader spends reading before the student does depends upon the student's age: for K–1 students, the amount of time should be short, between 45 seconds and 1 minute; for students in grades 2–4, the amount of time can be longer (1 to 3 minutes). Repeat the process as time allows.

Choral Reading. First, the teacher or model reader previews a passage for the students, and they all make predictions about what the passage will be about. Then the teacher reads the passage aloud—first by herself, then with the students joining in. Next the teacher fades her voice and allows the students to take the lead reading the passage aloud. During this exercise, students should read as quickly as possible as a group without speed-reading. If there is time available, the teacher should select pairs of students to read the passage again.

Tape-Recorded Readings. These can be books on tape or books on CD-ROM accessed through the computer. In either case, the books are available to students and read aloud by a model. The important role of the teacher is to determine that students are following along and reading the text while the story is read aloud. Vocabulary and key concepts can be reviewed with students prior to the use of recorded readings.

Readers' Theater or Reading Performances. Students rehearse the script from a book, play, short story, or poem until they are highly fluent. Then they perform for a small group, their class, another class, or in front of parents and relatives. The critical aspect of the exercise is that students read a text repeatedly until they can recite it fluently and with prosody.

Partner Reading. This is when students read and reread passages with classmates. Teachers can pair more proficient readers with less proficient ones. The less proficient reader reads the passage first, followed by his or her partner. The students continue taking turns until they complete the text. (More partner reading exercises can be found in the "Instructional Activities" section of this chapter. Figure 4.1 provides some guidelines for partner reading.)

In summary, here are the critical elements that have been documented to improve reading fluency:

- Providing an explicit model of fluent reading. This model could be the teacher, a well-trained adult, another student, or even a cassette.

- Giving students multiple opportunities to read the same text. Students need many opportunities to read the same text over and over again. Teachers, trained adults, or students should provide corrective feedback. Two research studies suggest that students who reread passages at least twice outperform those who read a passage only once in both fluency and storytelling ability (O'Shea, Sindelar, & O'Shea, 1987; Sindelar, Monda, & O'Shea, 1990).

- Establishing performance criteria for the speed and accuracy of reading text. Teachers should establish baselines for the number of words students read correctly per minute in a specified text level, as well as systematically monitor fluency progress.

Some common instructional practices are not associated with improvements in fluency. In turn-taking or round-robin reading, for instance, teachers work with a small group of students, each of whom takes turns reading aloud briefly. This is not a fluency practice. Neither is Sustained Silent Reading, or Drop Everything and Read, an exercise in which teachers allocate a designated amount of time to reading and everyone including the teacher reads. As the National Reading Panel (2000) notes, "The demonstrated effectiveness of guided oral reading compared to the lack of demonstrated effectiveness of strategies encouraging independent silent reading suggests the importance of explicit compared to more implicit instructional approaches for improved fluency" (pp. 3–4).

FIGURE 4.1 ➤ **Guidelines for Partner Reading**

Procedures

1. First reader reads.
2. Second reader reads the same text.
3. Students discuss text, with one student asking questions and the other one answering.
4. Repeat until story is complete.

Rules

1. Talk only to your partner.
2. Talk only about reading.
3. Work together.

Possible Errors

1. Reading the word incorrectly.
2. Leaving out a word.
3. Adding a word.
4. Waiting longer than four seconds.

Feedback on Incorrect Pronunciation

The first partner points to the incorrectly read word and asks the second partner, "Do you know this word?" When the second partner says the word correctly, the first partner says, "Yes, that word is _____. Now read the sentence again."

Source: Adapted from Bos and Vaughn (2002, p. 181), and based on the work of Greenwood, Delguardri, and Hall (1989) and Fuchs, Fuchs, Mathes, and Simmons (1997).

Progress Monitoring

Providing ongoing assessment of student reading progress may be one of the most valuable things you can do as a teacher. Students who monitor their fluency progress improve their reading skills. As with those who monitor their progress when weight-lifting or on a diet, the process contributes to success.

The most valuable way to monitor student progress in fluency is to take timed measures of the number of words they read correctly in one minute (WCPM). The passages students read should remain at a consistent level of difficulty during this period. As students meet benchmarks—for example, increasing the number of accurate words by an average of two a week over six weeks—teachers may want to begin increasing the difficulty level of the text while continuing to monitor progress by documenting WCPM. To ensure that students continue to improve their fluency rates, teachers should increase the difficulty of the text or raise the WCPM goal (e.g., from 60 WCPM to 70).

Teachers can use the following sequence to monitor the progress of each student:

1. Select two or three unfamiliar but independent-level passages, such as those in the activities section of this chapter.
2. Make two copies of each passage.
3. Give one copy of the first passage to the student, and keep the second copy to mark errors.
4. Tell the student, "When I say 'begin,' start reading aloud at the top of the page. Do your best reading. Read as quickly as you can but do not race."
5. Use a stopwatch to time the student's reading for one minute.
6. As the student reads, mark any errors on your copy of the passage. The following are considered errors: failure to read the word in three seconds (in which case you should tell the student the word), mispronunciations, substitutions, omissions, and reversals. If the student self-corrects or repeats, do not count it as an error.
7. If the student is in the middle of the sentence when the time is up, let him or her finish the sentence, but don't count any words beyond the one-minute mark.
8. Count the number of WCPM. Repeat the above procedure with one or two more passages. Average the number of WCPM.
9. Chart the average WCPM. For students who are even slightly below average, monitor progress every two weeks and implement additional fluency activities. For average or above-average students, monitor progress three times a year—at the beginning, middle, and end. Figure 4.2 presents a sample chart that documents a student's fluency progress over time.

The best way to determine whether student rate and accuracy levels are within the norm for their grade is to compare their WCPM to the national norms available. The national norms for grades 2–4 are provided in Figure 4.3. There are no national norms for 1st grade. Oral fluency measures are not useful once students can read above the 4th grade level. As you can see from Figure 4.3, the number of WCPM varies according to grade level and time of year. The percentile column shows reading norms for the 25th percentile, 50th percentile, and 75th percentile. These correspond to below-average, average, and above-average performance, respectively.

Let's use Figure 4.3 to help Mrs. Galileo with three of her students. In November of 2nd grade, Mrs. Galileo is concerned about the fluency rate of three students: Maria (44 WCPM average), Lydia (26 WCPM average), and Michael (51 WCPM average). Considering the time of year and grade level, how concerned should Mrs. Galileo be about each of these students?

FIGURE 4.2 ➤ **Sample Reading Fluency Chart**

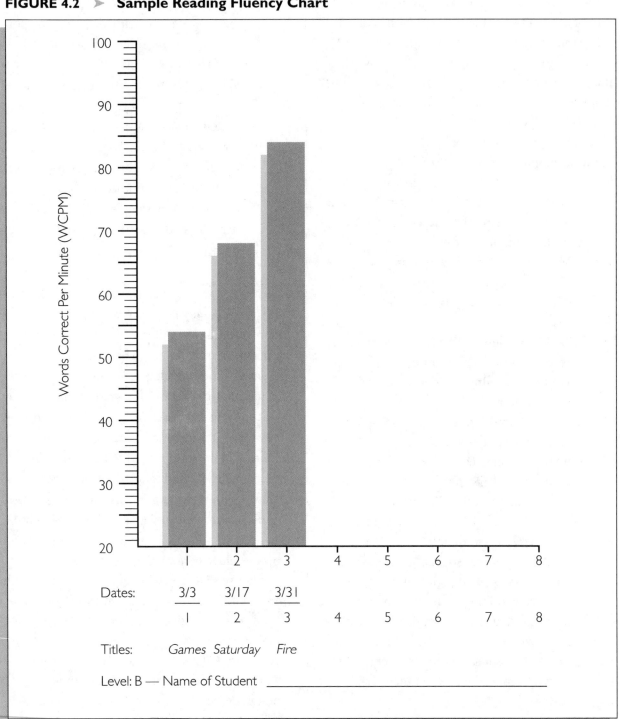

FIGURE 4.3 ➤ **Reading Fluency Guidelines for Grades 2–4**

Grade	Percentile	Fall WCPM	Winter WCPM	Spring WCPM
2	75	82	106	124
	50	53	78	94
	25	23	46	65
3	75	107	123	142
	50	79	93	114
	25	65	70	87
4	75	125	133	143
	50	99	112	118
	25	72	89	92

Source: Adapted from Hasbrouck and Tindal (1992), pp. 41–44.

By examining the figure, you can see that the average WCPM for 2nd grade in the fall is 53, and the average in the winter is 78. In November, we would expect average 2nd graders to be somewhere between 53 and 78 WCPM. Since Maria is slightly below average (44), prioritizing fluency activities for her would be a good strategy. At 26 WCPM, Lydia is in the 25th percentile, so additional activities and time should be made available to her immediately. Finally, because Michael is close to average, he can continue with the fluency activities already in place. Teachers can use these fluency guidelines to help make instructional decisions.

What Measures Are Useful to Monitor Progress in Fluency?

The following two measures may help teachers monitor students' fluency progress:

DIBELS Oral Reading Fluency (DORF) and Retell Fluency. This one-minute oral reading fluency measure is a standardized, individually administered test followed by a retell fluency comprehension check. The measure is intended for children from mid-1st grade through 3rd grade; tests are given in the winter and spring of 1st grade, and in the fall, winter, and spring of 2nd and 3rd grades. Materials include student and examiner copies of grade-level passages. Students read a grade-level passage aloud for one minute, and teachers mark errors such as omitted or substituted words and hesitations of more than three seconds on their copy of the text. Students then retell the passage in their own words while teachers tally the number of words that they produce (Good, Kaminski, Smith, Laimon, & Dill, 2001).

Test of Oral Reading Fluency (TORF). This test is administered individually and is designed for children in mid-1st to 6th grade. Students read passages aloud for one minute. As in the DORF measure, teachers mark errors while students read to determine their oral fluency scores. The test is divided into four reading levels from 1st grade to 6th grade, with 18 passages per level to allow for regular monitoring. The manual includes procedures for ongoing progress monitoring and goal setting (Children's Educational Services Inc., 1987).

Instructional Activities

A wealth of research supports the value of oral reading fluency as an indicator of overall reading competence and its utility for helping teachers plan better instruction and effect superior student outcomes. (Fuchs, Fuchs, Hosp, & Jenkins, 2001, p. 252)

Note: If you do not have all of the materials necessary for any of the following activities, feel free to substitute any reasonable materials you do have.

Letter Fluency

Objective. Given a set of random letters, students will name the letters fluently.

Materials. Letter tiles or letters written on a board, using previously learned letter names.

Sequence.
1. Place the letter tiles in random order in front of students, or write letters on the board. For example: R, T, W, B, N, E.
2. Point to each letter and ask students to say the letter's name. Repeat until they can accurately name all the letters.
3. Model the task by naming the letters slightly faster than the students can.
4. Ask students to name the letters at the modeled rate. Point to the letters quickly, and say the names of the letters with the students.
5. Repeat until students can name all letters accurately and quickly.
6. Ask students to point to and read the letters again. This time do not say the letters with students, but provide assistance if needed.
7. Repeat with a different set of letters, or vary the letter order.

Variations. Use letter sounds instead of letter names; point to letters and ask students to name a word that begins with that letter.

Word Power

Objective. Given a list of words, students will read the words fluently.

Materials. 30–35 sight words—familiar regular or irregular high-frequency words with sounds students have mastered written on index cards.

Sequence.

1. Tell students that the goal is to read as many words as possible in 30 seconds.
2. Show students the word cards, one at a time.
3. Place correctly read words in one stack and missed words in another stack. If a student hesitates or has difficulty for more than six seconds, say the word and place it in the stack of missed words.
4. After 30 seconds, count how many words the student has read correctly and review incorrectly read words with the student.
5. Have the student practice reading the word cards as you proceed to work with each student individually.
6. Give each student a second turn to read the word cards in 30 seconds.
7. Explain that the goal is to read more words than the first time.
8. Follow the same procedure. Compare the second reading to the number of words the student read the first time.
9. Provide feedback on accuracy and student progress.

Note: This activity was adapted from the University of Texas Center for Reading and Language Arts (2002a).

Irregular Word Reading

Objective. Students will increase their fluency with irregular words.

Materials. A tape recording of irregular words, a tape player, headphones, copies of a word grid with irregular words from the tape recording (see Figure 4.4).

Sequence.

1. Determine irregular words for instruction. Construct a grid and make a tape recording of the words.
2. Model the task by showing students how to use the tape player and the headphones, and how to point to the words and read quietly.
3. Explain that students will listen to the tape three times. The first time, they are to listen and point to the words. The second and third times, they are to read quietly along with the tape.
4. As students listen to the tape, ensure that they are pointing to the words, pronouncing them correctly, and not skipping words or lines. Provide assistance if needed.
5. Provide corrective feedback if students have trouble pronouncing words. For example: For mispronunciations, point to the word and say, "This word is _____. What is this word?" When the student responds, tell him or her to go back and read the words from the beginning of the grid.
6. Monitor student progress by answering the following questions:
   - Were the students able to track the words as they were read?
   - Did students have difficulty pronouncing any words? If so, did they require additional response time to read these words?
   - Will any specific words require more instructional time? If so, how will this time be scheduled?

FIGURE 4.4 ➤ **Sample Irregular Word Grid**

the	to	of	you	was
of	the	was	to	you
to	was	you	the	of
you	of	to	was	the
was	you	the	of	to

Note: This activity was adapted from the University of Texas Center for Reading and Language Arts (2002a).

Echo Reading

Objective. Given a reading passage and a model of fluent reading, students will read the text fluently and with prosody.

Materials. Copies of instructional-level texts.

Sequence.

1. Give students a copy of the text.
2. Explain that you will read part of the text while students follow along, and then they will "echo read" the same text, trying to repeat your rate and expression.
3. Model the task by fluently reading two to four sentences of the text.
4. Have students read the same section of text while trying to copy your rate and expression.
5. Read the next two to four sentences fluently. Again, have students read the same sentences while trying to echo your rate and expression.
6. Continue the procedure by reading the passage in two-to-four-sentence sections.

Variations.

- Tape record two to four-sentence sections of a reading passage. Pause between sections to allow time for students to echo read. Have students listen to the tape while following along in the text, and reading aloud during pauses on the recording.
- Have a student serve as the model reader.
- Read each section of text using different character voices, as long as you do not sacrifice fluency or prosody. Students then echo fluent reading using the character voices.

Note: This activity was adapted from the National Institute for Literacy (2001) and Reutzel and Cooter (1999).

Choral Reading

Objective. Given a reading passage and a model of fluent reading, students will read the text fluently and with expression.

Materials. Copies of instructional-level texts.

Sequence.

1. Give students copies of texts.
2. Model the task by reading the first part of the text out loud. Set the pace and read

with the proper phrasing, rate, and expression.

3. Read the same part of text again, and have students read along with you.

Variations. Use choral reading with the whole class, in small groups, or with individual students.

Note: This activity was adapted from Bos and Vaughn (2002); the National Institute for Literacy (2001); and Reutzel and Cooter (1999).

Chunking

Objective. Given a reading passage, students will read the text phrase by phrase to build fluency.

Materials. Copies of independent- or instructional-level texts.

Sequence.

1. Pair students so that more proficient readers are paired with less proficient ones.
2. For each pair, select a reading passage at the less proficient reader's instructional level.
3. Prepare each passage by placing slash marks between two- to five-word sentence segments and prepositional phrases. For example: "The big dog/chased the cat/through the house." (A slash indicates how the sentence should be chunked for practicing fluency.)
4. Explain to students that phrase-by-phrase reading can help improve fluency.
5. Model fluent reading from a passage while students follow along. Pause to emphasize the chunking of words into phrases.
6. Give students copies of the prepared passages.

7. Have pairs take turns reading aloud. Encourage students to pause briefly between marked phrases. As one student reads, the other can help decode any unfamiliar words.
8. Monitor each pair.

Variations.

- Write phrases on strips of paper and on chart paper for practice.
- For students having difficulty, cut the sentences into phrases, reorder the phrases, and have students practice reading the phrases individually.

Note: This activity was adapted from The University of Texas Center for Reading and Language Arts (2002a).

Tape-Assisted Repeated Reading

Objective. Given a reading passage and a model of fluent reading, students will read the text fluently and with prosody.

Materials. A tape recorder, headphones, assisted reading logs (see Figure 4.5), and copies of independent-level passages or books (for younger readers, use decodable texts or pattern- language books; for older readers, select high- interest low-vocabulary texts).

Preparation.

1. Tape record a passage or a whole book using a conversational rate, good expression, and appropriate phrasing.
2. Provide students with cues to assist them as they read. For example:
   - Tell them to allow 10 seconds of blank tape.

FIGURE 4.5 ➤ Sample Assisted Reading Log

		Assisted Reading Log			
		Read With			
Date	**Title**	**Tape/ Computer**	**Self**	**Student**	**Teacher**
	1.				
	2.				
	3.				
	4.				
	5.				
	6.				
	7.				
	8.				

- Remind them to use strategies they already know, such as pointing to each word as they read.
- Use a signal or cue for turning the page, and say each page number.
- Direct students to place a finger on the first word of the page.

3. On each side of the tape, include about 10 minutes of text. Label each side of the tape with the title and the corresponding page numbers.

Sequence.

1. Model the task by showing students how to insert cassettes into tape recorders and how to start, stop, and rewind tapes. Show students how to handle and wear headphones.

2. Model reading along, for example, by pointing to words and reading quietly.
3. Have students read the book along to the tape.
4. Monitor students to ensure they are following along with their fingers and reading quietly. Provide individual assistance if needed.
5. Have students read the passage three times: with the tape, with another student, and with the teacher.
6. Encourage students to document their readings using the assisted reading log.
7. Help students evaluate their reading. For example, ask them what they do well when they read orally, or to name one thing they can do to improve their reading.

Variations.

- Have students follow the above procedures as they listen to computer-based books or commercial software reading programs. Many software programs are available in both English and Spanish, with built-in recordkeeping systems to monitor progress.
- After reading along with a tape or computer, have students record part of the passage or book and then listen to it.
- Provide additional opportunities for students, especially struggling readers and ESL students, to repeatedly read taped passages and books at home. Send notes home explaining the procedures for listening and reading along to tapes.

Note: This activity was adapted from Bos and Vaughn (2002).

Make Your Goal

Objective. Given a reading passage, students will read it in one minute with accuracy of 95 percent or greater.

Materials. Copies of independent-level reading passages (can be a portion of a longer text).

Sequence.

1. Provide each student with a reading passage at his or her reading level. The passage should be slightly longer than the student's current WCPM rate (e.g., if a student reads 55 WCPM, the passage should be about 70 words long).
2. Explain that students will independently practice reading the passage aloud before reading it to you.

3. Have students repeatedly practice reading the passage. Stop at each student's desk to listen to him or her read. If the student does not reach the goal on the first reading, encourage him or her to continue practicing while you monitor other students. Return later and listen to any students who did not reach the goal on the first try.

Variations.

- Give students longer passages to read. Time their reading and count the number of WCPM. Have them continue practicing to see if they can improve their WCPM, and return to each student two or three times to see if he or she has improved.
- Each week during the activity, designate one day to graph the number of words read correctly as a way to document student progress.
- Pair students and have them take turns reading and rereading a passage until they reach their goals.

Partner Reading

Objective. Given a selected text, students will increase fluency by rereading it.

Materials. Copies of short and interesting texts at the lower-performing reader's instructional level for each pair of students and a list of high-interest low-vocabulary texts (see Figure 4.6).

Sequence.

1. Pair higher-performing readers with lower-performing readers for fluency

63

practice. Rank the students according to performance level, then split the class in half, pairing the highest-performing student in the class with the top-ranked student from the lower half, the second-highest performing student with the second-highest performing student from the lower half, and so on for the remaining students.

2. Provide each pair with reading texts at the lower-performing student's instructional-reading level. An easy way to match books to students' reading levels is to give students a list of words from the text; if they have difficulty with no more than about one in ten words, then the text is considered to be at their instructional level. (Independent-level text can also be used.)

3. Model and explain partner reading procedures.

4. Assign roles to student pairs, with Partner A being the stronger reader and Partner B the lower-performing reader. Do not explain to students what A or B stands for.

5. Have students take turns reading. Partner A reads the text aloud, modeling fluent reading, for one minute. Partner B follows along. Then Partner B reads aloud the same text for one minute.

6. The whole class can participate at the same time while you time the readings.

Variations.

• Have students read one page at a time, rather than read for a specific time. This allows time for you to work with other students, or to teach a small reading group.

• Incorporate content-area texts and other reading materials, such as children's magazines or newspaper articles.

Note: This exercise is adapted from the University of Texas Center for Reading and Language Arts (2001b) and based on the work of Fuchs, Fuchs, Mathes, and Simmons (1997).

Partner Reading with Graphing

Objective. Given a selected text, the student will increase fluency by rereading it.

Materials. Copies of 100- to 200-word instructional-level passages, individual student fluency graphs (see Figure 4.7), an Error Correction Card, and one timer for each student pair.

Sequence.

1. Select a series of short instructional-level passages for each student. Cumulatively count the number of words in each row, and write a running total beside each line. This makes it easier to determine the number of words read. (Note: Commercially available fluency-building passages are acceptable for this activity. These programs generally include a series of passages at different grade levels with the number of words per line already noted in the margin.)

2. Identify an appropriate fluency goal for each student using grade-level norms.

3. Place a bracket after the word that indicates the student's fluency goal.

4. Explain that students will be working with a partner to improve their fluency.

FIGURE 4.6 ➤ **Publishers of High-Interest/Low-Vocabulary Texts**

Publisher	Contact Information
Academic Communication Associates	Phone: 888-758-9558; Web site: http://www.acadcom.com
Capstone Press	Phone: 888-747-4992; Web site: http://www.capstone-press.com
High Noon Books	Phone: 800-422-7249; Web site: http://www.academictherapy.com
Incentives for Learning	Phone: 888-444-1773; Web site: http://www.incentivesforlearning.com
Modern Curriculum Press	Phone: 800-321-3106; Web site: http://www.pearsonlearning.com
National Geographic	Phone: 800-647-5463; Web site: http://www.nationalgeographic.com
National Reading Styles Institute	Phone: 800-331-3117; Web site: http://www.nrsi.com
National Wildlife Federation	Phone: 800-822-9919; Web site: http://www.nwf.com
New Readers Press	Phone: 800-448-8878; Web site: http://www.newreaderspress.com
Perfection Learning	Phone: 800-831-4190; Web site: http://www.perfectionlearning.com
Phoenix Learning Resources	Phone: 800-526-6581; Web site: http://www.phoenixlr.com
Remedia	Phone: 800-826-4740; Web site: http://www.rempub.com
Rigby	Phone: 800-822-8661; Web site: http://www.rigby.com
Saddleback Educational	Phone: 888-735-2225; Web site: http://www.sdlback.com
Scholastic (Includes Book Clubs & Software Club)	Phone: 888-246-2986; Web site: www.scholastic.com
Smithsonian Institute	Phone: 800-766-2149; Web site: http://www.siedu.com
Steck-Vaughn	Phone: 800-531-5015; Web site: http://www.steck-vaughn.com
Sundance	Phone: 800-343-8204; Web site: http://www.sundancepub.com
Wright Group	Phone: 800-523-2371; Web site: http://www.wrightgroup.com

Source: Adapted from Bos and Vaughn (2002).

5. Pair students, partnering higher-performing readers with lower-performing readers.

6. Explain that fluency goals are marked on the passages and vary from student to student.

7. Have the higher-performing reader read the lower-performing reader's passage. Next, have the lower-performing reader read the same passage three times, while the higher-performing reader provides feedback using the Error Correction Card. The higher-performing reader should time his or her partner's third reading for one minute. When done reading, the lower-performing reader should graph his or her WCPM.

8. As pairs read, check that students are modeling, providing appropriate feedback, reading the passages the required number of times, and graphing their progress.

9. Monitor students' fluency progress, making note of how many words students read in one minute and whether

   • Students meet their fluency goal during the timing, and if so, whether this occurred over multiple passages;

   • Any student requires more or less difficult reading material; and

   • There are any consistent error patterns.

Variations.

• Use decodable books for students with low reading fluency.

• For English language learners, be sure to preview any unfamiliar vocabulary.

• To reinforce comprehension, stop at intervals and review what happened.

Note: This exercise is adapted from Delquardri, Greenwood, Wharton, Carta, and Hall (1986) and Fuchs, Fuchs, Mathes, and Simmons (1997).

Previewing and Fluency

Objective. Given a reading passage or text, students will increase fluency by previewing it before reading.

Materials. Copies of independent- or instructional-level passages or texts.

Sequence.

1. Give students copies of the passage or text.

2. Explain that previewing before reading can help them understand texts as well as improve their fluency.

3. Introduce the passage or text using the title and looking through the text or section. (For longer texts, preview only one section of the text or book at a time.)

4. With students, make predictions about the content.

5. Introduce new or difficult words, including those that may be difficult for students to recognize automatically or have unfamiliar meanings. Have students write the words in personal dictionaries or on word cards.

6. Read a section of the text aloud at a slow conversational rate (about 130 words per minute). Have students follow along.

7. Pair students, partnering more proficient readers with less proficient readers.

FIGURE 4.7 ➤ **Fluency Graph**

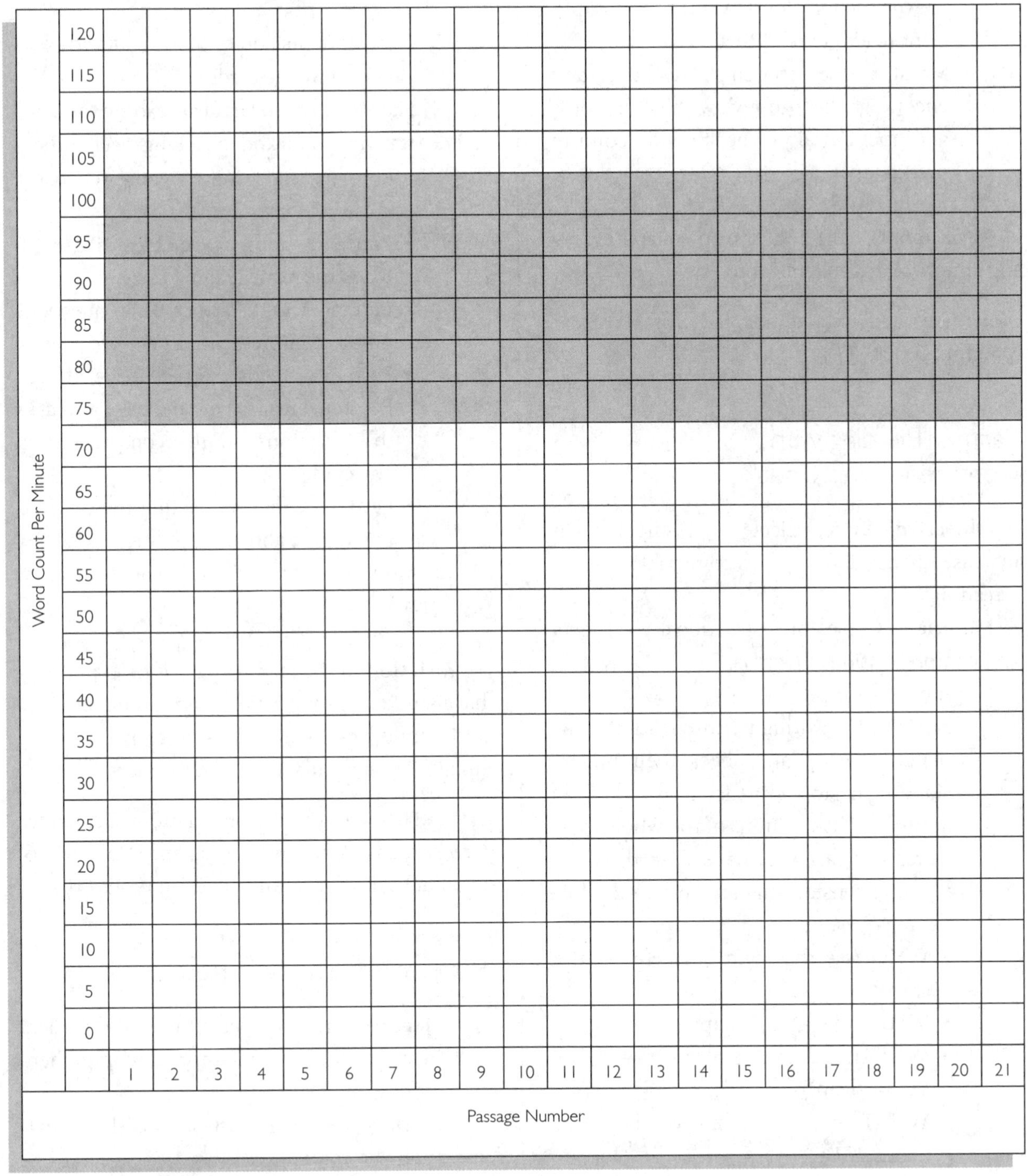

8. Have students take turns reading the previewed section aloud. Ask the more proficient reader to read first.

9. Monitor the students' reading, and encourage them to review difficult words and periodically check and confirm predictions.

Variation. Use big books to enhance previewing and to spark students' interest.

Note: This activity was adapted from Bos and Vaughn (2002).

Partner Reading with Comprehension Check

Objective. Given a selected text, students will increase fluency and improve comprehension by rereading it.

Materials. Copies of instructional-level texts and comprehension cue cards.

Sequence.

1. Explain that during partner reading, students can stop and check their understanding of stories as they read.

2. Model the task in front of the whole class using a passage they have all read. While reading, consider the answers to the following questions:
   - **WHO** was the main character in the story?
   - **WHEN** did _____ happen?
   - **WHERE** did _____ live (or work, or eat, or sleep)?
   - **WHAT** is the meaning of the word "_____"?
   - **WHY** do you think _____ happened?

3. Give students copies of the text and comprehension cue cards.

4. Have students take turns reading the same text in pairs and checking each other's understanding using the comprehension cue cards. For example:
   - Partner A reads a page of text. Partner B reads the same text.
   - Partner A asks Partner B the questions on the comprehension cue card.
   - Partner A reads the next page of text. Partner B reads the same page and asks the questions on the comprehension cue card.
   - Partners continue reading the text following the above procedure.

5. Monitor pairs. Provide assistance as needed.

Variation. If the reading passage is expository, have students ask questions about the main idea and supporting details; be sure to preview any unfamiliar vocabulary for ESL Learners.

Note: This activity is adapted from Delquadri, Greenwood, Whorton, Carta, and Hall (1986) and Fuchs, Fuchs, Mathes, and Simmons (1997).

Partner Reading with Retell

Objective. Given a selected text, the student will increase fluency and improve comprehension by rereading it.

Materials. Copies of instructional-level texts and retell cue cards.

Sequence.

1. Pair students and give them copies of the text and retell cue cards.
2. The higher-performing reader reads first, then the lower-performing reader reads the same text. At the beginning of each section, the higher-performing reader should ask his or her partner, "What did you learn first?" Then, as often as necessary to cover all the information presented by the text, he or she should ask, "What did you learn next?"
3. Have the pairs continue the above procedure with the lower-performing reader retelling each section after reading it.

Variation. Have students take turns retelling sections of text.

Note: This activity is adapted from Delquadri, Greenwood, Wharton, Carta, and Hall (1986) and Fuchs, Fuchs, Mathes, and Simmons (1997).

Showcase Readers

Objective. Given a previously read passage, students will read it fluently and with good expression.

Materials. Copies of previously read stories, books, or passages.

Sequence.

1. Give students a copy of the reading selection.
2. Explain that three students will be showcase readers today. These students will read fluently for the class.
3. Pair students and have them take turns reading the passage aloud.
4. After students have practiced the passage with their partners, call on several of them, one at a time, to be showcase readers for the day.
5. Have each showcase reader stand in a special place, such as in front of a small podium or table.
6. Assign a short section of the reading passage for the student to read aloud to the class for about 30 seconds to a minute.
7. Remind each student to read in a loud, clear voice so that everyone can hear. Offer assistance with difficult words.
8. After the reading, have the class applaud.
9. Repeat with a second and third student.
10. Use this activity a couple of times each week so that all of the students get an opportunity to be showcase readers during the month.

Reader's Performance

Objective. Given a reading passage in script format, students will read the text fluently and with good expression.

Materials. Copies of instructional-level texts converted into script format.

Preparation. Select instructional-level texts that consist of dialogue for several characters. Rewrite the text in a play format. For example:

Original Text: One day Mrs. Duck went to the pond. It was hot and she wanted a cool drink. Mr. Fox was sitting by the side of the pond. He told

Mrs. Duck that she could not get a drink because he was in a bad mood and did not want anyone near his pond. Mrs. Bird heard Mr. Fox say this, and she called down sweetly from her branch....

Adapted Text:

Mrs. Duck: I have been working so hard. Now I am so thirsty. I need to go to the pond for a nice, long drink.

Mr. Fox: Hello, Mrs. Duck. I am in a very bad mood. No one can drink from my pond today.

Mrs. Bird: Mr. Fox, this is not your pond. It belongs to everyone.

Note: You can also use commercially prepared scripts or plays from reading programs for this activity.

Sequence.

1. Highlight individual characters' parts on each script.
2. Explain that students will perform a play, and will practice rereading their parts to rehearse. Clarify that a reading performance is *not* a big production with costumes and props, and does not require students to memorize their parts.
3. Set a day and time for the reading performance.
4. Model by reading the text aloud at an appropriate rate with proper phrasing and expression to convey each character's feelings.
5. Group students, and assign them their individual roles or parts.

6. During class, have students practice reading and rereading their assigned roles, both independently and with their group. Encourage them to practice at home.
7. Have students perform their readings in front of the class or for another audience, such as family, friends, or other classrooms.

Variations.

- Use poems instead of scripts, and have students read alternating lines or stanzas.
- Have students perform their reading within their small group, with you as the audience.
- Have the audience sit in the center of the room with the readers surrounding the group.

Note: This activity is adapted from the University of Texas Center for Reading and Language Arts (2001b).

Who I Read To

Objective. Given a reading passage, students will read it fluently and with good expression.

Materials. A "Who I Read To" chart and copies of previously read stories, books, or passages.

Sequence.

1. Across the top of the "Who I Read To" chart, list names of people to whom students can read aloud. For older students, brainstorm five or six different people to whom they can read and have students complete their own charts. Examples of people to whom students can read

include parents, older siblings, other teachers, paraprofessionals, peers, grandparents, neighbors, and parent volunteers.

2. Give students a copy of a text that has previously been read in class and a copy of the "Who I Read To" chart.

3. In the left-hand column of the chart, write the title of the text beside the number.

4. Explain that students will read the passage to each person on the chart, who will in turn sign and date the chart. When the chart is completed for one reading passage, students will read the story to the principal (or some other designated person).

Variations.

1. Allow students to complete the chart over time. Periodically check on their progress and provide feedback.

2. After one passage is completed, the chart can be used again for additional texts.

✦   ✦   ✦

Annotated Bibliography

Blevins, W. (2001). *Building fluency: Lessons and strategies for reading success*. New York: Scholastic.

This book presents lessons, activities, fluency charts, oral reading passages, and word lists for helping students read words and connected texts fluently. The author explains how to measure fluency, calculate student fluency scores, and set goals based on fluency norms. Twelve quick-and-easy lessons for building fluency address a variety of fluency-building techniques, such as echo reading, audio book modeling, phrasing, repeated reading, and speed drills.

Great leaps. Contact: Diarmuid, Inc., Box 35780, Gainsville, FL 32635; 877-GRL-EAPS; Web site: http://www.greatleaps.com; e-mail: info@greatleaps.com.

This program addresses three levels of fluency. For the first level, phonics, students identify sounds and decode simple word patterns quickly and accurately; for the second level, sight phrases, they read phrases with sight words; and for the third level, text fluency, students read stories and graph their fluency progress.

Hiebert, E. H. (2002). *Quickreads: A research-based fluency program*. Parsippany, NJ: Modern Curriculum Press. Contact: Modern Curriculum Press, 299 Jefferson Road, Parsippany, NJ 07054; 800-321-3106; Web site: http://www.pearsonlearning.com.

This program features short, high-interest nonfiction texts at the 2nd, 3rd, and 4th grade levels. The program focuses on improving student fluency, comprehension, and background knowledge. Each grade level builds sequentially across the three texts, with increasingly difficult high-frequency words and phonics elements. The program also includes a pre- and post-test for placement, 12 copies each of the three texts and three read-along audio CDs per grade level, and a teacher's resource manual. Additional comprehension strategies and extension lessons can be used to support ESL students.

Peer-assisted learning strategies: Reading. Contact: Sopris West, 4093 Specialty Place, Longmont, CO 80504; 303-651-2829; Web site: http://www.sopriswest.com; e-mail: customerservice@sopriswest.com.

In this program for kindergarteners and 1st graders, students work with partners using peer-tutoring methods. First grade peer-assisted learning strategies (PALS) include 35-minute sessions performed three times a week and designed to improve reading skills. The sessions consist of two segments: a code-based activity in which students practice phonological awareness, decoding, and the application of both in connected text; and an activity in which students read, reread, and summarize stories with partners. Kindergarten strategies (K-PALS) include 20-minute game-like sessions. During the first five minutes of each session, the teacher demonstrates activities with the class as a group. In the remaining 15 minutes, students perform the same activities with a partner. Sessions focus on developing pronunciation, letter knowledge, and phonological and phonemic awareness.

Practices for developing accuracy and fluency. Contact: Neuhaus Education Center, 4433 Bissonnet, Bellaire, TX 77401; 713-664-7676; Web site: http://www.neuhaus.org.

This manual presents a set of decodable grade-level passages and a set of rapid word-recognition charts for students in grades 1–4. The charts can be used with the whole class to help students read words automatically. Students are timed as they read the first 100 words of a passage aloud. Record forms are included for students to document each story read, the date and time, their fluency rates, and any errors.

Read naturally. Contact: Read Naturally, 2329 Kressin Avenue, Saint Paul, MN 55120; 800-788-4085; Web site: http://www.readnaturally.com; e-mail: info @readnaturally.com.

This program helps students improve fluency by reading along with a tape of a model reader reading the same passage. The text is leveled, so students can gradually increase the level of text as their reading rates improve.

Students graph the number of words they read correctly prior to and after practicing. Vocabulary and comprehension questions are also provided to reinforce students' knowledge of words and concepts and to determine if they understand what they read. Each sequenced level includes 24 high-interest nonfiction stories; 12 cassette tapes, with one story per side; a teacher's manual; and software programs and computer-based progress monitoring tools.

◆   ◆   ◆

Web Sites That Teach

http://www.ldonline.org/ld_indepth/reading/reading _fluency.html.

This Web site provides information on how to determine and adjust a student's reading rate, and includes a variety of fluency activities, including repeated reading, choral reading, and commercial fluency programs.

http://ecot.rice.edu/conferences/acpweb/UST/ EDUC5325/fluency.html.

This Web site provides a video clip of the partner reading technique. The clip explains this strategy in detail and shows how to implement it in the classroom.

http://www.sil.org/lingualinks/literacy/referencematerials/ glossaryofliteracyterms/whatistheneurologicalimpress me.htm.

This Web site introduces the neurological impress method (a form of repeated or echo reading) to improve fluency, and includes various reading activities that incorporate the method, such as echo reading, repeated reading, and shared reading.

http://reading.uoregon.edu/big_ideas/flu.php.

This Web site provides information on how and when to teach fluency, how to sequence fluency skills, and available research-based fluency programs.

http://www.usu.edu/teach/text/fluency/Fluency
 Synthesis.pdf.

This Web site presents a review of fluency practices. The review provides stages of reading development, findings from research on fluency instruction, and implications for classroom approaches.

http://npin.org/library/2002/n00753/fluency.html.

This Web site provides science-based research findings about fluency instruction, and shows how to tell the difference between more and less fluent readers, model fluency reading, and prepare activities for repeated oral reading practice.

http://readingserver.edb.utexas.edu/downloads/
 1998_enhance_read_1.pdf.

This Web site provides a downloadable professional development guide for using partner reading to enhance fluency.

5 | Vocabulary

GOOD VOCABULARY INSTRUCTION HELPS CHILDREN GAIN OWNERSHIP OF words, instead of just learning them well enough to pass a test. Good vocabulary instruction provides multiple exposures through rich and varied activities to meaningful information about the word. (Stahl & Kapinus, 2001, p. 14)

This chapter provides an overview of vocabulary instruction for beginners. It is designed to provide a clear understanding of what we know about vocabulary instruction, and to show how to implement effective vocabulary practices in your classroom. The chapter includes key descriptions of vocabulary, practices for assessing vocabulary and comprehension, procedures for monitoring students' progress in vocabulary, and activities to promote vocabulary learning. The practices presented are based on the best documented research and are sensitive to the realities of classroom teachers.

What Is Vocabulary Instruction?

Oral and written vocabulary instruction is a valuable component of beginning reading, because student understanding of word meanings and how words are used in text contributes significantly to general reading comprehension. Although understanding the meaning of words is not the only contributing factor to reading comprehension, it is a significant one. Vocabulary knowledge is the tool that unlocks the meaning of text.

How often have you wondered what you might do to improve your students' vocabulary knowledge? Have you ever found yourself saying, "They can read the words, but they don't understand what they mean"?

Ms. Garcia, a 2nd grade teacher, who is concerned about the reading performance of her students. Most of them can read the words, but they often don't seem to understand what they read. Sometimes they partially understand what critical words mean, but not enough to grasp the author's intentions. Ms. Garcia is aware that many of her students cannot tell the main idea of a text after reading it, and is concerned that her students have more difficulty comprehending expository text than narrative text.

Ms. Garcia knows that understanding text is a critical skill that will be assessed on the statewide reading assessment to be given in the spring. She has spent considerable time asking her students questions, encouraging them to reread text to put together answers, and expanding on the ideas of students who interpret the text well, but she is very concerned that some of her students are not making progress. She knows that their understanding of the meanings of many of the words is limited, and they need additional vocabulary knowledge.

What will help Ms. Garcia's students? We can begin by understanding the two areas that her students have difficulty with: vocabulary and comprehension.

Oral vocabulary represents words that students learn to understand by listening to others speak and by using them themselves. When students learn to read, they bring their knowledge of oral vocabulary to print. When new words that are not part of a student's vocabulary appear in print, they are not readily understood. Students can expand their understanding of word meanings through explicit instruction, information

provided in text, or repeated exposure to the word. *Reading vocabulary* consists of the words that students understand when they read them in text.

While reading is a helpful means for improving word knowledge, many of the students with the poorest vocabularies are also those who read the least. The high road to vocabulary for all students is to read, read, read.

Hayes and Ahrens (1988) analyzed the types of words used in various print sources and oral language settings, as shown in Figure 5.1. The first column of the figure lists the major print sources, which vary from simple (preschool books) to difficult (scientific articles). The second column shows the rank of the average word in each source based on difficulty. Higher numbers indicate that more challenging, less common vocabulary is used. Some of the findings, such as the fact that less common words are found in scientific articles, aren't surprising, but others are. For instance, did you realize that preschool or children's books expose you to more challenging vocabulary than do prime-time adult TV shows? With the exception of courtroom testimony, reading is a more valuable way to extend your vocabulary than watching TV or listening to others talk.

For young students teachers can make a huge difference in vocabulary knowledge by

- Teaching words and their extended meanings systematically,
- Providing multiple opportunities to practice using key vocabulary and engaging in oral language,
- Ensuring that word knowledge is an ongoing part of the instructional day, and

• Reading and listening to texts.

Of course, teachers need to select age-appropriate texts that are rich sources of new words.

Why Should I Promote Vocabulary Acquisition Implicitly and Explicitly?

There is evidence that language can be substantially affected by experiences in which children are exposed to a wider range of meaningful vocabulary and the meanings of unfamiliar words are explained. (Biemiller, 1999, p. 29)

Students can improve their vocabulary both indirectly and directly. Indirect or implicit vocabulary acquisition occurs when students engage in extensive oral interactions with adults and peers and when they read and are read to. Figure 5.2 shows how reading is connected to vocabulary acquistion. The first column in the figure shows an average number of minutes per day of independent reading, and the second column shows how many words read per year that number translates to. Students who read more are exposed to more words and thus know more words.

Students also benefit from being taught vocabulary directly or explicitly—their knowledge of words and understanding of what they read improves. Teachers who actively engage their students in vocabulary activities, such as teaching them vocabulary words prior to reading, realize

FIGURE 5.1 ➤ **Types of Words in Print**

Major Sources	Median Words
Printed Texts	
Abstracts of scientific articles	4389
Newspapers	1690
Popular magazines	1399
Adult books	1058
Comic books	867
Children's books	627
Preschool books	578
Television Texts	
Popular prime-time adult shows	598
Popular prime-time children shows	543
Cartoon shows	490
Mr. Rogers and *Sesame Street*	413
Adult Speech	
Expert witness testimony	1008
College graduates to friends, spouses	496

Source: Adapted from Hayes and Ahrens (1988), pp. 395–410.

measurable gains in student understanding of words and texts.

Teachers who provide systematic and explicit instruction in vocabulary will see improvements in their students' progress on state-mandated accountability assessments. Furthermore, learning word meanings and how to better understand text can be fun for students.

FIGURE 5.2 ➤ Effect of Daily Independent Reading on Words Read Per Year

Average Number of Independent Reading Minutes Per Day	Words Read Per Year
65.0	4,358,000
21.1	1,823,000
14.2	1,146,000
9.6	622,000
6.5	432,000
4.6	282,000
3.2	200,000
1.3	106,000
0.7	21,000
0.1	8,000
0.0	0

Source: Adapted from Cunningham and Stanovich (1998), p. 11.

How Can I Teach Vocabulary Skills and Strategies?

Some words are not likely to become part of one's vocabulary without direct instruction. In addition, effective vocabulary instruction helps students understand what they must do and know in order to learn new words on their own. (Stahl & Kapinus, 2001, p. 13)

Most vocabulary instruction practices supported by research can be organized into one or more of the following types:

- **Explicit.** Students are given descriptions or definitions of the target words. For example, teachers may help students learn the attributes and meanings of key words prior to reading text.
- **Indirect.** Students are encouraged to read widely and be exposed to different types of texts.
- **Multimedia.** Students are provided with media other than text to help them understand word meanings. For example, the teacher might provide graphic organizers or semantic maps, or use hypertext.
- **Association.** Students are encouraged to make connections between words and meanings they already know and new words they are learning. This can be taught using context, semantics, or visual imagery.

The National Reading Panel (NRP, 2000) emphasizes that students benefit when they are taught the meanings of words before encountering them in the text and when they are provided consistent, ongoing opportunities to learn new words through reading. However, a single exposure to words through preteaching is not nearly as valuable as multiple opportunities to learn the meanings of words, encounter them in print, hear them from the teacher and other students, and practice using them.

What Instructional Factors Contribute to Vocabulary Learning?

The following practices are especially effective for teaching vocabulary (NRP, 2000):

- Students need to be taught vocabulary words explicitly and provided with opportunities to link the meanings of these words to the texts they read. Teachers should select key words, provide their meaning, and link them to the text prior to reading.
- Students need to be encouraged to develop vocabularies indirectly. Teachers should ask them to keep a "new word" notebook in which they record new words they are exposed to through listening or reading. The meaning of these new words can be recorded and elaborated on as they are encountered later. Students can occasionally share or exchange notebooks.
- Students acquire vocabulary readily when actively engaged in learning tasks. Teachers should list new words on a vocabulary board or word wall, use them, and celebrate when students use them. Teachers should promote the use of key vocabulary words daily. Most important, they should encourage students to be "word detectives" who recognize, use, and have fun learning the meanings of words.
- Computers offer an effective way to enhance vocabulary knowledge. Every year there are new vocabulary programs that integrate words and word meanings.
- Teachers should teach synonyms and antonyms as a way to understand new words and identify different aspects of them. This gives students a way to contrast words by saying what they mean, and the opposite of what they mean, while learning them.

How Do I Determine Which Words Need to Be Taught Directly?

Perhaps one of the most important considerations when selecting words to teach directly is the *utility* of knowing the word. Beck, McKeown, and Kucan (2002) ask teachers to consider grouping words into three tiers:

- **Tier 1.** The most basic words. These do not need to be taught to any but the most learning disabled students. Examples: *car, water, man, candy.*
- **Tier 2.** Words that are used often and help readers understand a passage. Examples: *considerate, altitude, mobilize, concentrate, industry.*
- **Tier 3.** Words that are infrequently used and that may be associated with specific fields or domains. Examples: *isosceles, algorithm, bellicose, corpus, exacerbate, sedentary.*

Teachers should focus on Tier 2 words for explicit instruction. One way to determine whether a word belongs to Tier 2 is to consider whether it allows students to express themselves in a more interesting and mature way than they otherwise might. For example, examine the following sentence and determine which word might be a good candidate for Tier 2:

The twin girls looked and acted alike, although all they seemed to have in common with their brother was that they were enthusiastic.

Do you agree that *enthusiastic* is probably a good Tier 2 word for 2nd graders? Teachers should ask students what other words they know that have the same meaning, and to use the word both in reading and oral language.

When selecting words to teach students, consider the following questions:

- Is this word highly useful to students?
- What is the likelihood that the majority of the class already knows this word?
- Do students know related words that are simpler or less sophisticated so they can relate to this word and use it when appropriate?
- Will this word help students understand text?

There is little chance that you will be able to teach all of the words that your students do not know directly, and there are several reasons that you shouldn't:

- The number of words would be too many. Early elementary students cannot possibly acquire the meaning of too many new words, and teaching them can be time consuming, so students should be limited to about three new words per reading story.
- Teachers need time to review previously taught words, and adding too many new ones can reduce the effectiveness of instruction.
- Students are able to figure out the meaning of text without understanding the meaning of every word they read.

- Students can be encouraged to use the strategies that you teach them, such as context and word chunking, to understand the meaning of some unfamiliar words.

What Practices Can I Use to Teach Vocabulary Directly?

During early reading instruction it may be valuable if teachers monitor how students incorporate vocabulary learning strategies so they can reinforce students for engaging in these activities correctly. (Baker, Simmons, & Kame'enui, 1998, p. 227)

Teachers should ask themselves the following questions to see if they need to adjust their instructional methods:

- Do you create a learning context that promotes language and word learning?
- Do you create a learning context that provides ample opportunity to read a wide range of print, including informational, expository, and narrative text?
- Do you allow students to read and reread to classmates, older and younger students, and adults?
- Do you teach and review vocabulary words and word learning strategies explicitly?
- Do you encourage students to read independently outside of school, including at home, after school, and during the summer?
- Do you promote thinking and extended discourse by engaging students in conversations about what they read and the conclusions they draw?

- Do you encourage students to use new vocabulary and determine synonyms and antonyms for words they know?
- Do you provide students with a range of reading materials that challenge them to think about what they read and learn?
- Do you monitor students' vocabulary and comprehension, and provide feedback for misunderstandings?
- Do you ask silly questions about the new words students are learning and ask them to respond so as to indicate that they understand the real meaning of the word?

Good strategies for direct instruction include:

Semantic mapping. Semantic maps provide a web for understanding the key features of a word or concept that is critical to understanding a text or theme.

Teaching word parts. An effective way to help students extend their word knowledge is to teach them to recognize and use information from word parts such as prefixes, suffixes, and root words. Figure 5.3 provides a list of frequently seen prefixes and suffixes in English text.

How Well Do Students Need to Know the Meaning of the Word?

We do not know the meanings of all words equally well. According to Dale (1965), there are four stages of word knowledge:

1. Words we've never heard before;
2. Words we've heard, but don't know what they mean;
3. Words we know the general meaning of, but cannot specifically define; and

4. Words we know well and understand the meaning of, whether they're spoken or written.

Teachers can use these four stages to determine students' word knowledge and scaffold their learning. The following example shows how a teacher can begin with Stage 1 and work through Stage 4:

Teacher: "I would like you to raise your hand if you have ever heard of the word *deteriorate*. Some of you have heard of the word and some of you have not. Now, how many of you have some idea what *deteriorate* means? Raise your hand if you can tell me something about the word *deteriorate*."

The teacher asks students to brainstorm the meaning of *deteriorate*.

Teacher: "Now, I'm going to show you a sentence that we will read today with the word *deteriorate* in it. Let's see if we can elaborate on our understanding of the word *deteriorate*."

Progress Monitoring

Monitoring student progress in vocabulary is challenging. Vocabulary is difficult to assess, and it's hard to identify all of the new words that students are learning. However, teachers *can* monitor the progress of key concepts and vocabulary that they teach explicitly. When preparing students to read narrative stories or learn from expository text, teachers can identify words and

FIGURE 5.3 ➤ The Most Frequent Affixes

Prefix	Suffix
un-	-s, -es
re-	-ed
il-, ir-	-ing
dis-	-ly
en-, em-	-er, -or
non-	-ion, -tion, -ation, -sion
in-, im-	-able, -ible
over-	-al, -ial
mis-	-y
sub-	-ness
pre-	-ity, -ty
inter-	-ment
fore-	-ic

concepts that are likely to help students understand what they read. The key words should be taught prior to reading, and teachers should provide students with tasks, such as the instructional activities below, to ensure that they are engaged with the words over time. Teachers can keep and periodically revisit a chart of key words, monitoring the progress of all students to ensure that they remember and can use the words. To accomplish this, the class should participate in ongoing activities related to the words and use the words during classroom dialogues.

Instructional Activities

Dependence on a single vocabulary instruction method will not result in optimal learning. A variety of methods was used effectively with emphasis on multimedia aspect of learning, richness of context in which words are to be learned, and the number of exposures to words that learners receive. (National Reading Panel, 2000, sec. 4, p. 4)

Using Examples and Nonexamples

Objective. Students will learn vocabulary words using examples and nonexamples.

Materials. Vocabulary words, pictures that provide examples and nonexamples of the words (see Figure 5.4), a transparency, an overhead projector, and an overhead marker.

Sequence.

1. Write a vocabulary word (e.g., *gigantic*) on a transparency.
2. Say the word, and have students repeat it.
3. Ask what the word means and provide appropriate feedback. If students respond correctly, say: "Yes, *gigantic* means huge." If they respond incorrectly, immediately model the correct response: "*Gigantic* means huge."
4. Discuss pictures that represent examples and nonexamples of the word. For example, point to a picture of a dinosaur and say, "The dinosaur is gigantic." Then point to a picture of a dog and say, "The dog is *not* gigantic."
5. Present the pictures one at a time. Have students determine if they are examples or nonexamples. For example, "The tall building is gigantic; the toy house is not gigantic."

FIGURE 5.4 ➤ **Sample Pictures for the Vocabulary Word *gigantic***

6. Provide opportunities for students to practice discriminating whether a picture represents an example or nonexample of a word. For example:
   • Have students sit in a circle.
   • Within reach of everyone, place the stack of pictures face down in the middle of the circle.
   • Have students take turns identifying whether the picture represents an example or nonexample of a word.

Note: This activity was adapted from the University of Texas Center for Reading and Language Arts (2002a).

Elaborating Words

Objective. Students will provide at least one detail to describe a word in a sentence.

Materials. Familiar words (*dog, ocean, hat*), words that describe the familiar words (see Figure 5.5), an overhead projector, a marker, and a transparency.

Sequence.

1. Explain that students can elaborate on or say more about words to make sentences more interesting.
2. On the transparency, write a sentence that uses a familiar word. Be sure to underline the word. Example: "The dog chased the cat."
3. Read the sentence, and have students read it aloud.
4. Model how to elaborate and add more words to describe the word. Example: "I will think of some words that tell more about the dog."
5. Add several descriptive words (*large, black, white*) to the sentence.

6. Rewrite the sentence, adding the descriptive words. Example: "The large black and white <u>dog</u> chased the cat."

7. Read the sentence, and have students repeat it.

8. Write another sentence on the transparency. Be sure to underline the familiar word. Example: "The shark lives in the <u>ocean</u>."

9. Read the sentence, and have the students repeat it.

10. Ask students to think of words that tell more about the familiar word. Example: "What are some words that tell more about the ocean?"

11. Prompt students if necessary. Example: "Tell me about the size of the ocean."

12. Rewrite the sentence, adding the descriptive words. Example: "The shark lives in the huge, blue, and salty <u>ocean</u>."

13. Read the sentence, and have students repeat it.

14. Write another sentence on the transparency. Be sure to underline the familiar word. Example: "My sister bought a <u>hat</u>."

15. Read the sentence, and have students repeat it.

16. Ask students to independently think of at least three words to describe or tell more about the familiar word.

17. Have several students share their descriptive words. Rewrite the sentence, adding the words.

Variation. Use pictures of objects with specific details.

FIGURE 5.5 ➤ **Examples of Words That Describe Other Words**

For the word *dog*:
- Large
- Black
- White

For the word *ocean*:
- Huge
- Blue
- Salty

For the word *hat*:
- New
- Red
- Spotted

Note: This activity was adapted from the University of Texas Center for Reading and Language Arts (2002a).

Using Synonyms or Definitions

Objective. Students will learn how to use synonyms or definitions to increase their word knowledge.

Materials. Vocabulary words.

Sequence.

1. Introduce the first word (e.g., *immigrant*). Say the word, and have students repeat it.

2. Define the word for the students. Example: "*Immigrant* means someone who comes from abroad to live permanently in another country."

3. Ask students to restate the definition in their own words.

4. Scaffold students' responses by asking questions. Example: "Where does an immigrant come from? Where does an immigrant go? Why does an immigrant come from abroad to another country?"

5. Provide sentences using the word. Example: "Tom's grandparents came to the United States from England in 1912. They lived in the United States until they passed away."

6. Ask questions to determine students' understanding of the word. Example: "Are Tom's grandparents immigrants? How do you know?"

7. Scaffold responses, if necessary. Example: "Tom's grandparents came from abroad and lived in the United States for the rest of their lives."

8. Repeat the same procedure with other sentences.

9. Provide several nonexample sentences using the word. Example: "Recently, many international students have come to the United States to study."

10. Ask questions to determine students' understanding of the word. Example: "Are the international students immigrants? How do you know?"

11. Scaffold responses, if necessary. Example: "International students do not intend to live in the United States permanently."

12. Repeat the same procedure with several more nonexample sentences.

Note: This activity was adapted from Carnine, Silbert, and Kame'enui (1997).

Creating Word Maps

Objective. Students will learn how to create a word map for a targeted vocabulary word in a text.

Materials. A targeted vocabulary word, an overhead projector, a marker, a copy of a word map for each student (see Figure 5.6), and a transparency of a word map.

Sequence.

1. Introduce the targeted word. On the transparency, write the word (e.g., *wicked*). Say the word, and have students repeat it. Then have students write the word on their individual word maps.

2. Ask students to define the word. Example: "What does the word *wicked* mean?"

3. Discuss responses. As a group, determine the best definition. Write the definition on the transparency and read it, then have students repeat the definition and write it on their word maps.

4. On the transparency, write one example sentence ("Tom always lies to his friends") and one nonexample sentence ("Diana is a considerate boss who is always willing to listen") for the word. Label each.

5. Have students turn to their neighbors. On their word maps, have each pair write one example sentence and one nonexample sentence of the word.

6. Have students read their sentences. Provide corrective feedback.

FIGURE 5.6 ➤ **Word Map**

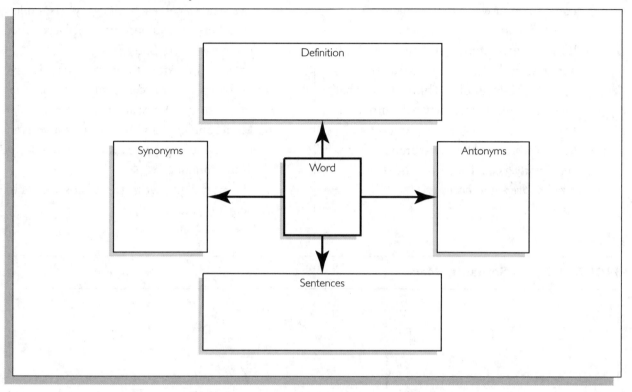

7. Ask students to identify synonyms and antonyms of the word. Example: "What is a synonym for *wicked*? What is an antonym for *wicked*?"

8. Have students record synonyms (*unkind*, *bad*) and antonyms (*good*, *considerate*) on their word maps.

9. Encourage students to use the word in conversation and to look for it in print.

Note: This activity was adapted from the University of Texas Center for Reading and Language Arts (2003).

Semantic Mapping

Objective. Students will create a semantic map to illustrate their understanding of a targeted vocabulary word in a text.

Materials. A targeted vocabulary word, an overhead projector, an overhead marker, a copy of the semantic map for each student (see Figure 5.7), a transparency of a semantic map, and a blank transparency.

Sequence.

1. Introduce the targeted word (e.g., *owl*). Write the word on a blank transparency. Say the word and have students repeat it.

2. Have students brainstorm words that come to mind when they think about the targeted word.

3. If necessary, prompt students to think about words that are related to the targeted word. Example: "Think about what owls look like, what they eat, and what they do."

4. Record words on the transparency. Example: *Feathers, talons, rodents, bugs, fly around, sleep,* and *hoot.*

5. With students, group words into categories and label each category. Example: "Feathers and talons can be placed in a category called 'Body Parts.'"

6. Project the semantic map transparency and explain the different parts on the map using the key at the bottom.

7. Model and explain how to create a semantic map using the words generated by your students.

8. Have students write the words on their semantic maps.

FIGURE 5.7 ➤ **Semantic Map**

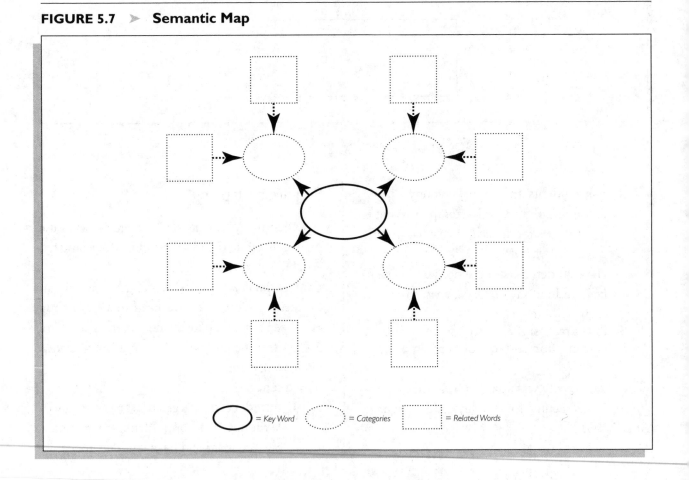

Variations.

- Draw a simplified semantic map with students to represent the words that they generate.
- Introduce a new vocabulary word and its meaning. Have students work in small groups or in pairs to construct semantic maps for the new word. After students read the passage, they can add more words to their maps.

Note: This activity was adapted from the University of Texas Center for Reading and Language Arts (2003).

Four-Square Vocabulary Maps

Objective. Students will use a four-square vocabulary map to better understand a word from their text.

Materials. A vocabulary word, an overhead projector, an overhead marker, a copy of a four-square vocabulary map for each student (see Figure 5.8), and a transparency of a four-square vocabulary map.

Sequence.

1. On the transparency, write a targeted word (e.g., *respite*) in the first box below the heading "Word."
2. Say the targeted word and have students repeat it.
3. Have all the students write the word on their four-square vocabulary maps.
4. State the definition of the word. On the transparency, write the definition in the box under the heading "What Is It?" Example: "*Respite* means a short rest."
5. Have students repeat the word's meaning and write it on their maps.
6. Provide example sentences to check students' understanding of the word, and ask questions about the sentence. Example: "Jane ran for three miles. Then she washed her face with cold water and relaxed for a while. Then she ran for another three miles." Then ask, "Did Jane take a respite? How do you know?"
7. Scaffold student responses, if necessary. Example: "She took a short break between runs."
8. On the transparency, write the sentences underneath the question, "What are some examples?"
9. Have students copy the sentences on their vocabulary maps.
10. Repeat the same procedure with several more example sentences.
11. Provide nonexample sentences to check students' understanding of the word. Example: "Tom worked hard at work. When he went home, he stayed up all night to finish the work." Then ask, "Did Tom take a respite?" "How do you know?"
12. Scaffold students' responses, if necessary. Example: "He did not take a rest, so he did not take a respite."
13. On the transparency, write the sentences under the question, "What are some nonexamples?"
14. Have students copy the nonexample sentences on their vocabulary maps.
15. Repeat the same procedure with several more nonexample sentences.

Note: This activity was adapted from Stahl (1999) and the University of Texas Center for Reading and Language Arts (2001b).

Personal Vocabulary Books

Objective. Given a vocabulary word, students will identify synonyms, pictures, and text related to the word.

Materials. Notebooks or blank books for each student, vocabulary words, assorted old magazines, newspapers, trade books, and textbooks.

Sequence.

1. As new vocabulary words are introduced, have students write the words, one per page, in their vocabulary books.

2. Encourage students to hunt for those words or their synonyms in old magazines, newspapers, or books.

3. When students find the words or synonyms in magazines or newspapers, have them cut them out and paste them on that word's page in their vocabulary books. When they find the words in the trade

---

FIGURE 5.8 ➤ **Four-Square Vocabulary Map**

Word	What are some examples?
What is it?	**What are some nonexamples?**

books and textbooks, have them copy the relevant sentence and underline the word.

4. Have students occasionally share the pages in their vocabulary books with peers or with the class.

Variations.

- Have students find antonyms for the words.
- Provide a template for entries that includes the name of the source where students found the word, the date they found it, how the word was used (e.g., a headline, a sentence, a phrase in an ad), and the page number.

Vocabulary Word Sorts

Objective. Students will sort previously introduced vocabulary words into categories according to word meanings.

Materials. Index cards, a marker, and previously introduced vocabulary words.

Sequence. First, model and demonstrate steps 1–7. Next, have students work in pairs or in a small group. Provide support as needed.

1. Identify two or more vocabulary words to use as word sort categories (e.g., *drowsy* and *amusing*). Write each word on an index card. These cards will be the heading cards for the two categories.
2. Identify several words or phrases related to the categories (e.g., words related to *drowsy*: *sleepy*, *tired*, *closing eyes*, and *snooze*; words related to *amusing*: *funny*, *laughing*, *comedy*, and *jokes*). Write each word on a separate index card.
3. Place the heading cards on a table (or in a pocket chart).

4. Ask students to read the words on the heading cards aloud.
5. Review word meanings by asking students to describe or define each word.
6. Hold up each related word card. Ask students to read each word aloud.
7. Have students sort the related words into the two categories.
8. To check students' word sorts, have them read each heading card and the related words in that category.

Variations.

- To make the word sort more challenging, have students complete an "open sort," where you do not present the categories. Give students several index cards with vocabulary words written on them, and have them sort the words into two or more categories of their choice. After they complete the sort, ask students to describe the categories they have chosen and how the words in each category are related.
- Include a few words that do not fit either category. You can create a "wild card" or "other" category for these.
- Have students copy categories of related words in their personal vocabulary books.

Vocabulary Posters

Objective. Given a vocabulary word, students will identify its meaning using simple definitions, synonyms, examples, and nonexamples of the word.

Materials. Poster boards, previously taught vocabulary words, and markers.

Sequence.

1. Write a previously taught vocabulary word at the top of a poster board.
2. Review the word's meaning.
3. Ask students to write a sentence using the word.
4. Have students read their sentences to a partner.
5. Call on several students to read their sentences to the whole class.
6. Encourage students to listen and watch for the word all week in conversations or in print.
7. Model and explain that when students find the word, they should write the context of the word on the poster. For younger students, write the words on the poster yourself. Example: *region* (see Figure 5.9).
8. At the end of the week, read and discuss the vocabulary poster with students.
9. Each week, add a new vocabulary poster.

Variation.

- Give each student half of a poster board (or a piece of construction paper) and one vocabulary word. Have them make a poster to advertise their word. Ask them to decorate the poster with the word's definition, synonyms, drawings or pictures that illustrate the word's meaning, and sentences that use the word.
- Display posters in the classroom.
- Use posters to review words.

Add-a-Part: Prefixes and Suffixes

Objective. Students will use prefixes and suffixes to create words.

Materials. Pocket chart, index cards with prefixes and suffixes (see Figure 5.10), root words that can be combined with the prefixes and suffixes, and a plastic bag.

Sequence.

1. Explain that combinations of letters called prefixes can be added to the beginning of words to form new words, and that suffixes can be added to the end of words to do the same.
2. On a pocket chart, place a card with a prefix. Point to the prefix and pronounce it.
3. Give the meaning of the prefix. Example: "*Dis-* means not."
4. Check students' understanding by asking them to say the prefix and repeat its meaning. Example: "What is the prefix?" (Answer: "*dis-*.") Say, "What does the prefix *dis-* mean?" (Answer: "*not*.")

FIGURE 5.9 ➤ **Sample Context Notes for the Word *region***

Region			
Source	**How It Is Used**	**Name**	**Date**
The Daily Times	The population in the southwest region doubled.	Jake W.	1/13

5. Place a card with a root word (e.g., *honest*) after the prefix.

6. Point to the root word and pronounce it.

7. Have individual students read the prefix and the root word.

8. Model by saying the whole word without pausing between each word part. Example: "*dishonest*."

9. Point to the prefix (*dis-*) and the root word (*honest*). Have students say each word part as you rapidly point to each part ("*dis*," "*honest*").

10. Give the meaning of the root word. Example: "*Honest* means truthful."

11. Model and explain that looking at each word part and thinking about what it means can help students determine the meaning of a word. Example: "*Dis-* means 'not' and *honest* means 'truthful.' *Dishonest* means 'not truthful.'"

12. Repeat the same procedure with other prefixes and suffixes.

13. Provide students with opportunities to practice. Example:
    - Have students sit in a circle. Place the plastic bag of cards with prefixes and suffixes in the middle of the circle, within reach of everyone.
    - Model playing the "add-a-part" game. Draw one card out of the bag, and say the affix on the card (*-less*). Create a new word with the affix (*careless*). Ask students to create other words with the same affix.
    - Continue, with students taking turns.

Note: This activity was adapted from The University of Texas Center for Reading and Language Arts (2001b).

Pairing Words

Objective. Given pairs of vocabulary words, students will identify similarities and differences between their meanings.

Materials. A list of new and review vocabulary words.

Sequence.

1. Introduce new vocabulary words using simple definitions, synonyms, or pictures.

2. Make a chart on the board with two columns, labeled "Similarities" and "Differences." Write two vocabulary words from the list of words.

3. Model identifying one similarity and one difference between the meanings of the words. Example: "The words *governor* and *state* are similar in some ways. For instance, a governor works for the state. The words are also different in some ways. A governor is a person; a state is a place."

4. Have students identify other ways in which words are similar or different. List their responses on the chart.

5. Have students work in pairs. Give two words to each pair, and have students list ways in which the words are similar and different.

Variations.

- Use pictures or demonstrations to compare and contrast the words.

FIGURE 5.10 ➤ **Common Prefixes and Suffixes**

Common Prefixes		
Prefix	**Meaning/Function**	**Example Words**
un-	not, opposite of	unable, unchangeable
re-	again	reread, redo
in-, im-, ir-, ill-	not	inactive, immature, irregular, illegal
dis-	not, opposite of	dishonest, disagree
en-, em-	cause to	enable, embrace
non-	not	nonfiction
in-	in or into	inside, interior
over-	too much	overdue, oversleep
mis-	wrongly	misbehave, mispronounce, misspell
sub-	under	submarine, subway
pre-	before	preheat, preschool
inter-	between	international, intersection
fore-	before	foreground
de-	opposite of	deactivate
trans-	across	transport
super-	above	supernatural
semi-	half	semicircle
anti-	against	antislavery, antisocial
mid-	middle	midnight
under-	too little	underpaid
ex-	out, out of	exterior, exhaust, expose

(continued)

FIGURE 5.10 ➤ **Common Prefixes and Suffixes—*cont.***

Common Suffixes		
Suffix	**Meaning/Function**	**Example Words**
-s, -es	plurals	cats, dishes
-ed	past-tense verbs	landed, smelled, wished
-ing	verb form/present participle	renting
-ly	characteristic of	gladly, happily
-er, -or	person connected with	painter, director
-ion, -tion, -ation, -ition, -sion	act, process	tension, attention, imagination
-ible, -able	can be done	comfortable, changeable
-al, -ial	having characteristics of	natural, remedial
-y	characterized by	rainy
-ness	state of, condition of	kindness, happiness
-ity, -ty	state of	necessity, honesty
-ment	action or process	government
-ic	having of	poetic
-ous, -eous, -ious	having of	joyous, gracious
-en	made of	wooden
-er	comparative	smarter
-ive, -ative, -itive	adjective form of a noun	active, affirmative
-ful	full of	fearful, beautiful, hopeful
-less	without	fearless, tireless, hopeless
-est	superlative	lightest, strongest
-ance, -ence	state of	importance
-ness	having of	illness

- Give students a word with multiple meanings, and have them complete the activity by comparing and contrasting the different meanings.
- Identify a set of word pairs that can be compared and contrasted. Write each word on a separate index card, shuffle the cards, and have students match the word pairs that can be compared or contrasted.

Figures of Speech

Objective. Students will learn figures of speech.

Materials. A pocket chart, index cards with figures of speech (see Figure 5.11), and index cards with the meanings of the expressions.

Sequence.

1. Explain that a figure of speech consists of a group of words that has a different meaning from each individual word's meaning (e.g., *down and out* means "without hope," *heavy heart* means "sad," *burn a hole in one's pocket* means "a desire to spend money as soon as possible").
2. In a pocket chart, place a card with a figure of speech (*on the carpet*).
3. Say the phrase, and have students repeat it.
4. On the board, write a sentence that contains context clues to help students figure out the meaning of the phrase. Example: "Chang's teacher called him *on the carpet* after he broke the window."
5. Help students look at the other words in the sentence to determine what the phrase means.
6. Scaffold students' responses, if necessary. Example: "Because Chang broke the window, he would probably be in trouble with his teacher. So, *on the carpet* means 'in trouble.'"
7. In the pocket chart, place the meaning card beside the phrase card.
8. Repeat the same procedure with other figures of speech.
9. Provide opportunities for students to practice. Example: After modeling all the phrases and their meanings, remove the cards from the pocket chart, shuffle them, and ask students to match the phrase cards (*on the carpet*) with their corresponding meaning cards ("in trouble").

Note: This strategy was adapted from Carnine, Silbert, and Kame'enui (1997).

✦   ✦   ✦

Annotated Bibliography

Beck, I. L., McKeown, M. G., & Kucan, L. (2002). *Bringing words to life: Robust vocabulary instruction*. New York: Guilford Press.

FIGURE 5.11 ➤ **Examples of Easy, Intermediate, and Difficult Idioms**

Teachers may want to refer to this list to teach idioms.

Easy Idioms

- To give up
- A can of worms
- To be even Steven
- To make believe
- To be out in left field
- To smell a rat
- To talk back
- To rain cats and dogs

Intermediate Idioms

- To stack the cards against someone
- To bring off
- To cook someone's goose
- To do in
- To sniff out
- To stand firm
- To get in someone's hair
- To read the riot act
- To take to the cleaners
- To carry out a task
- To be undercover
- "Go jump in the lake"

Difficult Idioms

- To kick the bucket
- Across the board
- To bury the hatchet
- To buttonhole
- To gild the lily
- To run amok
- To be a wet blanket
- To be on the dole
- To do a double take
- To keep it under your hat

This book provides teachers with practical ideas and activities for vocabulary instruction, guiding teachers through the steps necessary to develop strong and powerful vocabulary lessons, from selecting vocabulary words to teach to getting students to think about and use new words. Vocabulary strategies and instructional examples for early (K–2) and later grades are included, and appendices list trade books by grade level that are rich with vocabulary.

Blachowicz, C. L., & Fisher, P. (2001). *Teaching vocabulary in all classrooms* (2nd ed.). Upper Saddle River, NJ: Pearson Education.

This book presents practical instructional strategies and activities for developing vocabulary that can be applied across grade levels, from kindergarten through high school. Although the focus is on teaching vocabulary to enhance content knowledge acquisition, the ideas can be used with younger students as well as those with special needs. The chapters include easy-to-read descriptions and examples for building vocabulary, from wordplay activities to contextual and structural analysis.

Bowers, L., Huisingh, R., LoGiudice, C., Orman, J., and Johnson, P. F. (2000). *125 vocabulary builders*. East Moline, IL: LinguiSystems.

This book contains paper and pencil activities designed to provide practice with newly acquired vocabulary words.

Fry, E. B., Kress, J. E., & Fountoukidis, D. L. (2000). *The reading teacher's book of lists with CD-ROM* (4th ed.). San Francisco: Jossey-Bass, Inc.

This updated book, with additional CD-ROM, presents various lists for K–12 teachers, including word lists that they can use to plan lessons and develop instructional materials. The book organizes 190 lists into 15 sections, from phonics to the Internet. Vocabulary-related lists include "Compound Words," "Homophones," "Prefixes and Suffixes," "Common Word Idioms," "Synonyms and Antonyms," and "Ways to Define a Word."

Stahl, S. A., & Kapinus, B. (2001). *Word power: What every educator needs to know about teaching vocabulary*. Washington, DC: National Education Association.

This book provides guidelines and instructional activities for enhancing student vocabulary and helping students understand how words function in communication. Strategies are also provided for teaching students the appropriateness, value, and potential effects of words.

❖   ❖   ❖

Web Sites That Teach

http://reading.uoregon.edu/big_ideas/voc.php.

This Web site provides information about vocabulary, including research findings, a definition of the term, a discussion of the importance of vocabulary, and guidelines for teaching vocabulary to K–3 students.

http://reading.uoregon.edu/instruction/instruc_voc_q2.php.

This Web site provides strategies for teaching vocabulary by modeling with examples and using synonyms and definitions.

http://www.mcps.k12.md.us/departments/dsd/70plus/VOCAB.pdf.

This Web site provides readers with the principles of vocabulary instruction and with downloadable resources on such strategies as semantic mapping and contextual analysis.

http://www.ed.gov/offices/OESE/SASA/rb/slide020.html.

This Web site provides a summary of research-based vocabulary instruction and strategies.

http://www.allamericareads.org/lessonplan/vocab.htm.

This Web site introduces strategies to promote vocabulary development, including use of contextual clues, idiomatic expressions, and word mapping.

http://www.ldonline.org/ld_indepth/teaching_techniques/ellis_clarifying.html.

This Web site introduces elaboration techniques for teaching new vocabulary words.

http://idea.uoregon.edu/~ncite/documents/techrep/tech13.html.

This Web site presents findings from a synthesis on vocabulary acquisition.

http://idea.uoregon.edu/%7Encite/documents/techrep/tech14.html.

This Web site presents converging evidence on vocabulary acquisition, and discusses the curricular and instructional implications.

http://www.sd129.org/jpetzke/vocab_web/vocab_research.html.

This Web site provides research findings on vocabulary instruction and acquisition.

◆　　　◆　　　◆

6 Comprehension

THE EVIDENCE IS GROWING THAT ELEMENTARY CHILDREN CAN BE TAUGHT TO use the comprehension strategies used by excellent, mature comprehenders. Moreover, when they learn such strategies, their comprehension improves. (Pressley & Afflerbach, 1995)

Most teachers have wondered what they might do to improve the reading comprehension of their students. They may be frustrated that students can read words but often have only surface understanding of what they read. Though phonics and word reading are building blocks of literacy, comprehension—appreciating and understanding text—is the ultimate goal. Without comprehension, reading for pleasure and knowledge is impossible. This chapter addresses the critical elements of reading comprehension, including assessment practices and instructional activities.

What Is Comprehension Instruction?

Teachers must be skillful in their instruction and must respond flexibly and opportunistically to students' needs for instructive feedback as they read. To be able to do this, teachers must themselves have a firm grasp not only of the strategies that they are teaching the children but also of instructional strategies that they can employ to achieve their goal. (National Reading Panel, 2000, pp. 4–7)

Comprehension is the active process of constructing meaning from text; it involves accessing previous knowledge, understanding vocabulary and concepts, making inferences, and linking key ideas. Comprehension cannot be learned through rote instruction, but requires a series of strategies that influence understanding of text. Reading comprehension includes the following:

- Applying one's knowledge and experiences to the text,
- Setting goals for reading, and ensuring that they are aligned with the text,
- Using strategies and skills to construct meaning during and after reading,
- Adapting strategies that match the reader's text and goals,
- Recognizing the author's purpose,
- Distinguishing between facts and opinions, and
- Drawing logical conclusions.

With this in mind, the teacher's role during reading comprehension instruction is to ensure that students participate actively prior to reading, have the strategies and skills to use when reading, and try to make sense of the text by understanding the author's intention and bringing their own experiences to bear on the text.

Text can be divided into three types for comprehension purposes:

- **Textually explicit**, which requires little of the readers' background knowledge, stating information clearly so that the reader can refer back to the text to obtain it;
- **Textually implicit**, which provides discrete information but requires readers to use their own knowledge and experience to assemble ideas; and
- **Implicit only**, where information is not stated directly, and readers are required to make inferences by combining information from previous experience and reading to the text.

Understanding these text types helps teachers determine the types of comprehension difficulties their students are most challenged by and design practices to assist them. Read the story below and consider the questions that follow. Decide what type of text you used to answer the questions, and think about how you might help your students answer these questions now that you know more about text types.

"The Drive to Big Lake"

Pat and her father were driving to Big Lake in the Blue Mountain. They were going to Big Lake to go fishing. As they drove, Pat watched her father talk on the CB radio and watched the sun come up over the mountains.

When Pat and her father were near Big Lake it became very foggy. Pat's father drove very slowly but did not see a sharp bend in the road. The car ran off the road and into a ditch. Pat was OK, but she knew that she needed to get help for her father.

She climbed out of the car and went to the road. She thought maybe a car would come by, but none did.

She walked down the road. She was looking for a house. As she walked, she yelled for help.

Then she remembered the CB radio that was in the car. She ran back to the car. She had never used the CB, but she tried to call for help on it. A fisherman at Big Lake was listening to his CB. Pat told him where she and her father were. Fifteen minutes later help came.

By this time Pat's father had opened his eyes and was OK. The police helped Pat and her father get the car out of the ditch and back on the road. Everyone was proud of Pat. (Bos, 1979, p. 164)

Now consider the following questions:

1. Where was the lake that Pat and her father were going to?
2. Were Pat and her father in an urban or rural area?
3. What time of day was it when they had their accident?
4. Was Pat able to call for help on the CB radio?

Why Should I Teach Reading Comprehension?

Children are routinely asked questions after reading but are infrequently provided with demonstrations of the comprehension strategies needed to answer the questions posed. In short, too often assigning and asking are confused with teaching. (Cunningham, 1998, p. 47)

For some teachers, comprehension instruction is little more than determining students' understanding of a story by asking questions. Too often, teachers are satisfied that students who seem to answer questions reasonably well are making adequate progress; for those who are unable to answer questions completely or prove any genuine understanding of the text, teachers often provide the answers or scaffold responses by cueing them to critical information or asking additional questions. This is not enough. The best way to ensure improved literacy among students is to directly and explicitly teach comprehension strategies.

More than 20 years ago, Durkin (1978–79) found that in a study of over 4000 minutes of 4th grade reading instruction, only 20 minutes of comprehension instruction was recorded. These findings shocked researchers and teachers at the time. More recent studies reveal that explicit comprehension instruction is still not being provided as often as it should be. This situation must be improved (Pressley & El-Dinary, 1997; Schumm, Moody, & Vaughn, 2000; Vaughn, Moody, & Schumm, 1998).

The current emphasis on high-stakes reading tests at the district and state level is perhaps one of the biggest motivators for teaching comprehension. Every state is required by law to document student progress in reading. Teachers who provide systematic and explicit comprehension instruction will see real gains in their students' progress on these assessments, and will enhance their students' joy in reading.

What Do Good and Poor Readers Do Related to Reading Comprehension?

We know from working with good readers that what appears to be relatively effortless reading actually involves a series of sophisticated practices in which skills and abilities are well integrated. Good readers read words rapidly and accurately, set goals for reading, note the structure and organization of text, monitor their understanding while reading, create mental notes and summaries, anticipate what will happen in the text, and revise and evaluate their thinking as they read. In summary, they are active processors of text.

Poor readers, on the other hand, lack the automatic word reading skills of good readers. They typically read slower and less accurately, understand the meaning of fewer words, rarely monitor their understanding, and use few of the effective strategies of good readers (Pressley & Afflerbach, 1995). They struggle with comprehension because of slow and inadequate decoding skills, low interest, minimal preparation, and inadequate background knowledge and vocabulary to aid in interpreting text. Teaching students to use strategies that address these difficulties results in greater reading comprehension (Gersten, Fuchs, Williams, & Baker, 2001; Mastropieri & Scruggs, 1997; Swanson, 1999).

How Can I Promote Reading Comprehension?

There is substantial evidence that children become much better comprehenders if they are taught to use the active comprehension processes that skilled readers use. As is true for phonemic awareness and word-recognition skills, students do not seem to discover sophisticated comprehension strategies through immersion in reading alone. (Pressley, 1998, p. 277)

Progress Monitoring

Of all the critical elements of reading, the most challenging to monitor and assess are comprehension and vocabulary. While there are a number of tests available to assess comprehension, we have reservations about them. Figure 6.1 shows a list of 10 tests that can be used to make some rough beginning judgments. Because these tests may not completely represent the comprehension skills of their students, teachers should combine them with their personal knowledge of student progress.

When choosing tests, teachers should consider

- The tests' purpose (screening, monitoring, or assessing reading level or competence compared to peers);
- The specific information needed about the student's reading comprehension (types of questions missed and level of understanding);
- The number of students being tested, and whether the tests can be administered individually, in small groups, or to the whole class; and
- The experience or qualifications required to administer the tests.

FIGURE 6.1 ➤ **Reading Comprehension Assessments**

Title	Ages/ Grade Levels	Estimated Testing Time	Key Elements and Strategies	Administration
Clay Observational Survey (Clay, 1993)	Grades K–3	15 minutes	• Oral reading • Reading vocabulary (words known in reading)	Individual
Comprehensive Reading Assessment Battery (Fuchs, Fuchs, & Hamlett, 1989)	Grades K–6	30–40 minutes	• Fluency • Oral comprehension • Sentence completion	Individual
Gates-MacGinitie Reading Tests (MacGinitie et al., 2000)	Grades K–12 and adult	55–75 minutes	• Word meanings (levels 1 and 2) • Comprehension (short passages of 1–3 sentences for levels 1 and 2; paragraphs for levels 3 and up)	Group
Gray Oral Reading Test 4 (Wiederholt & Bryant, 2001)	Ages 6–19	15–45 minutes	• Comprehension (14 separate stories, each followed by 5 multiple-choice questions)	Individual
Gray Silent Reading Test (Wiederholt & Blalock, 2000)	Ages 7–26	15–30 minutes	• Comprehension (13 passages with 5 questions each)	Individual, small group, or entire class
Qualitative Reading Inventory (Leslie & Caldwell, 2001)	Emergent to high school	30–40 minutes	• Comprehension • Oral reading • Silent reading • Listening	Individual

(continued)

FIGURE 6.1 ➤ **Reading Comprehension Assessments—*cont.***

Title	Ages/ Grade Levels	Estimated Testing Time	Key Elements and Strategies	Administration
Test of Early Reading Ability 3 (Reid et al., 2001)	Preschool– 2nd grade	20 minutes	• Comprehension of words, sentences, and paragraphs • Vocabulary • Understanding of sentence construction • Paraphrasing	Individual
Test of Reading Comprehension (Brown et al., 1995)	Ages 7–18	30–90 minutes	• General vocabulary • Understanding syntactic similarities • Paragraph reading (6 paragraphs with 5 questions each) • Sentence sequencing (5 randomly ordered sentences that need reordering) • Diagnostic supplement: Content area vocabulary in Math, Social Studies, and Science • Reading directions	Individual, small group, or entire class
Standardized Reading Inventory 2 (Newcomer, 1999)	Ages 6–14- and-a-half	30–90 minutes	• Vocabulary in context • Passage comprehension	Individual
Woodcock Reading Mastery (Woodcock, 1998)	Ages 5–75	10–30 minutes	• Word comprehension (antonyms, synonyms, analogies)	Individual

Instructional Factors

To reflect on the critical aspects of reading comprehension instruction, teachers should ask themselves how often they implement the practices below: (1) never; (2) some of the time, but not enough; or (3) whenever needed. Practices rated 1 or 2 should be implemented more frequently.

The practices are as follows:

- Asking students to predict what they are going to read based on such features as title, pictures, and key words.
- Providing students with opportunities to integrate their background knowledge with the critical concepts in the text.
- Requesting that students monitor the words and concepts they do not understand while reading and make note of them for further discussion.
- Modeling and providing opportunities for students to construct mental images that represent text so they can better remember and understand what they read.
- Allowing students to seek clarification about confusing aspects of what they read.
- Giving students adequate time to develop questions about what they read and to ask these questions to classmates.
- Providing practice summarizing and integrating information from text.

What Intervention Practices Facilitate Reading Comprehension?

In 2000, the National Reading Panel published a synthesis of reading comprehension intervention strategies associated with effective outcomes based on a review of over 200 articles. The strategies include the following:

- Providing students with guided practice and suggestions for how to monitor their comprehension and adjust how they read when difficulties arise.
- Encouraging cooperative learning practices for reading.
- Using graphic and semantic organizers that help students draw connections, relationships, and word meanings.
- Designing questions that address the story structure.
- Providing extended feedback for student responses.
- Allowing students to elaborate on one another's responses to questions.
- Preparing students to ask and answer their own questions about what they read.
- Teaching students to write key information about what they've read while they are reading and to summarize these key points after reading longer passages.
- Teaching students strategies that can be combined to understand text.

Teachers should also consider whether the strategies they choose are best taught before, during, or after reading.

Before Reading

For many students, connecting what they already know to what they are going to read may mean extending their prior knowledge by building key concepts and vocabulary. Good teachers are aware that the background knowledge of a few students does not represent that of the whole class. They should help students make connections based on what they know and set a purpose for reading.

Graves, Juel, and Graves (2001) suggest that teachers do the following prior to having students read:

- Teach students to set a purpose for reading.
- Provide questions and connections that motivate students to be engaged when they read.
- Pre-teach key vocabulary and concepts.
- Link students' background knowledge and experiences with what they are going to read.
- Relate the text to the students' lives.
- Teach students text features and how to use them to understand what they read.

Text preview is another way to engage students before reading (Graves, Prenn, & Cooke, 1985; Graves, Juel, & Graves, 2001). To do this, teachers should design a preview of the text that includes three parts: an idea or question that piques their interest, a brief description of the theme or story organization, and student- and teacher-generated questions to guide reading. For 5 to 10 minutes, teachers should guide students about what they are going to read, discuss interesting or important parts of the story, connect students' experiences and knowledge to key ideas in the story, and present and generate questions to consider while reading.

During and After Reading

To ensure that students are active, engaged, and likely to understand and respond to text during and after reading, teachers should do the following:

- Teach students through demonstration and think-alouds how to monitor their understanding while they read and recognize difficult concepts or words.
- Provide students with student- or teacher-generated questions to consider while reading.
- Help students draw inferences from text.
- Have students summarize the main idea of a selected paragraph.
- Ask students to confirm, disconfirm, or extend predictions and questions generated prior to reading.

Questions are windows into student reading comprehension. The most effective practice teachers can develop is how to ask, extend, and teach students to generate questions that teach and motivate understanding of text. Some examples of good question starters include the following:

- Why do you think the author _____?
- How would you have ended this story?
- What character was your favorite, and why?
- What information helped you decide where this story took place?
- How would you sequence the three most important findings?

- How would you compare the main character in this story to a main character from a previous story?

Another effective strategy is "Questioning the Author," where teachers provide students with distinct goals, and queries that help them reach those goals (see Figure 6.2).

To do well on high-stakes achievement tests, students need to know how to identify the main idea and summarize. Williams (1988) indicates that identifying main ideas is essential for reading comprehension. Explicit and systematic instruction in the main idea is associated with improved outcomes in reading comprehension (Graves, 1986; Jenkins, Heliotis, Stein, & Haynes, 1987; Jitendra, 1998; Jitendra, Hoppes, & Xin, 2000; Wong & Jones, 1982). One good strategy is to ask students the following questions about a text:

- What or who the subject is
- What the action is
- Why something happened
- Where something is or happened
- When something happened
- How something looks or is done

Figure 6.3 shows an example of a rule-based instructional strategy.

Identifying Themes. Students should learn to identify themes from stories and to determine the extent to which they apply to their own lives (Williams, 1998). After identifying text that contains a theme, such as cooperation, responsibility, or respect for others, teachers can use it as the source for the following lesson:

- **Step 1.** The teacher initially identifies the theme, slowly turning more responsibility over to the student.
- **Step 2.** The teacher reads the story and stops to ask questions to determine whether students are connecting what they are reading to the story theme.
- **Step 3.** The teacher helps students organize information from the text by asking the following three questions:
  —Who is the main character?
  —What did the main character do?
  —What happened?

Once students understand the organization of the story, the teacher asks them questions about the story.

- **Step 4.** Students learn to state the theme in a standard format that tells what the character should or should not have done and what they (the students) should or should not do. The teacher should encourage them to consider whom the theme applies to and under what conditions.

The main way to actively engage students in reflecting on text while they read is to ask them who or what the story is about, and what is happening in it (Jenkins et al., 1987; Malone & Mastropieri, 1992). For narrative text, story retelling can be an effective way to assure reading comprehension (Bos, 1987). The teacher can model retelling the story by identifying the key components: character, setting, problem, and resolution. For students who struggle with these components, teaching them separately and then

FIGURE 6.2 ➤ **Questioning the Author**

Goal	Queries
Initiate discussion	• "What is the author trying to say?" • "What is the author's message?" • "What is the author talking about?"
Help students focus on the author's message	• "That's what the author says, but what does it mean?"
Help students link information	• "How does _____ connect with what the author already told us?" • "What information has the author added here that connects to or fits in with _____?"
Identify difficulties with the way the author has presented information or ideas	• "Does _____ make sense?" • "Is _____ said in a clear way?" • "Did the author explain _____ clearly? Why or why not? What's missing? What do we need to figure out or find out?"
Encourage students to refer to the text either because they've misinterpreted a statement or to help them recognize that they've made an inference	• "Did the author tell us _____?" • "Did the author give us the answer to _____?"

Source: Beck, McKeown, Sandora, and Kucan (1996). Reprinted by permission.

combining them can be effective. For a simple retelling, students should

- Identify and retell the beginning, middle, and end of the story;
- Describe the setting; and
- Identify the problem and resolution.

For a more complete retelling, students should

- Identify and retell events and facts in sequence,
- Draw inferences to fill in missing information, and
- Identify and retell the causes of actions and their effects.

For the most complete retelling, students should

- Identify and retell a sequence of actions or events,
- Draw inferences to account for actions, and
- Offer an evaluation of the story.

FIGURE 6.3 ➤ **Rule-Based Instructional Strategies**

1. Rule Statement

Teacher: Here is a rule about motive: The reason a character does something is called motive. Listen again: The character motive is the reason a character does something in a story. Now it's your turn: Say the rule about character motive.

Teacher repeats the rule until firmly understood.

2. Individual Test

Teacher calls on students to state the rule about motive and character motive.

3. Demonstration of Examples

Teacher: We will find the character motive of a story together. First listen to the story, and then we will find the character motive. Here is the story. Listen: "It was late. Jim was mad. The bus was not on its way. Jim stomped his foot and said, 'I didn't really want to go on the bus anyway.'"

4. Multiple Procedure

Teacher: Everybody: Who is this story about?
Students: Jim.
Teacher: Everybody: What is Jim doing?
Students: Waiting for a bus.
Teacher: Everybody: How does Jim feel?
Students: Mad.
Teacher: Everybody: Why was he mad?
Students: Because the bus was late.
Teacher: Everybody: How do you know he was mad?
Students: He stomped his foot.
Teacher: Everybody: Why did he say he did not want to ride on the bus?
Students: Because the bus was late.
Teacher: Everybody: Did Jim say what he meant?
Students: No.
Teacher: Everybody: What did Jim really want to do?
Students: Ride on the bus.
Teacher: My turn. Listen carefully: The character's motive is the reason a character does something. Jim wanted to ride the bus, but he said he didn't because he was mad. Now it's your turn.
Students: The character's motive is the reason a character does something. Jim wanted to ride the bus, but he said he didn't because he was mad.

Teacher repeats the process until understood.

Source: Adapted from Rabren, Darch, and Eaves (1999).

Prioritizing instruction in listening comprehension for kindergarten and 1st grade students is essential. As students progress from 2nd through 5th grade, they should likewise progress from listening to reading comprehension as needed.

Instructional Activities

Strategy instruction seems to consistently improve students' ability to see relationships in stories, answer comprehension questions, and retell what they have read in a more focused fashion. (Gersten, Fuchs, Williams, & Baker, 2001, p. 296)

Making Predictions (Before Reading)

Objective. Students will learn how to make predictions about narrative and expository texts.

Materials. Student copies of narrative or expository text with previewing cues (e.g., title, pictures), an overhead projector and marker, and a blank transparency.

Sequence.

1. Give a copy of the text to each student.
2. Introduce the topic of the text (e.g, friendship, oceans).
3. Explain that before reading, students will take a "book walk" (skim the pages of the text).
4. With students, skim information presented on each page, such as title, subheadings, pictures, graphs, and bolded or italicized words.
5. Encourage students to predict one thing they may learn by reading the text.

6. Have students share their predictions. Ask them to give reasons or evidence to support their predictions. Example: "Why do you think you will learn about that?"
7. Ask other students to provide feedback. Example: "Do you agree with the prediction? Why?"
8. Record students' predictions on the transparency.

Purposeful Reading

Objective. Given the title and pictures from a narrative text, students will set a purpose for reading by generating questions they want the text to answer.

Materials. Instructional-level narrative text with pictures or subheadings (e.g., chapter titles, section headings), a chart paper with the story web (see Figure 6.4).

Sequence.

1. Give a copy of the text to each student.
2. Ask students to read the title aloud.
3. Write the title in the center circle of the story web.
4. Model how to generate a question about the story from the title. Example: "I wonder why Sal goes to France. I will write that question: 'Why does Sal go to France?' I want see if I can find the answer when I read the story."
5. Write the question in one of the ovals that are connected to the title circle.
6. Ask students if they have any other questions about the story.

7. Write each additional question in a separate oval.
8. Continue to preview the text, looking at the pictures and subheadings.
9. After each picture or subheading, have students generate questions they want answered in the story. Record these questions on the web.
10. Before reading the story, review each question.
11. Encourage students to look for the answers to the questions as they read the story.

12. Have students read the story aloud.
13. When students find an answer to a question, stop and write the answer under that question on the story web.
14. After reading, discuss any unanswered questions on the web.

Variation. Use the web with expository texts. Change the title from "story web" to "content web," and begin the lesson by writing the topic of the text in the center circle.

FIGURE 6.4 ➤ **Story Web**

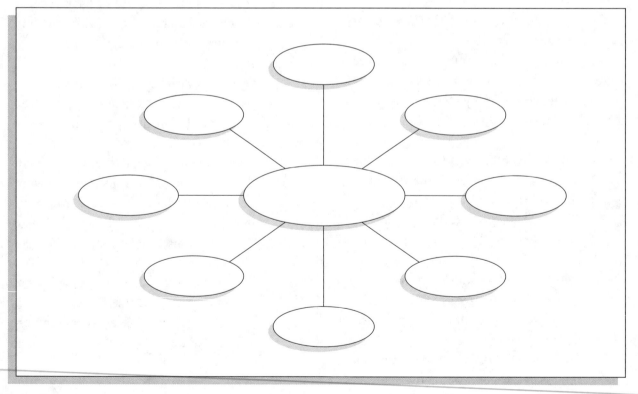

Getting the Gist (During Reading)

Objective. Students will learn how to get the gist (the main idea) of each paragraph in expository text.

Materials. Copies of three four- to seven-paragraph short expository texts for each student, an overhead projector and marker, student copies of the gist log (see Figure 6.5), and a transparency of the gist log.

Sequence.

1. Give a copy of one of the expository texts to each student.
2. Explain that a gist statement represents the main idea of a paragraph, which is also the most important information in a paragraph.
3. Explain the three steps of the "getting the gist" strategy:
   - Naming the subject of the paragraph (who or what the paragraph is mostly about).
   - Telling the most important information about the subject.
   - Stating the main idea in 10 words or less.
4. Read a paragraph of the text aloud.
5. Model how to identify the subject of a paragraph. Example: "What is the paragraph mostly about?"
6. Record the subject of the paragraph on the transparency.
7. Model how to identify the most important information about the subject. Example: "What is the most important information about the subject?"
8. Record the most important information on the transparency.
9. Model how to combine the subject with the most important information about the subject to create a gist statement of 10 words or less. Ask students to count the words if necessary.
10. Record the gist statement on the transparency.
11. Allow students to practice the strategy collaboratively, providing them with corrective feedback as needed. Example:
    - Give a copy of another expository text to each student.
    - Have one student read aloud the first paragraph.
    - Have several students tell who or what the paragraph is mostly about. Discuss responses, and record information on the transparency, in the first box of the gist log.
    - Have several students tell the most important information about the subject. Discuss responses, and record information on the transparency, in the second box of the gist log.
    - Have several students read a gist statement of 10 words or less using the information in the first and second boxes. Discuss responses, and record the gist statement on the transparency, in the third box of the gist log.
    - Continue the same procedure until the entire text has been read.

FIGURE 6.5 ➤ **Gist Log**

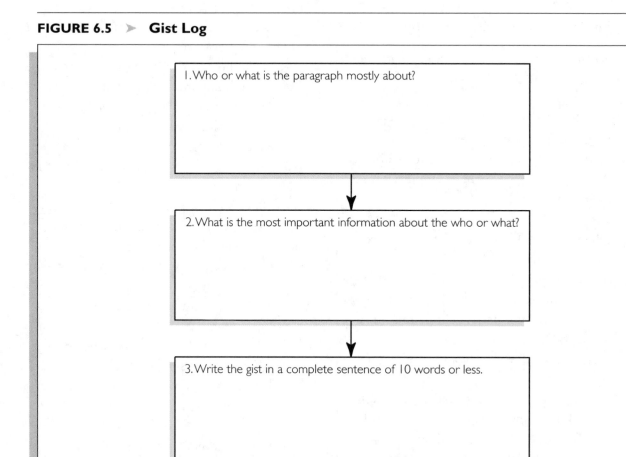

1. Who or what is the paragraph mostly about?

2. What is the most important information about the who or what?

3. Write the gist in a complete sentence of 10 words or less.

12. Provide opportunities for students to independently practice the strategy with a partner. Example:
    - Give a copy of another expository text and a gist log to each student.
    - Review the three steps of the strategy.
    - Pair students and have them take turns reading each paragraph aloud.
    - After each pair reads a paragraph, have the students use the strategy and record the gist of the paragraph on their gist logs.
    - Monitor students to ensure that they take turns reading and correctly follow the steps to determine the gist of a paragraph.
    - As a whole-group activity, have pairs read some of their gist statements.

Variation. Use "Get the Gist" with narrative texts.

Note: This activity was adapted from Klinger, Vaughn, Dimino, Schumm, and Bryant (2001).

Story Map (During Reading)

Objective. Students will learn how to use a story map to improve their comprehension of narrative texts.

Materials. Copies of a narrative text for each student, an overhead projector and marker, student copies of a story map (see Figure 6.6), and a transparency of the story map.

Sequence.

1. Give a copy of the narrative text to each student.
2. Explain that story elements are like cooking ingredients: Just as flour, sugar, butter, and chocolate chips are needed to make chocolate chip cookies, so are characters, setting, and plot needed to make a story.
3. Introduce and discuss the common story elements of narrative text:
   - Setting (where and when the story takes place)
   - Characters
   - Problem or goal
   - Plot (a series of events in which the characters try to solve a problem or achieve a goal)
   - Resolution (the solution or achievement of a goal)
4. Introduce a story map template.
5. Read the text aloud.
6. While reading aloud, stop periodically to model how to identify each story element.
7. Record the information on the transparency.
8. Provide opportunities for guided practice. Example:
   - Give each student copies of the text.
   - Have students take turns reading the text aloud.
   - Periodically stop students and ask some of them to identify story elements. Discuss responses, and record information on a story map transparency.
9. Provide opportunities for independent practice. Example:
   - Give copies of the text and a story map template to each student.
   - Remind students to look for story elements while reading.
   - Pair students and have them take turns reading.
   - Have students record story elements on the story map template as they read.
   - Monitor students to ensure that they take turns reading and correctly identify story elements.
   - As a whole group, discuss story maps.

Note: This activity was adapted from the University of Texas Center for Reading and Language Arts (2002b, 2003).

Asking Different Types of Questions (After Reading)

Objective. Students will learn how to generate different types of questions about narrative and expository texts.

Materials. Copies of a three- to five-paragraph narrative or expository text for each student, an overhead projector and marker, and a blank transparency.

FIGURE 6.6 ➤ **Story Map**

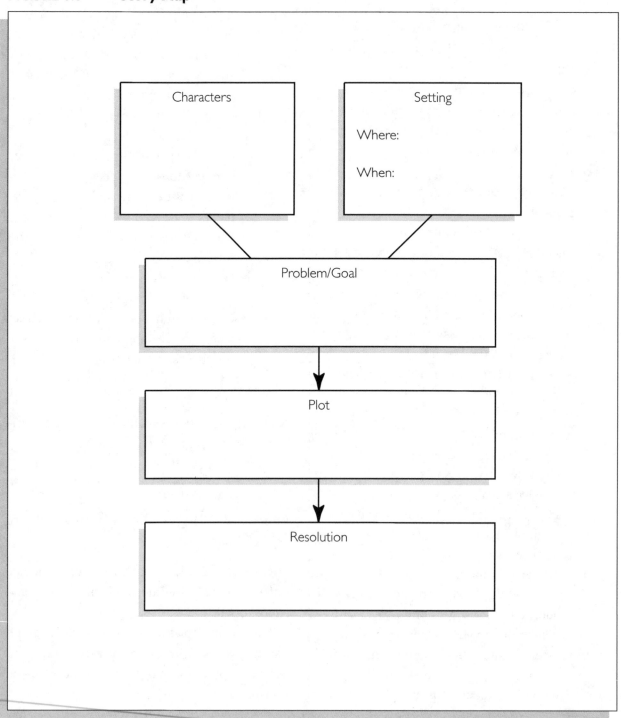

Sequence.

1. Give each student a copy of the text.
2. Explain that there are three types of questions:
   - "Right There" questions, the answers to which are explicit in the text ("Who is the main character?");
   - "Think and Search" questions, the answers to which are in the text, but need to be composed by students based on what they have read ("What causes a volcano to erupt?"); and
   - "On My Own" questions, the answers to which are not in the text, and need to be inferred by students based on a combination of their previous experiences and what they learned from the text ("How do you know that saber tooth tigers will not be in a zoo?").
3. Read the entire text aloud.
4. Model how to ask each type of question using who, what, when, where, why, and how questions.
5. Provide opportunities for guided practice. Example:
   - Give each student a copy of the text.
   - Have students take turns reading aloud.
   - Have several students ask "Right There" questions and say why they are "Right There" questions, using evidence from the text.
   - Record student-generated questions on the transparency.
   - Repeat the same procedure for "Think and Search" and "On My Own" questions.
6. Provide independent practice. Example:

- Give each student a copy of the text.
- Review the three types of questions.
- Pair students and have them take turns reading aloud.
- After reading the entire text, have pairs write one of each question type.
- Monitor students to ensure that they take turns reading and correctly generate the three types of questions.
- As a whole group, discuss questions generated by student pairs.

Note: This activity is adapted from Klingner, Vaughn, Dimino, Schumm, and Bryant (2001) and Raphael (1986).

Where's the Evidence? (During Reading)

Objective. Students will generate questions that can be answered in an expository or narrative text.

Materials. Copies of instructional-level text (narrative or expository) for each student.

Sequence.

1. Distribute text to students.
2. Read a short section of the text aloud.
3. Model how to generate questions. Example: "How did the girls find the bracelet?"
4. Write the answer on the board.
5. Ask students to find the answer to the question in the text.
6. Have students give the answer and identify the words in the text that helped them determine the answer.
7. Write the answer next to the question.

8. Ask students to generate a question from the text. On paper, have them write the question, its answer, and the page number wherever the answer is located in the text.

9. Have students ask their questions without revealing the answers.

10. After other students respond, have the student who asked the question confirm whether the answer is correct or incorrect. If incorrect, the student gives the correct answer and the page number in the text where the answer is located. Other students locate the answer in the text.

11. Have students read the next section of text.

12. Ask students to generate three or four questions, the answers, and the page numbers where the answers are located in the text.

13. Assign one student to be the "teacher." Have this student ask a question and call on classmates to provide the answer and the page where the answer is located. Have the student repeat the procedure with other questions.

14. Have students take turns being the "teacher."

Variation. After generating questions, students ask the teacher to answer them without using the text. Students confirm whether the teacher's answers are correct by looking in the text.

Making Inferences (During Reading)

Objective. Students will make inferences using information stated in a short reading passage.

Materials. Two- to three-sentence passages that contain "clues" about a situation.

Sequence.

1. Give copies of each short passage to students.

2. Explain that sometimes an author doesn't tell you everything, so you have to figure out what is happening using clues in the text.

3. With students, read the first passage aloud. Example: "Jill was running up the street with her mom. She was crying and looking everywhere. She loved Fluffy so much. Jill wondered if they would ever find her."

4. Ask, "What happened?"

5. Model how to answer the question by thinking aloud. Example: "Jill is crying. That means she is sad. It says she is looking everywhere. I wonder what she is looking for. It says Jill loves Fluffy and she wonders if they'll find her. Somebody is missing, but Fluffy is not a person's name. I think Jill has lost her pet."

6. Ask, "What happened?"

7. Have students repeat the answer. Example: Students say, "She lost her pet" or "She lost her dog."

8. Have students read the next passage aloud.

9. Ask, "What happened?"

10. Have students describe clues from the story that helped them determine what happened.

Directed-Reading Thinking Activity (DRTA; Before/During/After Reading)

Objective. Students will learn how to make and confirm predictions.

Materials. Student copies of narrative or expository text, including stopping points marked by the teacher; student copies of a DRTA organizer (see Figure 6.7); a transparency of a DRTA organizer; and an overhead projector and overhead marker.

Sequence.

1. Give a copy of the marked text and a DRTA organizer to each student.
2. Explain how DRTA can be used before, during, and after reading to help improve comprehension.
3. State the topic of the text.
4. Ask students to think about the topic and predict what the text will be about.
5. Have several students share their predictions.
6. Discuss the predictions, and record them on the transparency.
7. Have students write the predictions on their individual DRTA organizers.
8. Ask students to skim the text by looking at the title, subheadings, pictures, and graphics.
9. Have students predict what they may learn by reading the text.
10. Have several students share their predictions.
11. Discuss the predictions, and record them on the transparency.
12. Have students write the predictions on their DRTA organizers.
13. Have students take turns reading the first part of the text (before the first stopping point).
14. Ask students to think back about the predictions they generated and to check if they were correct.
15. Ask students to revise or make new predictions if necessary.
16. Have several students give their new or revised predictions.
17. Discuss the new predictions, and record them on the DRTA organizer.
18. Have students write the predictions on their DRTA organizers.
19. Repeat the same procedure with the entire text.
20. Ask students to reflect on their predictions. Discuss their conclusions.

Variation. With younger students, complete a DRTA organizer during teacher read-alouds.

Note: This activity is adapted from Blachowicz and Ogle (2001).

Using Narrative Comprehension Cards (Before/During/After Reading)

Objective. Students will learn how to use narrative comprehension cards while reading text.

Materials. Student copies of short narrative texts, student and teacher copies of narrative comprehension cards (see Figure 6.8), and a pocket chart.

Sequence.

1. Give a copy of the narrative text to each student.

FIGURE 6.7 ➤ **DRTA Organizer**

Title: _____

Predictions based on the topic:

Predictions based on skimming information such as the title, pictures, etc.:

Predictions after reading the first part of the text: Pages _____ to _____

Predictions after reading the second part of the text: Pages _____ to _____

Predictions after reading the third part of the text: Pages _____ to _____

Source: Adapted from Stauter (1969).

2. Introduce the narrative comprehension cards, then place them in the pocket chart. Explain that the cards are color-coded to help students know when to use them: Green cards are used before reading, yellow cards are used during reading, and red cards are used after reading.

3. Point to the first card, read it aloud, and model how to answer the question. Example: "What does the title tell me about this story? The title tells me that this story is about a pony."

4. Continue the same procedure for each card.

5. Provide opportunities for guided practice. Example:
   - Give a copy of the text to each student.
   - Place the narrative comprehension cards on the left side of the pocket chart in the correct order.
   - Before reading, read the first green card question aloud (Card #1).
   - Have several students answer the question. Move Card #1 to the right side of the pocket chart to indicate that the question has been answered.
   - Repeat the same procedure for all the green cards.
   - Have students take turns reading the text aloud.
   - During reading, stop periodically. Ask several students to answer the first yellow question card (Card #4).
   - Move Card #4 to the right side of the pocket chart after it is answered.
   - Repeat the same procedure for all of the yellow cards.

   - After reading, ask the first red card question (Card #11).
   - Move Card #11 to the right side of the pocket chart after it is answered.
   - Repeat the same procedure for all the red cards.

6. Provide opportunities for students to independently practice the strategy. Example:
   - Give a copy of another narrative text and one set of narrative cards to each student.
   - Remind students to answer the green cards before reading, the yellow cards during reading, and the red cards after reading.
   - Pair students and have them take turns reading aloud.
   - Before, during, and after reading, have each pair answer the questions on the cards.
   - Monitor students to ensure they take turns reading and correctly answer the questions on the cards.
   - As a whole group, discuss how the cards helped students understand what they read.

Variations. Use the same procedure with expository texts and expository comprehension cards (see figure 6.8). With younger students, use the narrative and expository cards during teacher read-alouds.

Note: This activity was adapted from the University of Texas Center for Reading and Language Arts (2001b).

FIGURE 6.8 ➤ Narrative and Expository Text Comprehension Cards

Narrative Text

Before the activity, make sets of cards. Example:

Green Card Questions (Use Before Reading)
- Card #1: What does the title tell me about this story?
- Card #2: What do the pictures tell me?
- Card #3: What do I already know about _____?

Yellow Card Questions (Use During Reading)
- Card #4: Who is the story about?
- Card #5: What is the problem that must be resolved in the story?
- Card #6: When does the story take place?
- Card #7: Where does the story take place?
- Card #8: Why does _____ happen?
- Card #9: How is the problem resolved?
- Card #10: What do I predict will happen next?

Red Card Questions (Use After Reading)
- Card #11: Who were the characters in the story?
- Card #12: When and where was the story set?
- Card #13: What was the problem that had to be resolved in the story?
- Card #14: How was the problem resolved?
- Card #15: Why did _____ happen?

> #1
> What does the title tell me about the story?

Expository Text

Before the activity, make sets of cards. Example:

Green Card Questions (Use Before Reading)
- Card #1: What does the title of the story tell me?
- Card #2: What do I already know about the topic?
- Card #3: What do the pictures tell me?
- Card #4: What do I want to learn about _____?

Yellow Card Questions (Use During Reading)
- Card #5: Does the text make sense?
- Card #6: What have I learned so far?
- Card #7: What questions do I still have?

Red Card Questions (Use After Reading)
- Card #8: What new words did I learn?
- Card #9: What was the text mainly about?
- Card #10: What did I learn?
- Card #11: What else do I want to know about?

Source: Adapted from the University of Texas Center for Reading and Language Arts (2001b).

Story Logs
(Before/During/After Reading)

Objective. Given a narrative text, students will identify the story elements (the characters, setting, problem, important events, and solution).

Materials. An instructional-level narrative text, a story log on chart paper (see Figure 6.9), and student copies of story logs.

Sequence.

1. Give each student a copy of the text.
2. Introduce the story log on the chart paper. Describe each story element.
3. Have students read the text aloud.
4. As story elements are introduced, model by thinking aloud to help students identify each element. Example: "They are having a picnic in the park. The setting is the park. I wonder if this will be the setting for the whole story."
5. After reading, model completing the story log. Have students contribute their ideas. List the characters, setting, problem, important events, and resolution.
6. Give a copy of another instructional-level narrative text and a story log to each student.
7. With students, read each story element on the log. Ask students to define each element.
8. Pair students. Have them take turns reading each paragraph in the story aloud.
9. Encourage students to look for each story element as they read.
10. After reading the story, have each pair complete a story log.

FIGURE 6.9 ➤ **Story Log**

Characters	Setting	Problem	Important Events	Resolution

KWL for Narrative Texts (Before/During/After Reading)

Objective. Given a narrative text, students will identify what they know, what they want to learn, and what they have learned.

Materials. An instructional-level narrative text with multiple sections or chapters and student copies of the KWL chart (see Figure 6.10).

Sequence.

1. Give each student a copy of the narrative text.
2. Introduce the KWL chart by explaining each column. Example: "The K stands for what I know. The W stands for what I want to learn. The L stands for what I learned."
3. Read the first chapter aloud.
4. Model and explain that after reading the first part of the story, students should list in the K column on the chart what they know about the story up to this point. Example: List the characters, the setting, the problem, and important events that have been mentioned up to this point in the story.
5. Model and explain that the next step is for students to generate questions about the story and what may happen next. With students, generate several questions and write them in the W column. Example: "Where will they go on vacation? What will happen to the dog?"
6. Have students read the next section or chapter aloud.

FIGURE 6.10 ➤ **KWL Chart**

K What I Know	W What I Want to Learn	L What I Learned

Source: Adapted from Ogle (1986).

7. Ask students if they have learned any of the answers to the questions that they wrote in the W column. Write their responses in the L column of the chart.

8. Ask students to tell what they know about the story from the second chapter. List their responses on the chart.

9. Have students generate questions about the story that they hope will be answered in the next chapter. On the chart, list their questions in the W column.

10. After each chapter is read, look at the questions in the W column and ask students whether any of them were answered in the chapter they just read. On the chart, write answers to these questions in the L column. Continue to add important points to the K column and list student questions in the W column.

Variation. Use KWL charts with expository texts.

Note: This activity was adapted from Ogle (1986).

❖   ❖   ❖

Annotated Bibliography

Blachowicz, C., & Ogle, D. (2001). *Reading comprehension: Strategies for independent learners.* New York: Guilford.

This book presents a variety of strategies and examples for teaching comprehension based on the authors' classroom experiences. Chapters include creative ways to help students monitor their own understanding, engage in research, and successfully read informational texts. The final chapter focuses on what teachers can do to encourage lifelong reading.

Cunningham, A. E., & Stanovich, K. (1998). What reading does for the mind. *American Educator, 22*(1/2), 8–15.

This article for teachers illustrates the long-term benefits of reading and its influence on learning and knowing.

Hoyt, L. (1999). *Revisit, reflect, retell: Strategies for improving reading comprehension.* Portsmouth, NH: Heinemann.

This practical resource for elementary teachers presents comprehension assessment practices, instructional strategies, and other activities to help students improve their understanding of narrative and expository texts. Chapters focus on oral retelling and talking and writing about books, informational texts, and the arts. The author clearly explains how to use the ideas with young readers. Reproducible blackline masters include checklists, forms, profiles, parent pages, story maps, and step-by-step strategy procedures.

Klingner, J. K., Vaughn, S., Dimino, J., Schumm, J. S., & Bryant, D. (2001). *From click to clunk: Collaborative strategic reading.* Longmount, CO: Sopris West.

This book describes how to implement collaborative strategic reading (CSR) practices in school. An introduction to the strategy and its effectiveness for developing comprehension are provided, as is a detailed plan for teaching CSR (including complete lesson plans and sample materials). Steps for developing cooperative learning groups and adapting CSR for secondary students are also included.

Tompkins, G. E. (1998). *Fifty literacy strategies: Step by step.* Upper Saddle River, NJ: Pearson Education.

This teacher-friendly book presents fifty instructional strategies and activities for improving students' reading skills, including comprehension. The lesson plan format incorporates examples to help teachers implement the ideas with young students. Sample lessons include "KWL Charts," "Book Talks," "Cubing," "Story Boards," "Story Retellings," "Directed Reading-Thinking Activity," and "Shared Reading."

Wilhelm, J. D. (2001). *Improving comprehension with think-aloud strategies*. New York: Scholastic.

This book describes how to teach comprehension through thinking aloud and presents strategies for helping students recognize and make meaning from text. Instructional steps for modeling think-alouds, lesson ideas, examples of think-alouds in action, and teacher and student assessment checklists are also provided.

✦　　✦　　✦

Web Sites That Teach

http://reading.uoregon.edu/big_ideas/comp.php.

This Web site defines and discusses the importance of comprehension, and provides research findings on the topic.

http://reading.uoregon.edu/instruction/instruc_comp.php.

This site provides a variety of comprehension strategies, a general framework for teaching comprehension, types and critical features of comprehension instruction, and

directions on how to sequence comprehension skills in grades K–3.

http://www.readingrockets.org/lp.php?SCID=15.

This site provides an overview of reading comprehension, including research findings and practical tips for teachers.

http://www.aea11.k12.ia.us/Schrader/reading comprehension.html.

This site includes a variety of links to research and practical articles on reading comprehension.

http://www.readingonline.org/articles/ handbook/pressley/index.html.

This Web site introduces well-validated ways to increase student comprehension skills.

http://curry.edschool.virginia.edu/go/readquest/strat/.

This site introduces a variety of reading comprehension strategies including brainstorming, graphic organizers, and questioning.

http://www.ed.gov/offices/OESE/SASA/rb/slide024.html.

This site provides a summary of research-based comprehension instruction and strategies.

http://www.ncld.org/research/ncld_reading_comp.cfm.

This site provides a summary of research findings on reading comprehension instruction for students with learning disabilities.

✦　　✦　　✦

7 Putting It All Together

THIS FINAL CHAPTER SHOWS HOW TO INTEGRATE THE ESSENTIAL INSTRUCTIONAL elements of reading described in previous chapters, and is divided into three sections:

- A brief overview of the five core instructional areas and their essential elements,
- A discussion on the use of progress monitoring to inform instruction and identify student needs, and
- Tips for helping students who are having difficulty acquiring reading skills.

Overview of the Essential Elements of Reading

To read efficiently, students must apply letter-sound correspondences, blend sounds together to read words, and recognize that some words are irregular. In addition, they must learn that when they do not understand something they are reading, they can use comprehension and vocabulary strategies to construct meaning from the text. That is a big undertaking for both students and teachers.

In the first four years of school, children will gradually acquire the skills they need to read proficiently. Teachers can introduce these skills separately, but they should be integrated as quickly as possible. This pattern should continue each time students learn more complex skills. Different critical elements should be emphasized at different times; for example, whereas the focus in kindergarten is on phonological awareness, in 1st grade the focus is on phonics and word study. Nevertheless, teachers should include all the elements on a daily basis as appropriate for the grade. Figure 7.1 shows which elements to focus on at each grade level.

Though teachers may already incorporate many of the elements in this book into their reading programs, they should be certain that instruction in each is of sufficient length, focuses on the essential components, uses appropriate materials, and integrates such features of effective teaching as modeling, explicit language, multiple opportunities to practice and review, and corrective feedback.

The following is a summary of the essential elements of reading instruction. It will help teachers determine whether or not they should enhance their reading programs with additional instructional activities.

Phonological Awareness. This element is essential in kindergarten and 1st grade, and should be taught for approximately 15 to 20 minutes daily for instruction to be effective. Though most of the activities related to phonological awareness are oral, teachers should be sure to link sounds to letters and print as soon as possible. They should base activities on students' skill levels and degrees of knowledge, proceeding from easier to more difficult tasks; be sure to include such tasks as identifying, blending, and segmenting syllables, onset/rimes, and phonemes in their lessons; and remember that the two most important tasks are segmenting and blending words at the phoneme level.

Phonics and Word Study. These elements provide the foundations for literacy instruction in 1st grade, but related skills such as print awareness and alphabetic knowledge and understanding should be emphasized in kindergarten. Letters and their corresponding sounds should not be introduced in alphabetical order, but rather in a systematic sequence that allows students to decode and blend common consonant-vowel-consonant (CVC) words, both in isolation and in connected text. Students should learn to read decodable text in 1st grade, since doing so allows them to apply their other skills to reading as well. The goal is to help students develop independent word recognition strategies and automaticity.

Fluency. Fluency instruction should start the second semester of 1st grade, when students have built a strong foundation in word identification. Twenty minutes of fluency instruction daily is sufficient for most students, using independent-level text, especially if they are reading alone or with a same-age peer; for students reading with a tutor or a knowledgeable adult, instructional-level text is appropriate. Effective fluency-building activities include model reading and rereading or choral reading, paired reading with another adult or student, and reading with tape-recorded selections.

Vocabulary. This element should be an ongoing part of the instructional day in kindergarten through 3rd grade, and taught in the context of reading activities. Text should be age-appropriate and expose students to new words. Activities can be *explicit*, where teachers describe or define key words, or *implicit*, where students engage in oral language activities, are read to, or read independently to learn new words. When teaching

FIGURE 7.1 ➤ **Timeline for Teaching Literacy**

	Kindergarten	**1st grade**	**2nd Grade**	**3rd Grade**
Phonological Awareness	Syllables Onset/rime Phoneme level	Phonemic awareness		
Phonics and Word Study	Print awareness Alphabetic knowledge Alphabetic principle Decoding Irregular word reading	Alphabetic principle Decoding Irregular word reading Decodable text reading		
Fluency		Connected text (second semester)	Connected text	Connected text
Vocabulary	Oral vocabulary	Oral and reading vocabulary	Reading vocabulary	Reading vocabulary
Comprehension	Listening comprehension Sense of story	Listening comprehension Reading comprehension	Reading comprehension in narrative and expository text	Reading comprehension in narrative and expository text

vocabulary explicitly, teachers should target words that are used frequently, will extend students' vocabulary, and will help students understand the text.

Association methods that teach students to make connections among words, and multimedia approaches that expose students to words across different media, can also be used to enhance vocabulary. It's best if teachers use a variety of methods in their instruction, and remember that students cannot learn all the words they need to know from explicit instruction; they need many opportunities to read a variety of texts to build

their vocabulary. Reading good age-appropriate literature is the best vocabulary builder and a great source of engaging material for young students.

Comprehension. As with vocabulary, comprehension skills should be taught from kindergarten through 3rd grade. Kindergarten students start building these skills when teachers model strategies that develop comprehension before, during, and after reading a selection. Some students will be able to use these strategies as they begin to read text on their own, though others will need additional instruction. Effective reading comprehension instruction goes beyond asking students to answer questions about a text they have heard or read; it should also include teaching students how to use appropriate strategies and monitor their own progress.

Teachers should consider the following valuable practices, which are embedded into the instructional activities in this book, when teaching the above elements:

- Modeling.
- Being explicit about what students should do.
- Sequencing activities so that students learn and develop skills systematically.
- Providing multiple opportunities for students to practice, and
- Providing feedback so students practice new skills correctly.

Progress Monitoring to Inform Instruction

Progress monitoring is essential to reading instruction, enabling teachers to keep track of student learning and identify those who need additional help. Though teachers should monitor student progress in all aspects of reading, a few skills at each grade level serve as critical markers of development:

- In kindergarten, teachers should focus on letter recognition and phonemic awareness. By the end of kindergarten, students should know most of the letter names and sounds and be able to segment words at the phoneme level (Blevins, 1998). Both accuracy

and automaticity of letter names and sounds and phoneme segmentation should be assessed at this stage.
- In 1st grade, the focus should be on the alphabetic principle, which can be assessed through nonsense-word reading activities; regular and irregular word reading, which can be assessed using word lists; and oral reading fluency, which should begin in the second half of 1st grade.
- In 2nd and 3rd grade, teachers should concentrate on reading fluency and reading comprehension. Learning appropriate oral reading rates can help teachers identify students who need additional help with fluency.

Teachers can assess these critical skills formally or informally at each grade level using the measures described in previous chapters, in addition to those provided by their schools or districts.

To monitor progress efficiently, teachers should assess all students at the beginning of the year in the critical areas for their grade level. Once they determine the students that will need additional instruction, they should develop a plan for teaching those students in small groups, then monitor them on a regular basis, perhaps every six to eight weeks, to assess their progress. Students who are reading at grade level should be assessed approximately three times a year: at the beginning of the year, the middle of the year, and the end of the year. Assessment information can also be used to regroup students and to alter instruction as needed. Though monitoring progress is very important, the focus should be on providing students with solid instruction and enjoyable literacy experiences.

Supplemental Reading Instruction from Kindergarten to 3rd Grade

Students who do not make progress learning to read will need supplemental instruction that allows them to practice and master foundational skills and concepts before they get too far behind their peers. Two ways to intensify instruction are by increasing instructional time and reducing group sizes (Foorman & Torgesen, 2001); students who are behind should be taught in small homogeneous groups of three to five. The teacher, an instructional assistant, or a trained tutor can provide the supplemental instruction.

As with core instruction, supplemental instruction is most effective if it is systematic and explicit. Small homogeneous groups help teachers focus on one or two essential components, let students participate actively more often, and allow for more individualized scaffolding and corrective feedback. The instructional activities described in this book, along with the features of effective instruction noted at the beginning of this chapter, can all be used for supplemental as well as core instruction, and can be used individually or in combination depending on student need.

Kindergarten

In kindergarten, students develop the foundational skills of literacy. Because students enter school at different levels of literacy, it is important that they all have opportunities to acquire such skills as letter naming and phonological awareness. Students with limited reading experience and those who just need additional practice will benefit from 15–20 minutes of additional instruction.

Figure 7.2 identifies different types of activities suitable for kindergarten, along with their objectives and critical components. The activities provide students with additional practice following whole-group instruction, and can serve as a review of previously taught letters and lessons. Teachers should keep in mind that supplemental activities are for students who need more practice than their peers, and should not take the place of core instruction.

1st Grade

Progress monitoring will help you identify 1st grade students who are struggling with reading acquisition. Students who only know a few letters and sounds at the beginning of the year will benefit from intensive instruction in phonemic awareness, the alphabetic principle, blending, and word building. They will also need additional practice applying their decoding skills to connected text (see Figure 7.3), which can help them build the skills to become independent readers. Other students will have adequate decoding skills but trouble with fluency, and still others may need additional help with comprehension strategies.

2nd and 3rd Grade

Students in 2nd and 3rd grade who are still struggling with reading acquisition may need additional practice with fluency-building activities, vocabulary instruction that emphasizes

FIGURE 7.2 ➤ **Supplemental Reading Instruction for Kindergarten**

Instructional Component	Objectives	Activities	Lesson Components
Phonological Awareness	To accurately and automatically manipulate onset and rimes (first semester) and phonemes (second semester)	Identifying, blending, segmenting, and substituting words in sentences, and syllables in words, onset/rime, and phonemes with or without support	• Focus on one or two types of manipulation (e.g., blending and segmenting) • Conduct all activities orally initially, and then link to print • Allow students to respond individually and as a group • Use manipulatives if desired
Phonics and Word Study	• To understand that sounds are represented by letters • To apply sound-letter correspondences to reading words accurately and fluently	• Identifying letter names and sounds, consonants in initial and final positions, and short vowels • Blending sounds to read words • Dictating letters and words	• Introduce letters and sounds systematically • Have students combine sounds to form words • Allow students to practice writing the letters and words they are learning
Listening Comprehension	To construct meaning from stories using comprehension strategies	• Reading narrative and expository text out loud • Predicting and activating background knowledge before reading • Summarizing periodically during reading • Questioning and retelling activities after reading	• Introduce strategies systematically • Model strategies • Focus on the most important idea • Use different types of questions

FIGURE 7.3 ➤ **Supplemental Reading Instruction for 1st Grade**

Instructional Component	Objectives	Activities	Lesson Components
Fluency	To automatically recognize words, both in isolation and in connected text	• Partner reading (student-adult or student-student) • Choral reading • Tape-assisted reading	• Provide a good and explicit model • Provide opportunities to reread text • Have students reread text at least three times • Establish performance criteria
Phonological Awareness	To be able to manipulate phonemes	Blending and segmenting words at the phoneme level with or without support	• Focus on one or two types of manipulation (e.g., blending and segmenting) • Use print • Provide opportunities for students to respond individually and as a group • Use manipulatives if desired
Phonics and Word Study	• To apply sound-letter correspondences to read words accurately and fluently • To use decoding strategies to read unknown words	• Blending sounds to read words • Reading decodable text • Dictating words and sentences	• Read books that contain words students have learned • Let students use decoding strategies • Introduce patterns and rules systematically • Combine sounds to form words
Comprehension	To use comprehension strategies before, during, and after reading text to construct meaning	• Engaging in comprehension strategies before, during, and after listening to or reading a text • Predicting and activating background knowledge • Self-questioning, self-monitoring, and generating and answering questions	• Model use of self-monitoring and comprehension strategies • Provide opportunities for students to use self-monitoring and comprehension strategies

structural analysis and decoding multisyllabic words, and additional practice with comprehension skills (see Figure 7.4). Progress monitoring tools can help teachers identify students' areas of need. Students who are having difficulties in all areas will benefit from an additional 30–40 minutes of small-group supplemental instruction; those who are especially behind may need to receive phonics and word study instruction to solidify word recognition skills, which are essential for fluent reading and comprehension.

FIGURE 7.4 ➤ **Supplemental Reading Instruction for 2nd and 3rd Grade**

Instructional Component	Objectives	Activities	Lesson Components
Fluency	To automatically recognize words in connected text	• Partner reading (student-adult or student-student) • Choral reading • Tape-assisted reading • Fluency building at the word and phrase level	• Provide a good and explicit model • Provide opportunities for student to reread text at least 3 times • Establish performance criteria
Vocabulary	To use advanced word recognition strategies with unknown words	Teaching words and their extended meanings systematically	• Model and teach the use of both explicit and implicit vocabulary instruction activities • Provide multiple opportunities to practice and use key vocabulary
Comprehension	• To use comprehension strategies before, during, and after reading text to construct meaning • To use self-monitoring strategies	• Predicting and activating background knowledge before reading • Providing decoding support and monitoring comprehension during reading • Answering and generating questions and summarizing after reading	• Make sure books are at instructional level • Preview vocabulary when introducing books • Model the use of self-monitoring and comprehension strategies • Provide opportunities for students to use self-monitoring and comprehension strategies

Conclusion

Over the years, approaches to reading instruction have come and gone. Recently, however, several syntheses (National Reading Panel, 2000; Swanson, 1999; Vaughn, Gersten, & Chard, 2000) have examined reading strategies, leading the identification of effective, science-based practices. Though some of the phonics, comprehension, and vocabulary activities in this book have been around many years, some of the practices, such as fluency building and progress monitoring, are new or have been given new emphasis as a result of scientific research.

Whether you are a new teacher or a veteran, these are exciting times in reading education. We know more about teaching reading effectively now than ever before, so even the most experienced teachers can enhance their teaching. The changes to instruction may be minor or major, but the goal is for teachers to continue to integrate their knowledge and craft with science-based research to improve their effectiveness.

Now more than ever, the ability to read well is essential for academic and economic success (Juel, 1988). The primary grades are crucial in a child's education, and teachers are in a position to ensure that their students become proficient lifelong readers.

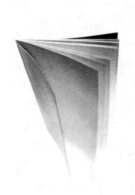

Glossary

Accuracy. The ability to perform a skill, such as reading words, correctly.

Affix. An element attached to the beginning or ending of a word. (See also *prefix* and *suffix*.)

Alphabetic principle. The principle that letters in written words represent sounds in spoken words.

Analogy. A connection drawn between letter-sound patterns in previously learned words and those in novel words to help read the latter. Example: the /ing/ sound in *ring* and *sing* is analogous to the same sound in *king* and *sting*.

Analytic phonics. The process of teaching letter-sound correspondences through previously learned words. Example: using the known word *cat* to analyze the individual letters and sounds /c/, /a/, and /t/.

At-risk. A term used to describe students who demonstrate low performance in one or more areas related to reading development, such as vocabulary or phonological awareness.

Automaticity. The ability to quickly and accurately recognize letters, sounds, and words without hesitation.

Basal reader. A book of graded stories developed as an accompaniment for a reading program.

Base word. A meaningful word to which prefixes, suffixes, and endings can be added. Example: *read,* which is a base word for *reread, readable*, and *reading*. Also referred to as the *root word*.

Blending. The process of combining individual sounds or word parts to form whole words either orally or in print. Example: combining the speech sounds /c/, /a/, and /t/ to form the word *cat*.

CCVC word. A word consisting of the consonant-consonant-vowel-consonant pattern. Examples: *crab, stop*.

Choral reading. Reading of text by several students in unison.

Comprehension. The ability to understand and draw meaning from spoken and written language.

Computer-assisted instruction. Instruction designed to be delivered via a computer.

Consonant blend. Two or more consecutive consonant letters at the beginning or end of a word that each represent their distinct sounds when the word is pronounced. Examples: *st* in *rust, str* in *strain*.

Consonant digraph. Two consonant letters that represent a single sound when a word is pronounced. Examples: *th* in *that, ch* in *much*.

Consonant letters and sounds. All letters and their corresponding sounds that are not vowels: *b, c, d, f, g, h, j, k, l, m, n, p, q, r, s, t, v, w, x, y,* and *z*.

Content word. A word, usually a noun or verb, important to the understanding of a concept or text.

Context. The words and sentences occurring before and after an unknown word that provide hints about its meaning.

Conventional spelling. The standard English spelling of a word.

Cooperative learning. An instructional process in which groups of students work together to learn academic content.

Cross-age tutoring. The process of pairing older students with younger ones for reading instruction, with one student serving as the other's teacher.

CVC word. A word consisting of a consonant-vowel-consonant pattern. Examples: *bat, men*.

CVCC word. A word consisting of the consonant-vowel-consonant-consonant pattern. Examples: *tent, lump*.

CVCE word. A word consisting of a consonant-vowel-consonant-silent *e* pattern. Example: *make, note*.

Decodable text. Connected text in which most of the words are comprised of previously taught letter-sound correspondences.

Decoding. Using letter-sound relationships and word knowledge to convert printed words into spoken language. Example: converting *c, a,* and *t,* into the /c/, /a/, and /t/ sounds to read the word *cat.*

Dialect. Regional language variations, including differences in pronunciation, grammar, or vocabulary.

Dyslexia. A neurological disorder marked by difficulties with written language, including reading, writing, spelling, or handwriting.

Explicit instruction. Overtly teaching the steps required for completing a task.

Explicit question. A literal comprehension question that can be answered directly from printed or spoken language without making inferences.

Expository text. Informational text that is designed to teach or explain a specific topic to the reader.

Fluency. The ability to perform reading skills such as naming letters, reading words, and reading connected text quickly, smoothly, and automatically.

Frustration-level text. Text for which the reader does not have sufficient skills to accurately recognize or comprehend words. Frustration-level text is often defined as that in which the reader is able to read less than 90 percent of the words accurately.

Genre. A text structure that is identified by a unique set of characteristics. Examples: science fiction, mystery, poetry.

Grade-level text. Text for which students of a given grade should have the necessary comprehension, vocabulary, and word recognition skills to read independently.

Grapheme. The smallest unit of written language representing the sounds in words. Example: the written letters *ai,* which represent the sound /ai/ in *rain.*

Graphic organizer. Diagram or other pictorial illustrating text organization or relationships among concepts or events in the text.

Graphophonemic knowledge. The ability to understand the relationship between letters and their sounds.

Guided reading. A teaching strategy in which teachers support student reading and rereading of leveled books, providing incidental word recognition instruction within the context of reading.

Implicit question. A comprehension question that requires the reader to connect information in the text to prior knowledge to deduce the answer.

Independent-level text. Text for which the reader has sufficient word recognition and comprehension skills to read the text easily and fluently without assistance. Independent-level is often defined as text in which the reader is able to read at least 95 percent of the words accurately.

Instructional-level text. Text for which the reader has sufficient word recognition and comprehension skills to read with few errors and some assistance. Often defined as text in which the reader can read between 90 and 94 percent of the words accurately.

Invented spelling. Attempts by young children with limited knowledge to spell words using their own conventions. Example: spelling the word *does* using the sounds /d/, /u/, and /z/ and the matching letters *d*, *u*, and *z* (*duz*).

Irregular word. A word in which some or all of the letters do not represent their most commonly associated sounds.

Learning disability. Disorder marked by achievement in one or more academic areas that is not commensurate with ability levels.

Letter-sound correspondence. The association between a specific letter and its corresponding sound. Example: the letter *m* and the sound /m/, as in the word *man*.

Letter knowledge. The ability to automatically identify the names and the most common sounds of the letters of the alphabet.

Listening comprehension. The ability to understand and get meaning from spoken language.

Listening vocabulary. The words people can understand when spoken.

Long vowel. A vowel sound that is the same as the name of the letters. Example: the sound /a/ in the word *make*.

Main idea. The most important point or idea in a text.

Matthew effect. A term used to describe the effect of good readers reading more print and, therefore, improving their reading skills faster than poor readers, who may have less contact with print.

Morpheme. The smallest meaningful unit of language; may be a word or a word element. Example: the suffix *-ed* in *jumped*, which conveys past tense.

Morphology. The study of the structure of words, including the use of base words and affixes, and their effect on word meaning.

Narrative text. Text that tells a story and follows a common story structure.

Onset-rime instruction. The use of word patterns to read unfamiliar words. The *rime* involves the vowel and final consonants of the word, such as the /at/ in *sat*; the *onset* refers to the initial consonants of the word, such as the /s/ in *sat* or the /tr/ in *train*.

Orthography. A system of written language that includes the formation of letters and spelling of words.

Partner reading. The process of reading in pairs.

Peer tutoring. The process in which students teach each other academic skills.

Phoneme. The smallest unit of sound.

Phonemic awareness. The ability to recognize and manipulate phonemes in spoken words by orally blending, segmenting, adding, and deleting them.

Phonics. The systematic process of teaching sound-symbol relationships to decode words.

Phonological awareness. The ability to manipulate the sound system of spoken language, including words, rhymes, syllables, onset-rimes, and phonemes. Phonological awareness is a broad term encompassing *phonemic awareness.*

Phonology. The study of the sound system of a language and the use of sounds in forming words and sentences.

Prefix. A meaningful word element attached to the beginning of a word. Examples: *un-* and *re-* in the words *unlock* and *refill.*

Print concepts. The components of written language. Examples: words, sentences, and (in English) print moving from left to right.

Progress monitoring. A system of frequent, dynamic assessment to measure student progress in a skill area.

Prosody. The use of appropriate intonation and phrasing when reading; reading with expression.

Reading. The process of transforming print into meaning.

Reading comprehension. The ability to understand and get meaning from written language.

Reading level. Information for teachers about the difficulty of a text for a particular student. Reading levels are *instructional, independent,* and *frustrational.*

Repeated reading. The process of reading text several times with feedback to develop speed and accuracy.

Rhyme. Words that have the same ending sounds, but not necessarily the same letters. Examples: *state, straight,* and *bait* all rhyme with each other.

Scaffolded instruction. Temporary supports provided during initial skill instruction, each task becomes increasingly more difficult until the skill is mastered. Examples: changing the difficulty of the content or task; changing the amount of support provided by materials or teacher guidance.

Segmenting. Breaking whole words into individual sounds or word parts. Example: breaking up the word *cat* into the speech sounds /c/, /a/, and /t/.

Sounding out. See *decoding.*

Sight words. Words that are read fluently and automatically at first sight.

Speaking vocabulary. Words people use when they speak.

Story structure. The components of narrative text, including characters, setting, events, problem, and resolution.

Summarizing. The process of synthesizing the main ideas in a text.

Syllable. A unit of pronunciation, usually containing a vowel.

Synthetic phonics. The process of teaching word reading through blending of known letter-sound correspondences. Example: using the known sounds /c/, /a/, and /t/ to read the word *cat*.

Systematic instruction. A planned, sequential program of instruction.

Tape-assisted reading. The process of reading text along with an audiotape of a fluent reader.

Text. The words composing written material such as a story, newspaper article, or sections of a textbook.

Text structure. The organization of the content in written material.

Think-aloud. The act of modeling independent comprehension by stopping periodically during reading to say aloud what the reader is thinking.

Word analysis. A strategy readers use to decode written words.

Word family. A group of words sharing the same rime. Example: *cat, bat, sat, mat*, and *flat* form a word family.

Word recognition. A strategy readers use to identify written words.

WPM. Words read per minute. The number of words read correctly per minute (WCPM) is often used to determine a student's fluency level.

Note: The authors would like to recognize the expert work of Jeanne Wanzeck on this glossary.

References

Adams, M. J. (1990). *Beginning to read: Thinking and learning about print.* Cambridge, MA: MIT Press.

Adams, M. J. (2001). Alphabetic anxiety and explicit, systematic phonics instruction: A cognitive science perspective. In S. B. Neuman & D. K. Dickinson (Eds.), *Handbook of Early Literacy Research* (pp. 66–80). New York: Guilford Press.

Allington, R. L., & Cunningham, P. M. (2002). *Schools that work: Where all children read and write* (2nd ed.). Boston: Allyn & Bacon.

American Federation of Teachers (June, 1999). *Teaching reading is rocket science: What expert teachers of reading should know and be able to do.* Washington, DC: Author.

Baker, S. K., Simmons, D. C., & Kame'enui, E. J. (1998). Vocabulary acquisition: Research bases. In D. C. Simmons & E. J. Kame'enui (Eds.), *What reading research tells us about children with diverse learning needs* (pp. 183–218). Mahwah, NJ: Lawrence Erlbaum Associates.

Ball, E. W., & Blachman, B. A. (1991). Does phoneme awareness training in kindergarten make a difference in early word recognition and development spelling? *Reading Research Quarterly, 26*(1), 49–66.

Beck, I. L., McKeown, M. G., & Kucan, L. (2002). *Bringing words to life: Robust vocabulary instruction.* New York: Guilford Press.

Beck, I. L., McKeown, M. G., Sandora, C., & Kucan, L. (1996). Questioning the author: A yearlong classroom implementation to engage students with text. *The Elementary School Journal, 96*(4), 385–414.

Biemiller, A. (1999). *Language and reading success.* Cambridge, MA: Brookline Books.

Blachowicz, C., & Ogle, D. (2001). *Reading comprehension: Strategies for independent learners.* New York: Guilford.

Blevins, W. (1998). *Phonics from A to Z: A practical guide.* New York: Scholastic Professional Books.

Bos, C. S. (1979). *Inferential operations in the reading comprehension of educable mentally retarded and average students.* Unpublished doctoral dissertation, University of Arizona, Tucson.

Bos, C. S. (1987). *Promoting story comprehension using a story retelling strategy.* Paper presented at a meeting of the Teachers Applying Whole Language Conference, Tucson, Arizona.

Bos, C. S., & Vaughn, S. (2002). *Strategies for teaching students with learning and behavior problems* (5th ed.). Boston: Allyn and Bacon.

Bradley, L., & Bryant, P. E. (1985). *Rhyme and reason in reading and spelling.* IARLD Monograph No. 1. Ann Arbor: University of Michigan Press.

Brown, V., Hammill, D., & Wiederholt, J. (1995). *Test of Reading Comprehension 3.* Austin: Pro-Ed.

Carnine, D. (1999). Perspective: Campaigns for moving research to practice. *Remedial and Special Education, 20*(1), 2–9.

Carnine, D. W., Silbert, J., & Kame'enui, E. J. (1997). *Direct instruction reading* (3rd ed.). Upper Saddle River, NJ: Prentice Hall.

Center for the Improvement of Early Reading Achievement. (2001). *Put reading first: The research building blocks for teaching children to read.* Washington, DC: Partnership for Reading.

Chall, J. S. (2000). *The academic achievement challenge: What really works in the classroom?* New York: Guilford.

Chard, D. J., & Dickson, S. V. (1999). Phonological awareness: Instructional and assessment guidelines. *Intervention in School and Clinic, 34*(5), 261–270.

Chard, D. J., & Osborn, J. (1999). Word recognition: Paving the road to successful reading. *Intervention in School and Clinic, 24,* 271–277.

Chard, D. J., Simmons, D. C., & Kame'enui, E. J. (1998). Word recognition: Research bases. In D. C. Simmons & E. J. Kame'enui (Eds.), *What reading research tells us about children with diverse learning needs: Bases and basics* (pp. 141–167). Mahwah, NJ: Lawrence Erlbaum Associates.

Children's Educational Services, Inc. (1987). *Test of Oral Reading Fluency.* Minneapolis, MN: Author.

Clay, M. (1993). *An observational survey of early literacy achievement.* Portsmouth, NH: Heinemann.

Cooper, H. (1996). Speaking power to truth: Reflections of an educational researcher after 4 years of school board service. *Educational Researcher, 25*(1), 29–34.

Cunningham, A., & Stanovich, K. E. (1998). What reading does to the mind. *American Educator, 22,* 8–15.

Cunningham, P. M. (1998). The multisyllabic word dilemma: Helping students build meaning, spell, and read "big" words. *Reading and Writing Quarterly: Overcoming Learning Difficulties, 14,* 189–218.

Cunningham, P. M. (1999). *Phonics they use: Words for reading and writing* (3rd ed.). Boston, MA: Addison-Wesley.

Dale, E. (1965). Vocabulary measurement: Techniques and major findings. *Elementary English, 42,* 895–901.

Delquadri, J., Greenwood, C. R., Whorton, D., Carta, J. J., & Hall, R. V. (1986). Classwide peer tutoring. *Exceptional Children, 52*(6), 535–542.

Durkin, D. (1978–1979). What classroom observations reveal about reading comprehension instruction. *Reading Research Quarterly, 14*(4), 481–533.

Ehri, L. C. (1991). Learning to read and spell words. In L. Rieben & C. A. Perfetti (Eds.), *Learning to read and its implications* (pp. 57–73). Hillsdale, NJ: Lawrence Erlbaum Associates.

Ehri, L. C., Nunes, S. R., & Willows, D. M. (2001). Phonemic awareness instruction helps children learn to read: Evidence from the National Reading Panel's meta-analysis. *Reading Research Quarterly, 36*(3), 250–287.

Elkonin, D. B. (1973). U.S.S.R. In J. Downing (Ed.), *Comparative reading* (pp. 551–579). New York: MacMillan.

Foorman, B. R. & Torgesen, J. (2001). Critical elements of classroom and small-group instruction promote reading success in all children. *Learning Disabilities Research and Practice, (16)*4, 203–212.

Fuchs, L. S., Fuchs, D., & Hamlett, C. L. (1989). Monitoring reading growth using student recalls: Effects of two teacher feedback systems. *Journal of Educational Research, 83,* 103–111.

Fuchs, D., Fuchs, L., Thompson, A., Al Otaiba, S., Yen, L., Yang, N., Braun, M., & O'Connor, R. E. (2001). Is reading important in reading-readiness programs? A randomized field trial with teachers as program implementers. *Journal of Educational Psychology, 93,* 251–267.

Fuchs, L. S., Fuchs, D., Hosp, M. K., & Jenkins, J. R. (2001). Oral reading fluency as an indicator of reading competence: A theoretical, empirical, and historical analysis. *Scientific Studies of Reading, 5,* 239–256.

Fuchs, D., Fuchs, L. S., Mathes, P. G., & Simmons, D. C. (1997). Peer-assisted learning strategies: Making classrooms more responsive to diversity. *American Educational Research Journal, 34*(1), 62–94.

Gersten, R., Fuchs, L., Williams, J. P., & Baker, S. (2001). Teaching reading comprehension strategies to students with learning disabilities. *Review of Educational Research, 71*(2), 279–320.

Good, R. H., Kaminski, R. A., Smith, S., Laimon, D., & Dill, S. (2001). *Dynamic Indicators of Basic Early Literacy Skills* (5th Ed.). Eugene: University of Oregon.

Goswami, U. (2000). Casual connections in beginning reading: The importance of rhyme. *Journal of Research in Reading, 22*(3), 217–240.

Gough, P., & Tumner, W. (1986). Decoding, reading, and reading disability. *Remedial and Special Education, 7,* 6–10.

Graves, A. W. (1986). Effects of direct instruction and metacomprehension training on finding main ideas. *Learning Disabilities Research, 1,* 90–100.

Graves, M. F., Juel, C., & Graves, B. B. (2001). *Teaching Reading in the 21st Century* (2nd ed.). Boston: Allyn & Bacon.

Graves, M. F., Prenn, M., & Cooke, C. L. (1985). The coming attractions: Previewing short stories. *Journal of Reading, 28*(7), 594–598.

Greaney, K. T., Tunmer, W. E., & Chapman, J. W. (1997). *Journal of Educational Psychology, 89*(4), 645–651.

Greenwood, C. R., Delguardri, J. C., & Hall, R. V. (1989). Longitudinal effects of classwide peer tutoring. *Journal of Educational Psychology, 81,* 371–383.

Hasbrouck, J. E., & Tindal, G. (1992). Curriculum-based oral reading fluency norms for students in grades 2 through 4. *Teaching Exceptional Children, 24*(3), 41–44.

Hayes, D. P., & Ahrens, M. G. (1988). Vocabulary simplifications for children: A special case of "motherese"? *Journal of Child Language, 15*(2), 395–410.

Henry, M. (1997). The decoding /spelling curriculum: Integrated decoding and spelling instruction from preschool to early secondary school. *Dyslexia, 3,* 178–189.

Hiebert, E. H. & Sawyer, C. C. (1984). *Young children's concurrent abilities in reading and spelling.* Paper presented at the annual meeting of the American Educational Research Association, New Orleans, LA.

Jenkins, J. R., Heliotis, J., Stein, M. L., & Haynes, M. (1987). Improving reading comprehension by using paragraph restatements. *Exceptional Children, 54,* 54–59.

Jitendra, A. K. (1998). Effects of a direct instruction mail idea summarization program and self-monitoring on reading comprehension of middle school students with learning disabilities. *Reading and Writing Quarterly: Overcoming Learning Disabilities, 14*(4), 379–396.

Jitendra, A. K., Hoppes, M. K., & Xin, Y. P. (2000). Enhancing main idea comprehension for students with learning problems: The role of a summarization strategy and self-monitoring instruction. *Journal of Special Education, 34*(3), 127–139.

Juel, C. (1988). Learning to read and write: A longitudinal study of 54 children from first through fourth grades. *Journal of Educational Psychology, 80*(4), 437–447.

Kame'enui, E. J., & Simmons, D. C. (2001). Introduction to this special issue: The DNA of reading fluency. *Scientific Studies of Reading, 5,* 203–210.

Kaminski, R. R., & Good, R. (1996). Toward a technology for assessing basic early literacy skills. *School Psychology Review, 25*(2), 215–227.

Klingner, J. K., Vaughn, S., Dimino, J., Schumm, J. S., & Bryant, D. (2001). *From clunk to click: Collaborative strategic reading.* Longmont, CO: Sopris West.

Learning First Alliance. (2000). *Every child reading: A professional development guide.* Washington, DC: Author.

Leslie, L. & Caldwell, J. (2001). *Qualitative reading inventory* (3rd ed.). NY: Longman.

Lundberg, I., Frost, J., & Peterson, O. (1998). Effects of an extensive program for stimulating phonological awareness in preschool children. *Reading Research Quarterly, 23*(3), 263–284.

MacGinitie, W. H., MacGinitie, R. K., Maria, K., & Dryer, L. (2000). *Gates-MacGinitie Reading Test* (4th ed.). Itasca, IL: Riverside Publishing.

Malone, L. D., & Mastropieri, M. (1992). Reading comprehension instruction: Summarization and self-monitoring training for students with learning disabilities. *Exceptional Children, 58*(3), 270–79.

Mastropieri, M. A., & Scruggs, T. E. (1997). Best practices in promoting reading comprehension in students with learning disabilities: 1976 to 1996. *Remedial and Special Education, 18*(4), 197–214.

Moats, L. (2000). *Speech to print: Language essentials for teachers.* Baltimore, MD: Brookes Publishing.

National Assessment of Educational Progress. (2003). *National Center for Educational Statistics.* Washington, DC: U.S. Department of Education.

National Institute for Literacy. (2001). *Put reading first: The research building blocks for teaching children to read.* Jessup, MD: Author.

National Reading Panel. (2000). *Teaching children to read: An evidence-based assessment of the scientific research literature on reading and its implications for reading instruction.* Reports of the subgroup. Bethesda, MD: National Institute of Child Health and Human Development, National Institutes of Health.

Newcomer, P. (1999). *Standardized Reading Inventory.* Austin: Pro-Ed.

The No Child Left Behind Act of 2001, PL 107–110, No Child Left Behind Act (2001, August 2).

Ogle, D. M. (1986). KWL: A teaching model that develops active reading of expository text. *The Reading Teacher, 39*, 564–570.

O'Shea, L. J., Sindelar, P. T., & O'Shea, D. J. (1987). The effects of repeated readings and attentional cues on the reading fluency and comprehension of learning disabled readers. *Learning Disabilities Research, 2*, 103–109.

Perfetti, C. A. (1977). Language comprehension and fast decoding: Some psycholinguistic prerequisites for skilled reading comprehension. In J. T. Guthrie (Ed.), *Cognition, curriculum, and comprehension* (pp. 20–41). Newark, DE: International Reading Association.

Perfetti, C. A. (1985). *Reading ability.* New York: Oxford University Press.

Pressley, M. (1998). *Reading instruction that works: The case for balanced teaching.* New York: Guilford.

Pressley, M., & Afflerbach, P. (1995). *Verbal protocols of reading: The nature of constructively responsive reading.* Hillsdale, NJ: Lawrence Erlbaum Associates.

Pressley, M., & El-Dinary, P. B. (1997). What we know about translating comprehension-strategies instruction research into practice. *Journal of Learning Disabilities, 30*(5), 486–488, 512.

Rabren, K., Darch, C., & Eaves, R. (1999). Teaching character motives to LD students. *Journal of Learning Disabilities, 28*, 15–36.

Raphael, T. E. (1986). Teaching question-answer relationships revisited. *The Reading Teacher, 39*(6), 516–523.

Reid, D. K., Hresko, W. P., & Hammill, D. D. (2001). *Test of Early Reading Ability.* Austin: Pro-Ed.

Reutzel, D. R., & Cooter, R. B., Jr. (1999). *Balanced reading strategies and practices: Assessing and assisting readers with special needs.* Upper Saddle River, NJ: Merrill.

Schumm, J. S., Moody, S. W., & Vaughn, S. R. (2000). Grouping for reading instruction: Does one size fit all? *Journal of Learning Disabilities, 33*(5), 477–488.

Share, D. L. (1995). Phonological recoding and self-teaching: Sine qua non of reading acquisition. *Cognition, 55*(2), 151–218.

Shaywitz, S. E., & Shaywitz, B. A. (1996). Unlocking learning disabilities: The neurological basis. In S. C. Cramer & W. Ellis (Eds.), *Learning disabilities: Lifelong issues* (pp. 255–260). Baltimore: Paul H. Brookes.

Sindelar, P. T., Monda, L. E., & O'Shea, L. J. (1990). The effects of repeated readings on instructional and mastery level readers. *Journal of Educational Research, 83*(4), 220–226.

Smith, S. B., Simmons, D. C., & Kame'enui, E. J. (1998). Phonological awareness: Research bases. In D. C. Simmons & E. J. Kame'enui (Eds.), *What reading research tells us about children with diverse learning needs: Bases and basics.* Mahwah, NJ: Lawrence Erlbaum Associates.

Snow, C. E., Burns, M. S., & Griffin, P. (Eds.). (1998). *Preventing reading difficulties in young children.* Washington, DC: National Academy Press.

Stahl, S. (1999). *Vocabulary development.* Cambridge, MA: Brookline Books.

Stahl, S. A. (2001). Teaching phonics and phonological awareness. In S. B. Neuman & D. K. Dickinson (Eds.), *Handbook of Early Literacy Research* (pp. 333–347). New York: Guilford Press.

Stahl, S. A. & Kapinus, B. (2001). *Word power: What every educator needs to know about teaching vocabulary.* Washington, DC: National Education Association.

Stanovich, K. E. (1986). Matthew effects in reading: Some consequences of individual differences in the acquisition of literacy. *Reading Research Quarterly, 21*(4), 360–406.

Stanovich, K. E. (2000). *Progress in understanding reading: Scientific foundations and new frontiers.* New York: Guilford.

Stauter, R. G. (1969). *Directing reading maturity as a cognitive process.* New York: Harper and Row.

Swanson, H. L. (1999). Instructional components that predict treatment outcomes for student with LD: Support for a combined strategy and direct instruction model. *Learning Disabilities Research and Practice, 14,* 129–140.

Texas Education Agency. (2000). *Guidelines for examining phonics and word recognition programs.* Austin Author.

Torgesen, J. (2000). Individual differences in response to early interventions in reading: The lingering problem of treatment resisters. *Learning Disabilities Research and Practice, 15*(1), 55–64.

Torgesen, J., & Bryant, B. (1994). *Test of phonological awareness (TOPA).* Austin: Pro-Ed.

Torgesen, J., Wagner, R., & Rashotte, C. (1994). Longitudinal studies of phonological processing and reading. *Journal of Learning Disabilities, 27,* 276–286.

University of Texas Center for Reading and Language Arts. (2001a). *Essential reading strategies for the struggling reader: Activities for an accelerated reading program* (expanded ed.). Austin: Texas Education Agency.

University of Texas Center for Reading and Language Arts. (2002a). *Reading strategies and activities: A resource book for students at risk for reading difficulties, including dyslexia.* Austin: Texas Education Agency.

University of Texas Center for Reading and Language Arts. (2002b). *Supplemental instruction for struggling readers, grades 3–5: A guide for tutors.* Austin: Texas Education Agency.

University of Texas Center for Reading and Language Arts. (2002c). *The Secretary's reading leadership academy: Effective reading instruction.* Austin Author.

University of Texas Center for Reading and Language Arts. (2003). *Effective instruction for elementary struggling readers: Research-based practices* (Rev. ed.). Austin Texas Education Agency.

Vaughn, S. & Dammann, J. E. (2001). Science and sanity in special education. *Behavioral Disorders, 27*(1), 21–29.

Vaughn, S., Gersten, R., & Chard, D. J. (2000). The underlying message in LD intervention research: Findings from research syntheses. *Exceptional Children, 67*(1), 99–114.

Vaughn, S., Moody, S., & Schumm, J. S. (1998). Broken promises: Reading instruction in the resource room. *Exceptional Children, 64*(2), 211–226.

Walberg, H. J. (1998). Foreword. In K. Topping & S. Ehly. *Peer-assisted learning.* Mahwah, NJ: Lawrence Erlbaum Associates.

Wagner, R., Torgesen, J., & Rasholte, C. (1999). *Comprehensive test of phonological processing.* Austin: Pro-Ed.

White, T. G., Sowell, J., & Yanagihara, A. (1989). Teaching elementary students to use word-part clues. *The Reading Teacher, 42,* 302–308.

Wiederholt, J. L., & Blalock, G. (2000). *The Gray Silent Reading Test.* Austin: Pro-Ed.

Wiederholt, J. L., & Bryant, B. R. (2001). *Gray Oral Reading Test* (4th ed). Austin: Pro-Ed.

Williams, J. P. (1988). Identifying main ideas: A basic aspect of reading comprehension. *Topics in Language Disorders, 8*(3), 1–13.

Williams, J. P. (1998). Improving the comprehension of disabled readers. *Annals of Dyslexia, 48,* 213–238.

Wong, B. Y. L., & Jones, W. (1982). Increasing metacomprehension in learning disabled and normally achieving students through self-questing training. *Learning Disability Quarterly, 5,* 228–240.

Woodcock, R. W. (1998). *Woodcock Reading Master Test* (rev. ed.). Circle Pines, MN: American Guidance Service.

Yopp, H. K. (1995). A test for assessing phonemic awareness in young children. *Reading Teacher, 49*(1) 20–29.

Index

About the Authors

Sharon Vaughn is Director and H.E. Hartfelder/Southland Corporation Regent's Chair of the University of Texas Center for Reading and Language Arts in Austin. She is also Editor-in-Chief of the *Journal of Learning Disabilities,* author of numerous books and research articles on learning and reading difficulties, and a consultant on translating research into practice for school districts and state departments of education.

Sylvia Linan-Thompson is Assistant Professor of Special Education at the University of Texas at Austin, and has engaged in large-scale research projects that examine reading interventions for struggling readers in primary grades, literacy acquisition of English-language learners, and Spanish literacy development. Sylvia has authored articles on these topics and has developed guides for supplemental reading instruction. She can be reached via e-mail at: sylvialt@mail.utexas.edu.